THE LIFE AND TIMES OF AUGUSTINE TATANEUCK

University of Regina Press designates one title each year
that best exemplifies the guiding editorial and manuscript
production principles of long-time senior editor Donna Grant.

THE LIFE AND TIMES OF
Augustine Tataneuck

An Inuk Hero in Rupert's Land, 1800–1834

Renee Fossett

© 2023 University of Regina Press

All rights reserved. No part of this work covered by the copyrights hereon may be reproduced or used in any form or by any means—graphic, electronic, or mechanical—without the prior written permission of the publisher. Any request for photocopying, recording, taping, or placement in information storage and retrieval systems of any sort shall be directed in writing to Access Copyright.

Printed and bound in Canada at Marquis Book Printing. The text of this book is printed on 100% post-consumer recycled paper with earth-friendly vegetable-based inks.

Cover art: Drawn by Lieut. George Back, R.N., in John Franklin's *Narrative of a Journey to the Shores of the Polar Sea, in the years 1819, 20, 21 and 22* (London: John Murray, 1823). Public domain.
Cover design: Duncan Campbell, University of Regina Press
Interior layout design: John van der Woude, JVDW Designs
Copyeditor: Alison Jacques
Proofreader: Rachel Taylor
Indexer: Judy Dunlop

Library and Archives Canada Cataloguing in Publication

Title: The life and times of Augustine Tataneuck : an Inuk hero in Rupert's Land, 1800-1834 / Renee Fossett.
Names: Fossett, Renee, author.
Description: Includes index.
Identifiers: Canadiana (print) 20230132650 | Canadiana (ebook) 20230133274 | ISBN 9780889779266 (softcover) | ISBN 9780889779297 (hardcover) | ISBN 9780889779273 (PDF) | ISBN 9780889779280 (EPUB)
Subjects: LCSH: Tataneuck, Augustine. | LCSH: Inuit—Biography. | LCSH: Fur traders—Canada, Northern—Biography. | LCSH: Fur trade—Canada, Northern—History—19th century. | LCSH: Canada, Northern—History—19th century. | LCGFT: Biographies.
Classification: LCC E99.E7 F67 2023 | DDC 971.9/01—dc23

10 9 8 7 6 5 4 3 2 1

University of Regina Press, University of Regina
Regina, Saskatchewan, Canada, S4S 0A2
TEL: (306) 585-4758 FAX: (306) 585-4699
WEB: www.uofrpress.ca

We acknowledge the support of the Canada Council for the Arts for our publishing program. We acknowledge the financial support of the Government of Canada. / Nous reconnaissons l'appui financier du gouvernement du Canada. This publication was made possible with support from Creative Saskatchewan's Book Publishing Production Grant Program.

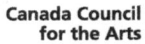   

*To the Inuit children I taught two generations ago.
They are all Elders now and have created Nunavut.
I am very proud of them.*

CONTENTS

List of Maps ◆ ix
Preface ◆ xvii

Introduction to Augustine's World ◆ xxiii
CHAPTER 1 The Inuit, the Company, and Churchill Post, 1812 ◆ 1
CHAPTER 2 The Apprentice, 1813–1820 ◆ 27

INTERLUDE 1 The First Arctic Overland Expedition, 1819–1822 ◆ 57

CHAPTER 3 First Journey to the Western Arctic, 1820–1821 ◆ 67
CHAPTER 4 Death and Survival, 1821–1822 ◆ 87

INTERLUDE 2 Reorganizing and Retrenching the Company, 1822–1824 ◆ 115

CHAPTER 5 The "Engaged Servant," 1822–1824 ◆ 121

INTERLUDE 3 The Second Arctic Overland Expedition, 1824–1825 ◆ 137

CHAPTER 6 Second Journey to the Western Arctic, 1824–1826 ◆ 149
CHAPTER 7 Journey to the Polar Sea, 1826–1827 ◆ 175
CHAPTER 8 Augustine, Ullebuk, and Moses, 1827–1830 ◆ 209

INTERLUDE 4 The Northeast Expedition, 1830 ◆ 237

CHAPTER 9   The Ungava Adventure, 1830–1833 ✦ 245
CHAPTER 10   "Faithful, Disinterested, Kind-Hearted Creature," 1833–1834 ✦ 275
CHAPTER 11   The Families, 1834–1863 ✦ 287
             Epilogue ✦ 307
             Memorials ✦ 317

             Acknowledgements ✦ 319
             Glossary ✦ 323
             Notes ✦ 327
             Index ✦ 369

LIST OF MAPS

MAP 1 The Far Northwest • xi
MAP 2 Northwest Coast and Mackenzie River • xi
MAP 3 Boreal Athabasca and the Central North • xii
MAP 4 West Coast of Hudson Bay and Inland • xiii
MAP 5 East Coast of Hudson Bay and Ungava Bay • xiv
MAP 6 Churchill River and Post • xv

All maps created by Weldon Hiebert.

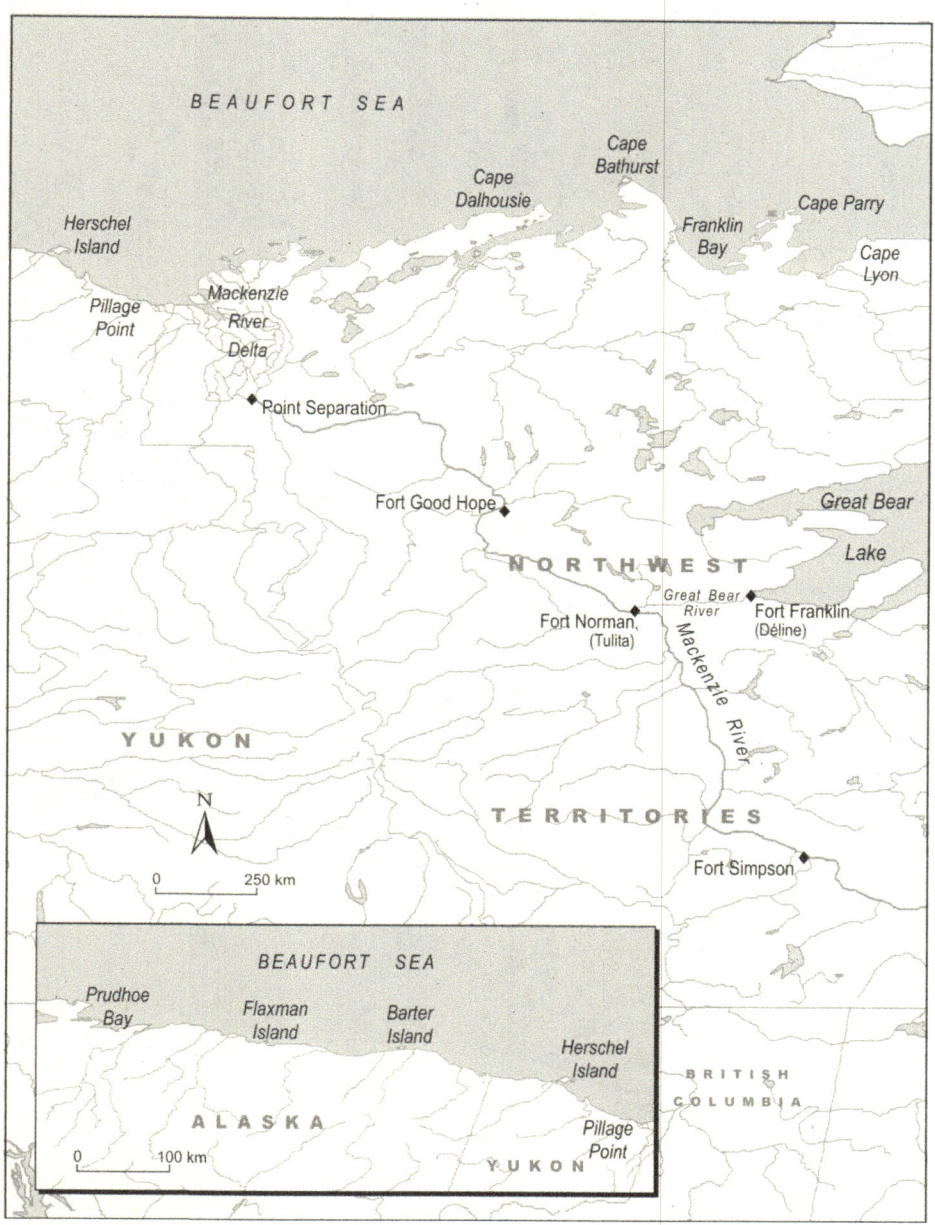

Map 1 (inset). The Far Northwest
Map 2. Northwest Coast and Mackenzie River

XII • THE LIFE AND TIMES OF AUGUSTINE TATANEUCK

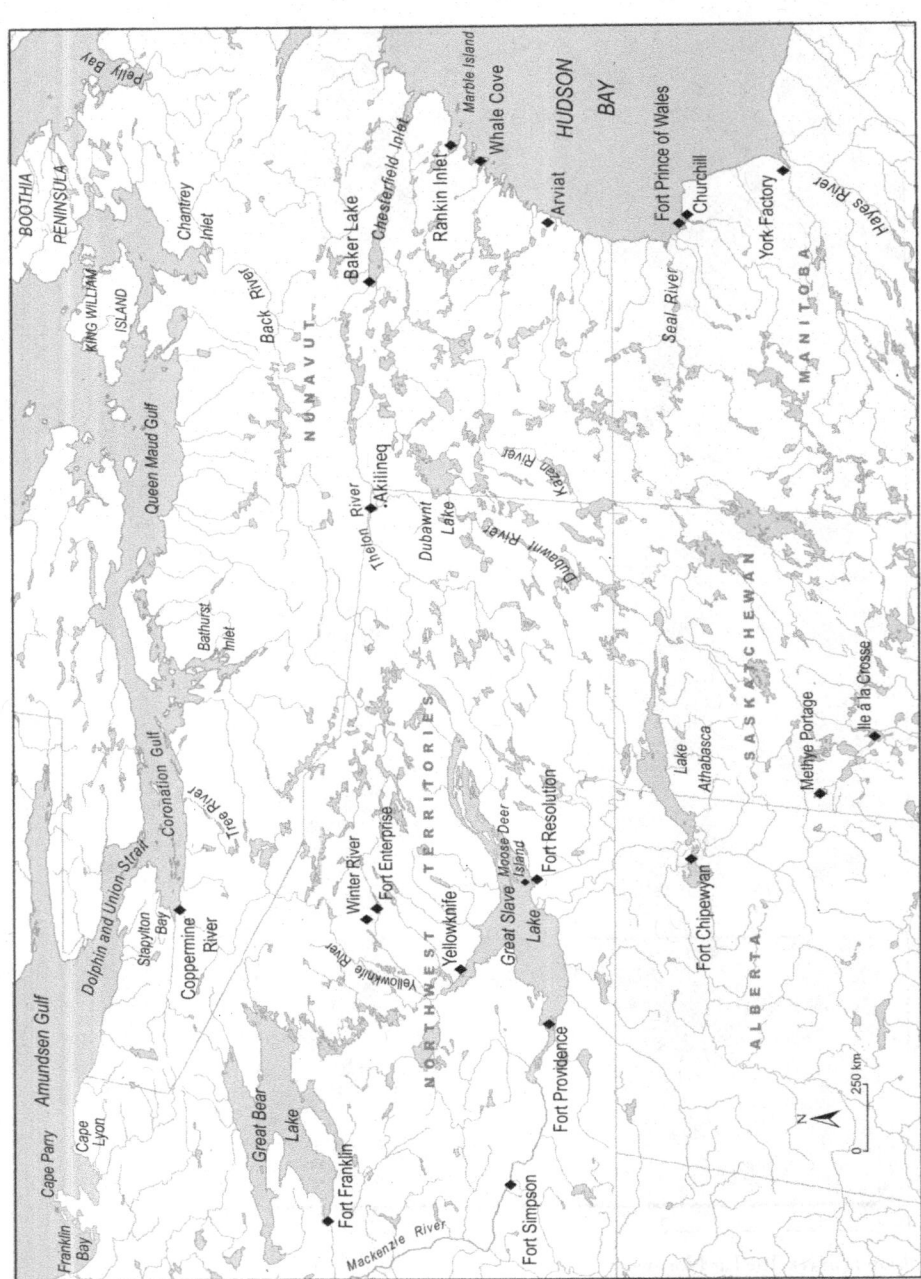

Map 3. Boreal Athabasca and the Central North

MAPS · XIII

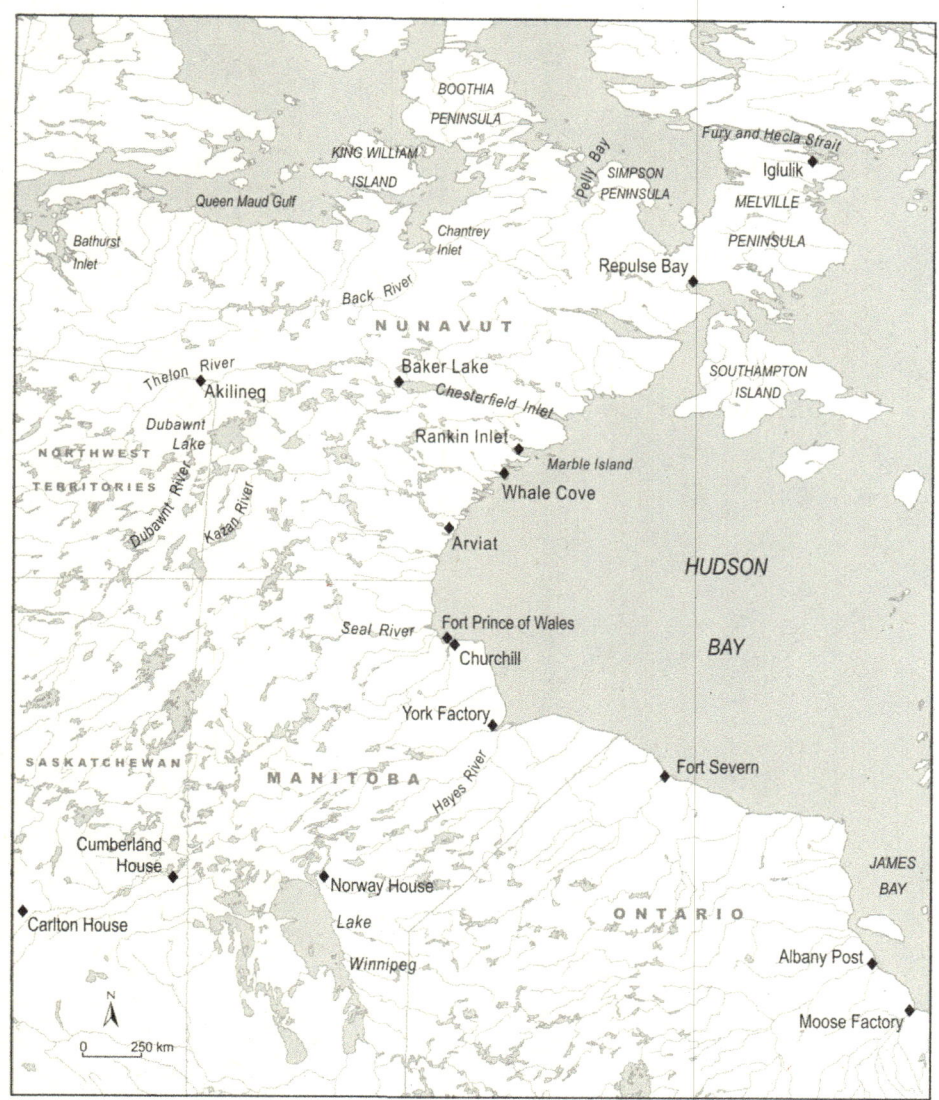

Map 4. West Coast of Hudson Bay and Inland

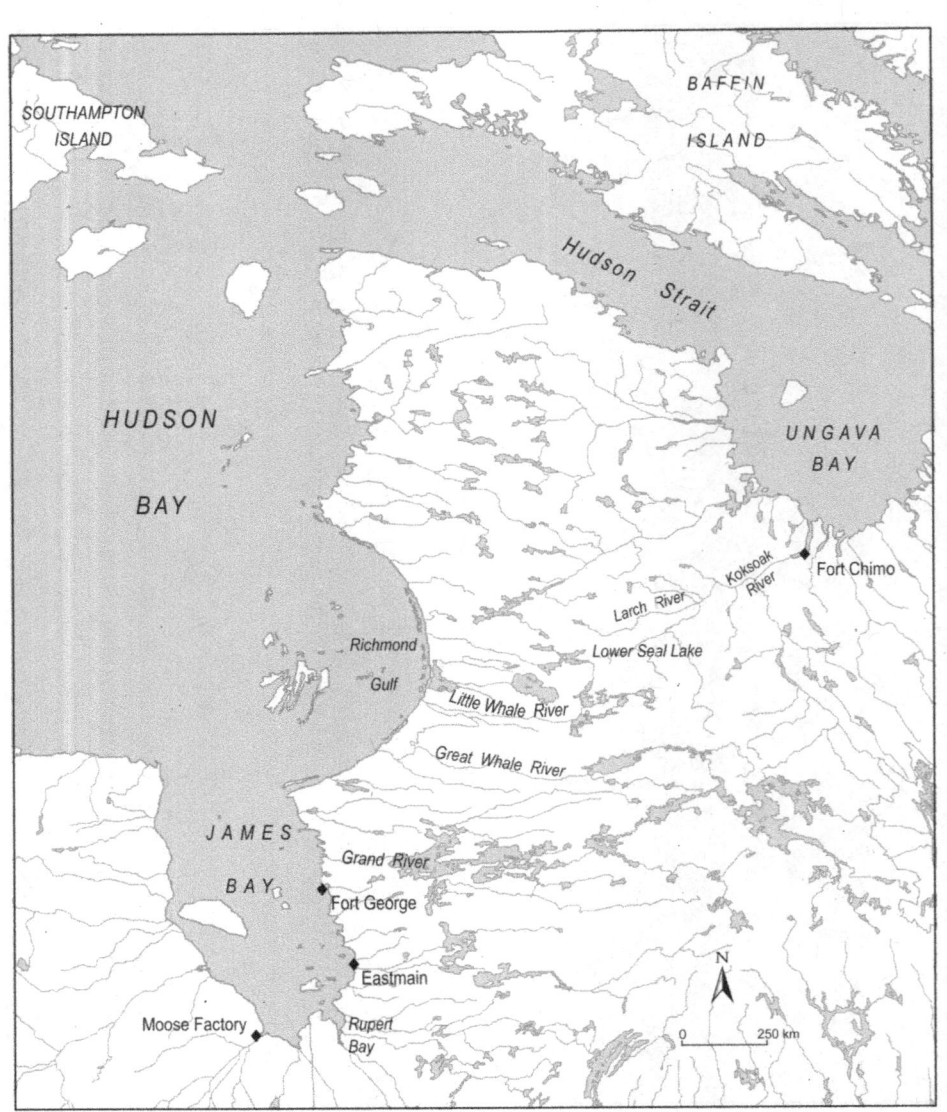

Map 5. East Coast of Hudson Bay and Ungava Bay

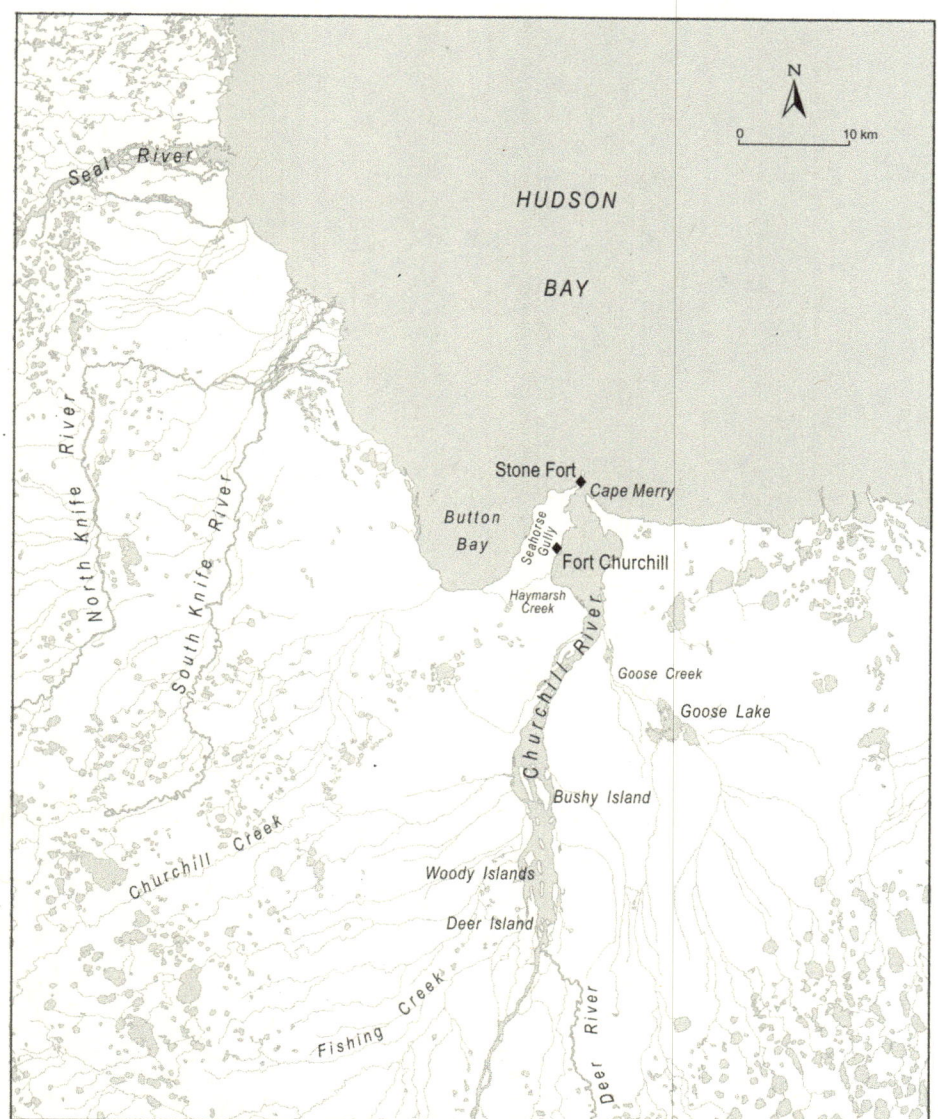

Map 6. Churchill River and Post

PREFACE

MY RELATIONSHIP WITH AUGUSTINE TATANEUCK BEGAN IN 1989, when I was reading the Hudson's Bay Company journals from Fort Churchill. My search then was for evidence of widespread Inuit trade routes along the west shores of Hudson Bay and through the Keewatin barren lands to the western Arctic. In the 1812 journal, I noticed that an Inuk—a "lad," as the journal called him, possibly just approaching his teenage years—was living and working at the trading post. His activities were noted in the post journals, more or less in passing, over the next few years.

I wondered about him. Who was he? Why was he in Churchill instead of with his family somewhere to the north in the great barren lands of Keewatin? I had sons of my own who had only recently left home to study at distant universities, so my natural first thought was for the well-being of the young Inuk. Did he long for his parents and family, and for his community? How was he coping with a new language and a new culture? As a new empty-nester myself, I also had thoughts for his mother, missing her son and worrying about him. For the next twenty years, as I read the Churchill journals for the second and third times, I collected all mentions of this youngster as he matured and took on the responsibilities of marriage, fatherhood, and earning a living. From time to time, brief comments hinted at his activities away from the trading post. When I followed up on them, I discovered that over the years he had travelled with John Franklin on long, difficult explorations of the Arctic coast, sometimes with tragic results, and that he had used his wages from the British Admiralty to sustain his community in a period of severe environmental stress. When clues led me to his birthplace, I began to understand, from my studies in historical climatology, that his family had chosen to send him to Churchill to live among strangers where he had a better chance to survive the perils of a brutally harsh climatic regime that had been causing widespread deaths among his people since before he was born. I wanted to write his story. I wanted Canadians everywhere and anywhere to know about him.

If he ever wrote a letter or made notes of his thoughts on the unstable and unforgiving climatic regime that prevailed during his lifetime or of the comings and goings of British ships and men, none have survived. He left no diaries or letters; his birth, marriage, and death were not registered in public records; his obituaries were written by men who did not include, or even know, anything about his parents or the surviving members of his family. No document ever mentioned the names of his parents, his wife, or his children. His story was told by other people who knew him, mostly upper-level employees of the Hudson's Bay Company (HBC or the Company), a few British explorers, and a missionary.

Written documents are the default first choice for the evidence that historians seek when beginning a study of any period in the past. But when the subject of a biography is a member of a minority group two hundred years in the past, written documents tend to be scarce. In spite of the absence of documents written by Augustine himself, we know more about his life than we know about any other Inuk who lived two centuries ago. His life story, fascinating in itself, also opens doors into the lives of men and women—Inuit, British, French Canadian, Orcadian—who did not belong to an upper ruling class, who did not have political influence, but who formed the economic base of an overseas chartered company, a colony, and eventually a country. In Augustine's case, the Hudson's Bay Company's detailed and carefully preserved journals, accounts, and correspondence books are abundant and accessible. From them, and from the narratives of explorers and missionaries, it is possible to plot a slim chronological narrative of Augustine's work history and some vital events.

The Hudson's Bay Company documents also provide surrogate evidence for Augustine's daily life. When the daily journal noted that Augustine was ill, the Company's yearly medical inventories suggested the medications and treatment he would have been given. Inventories of stored food, whether country provisions or items imported from England, and the weekly Rations Dispersal Ledger were useful in reconstructing the daily diets of men doing hard labour or travelling and the diets and nutritional details of the half rations given to women at the posts. The Servants' Accounts, with their specific descriptions of what Augustine and his companions bought, yielded small hints about the women and children in their households. The purchase of a large number of beads, for instance, was an indication that a woman was making clothing for her family, using glass beads to sew the necessary spirit symbols in the correct places.

Aside from the Company's records, medical practices of the period are described on numerous websites and in the history of medicine section of any university medical school library. These helped me sort out how the badly broken leg of a man at Cumberland House in 1826 was treated. Archaeological and wildlife studies are also sources that hint at the migrations of Inuit communities. When archaeological notes say that the usual site for an Inuit seal camp was unoccupied in any particular year, a published wildlife study may reveal where the seal would have been at that time. If we know where the food resources are, we can usually find the people who depend on those resources. An anthropologist, Franz Boas, and a whaling captain, George Comer, similarly provide surrogate evidence from oral histories of Inuit communities on the western shore of Hudson Bay.

Augustine's life story is embedded within the story of his times. Most of his working life was spent in the fur trade, which at the time meant in Rupert's Land, the nearly sovereign territory of the Hudson's Bay Company. He lived through climate disasters, years of diminishing food sources, and political upheavals on an international scale. He was an important but not widely recognized player in the struggle for possession of northwestern North America waged by Britain, Russia, and the United States.

The cast of characters is large. Augustine was in daily contact with the officers and servants at the trading post, ranging from as few as seven at a small post like Churchill to as many as one hundred at a large establishment like York

Factory or Moose Factory. Because of his fairly low rank within the Company's hierarchy, he spent much of his working time with Cree and Chipewyan hunters and with fellow Company employees who were "country born," that is, the sons of Company officers and men and their Cree and Chipewyan wives. On Augustine's overland expeditions to the western Arctic, his daily companions were French and Métis voyageurs, British marines, and even, in one case, an aging Italian soldier.

Some of life's conditions in Rupert's Land territory in the early nineteenth century were common to all labourers and tradesmen of the HBC, and their experiences also serve as surrogate evidence for Augustine's life. We know that he shared life circumstances with many others, some of whom left written evidence of their adventures, good and bad, and some whose life's experiences were described by others. When his companions were starving to death, we know that Augustine was suffering the same physical torments they were experiencing. When they suffered from blistered thighs and bloody, ice-torn feet, so did Augustine. In uncomfortable circumstances, the difference between Augustine and his companions was the attitude each brought to the experience. While hired canoe men spent long winters in crowded, drafty, and unhygienic log quarters and suffered the consequences of life on half rations, Augustine found another solution. He created a more peaceful life for himself by withdrawing to his own camp, where he built a warm snowhouse at a distance from the miseries of communal living and supplemented his diet by ice fishing and, from time to time, killing a rabbit or a squirrel.

The cast of institutions is equally imposing. The Hudson's Bay Company and the British Admiralty had authority and power over their employees. They dictated the goals and means of daily life, created and enforced the law, and influenced social behaviour. Augustine was employed by both corporate bodies, and the records of each note his work-related activities and his behaviour as an employee. The Company recorded almost nothing about his private life or his home community, while some of the Admiralty's officers took a keen interest in Inuit lifestyles and intellectual culture. An agent of a third institution, the Church Missionary Society, on a long visit to Churchill, sought to learn as much as possible from Augustine about Inuit views on the existence of a spirit world, recorded what he heard, and misunderstood much of it.

Perhaps most important, Augustine's actions and behaviours tell us a great deal about the kind of man he was. Epictetus, a philosopher in the Greek Stoic tradition, pointed out that biography is always incomplete. In response to Emperor Hadrian's question "What is it that man cannot see?" he answered, "The heart and the thought of others." While the response is clearly accurate, there is a great deal about another person that we can see. The fruit that a man produces in a lifetime tells us who he was, even if gaps remain. As individuals, we somehow manage to sustain various kinds of relationships with our families, friends, colleagues, compatriots, and strangers, all of which imply some two-way "knowing" of each other. Historians, by definition, write about societies that they do not inhabit, and the past is always a different country. We can, as Stephen Oates wrote, "live with another human being in another age."[1] Historians continue to write what are always partial histories and incomplete biographies, which, for the most part, manage to convey some truths about the past.

My own backstory was useful in interpreting Augustine and his companions for a later generation and a different cultural context. From 1961 to 1970, I lived as a community teacher and organizer, and as a Hudson's Bay Company "Arctic wife," in Rankin Inlet and Cambridge Bay. My experiences gave me some understanding of the physical difficulties Augustine and his companions faced. I know what it's like to kneel over a hole in the ice and clean fish in the slushy half-frozen river beneath. I did not do it hour after hour, and day after day, knowing that people might starve if I took time off, as Augustine knew. I did not have to do it at all, but I did it long enough on a few occasions to know that it was hard labour. I know what it's like to cross a few miles of barren ground in midwinter on a snowmobile and can make a good guess at how much more difficult it was to make a journey of a hundred miles following or leading a dog team and sled on foot. I also know, as Augustine's mother and wife must have known, the maternal anxiety of holding a sick infant while waiting for help to arrive.

From many conversations, mostly during language lessons with the late Leo Ussaq, I learned something about a universe in which there are human beings, other-than-human beings, terrifying creatures and dreamed realities, and animals that willingly arrange their own deaths in order to give humans the means to live. From my incredible teacher, I gained some understanding of the intellectual work that Inuit leaders and elders undertook in guiding their communities. It is one of my continuing regrets that I failed to learn Inuktitut beyond the simplest of daily exchanges. My greatest disappointment is that I will never know the names of Augustine's parents, wife, and children.

INTRODUCTION TO AUGUSTINE'S WORLD

AUGUSTINE TATANEUCK WAS BORN NEAR THE BEGINNING OF THE nineteenth century on the northwestern coast of Hudson Bay. Between 1812 and 1834, he was employed by the Hudson's Bay Company at Churchill River and Fort Chimo as a labourer, and by the British Admiralty as an interpreter for John Franklin's two overland expeditions in search of a northwest passage. He left no diaries or letters; most of what we know about him comes from people who knew him. His life was shaped by the inescapable environments he lived within. Climate and landscape set physical limits on what he could and could not do; the language, world view, and cultural traditions of his people predisposed him to certain behaviours; and the politics of Europe playing out in North America in the early 1800s created opportunities for him to act in ways new to Inuit. Together the various contexts of his life explain something about his character and his life choices.

THE PHYSICAL ENVIRONMENT

The Arctic is commonly defined as "the region lying within the Arctic Circle."[1] However, because the Arctic Circle, at just above latitude 66°33' north, is an imaginary line based solely on the number of hours of daylight without regard for landscape or habitation, it does not meet the definition of a "region."[2] A second definition describes the Arctic as any place where the average temperature for the warmest month (July) is below 50° Fahrenheit. Again the definition fails, because other regions meet the thermal criteria without being in any sense "Arctic," and because, in an era of noticeable climate change, whether warming or cooling, a thermal definition becomes useless.[3] A more meaningful and precise definition limits the Arctic to the land north of the treeline, characterized by low temperatures, extensive permafrost and tundra, and specific wildlife and vegetation.[4]

Planet Earth's climate is all pervasive. It not only affects every form of life but is also the slow and unstoppable creator of the geological and topographical world of mountains, deserts, seabeds, and continents. It limits what is possible within a region. Temperature, precipitation, and atmospheric activity control availability and suitability of vegetation and wildlife and, by extension, set limits on human economies, politics, and cultural behaviours.

Earth's most recent ice age, the Quaternary glaciation, lasted just over two and a half million years. During the Last Glacial Maximum, about twenty thousand years ago, all of Canada east of the Rocky Mountains was covered by the Laurentide Ice Sheet.[5] In some places, its burden of frozen snow reached as deep as two and a half miles. The great ice sheet began to melt around 9600 BCE and was not fully deglaciated until after 7000 BCE.[6] Over the next seven thousand years, the newly exposed landscape came to life with the material resources necessary for human habitation, including bacteria, fungi, lichens, mosses, grasses, seaweed, insects, fish, birds, and small and large mammals.

Climate scientists have identified and characterized eight climatic regimes in the last nine thousand years. The first was a long gradual warming as the North American ice sheets melted, known as the Boreal climatic episode (c.7000–6000 BCE). It was followed by the Atlantic episode (c.6000–c.3000 BCE), the warmest postglacial period, with average temperatures about 3.6° Fahrenheit higher than they were in the twentieth century. During the third climatic regime, the Sub-Boreal episode (c.3000–c.700 BCE), temperatures dropped enough that glaciers began to form at the highest elevations and sea ice thickened. The cooling trend continued through the Sub-Atlantic climatic episode (550 BCE–400 CE) and most of the Scandic episode (400–800 CE).

In the last decades of the Scandic period, temperatures and precipitation began to increase, leading to the Neo-Atlantic episode (c.900–c.1250 CE), also known as the Medieval Warm Period. Pronounced warming affected the flora, fauna, and human communities of northern North America, Europe, and Asia and of southern Greenland. It is also the period in which the ancestors of today's Inuit, the Thule people, migrated to the Canadian Arctic.

The Pacific Regime (1250–1550 CE) is characterized as a long, slow cooling period, followed by the Neo-Boreal Regime (1550–1850 CE), the coldest period since the end of the last ice age, with increased glaciation on the land and year-round pack ice. The six hundred years covered by the two regimes are often treated as two phases of the same cooling progression: the Little Ice Age.[7]

Within the Little Ice Age (1350–1850 CE), there were three periods of extreme cold with temperatures lower than were experienced during the last ice age: the Spörer Minimum, between 1460 and 1550; the Maunder Minimum, between 1645 and 1715; and the Dalton Minimum, between 1790 and 1830. Unusually cold climate episodes, the "minima," coincide with periods of greatly reduced or complete absence of sunspots. Exactly how sunspots affect Earth's climate is not yet fully understood, but climate scientists agree there is compelling evidence of a connection "between prolonged periods of low solar activity and the maxima of the Little Ice Age."[8] Even small changes in the sun's energy output affect the amount of ultraviolet radiation that enters Earth's atmosphere, which in turn changes the behaviour of Earth's northern and southern polar jet streams.[9]

Augustine Tataneuck lived in the Dalton Minimum during the last decades of the Neo-Boreal climatic episode. The landscape he called home was the central Arctic tundra, a treeless expanse of rocky flat lands and slightly elevated rock formations shaped by the Laurentide Ice Sheet as it flowed or melted during the last great ice age. Permafrost lies under the thin layer of tundra topsoil and varies in depth from sixty to ninety metres (two hundred to three hundred feet) on the continental mainland.[10] The tundra's shallow rivers can carry away only a small amount of meltwater, leaving the land dotted with small lakes and ponds amid soggy hummocks. The identifying characteristics of the tundra are the absence of trees, an extremely cold winter climate, low precipitation, a short growing season, permafrost with poor surficial soil and drainage, and low faunal and floral density and diversity.[11] The treeline separates the tundra from the subarctic boreal forest and follows a northwesterly trajectory from the west coast of Hudson Bay, about forty miles north of Churchill, to the eastern fringes of Canada's two large northern lakes, Great Bear and Great Slave.[12]

THE FIRST PEOPLE: THE PALEOESKIMO [DORSET]

The first people to live in the deglaciated North American Arctic appeared during the Sub-Boreal climatic episode, between 2500 and 2200 BCE.[13] Originally called the Paleoeskimo, they are now known as the Dorset people.[14] Their artifacts and their genetic lineage identify them as descendants of an unknown Siberian origin.[15] They settled in small coastal and island communities across the North American Arctic and Greenland where they adapted their economies and cultural traditions to suit the Sub-Atlantic and Scandic episodes.

As the early signs leading to the Medieval Warm Period began, the Dorset began to disappear. One reason for their disappearance may have been that warming caused marine animals, their main food resource, to move to cooler habitats where the Dorset, lacking boats, were unable to follow them and, without bows and arrows, could not hunt land-based animals. Other reasons for their disappearance may have been the lack of diversity in their DNA or diseases introduced by the Norse in Greenland. The arrival of the Thule people may also have played a part in their disappearance.

What we know about the Dorset—or Tuniit, as many Inuit call them today—comes not only from archaeological investigations but also from a body of oral history passed on by today's Inuit that focuses on the relations of Dorset and Thule. Sometimes the Tuniit and the newcomers lived peacefully as neighbours, and sometimes violence flared, forcing the Tuniit to withdraw to the safety of more remote places. How and when the last Dorset died remains a mystery, but we know from DNA sequencing that they were not absorbed into the Thule-Inuit gene pool, and they left no descendants.[16]

THE ANCESTORS: THE THULE

The Thule, like the Dorset, were the descendants of Siberian migrants. They settled on the North American coast of Bering Strait around 200 BCE.[17] As their Dorset predecessors had done, the Thule adapted their lifestyles and occupations to suit local conditions. By 1000 CE at least one of their western Alaskan communities had developed a high degree of expertise in open ocean travel and boat technology.[18]

Between 1200 and 1250 CE, in the last years of the Medieval Warm Period, the Thule began to move away from their Alaskan villages, in more than one event and more than one direction.[19] What we now call the "Thule migration" was a series of expansions across the treeless North American Arctic, each one most likely consisting of a few extended families. Among the earliest were the Siglit (Coastal People) who settled in the treeless tundra around the mouth of the Mackenzie River some time before or during the early 1200s.[20] Today they are known as Inuvialuit. They may have expanded along the Arctic coast to Amundsen Gulf and Coronation Gulf, but it is also possible that migrations from Alaska continued during the 1200s and that the gulf areas were occupied by newly arrived Thule migrants. In either case, the Thule continued to move east and by 1266 were hunting, and probably living, near Disko Bay on the west coast of Greenland, where their presence was noted by Norse explorers.[21]

Multiple excavations indicate that the Thule expansion through Lancaster Sound occurred "almost simultaneously" from Amundsen Gulf in the west to Ellesmere Island and northwest Greenland in the east.[22] None of the sites studied have yielded any date of Thule occupation earlier than the 1200s.[23] The Thule continued to move throughout Arctic Canada for more than four centuries, to Baffin Island, Ungava Peninsula, Melville Peninsula, and the west coast of Hudson Bay as far south as Rankin Inlet. By the 1500s, they had established themselves along the Labrador coast and in northern Newfoundland.

Some Thule families living on the Arctic coast of Amundsen Gulf and Coronation Gulf chose not to join the pioneers moving on to the eastern Arctic and Greenland. Instead, they moved north to Victoria Island, probably around 1400. We know them as the Copper Inuit, or, in more recent times, as Inuinnait.[24] During the Little Ice Age, food resources on Victoria Island and the mainland Arctic coast were often in short supply: seal, caribou, and fish were limited to particular seasons of the year; muskoxen were scarce, and dangerous in all seasons; and roots and berries were "almost non-existent."[25] In winter a dozen or so families might gather in a snowhouse village but in summer nuclear families went out on their own, living in tents, constantly on the move in search of food, and surviving as best they could.

Along the mainland coast near Queen Maud Gulf, some Thule societies expanded east and north to King William Island, Adelaide Peninsula, and Boothia Peninsula. Today they form a regional group known as the Netsilingmiut (People of the Seal Place), whose dialects are closely related to each other and to the western Canadian Inuktun dialect of the Mackenzie Delta people.[26] Somerset Island, just north of Boothia Peninsula, has typically been unpopulated but some oral histories from Rankin Inlet Inuit note that people driven out of their communities as punishment for serious crimes were sometimes exiled to the island, where their chances of survival were slim.

Environmental threats to the lives and livelihoods of people in some Arctic locations during the Maunder Minimum (1645–1715) led communities to consider relocating to more productive places. The Arctic coast Copper Inuit, already living with the harsh realities of climate and scarce food resources, recognized the signs of worsening climate and understood that their survival depended on moving to new and uninhabited territory. Archaeological surveys in the 1900s have shown that between 1600 and 1771, village sites along the Arctic coast were "unknown, or essentially so," suggesting that the region had "suffered a nearly complete population collapse."[27] While it is possible that entire villages of mainland Copper Inuit starved to death during a climate-induced famine, evidence from archaeology, architecture, language, and written and oral histories indicates that at least one community abandoned its territory in the late 1600s and sought safety elsewhere. Its preferred destination was a sparsely inhabited region north of the treeline on the Hudson Bay west coast, ideal for the community's marine-based economy. Importantly, the leaders and planners of the relocation knew how to get there.

For generations the ancestors of the Arctic coast communities had ventured inland to a biologically diverse boreal forest along the middle reaches of the Thelon River to harvest wood.[28] Until the late eighteenth century, their visits were probably sporadic, undertaken only when necessity demanded, and almost always in winter. They were not, however, the only people who depended on the forested sanctuary for wood: Inuit from the Hudson Bay west coast around Chesterfield Inlet and Baker Lake also made occasional trips inland, as did some Chipewyan who lived in the subarctic forests south of the Thelon sanctuary and hunted there in summer. From time to time, chance meetings happened between people from various Inuit communities as well as some Chipewyan, providing opportunities for an exchange of information about the lay of the land and the locations of occupied territory and the routes that connected them.

By Augustine's lifetime, gatherings at the wooded oasis in the heart of the barren lands had become routine. The meeting place was called Akilineq, based on the root word *aki*, which means "a place for exchange" and the concept of "two." People from all directions met every few years to exchange goods and information, enjoy athletic and song contests, and arrange marriages for themselves or their children.[29] Augustine Tataneuck never, as far as we know, claimed to have visited any of the trading sites, although he may have been there with his parents and fellow villagers as a small child, or during a three-year period, from 1816 to 1819, that he spent with his family in the North. He easily recognized artifacts of the Tree River People of Coronation Gulf, and, while he denied ever having been as far north as Marble Island on the west Hudson Bay coast, he was able to identify the island on a British Admiralty map.[30]

The Arctic coast Inuit relocation was a curated one.[31] Preparation for a journey of at least 600 miles to unknown territory with no intention to return began with gathering information. Elders and people who had travelled outside their own territory were highly valued for their knowledge and were probably the chief planners of the migration.³² People assembled and packed everything that might be needed during the exodus, as well as everything that would be useful for establishing their villages at their destination. If they had dogs, they would have included sleds and teams to haul bundles of tools and utensils, but most of the migrants would have been on foot, travelling at a pace that the elderly, the infirm, and the children could maintain day after day over several seasons. During the long trek they would, out of necessity, have paused for days or even weeks, to hunt and preserve meat. The migration probably took at least a year, possibly two, and may have numbered a hundred people.³³

From the Thelon woods to the bay coast there were two obvious routes. One was to follow the Thelon River east to Baker Lake and Chesterfield Inlet, in which case the migrants would have found a territory already occupied and risked having to fight their way south. The other possibility was to head south through sparsely populated or empty country and then east to the coast, crossing the Kazan and Dubawnt rivers along the way. We know from their oral history that they chose the second route and passed peacefully through mostly unpopulated territory.³⁴ They were first seen in small numbers at Knapp's Bay, a mile or two north of what is now Arviat, and at Neville's Bay (now Dawson Inlet) and Whale Cove, by an HBC boat crew in 1719, two years after Churchill Post was opened.³⁵ Almost a century later, around the time of Augustine's birth, some families began to move inland, where they established a caribou-based economy.³⁶

FROM THULE TO HISTORIC INUIT

During Augustine's lifetime, the people who lived on the southwest coast of Hudson Bay and its hinterland had no collective place name for the geographical region they lived in. The notion of "living in" or "being part of" a polity larger than a village and its hunting territory would not have held any meaning for them. As David Damas explained, "a Central Eskimo 'tribe' was not (and could not be) a self-perceiving entity, but is instead an abstraction, isolated and named by social anthropologists, mainly on linguistic grounds."³⁷

The lack of diversity and scarcity of food resources typical of the Arctic limited the size of Inuit territories and the populations that could survive within them, as did differences of terrain and climate. The sheer size of resource areas, even contiguous ones, meant villages were separated by many miles, leading to a high degree of linguistic and cultural change and to independence as a highly valued communal trait. The basic unit of a village before the mid-twentieth century was the extended family. Kinship was essential to group trust and the ethics of mandatory sharing, but there was always a degree of flexibility. In times of need the kin group could be extended by creating fictive kinships.

Until the late 1970s, there was little or no sense among Inuit of a Pan-Inuit body of communities whose territories stretched across the Arctic from Siberia to Greenland.[38] In Canada alone there were (and to some extent still are) at least two dozen Inuit communities, each independent within its own territory; each speaking, writing, and reading its own dialect in a variety of orthographies; each wearing its own distinctive clothing; each with its own cosmology; each with its own societal organization and social traditions. Until the late eighteenth century, relations between the northern coastal groups and the northern inland people tended to be hostile: conflicts over control of resources were not uncommon. By the early nineteenth century, most groups had peaceful trading relations with their neighbours, including summer gatherings at Akilineq and other venues to exchange material goods and information.

Within each group, people knew their own territory almost inch by inch and everything that stirred within it. They knew the routes that led to the territories of other people who spoke their language and they knew where to find necessary resources such as soapstone and pyrites. They saw themselves and their territories as distinct polities under their own control. Their emotional allegiance was to the village they were born into, where everyone had biological ties or carefully structured fictive kinship with everyone else.

Unknown to the people of Augustine's community, their village and hunting territory were part of Rupert's Land, a vast property created in 1670 by King Charles II. In a charter granted by the king to create the Hudson's Bay Company, Rupert's Land was defined as "all the land whose rivers and streams drain into Hudson Bay." Essentially a trading monopoly enforceable on British subjects, the charter allowed the Company to act as a de facto government over more than 40 percent of what later became Canada.[39] In 1869, the Company "sold" Rupert's Land back to the United Kingdom, which gave it to the fledgling Dominion of Canada. In 1876, when the first Canadian government took notice of its northernmost territory, it named the eastern tundra "the Keewatin Region."[40] In 1999, with the creation of Nunavut, it was renamed "the Kivalliq Region" by Inuit legislators. The collective name for people living in Kivalliq is Kivallirmiut (People of the South), which follows the Inuit practice of naming their communities after the territories they live in.

THE INTERLUDES AND THE BACKSTORY

Augustine Tataneuck would have known nothing, or next to nothing, about how sovereign states functioned, either independently or at the global level. The idea of independent polities with populations in the tens of thousands, separated from one another other by oceans and competing for control of enormous territories, would not have made any sense to him.

Readers, however, might be interested in the reasons behind the British push to explore and claim land and seas within the Arctic Circle in the early nineteenth century. To that end, I have included four "interludes," between the biographical chapters, that take the focus off Augustine for a few pages in order to describe why and how certain events came about and how they changed his life:

- *Interlude 1*: 1819–1822, The First Arctic Overland Expedition
- *Interlude 2*: 1822–1824, Reorganizing and Retrenching the Company
- *Interlude 3*: 1824–1825, The Second Arctic Overland Expedition
- *Interlude 4*: 1830, The Northeast Expedition

Readers can choose to read these interludes or, if they prefer to follow Augustine's life events without interruption, to skip them altogether.

SPELLING, WRITING, NAMING, AND USAGE

Today, nobody knows for sure how words were pronounced in the many subdialects spoken by Inuit more than two centuries ago or what the appropriate spelling would have been in English, French, German, or Danish, the languages spoken and written by observers.[41] Pronunciation and spelling in the documents that serve as sources for Augustine's life vary according to their Writers' ethnicity, hometown, social status, and education. Most recorded names of Inuit people and their villages suggest that the general rule was for European fur traders and explorers to "write it the way it sounds."

Inuit have rejected multiple attempts to create a dictionary and an orthography that all Inuktitut speakers could or would use. Dialect and orthography have become political symbols of a community's independence and are embedded in the history and ideology of each community. Among many groups, speakers' preferred orthography is connected to the orthography's creator. As Noelle Palmer notes, "The Qallunaat missionaries who first codified the way the Inuit spoke for translation purposes assumed control of the Inuit writing systems as they split the Inuit into orthographic camps along religious boundaries."[42] Those writing systems were, and often still are, sacred within some communities because, as Jose Kusugak noted when his carefully constructed universal writing system was rejected by his countrymen, "people were attached to the old writing system as the very symbol of our language and of their salvation."[43] Given the lack of agreement among Inuit communities on pronunciation, orthography, and sometimes meaning, my choice is to use and spell words in quotations exactly as they were written by their authors and sometimes to use the same spelling in my paraphrased comments related to them.

CHAPTER I

THE INUIT, THE COMPANY, AND CHURCHILL POST

1812

Late on the evening of August 29, 1812, nine Inuit hunters and a boy of about twelve years arrived at the mouth of the Churchill River. They had walked at least 150 miles, and possibly as many as 250, from somewhere along the west coast of Hudson Bay north of the trading post at Fort Churchill, carrying their tents and bedding and bundles containing the furs from their summer hunt—the pelts of forty-two wolves, nine wolverines, and 363 foxes—which they hoped to trade. Thomas Topping, the senior officer at the trading post, noted in the Company's daily journal that it was "night" and the men were "putting the boats away." The temperatures that day had been typical of late summer, ranging from 48° Fahrenheit at noon to 42° as twilight gave way to darkness around seven-thirty. A force 1 northeast wind had blown most of the mosquitoes away, and the sky was bright with stars.[1]

They pitched their skin tents at Seahorse Gully, an almost flat, gravelly space about a mile downriver from the Hudson's Bay Company trading post. Inuit coming from the north, on foot along the rocky beaches or paddling kayaks along the coast, nearly always chose to set up camp in the gully, where they knew the chances were good that they would be undisturbed. Chipewyan coming on foot from the northwest tended to pitch their tents on the high rocks behind the post and did not pass near the gully and its low hill. Cree approaching from the southeast ended up at Cape Merry on the river's east bank. Because of old enmities among them, each of the three groups preferred to settle down at a safe distance from the other two. The Hudson's Bay Company traders, aware that misunderstandings could flare up into open hostilities at any time, encouraged the separation. They also discouraged their Inuit, Chipewyan, and Cree clients from coming too near the post itself, except when they were actively engaged in trading. One reason was the well-founded fear that visitors' fires might get out of control and endanger the post's buildings. Another was that visitors got in the way of the Company's men going about their business.

Only a week earlier, on August 22, the Hudson's Bay Company vessel *King George III*, commanded by Captain John Turner, had anchored in deep water on Churchill River's east bank.[2] The ship carried a year's supply of trade goods and provisions for the post, along with a year's worth of mail from home in a pouch in the captain's quarters and new recruits who were crowded into tiny passenger cabins. The post's men worked around the clock off-loading cargo from the supply ship into shallow-bottomed *bateaux* and moving bales, barrels, sacks, and kegs to the long floating pier in front of the stockaded post on the west bank. Surplus trade goods, the year's fur returns, and labourers destined to return to their European homes were ferried out to the ship to be taken to its next port, York Factory, and from there north out of the bay, east through Hudson Strait, and across the North Atlantic to British ports. On August 27, Captain Turner took the vessel out of the river and headed down the bay.

On the morning of Sunday, August 30, the Inuit left Seahorse Gully with their bundles of pelts and headed south to the trading post. Even at a distance of a mile, they could smell the greasy, clogging reek of seal and whale oil from the Company's industrial rendering site. Their first glimpse of the post was its north palisade wall. Inside, they stepped into the hustle and bustle of two dozen men moving tons of freight from the beach and getting it under cover in various storehouses. Amid the controlled confusion, they managed to find

Thomas Topping and followed him to the trading room, where they exchanged their furs for a few useful tools.³

With their trading done, one of the Inuit stepped forward with the youngest member of the group, his son, and asked Topping if the youngster could spend the winter at the post.⁴ Encouraged by the other members of the travelling party, he came to an agreement with Topping: the youngster would stay at the post for the next year, doing chores and assisting the traders, and in return he would receive room, board, clothing, and various gifts to take back to his community the following summer. All business and arrangements made, the boy's father and his companions began the long walk home, and the young newcomer was left to fit himself into the life and routines of an alien world.

IN THE FIRST SEVENTY YEARS AFTER THE FOUNDING OF CHURCHILL in 1717, many young Inuit spent a year, and sometimes two, at the post. The first were two boys from the community at Knapp's Bay, who were invited by Henry Kelsey while he was exploring the coast north of the post in the Company's sloop. Other youngsters came and went sporadically between 1722 and 1756 when the Company's small vessels were able to make the trip. From 1757 to 1790, with few exceptions, one or two eager and adventuresome youngsters lived at Churchill every year.

The young apprentices worked around the post as hunters, fishermen, couriers, and general helpers, and in return they were given room and board, clothing, and a small credit on their accounts at the post. For the Company, the benefits it hoped to receive by keeping and teaching the youngsters went beyond the work they did at the post. The Company's major shareholders and directors, who made up the London Committee, its ruling body, hoped its temporary wards would act as interpreters and culture brokers between the Company and the northern communities, as well as becoming loyal customers.⁵

The boys were returned safely to their communities with some understanding of the greater world, as well as presents of desired items, such as metal kettles, awls, and hunting knives, which were distributed among all members of the home villages.⁶ They learned the basics of how the fur trade worked, how skins were graded and valued, and how to prepare and process pelts so they would fetch the highest prices. They became skilled in the use and care of firearms, picked up the basics of European-style arithmetic, and gained a familiarity with British attitudes, manners, and habits. Most of them learned to speak and understand some basic English, with varying degrees of fluency, and many also learned Cree and Chipewyan languages and dialects, also with varying degrees of fluency. Other benefits accrued to the apprentices and their communities. As well as gifts sent to their families, including guns and ammunition, the young men could count on favoured customer status with the Company in future years, both for themselves and for their families.

Inuit had their own reasons for sending their children south, other than the gifts and credit accounts. Among Inuit, "lending" or temporarily exchanging children created a family relationship within which all parties involved had certain rights and responsibilities, the most basic being the right to ask for help, and the obligation to share resources in times of need. Historic Inuit, living as they did in small communities in marginal environments, understood that a large network of family relationships was an effective defence against bad times. They recognized as family everyone with whom they had even the most distant of blood relationships. But because the number of such relationships that can exist within a small population is limited, they sought to expand family connections beyond the merely biological. In-laws, step-parents and step-siblings, and their familial connections were counted as family, and so were numbers of other people with whom there was neither a biological nor a marital relationship. Foster and adoptive parents, teachers and mentors, hunting partners, midwives, and strangers who happened to share one's name could all be recognized as kin.⁷

Captain George Francis Lyon—who spent two years, from 1821 to 1823, at Melville Peninsula in command of HMS *Hecla* under Captain Edward Parry and the summer of 1824 at Repulse Bay in command of HMS *Griper*—wrote a detailed account of child exchange among the Iglulingmiut.⁸ He saw the practice as a form of mutual adoption. "The most extraordinary connexion," he wrote, "is that by adoption, for there are few families which have not one or two adopted sons, their proper progeny being in like manner adopted by others. A wealthy man will, in this manner, take fine stout youths under his protection, and is thereby insured of being supported in his old age.... This curious connexion binds the parties as firmly together as the ties of blood." Lyon thought the term for the practice was *tegoo-u-gha* (possibly *tiguarivaa*, meaning "he has him in his family for a while").[9] The Churchill traders, as temporary foster parents, became part of the kinship network to which the boys belonged. From their parents' point of view, "lending" a child to the trading company was an effective insurance policy and hedge against future troubles.

Not all officers in the field were convinced that being host to young Inuit boys was worth the trouble. Samuel Hearne, chief at Churchill between 1776 and 1787, doubted that the Company received any benefits in return for "the great expense they have from time to time incurred.... [The boys] have not been any ways advantageous to the Company, by increasing the trade from that quarter."[10] Thomas Topping was one officer who believed that the young visitors, if welcomed and treated generously, would encourage their relatives and other members of their communities to come to the post in subsequent years. Applying this philosophy to the request brought to him by his visitors on August 30 and noting that the "young man wished much to stop the winter with us," Topping reasoned that if the newcomer spent a happy winter at the post, he would carry a good report of the fur traders back to his people the following summer.

❧

THE YOUNGSTER, REFERRED TO AS A "LAD" OR AS "OUR ESKIMAUX lad" in the post's journal, made his first acquaintance among the more than three dozen men at the post. The man Topping chose to take charge of the newcomer was twenty-one-year-old John Leask. A native of Orphir in Orkney, Leask had been hired as a labourer in 1808 and had consistently received good reports from his superiors. His employment record described him as 5 feet, 5¾ inches tall, "a strong man...a good servant, busy, ready and willing to do everything in his power." The Company's account books show him to have been careful with his money but generous when a friend needed help. His original contract specified an annual wage of £8, which he spent carefully. In the trading year 1808–9, his expenses amounted to £6/16/3, most of it for clothes more suited to the North American subarctic climate than those he had brought with him from Orkney. He had also donated five shillings to assist a fellow trader whose debt exceeded his income.[11] In his second year, from his wage of £8 plus £2 in wolf bounties, Leask spent a mere four shillings. In the third year, his income from wages and bounties was £11/16, of which he spent less than £3.[12]

Midway through his fourth year of service, Leask's responsibilities, and his wages, increased unexpectedly. On January 16, 1812, the post journal recorded the sudden collapse of Thomas Corston, the post's tailor, who had also acted as steward responsible for securing and apportioning provisions and other necessary supplies. Corston's illness proved painful, swift, and deadly. On the twenty-first of January, Topping recorded, "[We] buried the body of Thomas Corston. The thermometer this morning at 8 o'clock 50 deg below zero." Topping chose John Leask as Corston's replacement and promoted him to steward.[13]

Topping's choice of the post steward as temporary foster parent meant that the newcomer would have his bed in the kitchen, the warmest place on the post. Leask shared the kitchen with the post's cook, Thomas Spence, their beds and storage chests arranged near the post's only stove. There in the kitchen, the boy had his first lessons in English from men who spoke with a variety of Scottish accents. With gestures, and a few words of Inuktitut they may have known, Leask and Spence gave the young apprentice his first assignment: the never-ending chore of chopping and carrying in firewood. His second chore was to fetch provisions the cook wanted from various storehouses. A lesson in the geography of the post was added to his lessons in the English language.

IN RECORDING THE FACT OF THE YOUNG INUK'S ARRIVAL AT Churchill, Topping had nothing to say about his family, his birth date, or his ancestral history. All that Topping knew of him was contained in a single sentence entered into the post journal: "One of them, a young man, wished much to stop the winter with us, which was allowed, in hopes it would have a good effect in encouraging the farther natives to come down to us, he being one of them, after his report when he returns again to them."[14]

Topping did not record the young man's name in the journal entry for August 30, 1812, but the traders called him "Augustine" after the month of his arrival at Churchill.[15] Most journal entries continued to refer to him as a "boy" or a "lad," but by 1818 he was a married man, perhaps around seventeen years old. While we cannot be certain what name he was known by in his home community, in the opinion (and spelling) of British explorers who met him in later years, his name was Augustus Tattanoeuck. None of the observers spoke Inuktitut, nor was there then any Inuit system for recording the Inuit language. The explorers simply wrote, as best they could, a phonetic rendition of what they heard. Inuktitut speakers today do not recognize "Tattanoeuck" as a meaningful name, but *tata* sometimes means "full." The name may not have been the one by which he had been known in his home village. Among Inuit, name changes were common, with a new name often being given or assumed after a person has experienced a life-changing event, comparable to the practice of English speakers that requires people to or assumes they will adopt new names when they enter religious life, when they are elevated to high position, or, in the case of women in some societies, when they marry. The youngster or his father, or both of them, may have expected or hoped that among the fur traders his stomach might soon be filled. Years later, when he had mastered reading and writing skills, he signed his name "Augustine Tataneuck."[16]

Augustine Tataneuck's home community can be identified somewhat more certainly. The Churchill traders knew that Inuit occupied three areas along the western shore of Hudson Bay in the summer. The southernmost area was around Knapp's Bay near present-day Arviat, about 165 miles north of Churchill. People also occupied a stretch of the coast between Knapp's Bay and Whale Cove, roughly 245 miles north of Churchill. A third Inuit community was known to live at or near Marble Island, nearly 290 miles north of Churchill. None of the occupied areas seem to have been villages; instead, the occupants of the Knapp's Bay and Whale Cove communities were scattered in groups of two or three families over several miles along the coast. The people who frequented Marble Island in the summer spent the fall and winter months on the mainland. By describing the lad as one of "the farther natives," Topping made it clear that he was not from the Knapp's Bay community, and Augustine himself later said that although he had been to Marble Island, it was not near his home village. His birthplace must have been somewhere between present-day Arviat (*arviq*, "bowhead whale") and Rankin Inlet (*Kangirliniq*, "the solid part," "bedrock"; *Qairnirmiut* or *Qaernermiut*, "people of the bedrock").

AUGUSTINE WAS BORN AND LIVED HIS ENTIRE LIFE DURING ONE OF the coldest periods the northern hemisphere had experienced since the end of the last great ice age, more than ten thousand years earlier. A period of about five hundred years, from roughly 1350 to 1850, is known to climate scientists as the Little Ice Age, when drastically lower temperatures and new glaciations were common. Within the Little Ice Age were several periods of even colder weather. The last of them was the Dalton Minimum, a prolonged sunspot minimum between about 1790 and 1830.[17]

The signs were there before the full impact of the new climatic regime was fully felt. Subtle though they were, Inuit hunters, navigators, and seamstresses would certainly have noticed the ominous clues in the physical environment much earlier: summers that were wetter and chillier than they had been for most of the preceding century, and winters that were colder; snow that lay on the ground longer and in some years never completely melted; river ice that lasted a few days longer than usual in the spring; thickening of the sea ice that prevented seals from pupping; more rain days that made it difficult to dry wet bedding and tents; thicker caribou and seal skins that made cutting and stitching of kayak covers and clothing more arduous; and the disappearance of birds and animals that migrated to other regions or ceased to reproduce in sufficient numbers to provide sustenance for the people who depended on them. The miseries of cold, starvation, and exposure experienced by the Keewatin people between the 1780s and the 1830s too often ended in death.

In the spring of 1787, six Keewatin Inuit families foresaw a particularly severe winter ahead and took steps to deal with the impending crisis. They went to Churchill. Except for the boy apprentices, they were the first to do so since their initial meeting with the traders almost seventy years earlier. But they did not go to ask for help.

During the sloop years, between 1757 and 1790, the Keewatin coast Inuit had learned just how much metal tools and utensils lightened their workload. They had also learned from the youngsters they sent to winter at the post that bits and pieces of metal could be found for the picking in the ruins of the old Stone Fort five miles north of the post. Several families, numbering between twenty and twenty-five men, women, and children, made the 165-mile journey on foot from Knapp's Bay in late May of 1787. Their intention was not to trade their few country products but to search for highly valued scraps of lead, iron, copper, and brass. While sorting through the debris of the ruined Stone Fort, they took note of the large number of seals at the mouth of the Churchill River. After trading their pitiful bundles of cracked and hairy deerskins, they set about the serious work of killing seals and trading blubber and skins to the fur traders. A decade later, the presence of the Churchill seal herd became a significant factor in coping with the severe stress of the climatic regime. When the difficult conditions of the Dalton Minimum drove the seals away from their habitats on the northern coast, people knew where to find an alternate supply.[18]

Churchill's traders were also aware of the increasingly bad weather, noting that the storms and strong winds they had learned to expect at the fall equinox were about six weeks early and were unusually fierce. In the logbook entry for July 28, 1788, at Whale Cove, Captain George Taylor recorded offshore gales so strong that the little sloop *Churchill* was delayed a full six days before being able to get out to sea. When it was finally under sail, its crew spent three days beating against wind and rain to reach Marble Island. The fierceness of the weather resulted in the Company's decision in 1790 to end its regular summer trading voyages, which had brought little or no profit to the Company and which were becoming more dangerous as climatic conditions worsened.[19]

The year 1800, possibly the year of Augustine's birth, was "remarkably cold," wrote Chief Factor Thomas Stayner in the post journal for September. "The ground is entirely covered with snow," he noted, "and the shores with ice." In July of 1802–03, the Churchill traders heard reports of a great catastrophe among the Keewatin people. "They bring the dreadful intelligence of a great part of their tribe having perished by famine during the winter, which was remarkably cold," wrote HBC surgeon William Auld.[20] In September 1804, several families of Inuit asked if they could spend the winter in the safety of the post. Auld did not have enough food on hand to feed his own men and reluctantly turned them away. In the spring of 1807, he informed his superiors in London that it was "the coldest month of May I ever saw." Cold as it already was, the Arctic and subarctic coasts of Hudson Bay got even colder. In the early autumn of 1810, about eighty Inuit in family groups spent a few days near Churchill. Their close reading of the physical environment had led them to expect even harsher weather ahead, and they planned to carry on to York Factory for the winter. The Churchill traders knew that the large establishment at York was facing a winter of short rations and that, like Churchill, it would be hard pressed to feed its own complement of men. Once again, they persuaded the Inuit to return to their own country.[21]

In this time of trouble, Augustine was born. As a very young child, he lived through the terrible winter of 1802–3 and the difficult years that followed, when survival meant separation of communities into small family groups widely dispersed across a landscape emptied of its great caribou herds and a rocky coast deserted by seals. Only the sealing grounds at Churchill got them through, by yielding up a minimally adequate supply of the seal oil that had become the mainstay of their winter diet. The precarious nature of life and survival among the Keewatin people provided a strong motive for Augustine's father to bring his son to the security of Churchill Post.

⁂

ON HIS FIRST MORNING AT CHURCHILL, AS AUGUSTINE FOLLOWED John Leask on his daily tasks, the lad began to learn what the many buildings of his new home were used for and who worked in them. As a post, a fort, and a factory, by 1812 Churchill had been in operation for nearly a century. None of the buildings were new, and most of them had a rough, cobbled-together look.[22]

The first permanent establishment at Churchill River was a small station, built in 1717 on the west bank about five miles upriver. Its founder, James Knight, chose the site because it offered the only nearly level ground in the area, and it was at least partly sheltered by high rocks from the full blast of the northwest winds. But it was certainly not ideal. The ground was marshy, wet, and mosquito ridden, causing Knight to comment, "I never see such a miserable place in all my life." In 1719 the little post was designated a "fort" and named Prince of Wales's Fort.[23]

Nearly fifteen years later, in 1731, the Company began building a great stone fortress on the western peninsula overlooking Hudson Bay. In 1741, after ten years of construction, the traders moved into their new home. Life at the new Prince of Wales's Fort, known by its inhabitants as the Stone Fort, was far from comfortable. The astronomer William Wales, in Churchill in 1768–69 to observe the transit of Venus, complained of not being able to sleep because of the cold. "In the month of January," he wrote, "the cold began to be extremely intense; even in our little cabin, which was scarcely three yards square, and in which we constantly kept a very large fire, it had such an effect, that the little alarm clock would not go without an additional weight, and often not with that.... My bedding was frozen to the [wall] boards every morning.... [By early December] it was now almost impossible to sleep an hour together, more especially on very cold nights, without being awakened by the racking of the beams in the house."[24]

In 1782, forty years after the traders had moved into the Stone Fort, the miserably uncomfortable and militarily ineffective fortress was destroyed by French naval forces in their long struggle to wrest access to inland North America from the English. It lay empty and half in ruins for a year, until the Chief Factor, Samuel Hearne, was able to bring his workforce back to Churchill River from the Company's southern forts and posts that he had sent them to after the attack. He chose to abandon the Stone Fort and to rebuild on the site of Knight's original post. Hearne's first priority was to provide shelter for his men before winter set in. The 1783 supply vessel, *Prince Rupert III*, delivered the makings of a two-storey wood-frame building and lead sheets for roofing late in September, and by November a forty-by-twenty-four-foot two-storey All-Purpose House was ready for occupancy. Carpentry, cooperage, smithy, trading room, kitchen, and sleeping quarters for thirty-two men and officers with their country-born families were somehow all crammed into less than two thousand square feet of working and living space. Hearne hoped—fruitlessly, as it turned out—that none of his men would repeat William Wales's experience of waking to find their blankets frozen to the wall. Wind howling out of the northwest all winter made heating the living and working quarters impossible. It says much about living conditions at the factory that the entire year's supply of beer, wine, and spirits considered sufficient for the needs of thirty-two men had frozen solid by November 1784. When indoor temperatures were low enough to cause casks of beer to split open and bottles of wine to burst, human beings cannot have enjoyed many creature comforts.

Along with the minimal advantage of easy access to stands of stunted trees for firewood came other serious problems. In winter the only source of fresh water, melted snow, was abundant; in summer, murky, foul-smelling, barely potable water was taken from nearby ponds and swamps. In spring, water was plentiful but in the wrong places, flooding the post buildings at ground level and providing breeding grounds for intolerable clouds of mosquitoes. Tons of snow had to be shovelled and carried away from the buildings every spring, and trenches had to be dug and constantly maintained to drain off meltwater. The transfer of cargo from vessels in the river to the warehouses was another problem. Because rocky shoals prevented annual supply vessels from anchoring on the west bank, all cargo had to be off-loaded from the ships in a deepwater anchorage on the east bank at Cape Merry, rowed across the river in small bateaux, hefted onto an eighty-yard-long pier, and then carried another eighty to a hundred yards to the factory's storage sheds.

Next on the list of Hearne's priorities was a palisade fence around the three landward sides of the factory. The Company's owners required that the ground surrounding their establishments be cleared for a mile in all directions to prevent enemies from creeping unseen into the compound. On the cramped, rocky flats of Churchill, the area that could be fenced in was well short of the recommended mile—a mere 170 feet by 164 feet. The carpenters managed to cut and shape enough pickets from the stunted, spindly trees near at hand, and the armourer hammered out spikes to top them, giving at least the illusion of a defensive position. In reality, the post could not have been defended had an attack been made against it. Nearly thirty years later, the solid north wall of the palisade was Augustine's first view of Churchill Factory as he and his father, with their fellow villagers, approached what was to become the boy's new home.

When the London Committee failed to send more building supplies in 1784, Hearne improvised. Before freeze-up, the men had dug a cellar, lined it with stones rafted five miles from the abandoned Stone Fort, laid the foundation, and cut trees for an addition to the All-Purpose House. They spent most of the winter squaring logs with handsaws and axes. Like Inuit a decade later, the Company's men scavenged the ruins of the Stone Fort for lead, which they used to roof the expanded new building. The thirty-by-twenty-four-foot addition, called the Men's House, adjoined the All-Purpose House; like the first building, it stood two storeys and was bricknogged—that is, it was framed with timber and filled in with bricks taken from the ruins of the Stone Fort. The extra square feet provided each man with a bed-place about five by six feet, each fitted with a sliding door to provide at least minimal privacy.

The Men's House, unlike the All-Purpose House, had a state-of-the-art stove sent from London, but it did little to stop the cold and drafts. Like William Wales, the men came to expect a coating of frost on their bedding on winter mornings. The chief's quarters were no better than the men's. Chief Factor Thomas Stayner, who took over from Hearne in 1798, had trouble keeping his ledgers up to date during the dark winter days because wind blasting between the rough-hewn log walls and unchinked bricks snuffed his candles. He ordered the room lined with panelling but achieved only slight improvement. A quarter of a century later, the arrangement was still in place. It was in the Men's House trading room that Augustine, his father, and their countrymen traded their furs, selected the goods owed to them, and negotiated the terms on which Augustine would spend the winter.

The trading room in the Men's House, known as the "Indian House," was the only part of the post where the Company's clients were welcome. During its first years in Hudson Bay, uncertain relations with the local people had led to a policy of trading with clients through a window in the palisades, keeping the post itself completely off limits. Officers who lived there managed to convince the London Committee that Churchill was simply too cold to expect people to camp outside the stockade during the winter. The Committee waived its ruling and gave permission for a room adjacent to the kitchen on the ground floor of the Men's House to be set aside for the use of Cree and Chipewyan at the post in winter.

Hearne also managed to deal with the potentially dangerous problem of gunpowder storage. All available bricks and stones were used in constructing the Men's House, so once more Hearne and his men had to make do with very little. They built a partly underground new magazine with wood and bermed it thickly on top and sides with earth.

During the 1790s, the stockaded area became even more crowded with buildings than it had been in Hearne's time. Stayner supervised the construction of yet another addition to the 1783 All-Purpose House and the 1784 Men's House. Its exterior matched the earlier structures—timber-framed and bricknogged. Its comfort also matched that of the other two sections of the large building; the men continued to suffer from chilblains and woke on winter mornings to shake ice crystals off their blankets. The huge difficulties involved in producing firewood meant that stoves and fireplaces in the living, working, and storage rooms remained unlit most of the time. The ground-floor kitchen was the only place that was even close to being comfortably warm, and that was just in the winter. In the summer, the cook's fire burned only long enough to cook two meals a day. It was there that John Leask pointed Augustine to his sleeping place.

In the first few days of his stay at the factory, Augustine became familiar with the two-storey launch house and the wooden dock stretching eighty feet across the mudflats. Because it was impossible to make pilings stable in the gooey river flats, the new pier sat on floats. Each year after the supply ship left, the men took the pier apart to protect it from ice damage during the winter. Every summer after the river cleared, they set it in place again. Dismantling and storing the dock was one of the chores Augustine was assigned in his first week as a factory apprentice.

As assistant to the cook, Thomas Spence, Augustine visited the thick-walled ice house on a daily basis to fetch meat or fish for the day's meals. Half-filled with ice cut from the river every spring, the ice house kept butchered game in reasonably good condition for most of the summer. A comparison of the numbers of men who suffered from scurvy at Churchill and at York Factory indicates that meals at Churchill were more nutritious.

One of the buildings that Augustine would seldom, if ever, have had to visit was Stayner's new, thirteen-foot-square magazine, which replaced the dangerous earth-bermed gunpowder shed. The same size as the earlier powder house, it was lined with lead and sealed with a heavy copper door scavenged from the Stone Fort ruins. Other buildings that the young apprentice seldom needed to visit were a small warehouse and an abandoned still house that sat at either end of the western palisades. While it was Company policy not to give liquor to its clients, competition from the North West Company (NWC), which regularly used liquor to draw in customers, demanded that at some posts the regulations be set aside. Churchill was one of the few Company establishments where no rival traders threatened the trade, and spirits, wine, and beer were not given to clients. Competition did exist, however, near Churchill's summer outposts upriver, and the distillery produced liquor for their trade. In 1810, the inland posts were closed, and the distillery became obsolete. In 1812, in spite of it having been unused for two years, the rich aromas of moonshine and homebrew were added to the reek of rendered blubber from the beach.

Between the small warehouse and the old still house stood a 170-foot-long vegetable garden. All hands took turns at planting, watering, weeding, and harvesting minimal quantities of salad greens, potatoes, turnips, and cabbages. When spring came in 1813, Augustine was given the job of carrying water to the garden. He turned out to have something of a green thumb and took over some of the responsibility for starting seedlings indoors, planting them when the days were warm enough, and in the years the factory had chickens, he gathered and spread the kitchen garden with raw manure.

The men's personal hygiene suffered from a major problem: the absence of a decent supply of clean water. One of Augustine's first and daily chores was to fetch water for the cook and for the men's wash and laundry basins. During the first two months of his new life at the post, he made his way several times each day across swampy land on a narrow wooden causeway to a freshwater pond where he scooped endless pails of water for the kitchen. After the first heavy snowfall in late October, the job was less demanding; he simply filled buckets with reasonably clean-looking snow and carried them indoors.

The day-to-day work of the Company's men is noted in great detail in the daily journals, but nowhere is there any mention of latrines. Chamber pots were in use in the living quarters and presumably were emptied regularly. Where they were emptied is the question. At a guess, their contents were dumped on the river ice and carried off into Hudson Bay during spring thaw. How the daytime needs of up to fifty people were met is left to the imagination.[25]

Some of the old problems that had plagued James Knight, Samuel Hearne, and Thomas Stayner remained. Gusts of icy wind penetrated the uninsulated walls all winter, and mosquito hordes plagued the men during the summer months. Recurring scarcity of food kept the men almost continuously on short rations, and there was very little privacy when they had a few hours off. Added to the discomforts was the stress of dangerous work. Aside from the constant risks of frostbite and snow blindness, the men faced multiple hazards in their small boats and rafts on the turbulent, ice-strewn river and on their makeshift sleds on rough and icy ground. Moving incoming provisions and goods from ship to shore, and outgoing fur returns from storehouse to ship's hold, was arduous and dangerous during shipping season every year. In winter, accidents and fatal injuries on the frozen river were common.

EXPLAINING THE HUDSON'S BAY COMPANY'S HIERARCHY OF PERSONnel to young Augustine would have been a much more difficult undertaking for the boy's foster fathers, John Leask and Thomas Spence, than showing him what the different buildings were used for.

Company employees were divided into two major classes, officers and men, in semi-military fashion. Officers had to be able to read and write; most had at least some higher education, and most planned lifetime careers with the Company. Recruits from the "lower classes" signed on as labourers with contracts for periods ranging from one to nine years. Most were Orcadians who were hired on the dock when the Company's annual supply ship anchored at Stromness or Kirkwall to take on water and fresh food. A smaller number were Scots, and a much smaller number were English. Most planned to return to their home communities after a few years with enough savings to set themselves up as independent farmers, fishermen, or tradesmen.

Officers included Chief Factors, Chief Traders, Traders, Assistant Traders, Clerks in Charge, and Clerks. Their positions entitled them to be addressed as Mister, and their salaries were considerably higher than those of tradesmen and labourers. Accountants, Writers, and Surgeons occupied somewhat lesser officer positions, but depending on the way they performed on the job, they had a good chance of being promoted to higher-level ranks. Like the most senior men, they were "gentlemen" by virtue of their education and were accorded the dignity of being called Mister.[26]

Somewhere between officer and servant class were the skilled tradesmen—carpenters, blacksmiths, boatbuilders, and coopers. As was the case in the military world, their recognized abilities could earn them non-commissioned officer status. Post Masters, for example, were men who began as tradesmen, or even as labourers, and had proved themselves capable of running a small post. Because they had little formal education they were seldom considered for advancement to the highest ranks, but due to their supervisory positions they were accorded the courtesy title of Mister.

The servant class consisted of labourers, some of whom had special skills as tailors, sailors, whalers, hunters, and cooks. The word "servant" in the seventeenth century had a meaning somewhat different from later usage and applied to anyone "under the obligation to render certain services to, and to obey the orders of, a person or a body of persons, especially in return for wages or salary." The designation continued to be used by Britain's great chartered companies into the twentieth century, meaning simply "labourers."[27]

In theory, officers and servants lived as separately as possible. Officers had different living quarters with private rooms for sleeping, a shared officers' sitting room, and possibly a billiard room or library. At the largest posts such as Moose Factory, Fort Garry, or York Factory they had their own dining room, cook, and steward, and meals were of higher quality, with produce and wine brought from London every year. A Factor or Chief Factor often had a separate house for himself with a personal cook and baker. The Company's men were assigned to private sleeping rooms in a Men's House with their cook and waiter and a dining room that sometimes did extra duty as a recreation room. None of these hierarchical arrangements were part of life at Churchill. Social distinction between officers and men tended to be ignored. Everybody ate, worked, and slept without emphasis on class differences.

During much of the year, the main occupation at Churchill Post was the serious business of finding and stocking up on food and firewood. Most of the time the men lived in tents at hunting, fishing, and wooding sites generally at a distance from the post. It was John Leask's job to allot rations to each "mess" at each of the tent camps. Each mess prepared its own meals. A four-man mess got twenty-four pounds of flour per week to make bread, biscuits, or bannock, plus portions of cheese, oatmeal, barley, tea, and sugar provided by the Company. In addition, each mess had a share of meat, fish, or fowl hunted by the men themselves or bought from local people.

All hands received rations of alcohol or the materials for making it, as William Auld, Churchill's chief in 1810, explained. "In summer they get small beer almost *ad libitum* & 1 qt of English Brandy [per week]. In winter they get 3/4 of a [quart] of molasses as an equivalent for Beer & double or treble the above quantity of Brandy. This last is already curtailed & the rest will follow quickly & silently as we can get quit of our present stock. We mean not to replace it except in very small quantities when all will be glad to be content with Country provisions chiefly." Beer, on the other hand, was made at the post and distributed to all employees. Known as "small beer," it had a low alcoholic content, around two and a half percent, and was not handed out for recreational purposes. At posts where clean water for drinking was scarce—and Churchill was such a one—brewed and fermented beverages were the only means of quenching thirst and were, at the same time, the primary source of the vitamins and ascorbic acid needed to prevent scurvy.[28]

The highest-ranking officer in Augustine's first year at Churchill was Chief Factor Thomas Topping, seconded by John Charles, who held the rank of Inland Trader and spent the summers at the factory's upriver outposts and the winters at Churchill.[29] Charles's particular responsibilities when not inland were the annual seal and whale hunts and excursions to cut wood or carry mail to York Factory. A third officer, William Ross, was the post accountant during the 1811 to 1813 trading years.[30] John Pocock Holmes, a surgeon, was responsible for the medical care of all Churchill District's people—traders, inland crews, and local residents. Like most surgeons in the fur trade, and indeed in Great Britain, Holmes was barely twenty-two when he finished medical training; he joined the Company as a full-fledged doctor in 1805.[31] The early nineteenth century was not a time when aspiring physicians and surgeons spent years studying and served lengthy internships and residencies in order to qualify.

Also at Churchill when Augustine arrived in the late summer of 1812 were Assistant Trader William Oman, carpenter Alexander Ross, cooper Hugh Wood, and blacksmith Joseph Spence. The master boatbuilder Peter Wishart divided his time between Churchill and York Factory, depending on where his skills were most needed. Ross and Wood, at a yearly wage of between £25 and £30, could look forward to top wages of around £50 after ten years' service. Spence earned a substantial £50 a year, while Oman, in spite of his status as a junior officer, was on the payroll at £24 per annum, rather less than the post's three tradesmen.[32]

In Outfit 1812–1813,[33] Augustine's first year at the post, the workforce numbered thirty-nine. Among them were three men who became his life-long friends: John Charles, William Oman, and James Dunning.[34]

YET ANOTHER CLASS OF EMPLOYEE, "NATIVES OF HUDSON BAY," also lived and worked at Churchill.[35] The term was used to identify anyone who had been born in Rupert's Land and included young men of mixed parentage like James Dunning and William Oman, Augustine's contemporaries. The first James Dunning employed by the Hudson's Bay Company was a sailor born in Stockton-on-Tees, England. His son, also named James, was identified by the Company as Dunning Jr. and described as "the son of an Englishman" and a "Chipewyan mother." Born in 1797, he began working for the Company as a labourer and apprentice harpooner a year or two before Augustine came to Churchill. The two teenagers often did chores together, and as adults they worked together hunting ptarmigan and geese.[36]

Other men, also identified as "natives of Hudson Bay," made up Churchill's Homeguard, men and women who, for personal reasons, had chosen to live near a Company establishment at least part of the time. During Augustine's lifetime, they were Chipewyan, known as Caribou-eater Dene, and were probably the Sayisi people whose home village was northwest of Churchill in the vicinity of Little Duck Lake.[37] They spent most of the year following the Qamanirjuaq and Beverly caribou herds on the tundra, and after the establishment of the trading post they provided most of the meat used at the post. They had little or no interest in furs or trapping but participated in Churchill's goose hunt every spring.[38] When they were near Churchill their wives worked as tanners, tailors, gardeners, and laundresses and often ran small traplines.

Although the Sayisi home village was roughly 250 miles northwest of Churchill, there were members of the community who chose to live within a short distance of the palisade. Most were elderly men and women who could not keep up with the fast-moving hunters following the caribou herds. Some were younger people who were not able to live off the land independently because of physical handicaps and could not be cared for by hard-pressed families in tough times. They or their relatives, or sometimes the Company's men, built shelters for them near the post, and the Company provided them with essential provisions and fuel, as well as medical care. Some of them were able to join their families in the winter when travelling was easy and food resources were adequate, while some lived near the post year-round, as did the family of a youngster called Shenandoah. His name does not appear on the annual Servants' Lists because he was not a contracted employee but was paid in goods, usually provisions and clothing, or the materials for making clothing. The journals for the years 1812, 1813, and 1814 mention him almost daily as working at chores in company with Augustine.

WITHIN EACH OF THE RECOGNIZED GROUPS OF PEOPLE LIVING AT the trading posts, there was another "class" of people. Churchill, as fort, factory, and post, was never an entirely male establishment. Women lived and worked, flourished or starved, bore fur trade children, and raised them in log cabins or skin tents, and sometimes in the officers' quarters inside the palisade. At Churchill, in any given year, one, two, or more women—the Indigenous wives and bicultural daughters of the Company's officers—lived in the officers' quarters and took part in the post's social activities. All of them were of First Nations ancestry. Inuit women were not among them, nor were Inuit women involved in the fur trade except as skin tanners, cleaning animal pelts that their fathers, husbands, and sons traded at the post. Some Inuit women made sealskin and walrus-skin boots that the men in their family sold to the Company.

The paramilitary structure of the Hudson's Bay Company went hand in hand with its official premise that overseas employees would remain unmarried and celibate during their years of service and would, in time, retire unencumbered to their British homes. But even the mandates of the London Committee could not prevent its officers and men from recognizing the attractions of their clients' sisters and daughters.

The women at Churchill Post during Augustine's first years at Churchill were the First Nations wives of three officers and of two biracial men: James Dunning Jr., whose mother and wife were both Chipewyan, and William Oman, whose mother was Cree and whose wife was Chipewyan.[39] In 1812, Betsy Holmes, wife of the surgeon John Pocock Holmes, was there with her two Holmes children and two children from her previous marriage to Thomas Stayner.[40] In 1813–14, Mary Auld, wife of Superintendent William Auld, was there with her teenaged daughter Jane and three young sons. A year later, Jane Auld was married to John Charles and had a baby daughter. Betsy Holmes, Mary Auld, and Jane Auld Charles may have sewn winter clothing for Augustine, nursed him when he was ill, or called on him to do small chores for them, such as carrying out the garbage. Augustine had a particularly close relationship with William Auld and his family.

Less highly placed Company employees also undertook matrimony, although their wives did not receive the consideration from their superiors that the wives and children of senior officers did. From time to time there were rumblings from the Governor's office at York Factory about the cost of feeding wives and children, which the officers at the posts explained away by replying, truthfully, that the women earned their keep by snaring birds, cleaning pelts, sewing the men's clothing, doing the post's laundry, tending the gardens, and occasionally delivering babies.

In its inability to admit openly the full extent of women's contributions to the trade and their presence at trading posts, the Company's owner-managers in London were simply reflecting early nineteenth-century attitudes. Although married officers did not welcome the London Committee's strictures against marriage, they were aware that being open about their feelings and behaviour could rebound to their detriment. If women were officially not welcome on the post, then the keeper of the daily journal would do well not to draw the Committee's attention to the fact that they and their children were indeed living within the stockade. Because of the zone of silence concerning women, the daily journals, which tell us so much in other respects, have little to say about them.

IN THE FIRST FEW WEEKS OF HIS RESIDENCE AT CHURCHILL, besides struggling with a new language, the names and positions of his companions, and the physical layout of the post, Augustine had to learn the practical details of his chores. In bringing Superintendent Auld up to date on events at

Churchill in his report of December 4, 1812, Topping included a brief and not particularly enthusiastic assessment of Augustine. "He is active and willing," he wrote, "but backward in learning either Indian or English."[41] During his first month at the post, Augustine learned how to wield an axe and was assigned to work with a team of experienced timber cutters to cut and stack enough firewood to see the post through a long cold winter.[42]

The severe ice and gale-force winds that usually occurred in mid-winter began as early as September in 1812, resulting in poor catches of both fresh and saltwater fish and a decline in coastal seal colonies. As if this was not worry enough for Topping, none of the Chipewyan who frequented the post had yet arrived with meat or furs. The non-appearance of those faithful provisioners was a bad sign, as Topping knew only too well. If they had been killing enough caribou to supply themselves adequately, they would have made the journey from their own land territory to Churchill. Their failure to arrive could only be understood as a failure of the caribou hunt.

By mid-January of 1813, Augustine had learned how to use a firearm, and he, along with Shenandoah, was sent to the Eastern Tent, some twenty-four miles from the House, to hunt ptarmigan under the supervision of one of the Company's sailors, James Moore. The three of them returned to the House on January 30, because of "there not being birds sufficient to be worth while staying."[43] Their report on the absence of birds was just one of a series of signs that food resources around Churchill were disappearing.

Food resources were in short supply throughout most of the HBC's Northern Department. John Spence, at York Factory, told Topping, "We have no furs, very few geese, and everything appears to desert us." Three weeks later William Auld expressed his fear for the communities in Red River and Saskatchewan as well as those living near York Factory. While writing about the "unenviable" conditions of York Factory's people, he used stronger language to describe the suffering of the Cree living within a few days' march of York Factory. "It is not in my power," he wrote, "to tell how many wretches belonging to YF have died of hunger, suffice it to say that in one tent 8 perished whose carcasses supplied sustenance to two female survivors for a time."[44]

News from York Factory that England and America were at war barely caught Topping's attention. His concerns had to do with food. "YF not being able to accommodate us with any more pemmican," he wrote to Auld, "we are extremely sorry [to hear]." He was not alone in his anxiety. Early in March, Auld noted the "dismal" news that Adam Snodie, Clerk in Charge at Nelson River Post, had reported a "great scarcity of provisions at [his] house through the whole winter," adding that the local people were "suffering, of course." By the middle of April, Topping saw first-hand just how bad things were at York Factory. A new blacksmith arrived from the southern factory and within a few days was showing signs of advanced scurvy.[45]

AS THE FUR TRADERS STRUGGLED TO FEED THEMSELVES ON COUNtry provisions, however inadequately, Cree and Chipewyan in their winter communities were starving to death. The people at Churchill could only speculate on what was happening in Inuit communities to the north. News finally came nearly a year after Augustine's arrival at the post. Fifteen hunters from his village arrived on July 11, 1813, and reported a serious food shortage in their own country. Augustine's father was not among them.[46]

After their reunion with the boy they had left behind nearly a year earlier, his fellow villagers made arrangements for him to spend another winter at the factory, where starvation was less likely than in their home village. Augustine had apparently made some progress in learning English and was proving competent in the work assigned to him, enough so that Thomas Topping gave him a favourable report: "The lad who stopped this last winter requested to stop another year with us, and his friends...wished it also. We therefore consented, he being a very industrious, good tempered man, and very useful and universally liked by the whole of the factory people."[47] At Topping's urging, Augustine's kinsmen and fellow villagers reluctantly agreed to delay their return to their families in order to hunt whale for about ten days, and they set out for the whale fishery at Seal River.

John Charles, with a crew of men, intended to join them in about five days' time and planned to take Augustine along so he could see his countrymen once more before they left for the North. As it happened, the weather was either dead calm or too boisterous for Churchill's tiny sailboat towing the raft they needed to bring back barrels of whale oil. After a week of waiting for better weather, and worrying that the reluctant Inuit would abandon the hunt and return north, John Charles decided that if Augustine was to have a chance to say goodbye to his friends in person, the two of them had no choice but to walk the forty miles to Seal River.[48]

They reached Seal River "without seeing a single Esquimaux, but found the place they had slept at a night or two, but not any whales they had killed."[49] Charles faced the disappointment of not having his stores of oil for winter use increased. And any hopes young Augustine may have had of visiting with his kinfolk for a few more hours before another winter set in faded into the north as his people had done.

CHAPTER 2

THE APPRENTICE
1813–1820

ON AUGUST 14, 1813, AUGUSTINE WAS ON BOARD Churchill's sloop on his way to York Factory. Ten days earlier, William Auld, the newly appointed Northern Department Superintendent, had arrived on a tour of inspection and had singled out Augustine for special attention. When Auld left to return to York Factory, he took the youngster with him.[1]

Within the week, two Company supply ships, *Prince of Wales I* and *Eddystone*, entered Hudson Bay. They had been escorted across the Atlantic by the heavily armed Royal Navy frigate HMS *Brazen*, because, as the daily journal explained, "of there being war with America." Once they were safely through Hudson Strait, *Eddystone*'s passengers were transferred to *Brazen*, and *Eddystone* left the convoy to head south to the bottom of the bay. Late on the evening of August 18, *Prince of Wales* and *Brazen* anchored in deep water off the east bank of the Churchill River, with ninety-five Scottish and Irish colonists bound for Lord Selkirk's Red River Colony.[2] Also on board was a new Company recruit, twenty-year-old accountant Hugh Leslie, who in later years was a close friend and protector of Augustine.

Rain, fog, and rough water prevented the two captains, John Turner of *Prince of Wales*[3] and James Stirling of *Brazen*, from getting boats in the water until morning, when Stirling and two of his officers came ashore. Their first dreadful duty was to inform Chief Factor Thomas Topping that some of the passengers and crew of *Prince of Wales* were lying ill with a deadly typhus fever. Three men, including the party's leader, Peter Laserre, were already dead and had been buried at sea. Among the Red River settlers on board *Prince of Wales*, thirty were sick, in different stages of the disease.[4]

After the death of Laserre his second-in-command, Archibald McDonald of Argyllshire, became the new settlement leader, at least in title, but he was in unfamiliar territory, with no experience in leadership and no idea how to survive in the Subarctic or in the alien world of an isolated trading post under the rule of the Hudson's Bay Company. It was clear to McDonald that he was not qualified to make decisions on how his hosts should deal with the crisis and clear also to the three men who were both knowledgeable and experienced in managing potentially disastrous circumstances. Topping, Captain Turner, and Surgeon Nainsby from *Prince of Wales* stepped in and took control of the dangerous situation.

In the face of the terrible news, Topping had to make a series of quick decisions. Sending the two ships and their passengers away was not an option: thirty colonists were ill with the "malignant disease" and might not survive even a few more days at sea. A second consideration was that the ship itself was the source of the contagion and badly in need of cleaning.[5] Captain Turner urged that all passengers be moved ashore so that he could have his ship fumigated. Anxious to keep the sick and the healthy apart, Topping gave orders for a makeshift tent hospital and kitchen to be set up at Sloop's Cove under the supervision of Mr. Nainsby and a second tent camp erected on the uninhabited east bank of the river for the settlers who appeared to be healthy. To prevent the disease from spreading to his own people and, even worse, infecting the Chipewyan then camped near the factory, Topping declared a ban on all communication between ship and shore. He explained as best he could the nature of the disease to a gathering of Chipewyan who were at the post, emphasizing the need for strict isolation of the sick. He told them to keep away from Sloop's Cove and, recognizing that there might be a "temptation of seeing a European woman" for the first time, asked Captain Turner to land all the healthy women on the east bank of the river.[6]

Topping wrote to Superintendent Auld on August 21 to inform him of the crisis, noting that of ninety-five colonists aboard the two ships, thirty were "afflicted" and four had died since they came ashore. "It is a most distressing and unfortunate circumstance and I hope to God the disease may not be introduced to the country. We shall do our utmost to avoid it," he wrote. The good news was that the forty colonists who had transferred from *Eddystone* to *Brazen* were "in perfect health." On the twenty-third, Topping sent one of the Inland Traders, Joseph Howse, with thirty-six healthy settlers to York Factory in three boats borrowed from *Prince of Wales*. Howse carried with him a letter from Topping to Auld.[7]

During that night, more colonists were showing symptoms of the disease, and two more people died. One, possibly both, of those who died that night were sailors. Captain Turner told Topping that the "weak state of his ship's crew made it impossible for him to put to sea." Captain Stirling agreed that leaving "would be very imprudent."[8]

Topping assigned Augustine to the work parties delivering clean water and firewood to the hospital and to the campsite of the healthy colonists every day. Other Churchill men collected clothing and bedding from their own trunks, handed them out to the colonists, both ailing and well, and, in great fires on the beach, burned infested clothing to destroy disease-carrying fleas. To increase food supplies for a population suddenly more than tripled, Topping hired all the Chipewyan who were near the post to hunt and fish. "What fresh provision we had with vegetables was sent to Sloops Cove," he wrote, "as also everything that was in our possession for the relief of the sick people." Before all the patients could be moved from the infected ship to wood and leather cots in the tents, another colonist, Donald Stewart, died on the beach.[9] The only good news of the week was that the forty or so colonists who had been transferred from *Eddystone* to *Brazen* before reaching Churchill showed no signs of the deadly fever.

On August 25, Topping ordered quick repairs to one of his whaling boats and gave his clerk, Thomas Swain, the task of getting seven more healthy colonists away. In Swain's pack was Topping's second letter to Auld. "It is with an aching heart I am under the necessity to inform you," he wrote, "that the morning after Mr Howse left us [August 23] another of the seamen died, and three more people have been taken ill. We have stopt all communication with the ship." The letter ended with a request for assistance. "Could it be possible for you to come," he wrote, "it would be of the utmost benefit, as among the colonists there wants a person who has the power not only to order them, but also to enforce their acting for their own preservation as well as all around them."[10] Auld was certainly needed at Churchill. While he had no rightful authority over the colonists—that position officially belonged to Archibald McDonald—Auld did have the last word on what happened at the factory, and he was never slow to use his powerful personality to do what he thought best. He was also a partially trained physician, able to give useful advice on the care of the sick and the protection of the healthy.[11]

In addition to supplying vegetables and whatever fresh meat was on hand to the hospital tents every day, Topping set two men to making pine beer, which Mr. Nainsby thought would be good for the sick. The two medically trained men at the post—Nainsby and McDonald—would have understood that in the fermentation process the quantities of vitamin B6 in beer are increased and known from observation that beer had a strengthening effect. Topping then hired the Homeguard women to work around the clock making two new leather tents for the hospital. The same day, Surgeon Nainsby reported, prematurely, that the "contagion is at its crisis," which, Topping wrote, "we sincerely hope to God is the case." On the twenty-sixth, he sent two rafts with the new tents to Sloop's Cove, along with two hogsheads of the medicinal beer.[12]

On the thirtieth, another colonist died, and two more on the first two days of September. In spite of these most recent deaths, Surgeon Nainsby thought that in general his patients were beginning to improve.[13] A week later, the surgeon reported no new cases in the previous five days and declared *Prince of Wales* "in a state of health and no danger of infection." It was now safe, he said, to resume communications between ship and shore.

RELIEVED THAT THE SCOURGE HAD BEEN KEPT AWAY FROM THE local people, Topping ordered all hands to begin unloading the year's supplies from *Prince of Wales*. Moving the cargo did not go smoothly. Stress, exhaustion, haste, and, according to Topping, "the drunkenness of the [*Prince of Wales*'] crew" led to a collision between two of the boats jostling each other around the supply ship. The post's bateau, *Hope*, was rammed and settled deck-deep to the bottom, "full of public & private property, which is greatly damaged and much lost."[14] Loss of provisions, trade goods, and medicines, in any amount, was always a serious matter at isolated fur trade posts, where the lives of the Company's servants as well as its clients depended on adequate supplies. The loss of the men's private property was also a blow, considering that books and personal items from England had to be ordered at least twelve months in advance, and newspapers and letters from home came only once a year.

As Churchill's people coped with one crisis after another, the two parties Topping had sent racing to York Factory during the last terrible week of August reached their destination and delivered their letters, Joseph Howse on September 6 and Thomas Swain on September 7. On the same day, Superintendent Auld at York Factory started north on one of the Company's schooners with Augustine and a crew of ten.[15] They reached Churchill on the afternoon of September 9—"fortunately had a very short passage," Topping entered in the journal.[16] For the first time, Augustine saw men of the Royal Navy and was left with a lasting impression of their distinctive uniforms and the desire to have similar clothing some day.

On September 13 and 14, *Prince of Wales*'s panicked sailors staged a minor rebellion. By that time it was becoming obvious to everybody that Hudson Strait would be impassable before the ship could reach York Factory, unload, and put to sea again. The frustrated mariners faced a cold and tedious, as well as hungry, winter at York Factory. One of the officers came ashore, wrote Topping, "to inform us of this refractory behaviour."[17] Captain Turner, Superintendent Auld, and Archie McDonald went straight to Captain Stirling, the senior military man among them. Whatever authority Auld or McDonald passed on to Stirling resulted in the captain going aboard *Prince of Wales*, where he "made the seamen resume their duty." Topping did not say what measures Stirling took in demanding obedience, but the aura of naval discipline surrounding the uniformed captain, as well as his well-polished sidearms and sword, may have played a part.

The two ships, with the healthy colonists on board, were finally ready to sail on the sixteenth. *Brazen* left the anchorage first and cleared the river's mouth, only to return when *Prince of Wales* went aground. Floating the ship out of the mud proved difficult. All the healthy colonists were put ashore to lighten the load. With Topping, the two captains, and all able-bodied men absorbed in getting the grounded vessel into deep water, the colonists, left to their own devices for forty-eight hours and against all warnings, spent two nights visiting the sick in the tents at Sloop's Cove. The incident was to cost the colonists dearly; several more were infected and two of them died before *Prince of Wales* was finally lifted free by an incoming high tide and towed to deep water by Churchill's men.

York Factory's medical officer, surgeon Abel Edwards, and the colony's Surgeon Kinney arrived by boat from York Factory on September 19. In spite of Surgeon Nainsby's declaration that his patients were out of danger and that the fever showed no signs of spreading, Kinney and Edwards found eighteen people at Sloop's Cove still sick, three of them "in a dangerous state," and learned that one of the women had died during the morning—the eighth fatality since the vessels had anchored in the river on August 19. In consultation with Auld, Kinney and Edwards agreed that taking the sick on board would be unwise. "For the safety of the ship & crew [the colonists] would not be admitted to go on board [and] they must remain at CR [Churchill River]."[18]

Churchill's men, in the little spare time they had after stowing the year's supplies, opened and dried the wet goods salvaged from the wreck of *Hope*. The sorry fact that "the tea is all utterly useless, having imbibed so much of the salt water," was added to the miseries the men were already experiencing. There would be no comforting cups of hot tea during the next year. The good news was that there was a crate of chickens among the salvaged goods, raising hopes that there would be enough eggs to provide the semblance of a bland diet for the sick over the winter.

Finally, at about two in the afternoon of September 20, *Prince of Wales* and *Brazen* left the Churchill anchorage with a heavy north wind at their backs and headed south. Thomas Topping left Churchill around the same time, to return home for his furlough year. John Charles took over the management of Churchill Post and began keeping the daily journal. Superintendent Auld also left Churchill, on the Company's schooner *Eastmain*, and reached York Factory on the twenty-third. His stay there was brief. By the second week of October, he was back at Churchill with his wife, Mary, and their children. The family settled into the Men's House officers' quarters for the winter.[19]

THE ADDITION OF FIFTY SOULS TO CHURCHILL'S WINTER POPULAtion, many of them weakened from raging fevers, dehydration, and inability to take food, promised a more than usually difficult winter ahead. The Company's officers knew from long experience on the edge of the Arctic that providing their uninvited and unwelcome guests with food, medicine, clothing, bedding, and household utensils would create almost insurmountable problems for the post, which was hard put to supply its own needs in most winters. A major concern was the scarcity of firewood. The establishment could not adequately heat its own buildings, and keeping the unwelcome guests even minimally warm was going to be a challenge. Yet another potential problem was the unpreparedness of the colonists for life in the Subarctic and the inexperience and ignorance of their leaders. A final complicating factor was the lack of clear guidelines about who exactly had ultimate authority over the settlers.

Churchill's officers chose Churchill Creek, about fourteen miles upriver, for the colonists' temporary settlement.[20] John Charles approved of the site because it was "the only place there is wood sufficient for building, fuel, &c."[21] He sent a work crew to cut down the trees best suited for building a handful of small log cabins for the winterers. Two other reasons, lumped together in Charles's "&c," were that the site was far enough removed from the main establishment to keep the inexperienced newcomers from getting in the way of the post's business, or so the Company's officers hoped, and that the encampment was close enough to the post for Augustine to make daily trips to the colonists with rations. In a second decision, the officers decided that an old building at the hay marsh, known as Haymarsh House, could be fitted up as a hospital for the convalescents. Augustine was continuously on the trail for the next two months, supplying the hospital camp and the temporary village at Churchill Creek.

On the morning of September 21, Mr. Linklater and sixteen colonists started on foot for Churchill Creek, while the boats brought the colonists' "lumber" to the post.[22] In the afternoon, four boats, manned by eight of Churchill's men, headed upriver with seventeen more colonists, provisions, and "other necessaries." Linklater and Hugh Wood, the cooper, remained with the colonists to help them find a decent place to build their winter shelters. More provisions, clothing, and luggage, along with another batch of colonists, went upriver on the twenty-third. Fifteen settlers still too ill to be moved remained at Sloop's Cove, one of whom died the following day, the last of the typhus fatalities.[23]

The thirty-year-old building at the old hay marsh, once used as an overnight shelter for woodcutting and haying parties, had stood empty and decaying for almost two decades, but Charles thought that with some fixing up it would serve as a hospital for the convalescent colonists. Like Churchill, Haymarsh House was surrounded by stands of small trees, where, the Company's officers hoped, the colonists would be able to supply themselves with firewood. Surgeon Abel Edwards, with two colonists and boatbuilder Peter Wishart, began work "to fit it up in as comfortable a manner as possible for the reception of the sick…till they recover sufficiently to be removed to Churchill Creek without fear of infection."[24] Augustine and John Leask joined them to gather firewood, while Wishart finished making wooden beds. By September 29, under the supervision of Doctor Edwards, all of the still-ailing colonists were moved from Sloop's Cove to their new convalescent hospital. Winter homes for the healthy colonists were ready at Churchill Creek by October 17.[25]

The colonists had trouble settling into their new temporary homes. Doctor Edwards, who had given up his chance to go home to England in order to care for them, soon found that they needed a great deal of attention. "The greater part of them seem to be much like children," he wrote, "not capable of being trusted a moment out of sight." Their biggest problem was their unpreparedness for the hard climate they found themselves in. As the temperature fell to 48° Fahrenheit below zero, Edwards issued a circular addressed to "The Emigrants at Churchill Creek" with instructions on how to survive a subarctic winter. The circular included a mandatory dress code: "Every man & boy on leaving his residence to go to the woods or elsewhere [is] to have his waistcoat & jacket buttoned closely about his neck & breast, over which he is to wear his toggy or great coat." McDonald and Edwards visited the colonists every morning to ensure that they washed themselves and took their anti-scorbutic, probably pine-needle tea or beer.[26]

IN SPITE OF DISRUPTIONS TO POST LIFE CAUSED BY THE COLONISTS, the Company's business had to go on, and its men managed to attend to essential chores. On October 8, between trips to Haymarsh House and Churchill Creek, Augustine dug the frozen garden to take up the turnips and onions he had helped plant in early summer. A few days later he was wrenching up cabbages. When the usual fall hunting and fishing camps were set up, he and Shenandoah made regular trips to deliver rations and pick up fish and fowl when the hunts were successful, as well as taking supplies to Churchill Creek and the hay marsh hospital.[27]

William Auld continued to take an interest in Augustine, possibly because he was missing his oldest son, Thomas, who was about the same age as Augustine and had been sent to school in Scotland the previous year. On November 7, a Sunday, the two of them went for a walk, taking their guns and accompanied by Auld's pet dog. The Superintendent came home with twenty-three ptarmigan in his bag, and Augustine, still learning how to use a gun, brought back five. By mid-November, John Charles had men at three hunting tents and others on walkabout looking for caribou. Only the two senior officers, Charles and

Auld, their cook Thomas Spence, the steward John Leask, and Augustine were permanently stationed at the House.

In the semi-darkness of a subarctic winter, Augustine was constantly on the go between the House and the outlying tents. On November 19, he made the fourteen-mile walk to the hunting tent at Churchill Creek with provisions, returning the next day with a note from Hugh Leslie reporting careless and dangerous activities by the stranded, inexperienced, and probably bored colonists. Leslie worried that while wandering around with their guns, some of them would be lost in the woods, and in fact, some of them had already lost their way. But, he reported, they had "fortunately reached the river side before night, except one who did not reach his house till very late & from its then being mild weather received no hurt from the cold."[28]

Faced with the reckless behaviour of the colonists, the HBC officers took steps to safeguard them from their own ignorance. "To prevent these Strangers from losing themselves or getting themselves mutilated by the frost (very few of them being properly clothed) Mr Auld this morning went to Churchill Creek & desired those among them who had guns to deliver them in to Mr Edwards as well as to see that they attended to the regulations given them for their health and preservation during so long a winter as they must pass here." In their attempts to protect the colonists and make them more self-sufficient, the officers unwittingly set the scene for the worst of Arctic disasters.[29]

Charles assigned his steward, John Leask, the job of showing the colonists how to survive an Arctic winter. Leask was to show them "the nature of a hunting tent as well as direct them how to get the tent erected, and the best spot for fire wood and nearness to the hunting ground, things very requisite and essential at a hunting tent on Hudsons Bay," wrote John Charles, in one of his breathless sentences. Four settlers presented themselves at the main post on November 25 as directed, ready for Leask's lesson. The steward had already loaded small sleds with everything they needed to set up tents and stowed them in the Men's House trading room, where the four settlers bedded down for the night. John Leask, Thomas Spence, and Augustine went to their sleeping places in the kitchen on the other side of the adjoining wall.

During the night, the men sleeping in the kitchen woke to the smell of smoke and the sound of "cracking of fire on the roof." Rushing "half dres'd" into the next room they found the four settlers up, uncertain what to do next while flames filled the fireplace chimney. Leask hurried to alarm Auld in the officers' quarters and met him already halfway down the stairs. Amid suffocating smoke, and without water, the men found it impossible to quench the flames. As the roof, ceiling, and most of the second storey collapsed, all the trade goods stored upstairs went up in a fierce blaze. The men turned their attention to protecting the nearby buildings.

Their first panicked thought was to get the gunpowder out of the magazine and safely stowed at a distance before it exploded. They rescued the contents of the trading room and carried away most of the provisions stored in the sheds but lost the salted meat, butter, and molasses held in the cellars. "In less than three hours," wrote Charles, in anguish and indignation, "the whole of our dwelling House, ice house and coal shed was nothing but a heap of burning ruin, and the whole of us in a very weak and exhausted state from violent exertions, & the effects of the thick smoak, when trying to preserve the content of the upper warehouse, where the chief part of our trading goods was kept. As also our stores, the most of which with nearly all our books, lost, as well as the whole of the furs that were traded from the natives only a few days before this sad accident."[30]

John Charles's entry for the day went on at some length, in a turmoil of thoughts, words, and emotions:

> In this country where the buildings are generally of wood a greater calamity than fire can scarcely happen and particularly at this season of the year when no water can be obtained, but what is made from snow, and never more at once than is required for the domestic uses of the house. Snow certainly may in any quantity be had, but in a case like this, is of little service being hard froze in lumps, and cannot be put in the small places where the fire may be most violent. From the alarming state the fire was in when it was first observed, it must have been some time before our people in the kitchen were awoke, and

must have originated from the fire in the Indian House, it being in the roof of this place the fire was first observed which unfortunately was the cause of the destruction of the Factory. Our fire wood also, which was not the least of our losses, ready cut up, and nearly sufficient for the winter, in piles a short distance from the houses, as likewise in our shed could not be preserved from the devastating element. At break of day [on November 26], there being no fear of the sparks of fire communicating with our sheds, we were employed picking up the goods and carrying them into our launch house, as till then everything was laying about as it was thrown down. The powder also carried in…as the magazine was then occupied by our men to sleep in till we get a tent erected.[31]

Among those who escaped the fire in their nightclothes and wandered among the ruins of the fort the following day were Mrs. Auld, her daughter Jane, and the three boys. They had lost everything—clothes, books, small personal treasures, household furniture, and toys—and however drafty and uncomfortable their living quarters above the Men's House had been, they faced even greater discomforts in the tents that were to be their home for the next year.

The four settlers, who got the blame for careless handling of their fire and the consequent disaster, were, as Charles put it—for him, rather mildly—"sent back to Churchill Creek" on November 27.[32] They took with them a note to inform Hugh Leslie of the calamity and to request that the sailor James Moore, "a useful man," be sent to assist at the main establishment. All hands spent the morning pitching a tent in the garden patch against the western stockade and collecting useful items—ironwork, hatchets, chisels—from the ruins "before the rubbish could be covered with snow, as it was beginning to be bad weather." It was not only the falling snow that concealed tools and boxes; at latitude 58° north, the sun reached its nadir in late November, leaving the post in darkness for as much as sixteen hours out of the twenty-four and twilight for another four.

Moore arrived from Leslie's hunting tent on the twenty-eighth accompanied by one of the four repentant settlers ready to help out, and by evening a sleeping tent was ready for the Company's men. Those remaining at the factory continued to search through "the rubbish for everything that could yet be rendered serviceable" and considered themselves fortunate to have found the keys to the buildings that remained standing. During the next few days, blacksmith Thomas Halcrow was able to restore one of the stoves to working order and installed it in the packing shed, which was being turned into living quarters for the post's men.

Augustine made the twenty-six-mile trip to Mr. Linklater's tent at the Woody Islands on November 29, with a request that Peter Wishart, the boatbuilder, and one other man come home to help out. On the way, he paused at the Bushy Islands and informed the men at the fishery of the disaster. While Augustine continued on to the Woody Islands, one of the men from Bushy hurried downriver to the post, "as he said to get his gun repaired," wrote Charles, "though the real thing that brought him home was curiosity to ascertain if what he heard from our Esquimaux lad was true or not." Verifying Augustine's report was apparently necessary, Charles added, "The lad as yet not speaking English sufficient to make the men understand him."[33]

The stranded colonists continued to suffer from the cold and from the shortage of rations that the post's men took for granted every winter. On December 15, several of them presented themselves to Charles in need of supplies—"again," he wrote—and reported a case of scurvy. The hard-pressed senior trader did what he could. "Having nothing now in our possession to prevent its [scurvy's] influence but the partridges which they were constantly supplied with, and a few cabbages, a part of these were sent for the use of the patients and the rest conserved in case of a future demand." A month later, during the night of January 14–15, nineteen-year-old John Bannerman died from consumption.[34]

The old shed, finally refitted as a dwelling for all the post's people, was ready a week before Christmas. The men piled "snow all around it to keep out the wind," wrote Charles, "as it is only weather boarding nailed on the outside of square logs without anything stuffed in the seams," and "we shifted our residence...and took up our abode in our new House." The carpenters then turned their attention to an old, little-used summer cookhouse, "which is now our kitchen and residence for our cook, steward and Esquimaux lad," and began refitting it. Under the circumstances, Augustine again had reason to be glad he shared a living space with the cook and steward, where there was stacked firewood and a functioning stove.

THROUGH THE DARK WINTER MONTHS, THE POST'S MEN KEPT TO their day-in, day-out dull routine of hunting, chopping wood, and rebuilding the post. Augustine and Shenandoah continued to act as couriers and transporters, delivering oatmeal and ammunition to the men at the outlying tents and bringing home partridges for storage in the ice house. With one of the post's dogs for company, the boys set off every day before sunrise hoping to reach their destinations before the light faded in the afternoon.[35]

While the two boys were away on one of their errands, Charles sent James Moore and John Leask in search of "a place to erect a tent for our two men and Esquimaux lad to reside in." With firewood supplies dangerously low, Charles and Auld had reluctantly decided that a fire in the cookstove was a luxury they could no longer afford. With the men doing their own cooking over a barrel fire in their sleeping quarters, Spence, Leask, and Augustine might be more profitably employed in hunting.[36] The site chosen for the new tent was about three miles from the post. Its main advantage was its proximity to a small stand of trees, which could be used as fuel. On February 1, Augustine, Leask, and Spence moved into their canvas and caribou-skin home. In reporting the event, Charles made sure his superiors would understand that the three were not taking it easy. "They come to the factory in the morning to do what is required," he wrote, and "return in the evening." Reporting for work at the factory added six miles a day to Augustine's already rigorous routine.[37]

In February, the colonists began to wander again. Five of them left Churchill Creek "because they didn't have wood for fuel" and spent the night at the abandoned Haymarsh hospital, keeping warm by burning the beds that had been built for the sick. Charles exiled them to the Eastern Tent under the supervision of John Leask. On the eleventh, Archie McDonald reported that eight of his charges had gone off to Haymarsh hospital again. Charles concluded it was "highly requisite some person should be with them that has more authority," and he sent Augustine and Shenandoah to take them to Hugh Leslie's tent at North River. After just two nights the colonists refused to live in a tent and went back to Churchill Creek.

Eight settlers showed up at the House to get oatmeal on March 8, telling Charles that "the hospital [at Haymarsh House] was nearly burnt down by the party yesterday not putting out the fire." Their foolishness and obstinate refusal to accept the rules of the post aside, it is difficult not to have some sympathy for the troublesome colonists. The firewood they were expected to warm their tents and huts with was green, unseasoned wood from small stands of puny trees. Much of their fires' energy would have been lost in burning away sap and moisture. In addition to having very little heat, the colonists, living in very close quarters, had to breathe large amounts of tar and creosote formed by smouldering unseasoned wood.[38] With noses, throats, and lungs clogged with noxious fumes, they must at times have longed for the comfort of a simmering kettle over a clean-burning fire.

Warmer weather in March brought out the polar bears. When Shenandoah spotted one near his tent during the night, he urgently requested that Augustine follow its trail with him. After a long chase, Augustine returned with "the head of a small cub, having killed the old one also." Without pausing, he headed off to the Woody Islands with tools needed to build a sled to haul wood to the river's edge, ready for rafting to the post as soon as the ice cleared. He was home again on March 18 and immediately set off with Shenandoah and the dogs to North River to pick up 630 partridges and deliver them to the post's ice cellar. A day later, Charles gave him a sled and two harness dogs—a mark of approval for the young man's work. At the same time, Charles decided that deploying Augustine, Leask, and Spence in a tent three miles from the burned-out post was taking up too much time that could be used doing other things more important than saving fuel. On March 19, they loaded their tent and personal possessions on Augustine's small sled and again set up temporary quarters near the ruins of the Men's House. By month's end, the North River tent had produced 5,500 partridges, sufficient for the post's needs, and Charles sent Augustine to bring Hugh Leslie and his men home.

At the post, renovations made necessary by the great fire continued, following Charles's intricate reconstruction plan. Trunks belonging to the Inland Traders were taken from the Chest House and stored in the Destitute House, stores of flour were moved from the Flour House to the Chest House, and the Flour House was converted into a trading room. Charles recalled the blacksmith from the Eastern Tent to repair trading iron, hatchets, ice chisels, and everything else that had been damaged in the fire but could be fixed.[39] During the dark evenings, all hands netted snowshoes by firelight, probably enthusiastically as the snowshoes were meant for the Selkirk settlers while they walked to York Factory.

The colonists were also making preparations. Archie McDonald and twenty-six settlers brought "the lumber [excess baggage] they intend to leave here preparatory to their departure for York Factory." On April 5, Augustine took the last load of snowshoes to Churchill Creek, returning the next day with fifty-one colonists—thirty-one men, three women, and seventeen girls—ready to begin their long trek overland to York Factory.[40]

A month after the Selkirk colonists left Churchill, Charles recorded that Cree messengers had brought letters from York Factory reporting the safe arrival of the fifty-one settlers. Beyond that, he cared little and had nothing to say about his unwelcome winter guests. What excited him that day was the unexpected discovery of a bundle of useful metal tools. The carpenter, on finishing the new trading room, began laying a floor for a carpentry shop and in the process had to clean out a long-unused drain. Inside, he found twenty-four small hatchets and fifteen ice chisels, "which must have been put there at least twenty years ago, & fortunately for us had never been observed before, as with a little trouble our smith will make them as good as ever."[41]

Charles was not, however, completely free of Scottish colonists. Among them had been a few elderly settlers who would not have been able to walk 150 miles on snowshoes. Charles and the Selkirk leaders decided to wait until breakup and then send them to York Factory by boat. In the meantime, they were to remain at Churchill Creek.

WITH THE COMING OF THE NORTHERN SPRING IN EARLY MAY, GEESE began to arrive, and for about a month the partridge-hunting tents became stations for goose hunters. Between May 5 and June 4, 2,526 geese were brought in and 1,699 were salted in fifteen hogsheads for later use. The temporary workforce of Chipewyan hunters was paid off and started their summer trek north from the forest to the summer feeding grounds of the caribou herds.[42]

Most of the men at the post were busy rebuilding the stockade, tanning hides, making ropes, and, perhaps most importantly, "cleaning geese for meals."[43] A typical workday was as much as eighteen hours long. Travel was no longer as the crow flies. With the disappearance of ice on shallow lakes, routes between the post and the outlying tents necessitated walking around ponds instead of across them, greatly increasing the number of miles Augustine and Shenandoah had to walk each day. Without snow, sleds were not useful and all supplies and provisions had to be backpacked by the lads and their dogs.

The Sayisi people also suffered travel difficulties as melting snow bared the land and left a difficult terrain of hummocks and rocks. For the elderly or disabled, following the fast-moving caribou herd and its hunters was not possible. In such circumstances the presence of a trading post was a blessing. People knew that if they left their elderly and their invalids on one of the paths near the post, the Company would take them in and feed and care for them until snow once more covered the ground. By early June, Churchill Post was taking care of eight invalids, the last to be found a crippled boy left by his parents "just beyond the factory."[44]

John Charles recorded the story of one Sayisi family living near the post that casts light on the shadowy figure of Augustine's fellow courier, Shenandoah.

> There is a family of invalid Indians who depend upon us wholly for their subsistence, [he wrote,] to the number of eight, four of whom have been supported here for the last 6 years, constantly, owing to the decrepit and pitiful state of the relative of an Indian lad called Shenandoah, whom we always

employ; the old woman who is his grandmother has not stood on her feet for more than thirty years and having no relatives among her countrymen living, none of the latter can be persuaded to take her away, to be an encumberance to them, tho several *have* taken her, and the four others of the family consisting of her daughter and three children, but generally left them in a short time either to perish or find their way back to this place as they could. The other three are also cripples, whom their relatives were under the necessity of leaving in the month of June last [1814] with an intention of fetching them away on the first freezing of the river, when they can drag them in their sledges tho at the same time had no Europeans or settlement been near them, no doubt they would have left them in the same manner to perish, which is a custom far too often practised among the Chipewyans upon the friendless and infirm.[45]

The custom was inevitable in a time and place where no one could count on being able to care for another. If anyone was to survive at all, it was sometimes necessary for the less productive members of a community to stay behind while their hardier companions carried on the hunt. Often the hard decision was made voluntarily by the person who was left behind. When the "custom" was necessary, it was undertaken with some degree of hope. Those who went ahead left blankets and food if they had any and often made small shelters for those left behind. The hunters returned when they could to care for their kinsmen and fellow villagers.

On June 13, Surgeon Edwards, who was at Churchill Creek with Shenandoah, sent the young man to the post to tell Charles that one of the elderly colonists had reported seeing "strange Indians" lurking near their huts. Such reports were not uncommon among Algonquian and Athapascan peoples, whose oral literatures and legends described other-than-human persons with a taste for human flesh and the ability to turn true humans into cannibals. Despite skepticism on the part of the officers, only a shift in residence could calm the colonists' fears. Charles gave Augustine the job of preparing a new living site at Seahorse Gully for the elderly pioneers and settling them into it. Aided by one of the post's labourers he set up four tents ready for occupancy near the Stone Fort and on June 18 moved his elderly charges to their new home in a brigade of four canoes manned by the post's men. By evening, Augustine had his charges happily settled into their new homes.[46]

How the Scottish colonists knew about cannibal monsters remains unclear, unless someone who spoke English had been telling them ghost stories. Any of Churchill's labourers may have done so, but it is tempting to speculate that Shenandoah was the informant. What little we know about the Chipewyan youth suggests that he had lived at Churchill for most, perhaps all, of his life, in which case he was likely to be more fluent in English than Augustine was. Both youngsters saw the Selkirk colonists almost every day for the more than six months that they delivered provisions and carried messages to and from the post. There were many opportunities for the exchange of stories, including the cannibal monster story known among Athapascan peoples as *wechuge* and among Ojibwa and Cree peoples as *windigo*, *wittigo*, or *witiko*.[47]

WITH SUMMER FULL UPON THEM BY THE FIRST OF JULY, TRADING activity increased. On the morning of the tenth, five Inuit arrived with a few furs to trade—170 foxes, five prime wolves, two staged wolves, and two blue foxes—after a nine-day trip from their home country.[48] A few days later they left, and, to the astonishment of the Company's officers and men, Augustine went with them. A note of disappointment, and perhaps even annoyance, is apparent in John Charles's rough copy: "This day the 5 Esquimaux left us as also our Esquimax lad whom we have kept for these two years past. He could not be persuaded to remain on account of the promise he had made to a young girl previous to his remaining with us, the father of whom now came to solicit his return among his friends." The fair copy[49] of the journal entry tells a slightly different, and more precise, story: "Augustine...who has been with us nearly two years left with these 5 of his countrymen having been promised the hand of a young woman by one of the party."[50]

The "promise" was part of an Inuit social support system designed to provide children with assurance of care in the event that their biological or adoptive parents died or were otherwise unable to raise them. Wise and caring parents took the precaution of betrothing their infant, who, if orphaned, would be taken into the household of their future spouse and raised as a family member. Charles's use of the word "promise" indicates that Augustine's parents had made an agreement with the parents of a girl for an eventual marriage. From Augustine's point of view, it was time for him to marry, and he went with scarcely a backward glance. How he spent the next ten months, from July 1814 to May 1815, is not known, except that he was in the North, presumably with his family or with the family of his promised bride, in a community somewhere between Knapp's Bay and Rankin Inlet.

THE WINTER OF 1814—15 WAS NOT AN EASY ONE FOR THE COMPANY'S clients and employees. The severe climatic regime, known among climatologists today as the Dalton Minimum, had by 1814 prevailed for a quarter of a century. Caribou were scarce or absent altogether, and reports of suffering and starvation were more and more common among Inuit, Chipewyan, and Cree coming to the post.

Over the century and a half of the Company's existence, its officers in Rupert's Land had noted weather conditions daily in their post's journals or, in large posts, in a meteorological journal. Most records commented on long-term climatic trends only when something out of the ordinary seemed to be happening. Such was the case during the forty-year Dalton Minimum. In September of 1800, Chief Factor Thomas Stayner complained of a "remarkably cold" summer. William Auld applied the same words to the entire trading year of 1802–03, during which "a great part" of the nearby Inuit at Knapp's Bay died from starvation. In 1807 he described the Arctic spring as "the coldest month of May I ever saw." On June 17, 1815, Chief Trader John Charles declared, "The weather in general is very cold for this time of the year as we have frequent showers of snow, hail & rain, consequently our river is far from being open, tho the current above the place it ebbs & flows has opened it along the shore." When the river finally broke on June 30, Charles commented that it was "the latest it has been for several years, one year excepted."[51]

Two Inuit runners reached the post on May 3, 1815, with the news that a party from the North was approaching. After making their announcement they returned to their kinsmen with gifts of tobacco, gunpowder, and oatmeal, along with other small items that they could use as they travelled. The Inuit practice of sending runners ahead of their arrival gave the Company's men time to secure buildings they did not want visitors to enter and to stock the trading room with the merchandise most often wanted by the incoming group. Inuit did not expect anything like the ceremonial welcoming rituals the Company staged when the annual First Nations canoe brigades arrived at the large southern forts and factories. Instead, they practised their own unthreatening way of alerting other communities that they were nearby in what they would have seen as somebody else's territory. It was the polite thing to do as well as the safest way to approach a community that might be hostile. Perhaps even more importantly, the Inuit would have seen the gifts as an expression of hospitality and a readiness to share on the part of the Company.

One of the runners in 1815 was Augustine. "This morning," wrote John Charles, "the Esquimaux lad who left us in the month of July last [year] to go with his friends, arrived with another young man with intelligence that a party of their countrymen would be with us in a few days."[52] The weather, already blustery when Augustine and his companion arrived, grew worse as the day wore on, with heavy winds and thick falling snow. Rather than risk losing their way in bad weather, the two runners remained at the post until the storm let up two days later. They spent their time in the Men's House, sowing cabbage seeds in boxes of soil.

With weather "still boisterous, but not snowing as much" on May 6, the runners left to rejoin their fellow villagers. On the seventh and eighth, the weather was "excessive bad, blowing and drifting dreadfully." Four Chipewyan at the post were unable to leave, "as it was impossible to walk for the thick drift & snow." By May 9, the weather had improved somewhat, but it was still very cold. Another two days of "cold, disagreeable weather" were followed by a brief clear spell. Then, within an hour, the temperature fell from 47° Fahrenheit at noon to 26°, plummeting before evening to a freezing 16° of frost. Snow followed, with a hard wind blowing out of the west.

When Augustine's people had still not shown up by May 25, John Charles was seriously alarmed. "The two Esquimaux lads who left us on the 6 Inst [*instances*, meaning "on the sixth day of the month"] not having yet made their appearance with the rest of the party, we are afraid they may have lost themselves in the bad weather on their return." To his great relief, Augustine showed up on the twenty-ninth "to inform us that his friends would be with us in a day or two." Charles added that Augustine had told him the long delay was due to "the bad state of the ice in the bay which the Inuit had not foreseen."[53]

Twenty-two Inuit men, with their wives and children, arrived on the last day of May and set up their tents at Seahorse Gully. Sixteen of them came into the post on the morning of June 1 to trade their winter's catch. That done, they settled down to hunt seals at Button Bay.[54] For the three weeks following his countrymen's arrival, Augustine lived among them, hunting seals on the ice every day. In the third week of June, with a predicted five weeks of the hunt still to go before the hunters of his community planned to leave for their own country, he came to a life-changing decision. On the evening of June 22, Augustine walked to the factory, stowed his rifle, bedroll, harpoon, and backpack in an old shed newly fitted out as a kitchen, and declared his intention to throw in his lot with the Churchill traders forever. Pressed for an explanation, he revealed that the father of his promised bride had taken "most of the little prosperity he possessed" and had raised the "marriage price." In spite of his public announcement that he was "leaving his countrymen altogether," Augustine told Charles privately of his plan "to obtain if possible something to satisfy the father of the girl more than what he had given him already."[55] He apparently thought it would take a while to save up the necessary amount, and when Charles offered him a two-year contract as a labourer at a yearly wage of £10, he accepted.[56]

Augustine's first responsibility after accepting a contract as an engaged servant was to transplant the sturdiest of the cabbage plants he had seeded in May. He spent most of the summer on the year's biggest project: the construction of new buildings to replace those that had burned the previous year. His work involved excavating for a cellar, hauling stones for a foundation, and mudding walls as the carpenters raised them.[57]

In 1815, the Company began implementing some changes that the London Committee had agreed on five years earlier concerning how the posts were manned and governed. John Charles and John Leask were reassigned to the Nelson River District, along with three unnamed labourers. Replacing Charles as Master at Churchill was Adam Snodie, an Orcadian with fifteen years of service.[58] He arrived at Churchill on July 23 and officially took on his new responsibilities on July 29 when Charles signed over responsibility for keeping the journal.

On the afternoon of August 18, Snodie sent a bateau to York Factory with three men who were being transferred and four unnamed men whose contracts had expired and who planned to return to their English and Scottish hometowns. Augustine was also on board, his business at York Factory being to pick up and bring back the year's mail from the annual supply ship as well as the Governor's packet containing written instructions from the Company's Overseas Governor, Thomas Thomas. A ninth man was on board whose job was to accompany Augustine back to Churchill because of a Company rule that no one ever left the vicinity of a post without a companion in case of an accident in the wilderness.[59]

Two days later a group of Inuit hunters arrived ready to trade their furs for whatever goods they needed, including gunpowder. Snodie, still learning how things were done at Churchill, was dismayed to find that the post had run out of gunpowder. "Not knowing how to act," as he put it, he sent two men, James Moar and James Wood, to York Factory to get a new supply.[60] Less than a week later, on August 25, two Cree couriers arrived with a letter from York Factory's chief in charge, William Hemmings Cook, requesting Snodie's presence at York Factory.[61] Snodie left by boat the same day with Henry Hay, Robert Garrock, John Craigie, and the two Cree couriers, and he did not return until September 19.

During Snodie's twenty-five-day absence no one was keeping the daily journal, so we have no information on when Augustine returned to Churchill. We do know, however, that when Snodie arrived on September 19, Augustine was sick with "a violent cold," which had spread to other men at the post.

A month later, in the week of October 14, Snodie wrote in the daily journal that Augustine was still "very ill." His "violent cold" is not surprising. He had been at York Factory during ship time waiting to pick up the year's mail, forwarded from the London headquarters, and had been exposed to whatever germs and pathogens the newly arrived crews and passengers had carried with them from Britain. After a year of isolation, Augustine and the Churchill men would have had reduced immunity to the latest varieties of the common cold.[62]

SNODIE MADE NO MENTION OF HOW THE COLDS WERE TREATED. Churchill did not have a resident physician in 1815; whatever ills the post's people and clients suffered were dealt with by officers who had to depend on the medical books in their libraries to treat the sick. Most of them had experience in recognizing and treating the more common ailments of the time, but the state of the medical arts being what they were, many of the usual treatments were ineffective and some remedies were more dangerous than the ailments they were meant to cure.

Every post had a medicine chest with the curatives that were popular in England. In 1823, Churchill's supply of remedies included half a pound of sugar of lead, half a pound of liquor of hartshorn, half a pound of spirits of lavender, two bottles of Turlington's Balsam, two bottles of essence of peppermint, two ounces of camphor, and half a dozen "vomits." Along with the medicaments, there was one lancet for dealing with boils and infected slivers, a supply of small glass vials with corks, and a package of lint for washing wounds.[63]

Sugar of lead (i.e., lead acetate) was useful as a disinfectant and insecticide and as a remedy for canker in horses. It is an extremely poisonous substance used mainly in dyeing cotton fabrics and in the manufacture of varnish. While it is reasonably safe for human beings if used in small quantities to clean skin ulcers, it can cause lead poisoning and death when used internally as a specific for diarrhea, as it often was in the nineteenth century.

Turlington's Balsam, a mixture of essential oils and ammonia, was used to treat everything from a cough to kidney stones and paralysis. Its active medicinal ingredient was benzoin, which had expectorant qualities, relieved stuffy heads and chests when inhaled in steam, and was an effective antiseptic for mild skin irritations. When taken internally, it had diuretic properties and was known to cause stomach bleeding. Camphor, or camphorated oil, like the tincture of benzoin in Turlington's Balsam, was also inhaled in steam to treat asthma, colds, and stuffy heads and chests, and as a liniment for sore muscles. Liquor of hartshorn, a mild disinfectant, is basically ammonia in water. Lavender was, and still is, a staple of aromatherapy, used to treat stress and insomnia. Peppermint, for centuries past and into the present, is a basic remedy for stomach upsets of all kinds.[64]

The most appropriate remedy for Augustine's cold, given what was available, was inhalation of either camphor or Turlington's Balsam in steam. Augustine was very ill, and the cure took some time. Only on October 23 was he finally "fit to go to work," but apparently with a light duty roster. It was November 3 before Snodie judged him well enough to go to the Churchill Creek tent to hunt partridges with Thomas Halcrow and James Dunning.

BY EARLY WINTER IN 1815, CHIPEWYAN, CREE, AND BRITISH WERE all desperately short of food resources. Chipewyan arriving at Churchill Post on November 18 reported "great starvation"[65] among their people, which they said would prevent them from coming in to trade. They intended to spend the first part of the winter on the northern prairie, the only place they expected to find some deer. After that, they thought, they might go to Athabasca country, hoping to find enough deer to feed themselves and their families till spring.

In very cold weather in the first week of December, four Cree men came into the post on foot, unable to use their sleds for lack of snow. They too reported a great scarcity of deer, due to "those animals having taken a northern route in summer to avoid the torment of the musketoes in the woods and had not returned. The absence of deer and other food animals had left their families in great need of provisions."[66]

With the weather steadily growing worse, Snodie continued to fret over the scarcity of food resources in the new year. Augustine brought in sixty-six partridges from his tent at North River in late November and reported that though he had seen a great many, "owing to the very cold weather they were very wild and remaining in the woods." In the new year, Augustine reported to Snodie at the House that "since the weather has been cold, these birds have been very shy."[67] Snodie, having been asked by his immediate boss, James Swain Sr., why Churchill Post spent so much on food, tried to explain that it was the "great scarcity of partridges this winter, which has made our expenditure of European provisions more than it would otherwise have been."[68]

When Augustine was ready to return to North River after reporting to Snodie, falling snow reduced visibility so much that he had to wait out the weather before he could leave. Snodie, who was watching the temperature carefully, noted that "weather [was] very cold" in mid-January and by the end of the month "quick silver has remained in a malleable state [frozen solid] even in the middle of the day since [the] 21st." Quicksilver, or mercury, freezes at minus 40° on both the Celsius and Fahrenheit scales. At that temperature exposed human flesh will freeze in less than five minutes.[69] Again, at the beginning of February, Snodie noted, "Mercury or quick silver remained during whole of last week in a state of malleability both day and night." On Sunday, February 4, for the first time in two weeks, the mercury was not frozen. Even fur-coated animals were suffering from hunger and ready to take risks to get food. As Augustine set out for North River, he killed a white fox and "a very large wolf" scavenging for scraps only a few yards from the stockade.[70]

Augustine was barely back at his tent before dreadful cold set in again. "These two days [February 5 and 6] snowing and blowing very hard and extremely cold," Snodie recorded. "The longest continuation of bad and cold weather I have ever seen in this country being between four and five weeks during which there have been only three good days and not much oftener that Mercury had not been frozen."[71] Two days later, on February 8, a Chipewyan husband and wife walked into the post "in great want of provisions," according to Snodie.[72]

AFTER TWENTY-FIVE YEARS OF STEADILY WORSENING WEATHER, conditions became even more extreme with startling rapidity between the summers of 1815 and 1817. The cause, unrecognized at the time, was the eruption of Mount Tambora in Indonesia in the spring of 1815. The first sign of impending disaster was in 1812, when increased steaming and frequent small eruptions indicated that the volcano was becoming active. On April 5, 1815, the first major eruption was heard more than 800 miles away. On April 10 and 11, three great columns of fire shot more than 25 miles into the sky, spewing tons of dust and ash into the atmosphere. The collapse of the volcano's caldera caused earthquakes that were felt as far as 300 miles distant. Vulcanologists have estimated that about 12 cubic miles of magma and 36 cubic miles of ash circled the Earth, cutting off the sun's rays and lowering global temperatures by an average of around 5.5° Fahrenheit. The cloud cover produced what would today be considered nuclear winter conditions. The winter of 1815–16 was exceptionally severe, and the summer of 1816 scarcely differed from a normal winter.[73]

As the terrible "Year with No Summer" progressed, Churchill's men began to sicken. On the first day of April, the weather was still "very cold," and Snodie was concerned about Peter Wishart, the boatbuilder, who was unwell. By April 4, Wishart was experiencing "a violent pain in his breast, supposed to be what the people in this country call the country distemper." On April 8, he was still "badly," and "at his anxious desire" Snodie bled him. Thomas Halcrow was also unwell, with "a complaint in his breast" similar to what Wishart was suffering. Peter Baikie came down with the same disturbing symptoms on April 9. Country distemper is something of a mystery disease, especially common at York Factory. It may have been a variety of pneumonia, or perhaps the "epidemic bronchitis" mentioned frequently in the York Factory and Norway House journals of the time.[74]

While coping with one sick labourer and two tradesmen confined to their beds, Snodie had to deal with several Chipewyan families in deep distress. A family of four arrived on April 10. "They have been some time in great want of provisions," Snodie noted. Two more families arrived shortly after "in great starvation having seen no deer during winter."[75]

Suddenly, on April 19 the weather reversed itself and became unseasonably hot, just long enough to exacerbate existing problems. "Weather as warm as is generally in the month of June or July, most of the snow melted," wrote Snodie on the twentieth. The harried Post Master worried that families on their way to the post might be unable to cross the many small rivers, which were breaking up too soon, and there was "no snow in the woods to enable them to haul their furs on sleds." By the last week of April, the ground was bare and Snodie's fears were confirmed. A new arrival reported that he had been unable to get his furs across one of the small rivers and warned Snodie not to expect any new visitors. "This information is truly serious," wrote Snodie. "The ground is now entirely bare of snow…and several holes in the ice on this river." On May 6, a runner announced six men with their families who "were in great starvation and had very much difficulty in getting here, all the small rivers being open, they had been obliged to make several rafts of wood to enable them to cross them."[76]

Returning geese were affected by the unusual weather. At North River, Augustine and Dunning had killed thirteen—a long way from being adequate to feed the starving people now pouring into the post. To make sure his superiors understood the nature of the crisis he faced, Snodie explained in detail: "Their account and indeed appearance of having been in starvation is beyond discussion. Many of their relations died during winter, which both prevented them from killing furs and provisions for their own support and in addition to this they are now burdened with the families of the deceased relations, many of which is still sick." By May 15, fourteen men were at the post, with family members totalling seventy-eight. "When added to those at this place before is 106," wrote Snodie.[77]

Desperate people continued to stumble into the post. Two men who arrived on May 19 "have been walking in woods ever since [leaving their home territory]. And no snow on the ground to enable them to haul, they were obliged to carry some of their children on their backs as well as their guns. Their feet and legs are very much torn and swelled with the underwood." Others of their families were still some distance from the post. On the twenty-first, one man who had been ill for some time died. Snodie set two of his men to digging a grave. A day later, two more men arrived, who with their families brought Churchill's population to 140, "many of them existing skeletons."[78]

Temperatures were well below freezing again by the end of the month, and several Chipewyan families that had been hunting at North River left in an attempt to get back to their spring hunting grounds. "They were starving, in spite of every endeavour in my power to prevent it," Snodie wrote. Inuit were also starving. Three men from the North arrived with their families on the morning of May 28, with very little to trade. "They say that their hunt was very nigh to this place all the winter and no deer about them, their only subsistence was fish which occupied their time angling and prevented them from killing foxes. Have engaged them to kill seals about the Old Factory. They say that the very early spring is unfavourable to it, the ice being very much broken."[79]

Three more Inuit arrived a little over a week later. They brought the information that "very few Esquimaux are expected to visit this place during summer, the greatest part of those who denominate regular traders having gone to trade with more northern tribes of Esquimaux and will be here in spring 1817." The date of their arrival, late May to early June, and their readiness to remain near the post hunting seal for an extended period suggest that they were from Knapp's Bay. The fact that they brought their families with them indicates a lack of stored foods to sustain the women and children at their home base. By their own testimony, their seasonal living pattern was disrupted due to the lack of food animals. They had passed the winter in small residential groups of two or three families, a dozen individuals at most, in each of the two parties. It was usual for Inuit communities to split into smaller groups during bad economic times, and the winter of 1815–16 was one of the worst. Snodie recalled Augustine from the east side of the river, where he was hunting for geese, to supervise his countrymen's seal hunt.[80]

By mid-July the seal-hunting season was over, and Snodie paid off the half dozen Inuit who had been at the post since the end of May. "Sent the Esquimaux away," he wrote, "and Augustine in company with them, his service at this place was of very little importance to the Company."[81] The "firing" of Augustine was unexpected. No one, not Topping or Charles, not Auld or Snodie himself, had a harsh word to say against Augustine.[82] Almost three years after Augustine's dismissal, Snodie called him a "lad of an excellent character...faithfully attached to the servants of the Company," explaining that he had sent Augustine away because of the very real threat of starvation that faced the post. "From the contracted state of things, three years since, I was under the necessity of sending him with his country people."[83]

AUGUSTINE'S ACTIVITIES DURING HIS ABSENCE ARE UNKNOWN. When he left Churchill in 1816, he travelled with six hunters and their families who had come to the post from two different wintering stations and who were unlikely to have been part of his home village. How and when, perhaps even if, he got to his own community in the summer of 1816 is not apparent. Two facts only come to light: he returned to Churchill every year for the next four years to hunt seal and whale, and during those years, he married and had a son.

During the four years when Augustine's life was largely hidden from his friends in Churchill, events on another continent were leading to an adventure that would change the trajectory of his life. The British Admiralty decided to reopen its search for a northwest passage from the Atlantic Ocean to the Pacific. It proposed to send an overland expedition from York Factory to the mouth of the Coppermine River and eastward by boat along the Arctic coast. Lieutenant John Franklin was the naval officer chosen to lead the expedition. While preparing for the adventure, Franklin received a letter from Sir Alexander Mackenzie advising him to have an Inuit interpreter on the expedition. "If of this [Inuit] nation you could procure a young man who would be willing to accompany you, it might prove an object of great importance, as he could interpret for you on the seacoast and Copper Mine River." Franklin took Mackenzie's advice and asked the Hudson's Bay Company to recommend, and hire, a suitable person. His request was forwarded to Governor William Williams at Cumberland House and on to Adam Snodie at Churchill.[84] Augustine's was the name that came to mind.

INTERLUDE I

THE FIRST ARCTIC OVERLAND EXPEDITION

1819–1822

THE UNUSUAL CLIMATIC CONDITIONS OF 1815 TO 1817 HAD BEEN observed with interest by members of Britain's Royal Society. Its president, Sir Joseph Banks, heard reports of an unprecedented number of icebergs in the North Atlantic in 1816 and was more than interested when he received a letter from Captain William Scoresby, a veteran of the Greenland whaling fleet, reporting that the Greenland Sea had been ice free in 1816. Banks realized that open water in the Arctic offered an opportunity to investigate the new sciences—polar gravity, magnetism, electricity, optics, and variable atmospheric pressure. The Royal Society took up his cause and demanded that the Admiralty undertake a series of Arctic explorations for the purpose of scientific research and the discovery of a northwest passage.[1]

The British Admiralty also had reasons to be interested in the kind of exploration Banks had in mind. The British navy, having been built up to maximum strength during the long war against Napoleon, suddenly had far more ships and personnel—over 750 ocean-going vessels, 4,500 officers, and 140,000 ordinary seamen—than it needed or could afford after the defeat of the French in 1814.[2] In peacetime, Britain's naval officers were put on half pay, with no duties and no chance of promotion in their chosen careers. The redundant officers were greatly in favour of exploration, and the suddenly unemployed ordinary seamen, desperate for jobs that would support them and their families, welcomed any opportunity of a job, even one to the forbidding Arctic. The glut of officers, ordinary mariners, and mothballed ships could all be absorbed into a thriving merchant navy, if only someone could find a northwest passage from Europe to Asia. A highly publicized Arctic exploration seemed just the ticket for solving the problem.

Lieutenant John Franklin, after three years on half pay and with no prospects for advancement, was one of the lucky young officers to be offered just such an assignment. In 1818 the British Admiralty sent the Naval North Polar Expedition into the Greenland Sea to search for a northwest passage. Captain David Buchan in HMS *Dorothea* commanded the expedition, with Franklin as senior officer in the expedition's secondary vessel, HMS *Trent*. Heavy pack ice at the latitude of Spitsbergen Island forced Buchan to abandon the venture, but Franklin had been noticed by the Admiralty. In 1819 he was chosen to command the project so firmly demanded by Banks and the Royal Society: an overland expedition from York Factory to the mouth of the Coppermine River, to survey the Arctic coast eastward to Repulse Bay on the west coast of Hudson Bay. Success would confirm the existence of a northwest passage.

The Admiralty chose Dr. John Richardson, naval physician and naturalist, as second-in-command of the land exploration and assigned two midshipmen, George Back and Robert Hood, both talented artists, to the expedition. Back had served under Franklin in *Trent* in 1818; Hood was one of the hundreds of young officer candidates without assignment after the defeat of Napoleon's forces and, by 1818, had spent two years on the Admiralty's inactive list at half pay. Two enlisted sailors, John Hepburn and Samuel Wilkes, were seconded to the expedition as junior staff.

The expedition left Gravesend on May 23, 1819. After a particularly nasty passage across the North Atlantic, through Hudson Strait, and down the bay, the Company's supply ships anchored at York Factory on August 30, 1819. Governor William Williams, Chief Trader John Charles, and the newly appointed York Factory District Master Adam Snodie were all on hand to greet the officers of the Arctic overland expedition. Franklin was most anxious to talk to Snodie. At last there was some hard news, disappointing though it was, of a possible Inuit interpreter. "I found," Franklin wrote, "that as the Esquimaux inhabitants had left Churchill a month previous to our arrival, no interpreter from that quarter could be procured before their return in the following spring. The Governor, however, undertook to forward to us next season the only one amongst them who understood English, if he could be induced to go."[3] As Midshipman Robert Hood put it in his diary during the first week of September, "Our endeavours to obtain an Esquimaux interpreter were for the present ineffectual, but we were informed that a person of that nation had been employed as a servant at Churchill, and having lately taken a wife, [had] returned to live with his countrymen. As the Esquimaux visit Churchill every year in the spring, hopes were entertained that he might be prevailed on to accompany us, and in that case, means were to be adopted for conveying him after us to Cumberland House, or the Slave Lake."[4]

Having done what they could in the matter, the expedition members set out in canoes for Cumberland House, nearly 700 miles inland from York Factory. They arrived on October 23, to the surprise of the post's people, who were not expecting visitors. They were assigned to a half-finished house at the post, which Franklin immediately set his men to completing. Built of mudded wood with windows of scraped moose skin, it was, in Hood's words, "rather too airy for this climate." In spite of constantly blazing fires, the pens of the Writers and the brushes of the artists froze to the paper, and "extremes of cold and heat [were felt] at each side of our persons."[5]

Dr. Richardson described the typical trading-post meals as consisting almost exclusively of salted geese, fish, moose, and bison, adding that "a good many potatoes are also raised at this post, and a small supply of tea and sugar is brought from the depot at York Factory." His comment that the Cumberland House fishery had provided about three thousand fish averaging three pounds a piece hints that he would have enjoyed a more varied menu.[6]

The post's sled dogs were Hood's special grievance. "Domestication does not improve their manners, and no kindness attaches to them," he wrote. "They are cowardly, stupid and ravenous....Nothing is secure from them; they eat their way through the parchment windows and devour every animal substance without distinction." He particularly disliked their habit of waking at odd hours of the night to "exercise themselves in a long, melancholy, and unnatural howl... No rest," he continued, "can be procured by those unaccustomed to this dismal serenade." At the same time, he appreciated their ability to haul large loads—three of them could pull a sled with a two-hundred-pound load through snow that human beings could move about on only when wearing snowshoes and even then with great difficulty. None of the "creatures allotted to the use of man" had a harder existence, he thought. "Often they carry for many days a heavy load of provisions, of which they have no share, and are at last destined by necessity to supply its place."[7]

TWO AND A HALF MONTHS LATER, THE EXPEDITION WAS STILL AT Cumberland House and had received no positive news in the matter of an interpreter. Franklin worried that he was needed at Lake Athabasca but was reluctant to leave until he had word that an interpreter was on the way. He solved the problem by splitting the expedition into two parties. Hood's diary explains: "In the beginning of December, Mr. Franklin came to the resolution of going forward, accompanied by Mr. Back, to Lake Athapescow... The chief motive of our stay here was the hope of procuring the Esquimaux interpreter in the ensuing spring;... Mr. Franklin determined to commence his journey in the middle of January." The men of Cumberland House Post gave what help they could. One of them made a sled for hauling supplies and a carriole for Franklin's ease of travelling.[8]

Lieutenant Franklin, Midshipmen Back and Hood, the sailor John Hepburn, and the men who had already signed on as labourers left Cumberland House for Lake Athabasca on January 18, 1820, with the HBC's Roderick McKenzie and the winter packet of letters and supplies. Franklin rode in his new carriole; the others, with heavy backpacks, went on snowshoes and found it hard going. For nine miserable weeks, Franklin's party pushed forward. In the last week of March, they arrived at Fort Chipewyan on Lake Athabasca.[9]

By early June the rivers had opened enough for the fur trade brigades to get underway. Governor Williams, ready to start southeastward to York Factory, gave Franklin, whose route would take him to the northwest, a circular letter to all post managers along the route instructing them to give all possible assistance to the expedition.[10] Just as important, Hood wrote, Governor Williams "promised to exert every endeavour to forward the Esquimaux interpreter, upon whom the success of our journey so much depended."[11] Richardson and Hood, however, had neither canoes nor crews to begin their journey to Lake Athabasca. The doctor applied to the Hudson's Bay Company and the North West Company for two canoes, with crews and provisions sufficient for the river trip to Fort Chipewyan.[12]

An HBC brigade was the first to reach Cumberland House, on May 31, and from it Richardson managed to hire one canoe and two volunteers. On June 5, a North West Company brigade pulled up and the doctor hired another canoe and five Canadian voyageurs. Within the week, the HBC brigade from Ile à la Crosse arrived and Richardson hired a third canoe and crew. On June 14 they were on the river heading west, and a month later they joined their companions at Fort Chipewyan.[13]

THE REUNITED PARTY——FRANKLIN, RICHARDSON, BACK, HOOD, Hepburn, and sixteen voyageurs—left Fort Chipewyan on July 18, 1820, and reached Fort Resolution, the Hudson's Bay Company post on Moose Deer Island in Slave Lake, a week later. The Company's agent there, Robert McVicar, had already received instructions from Athabasca Department Superintendent Colin Robertson to assist the overland expedition in every possible way. Robertson's letter to McVicar, dated June 5, 1820, read, "Being given to understand that Pierrish St. Germent [Pierre St. Germain] has expressed a wish to join the Expedition under the command of Lieut. Franklin and others—and as I consider St. Germent particularly calculated for rendering much service to these Gentlemen, not only from his knowledge of the country but the languages and habits of the natives, I therefore give him full permission to enter into a new engagement with the above party." By obeying orders, McVicar lost the services of Pierre St. Germain, the son of a Canadian voyageur father and a Chipewyan mother, who was perfectly fluent in the Yellowknives' language. According to McVicar, St. Germain was intelligent, able to travel without a blanket or provisions, and an indispensable worker at the post. He was also a "scoundrel," too independent, and overly fond of alcohol.[14]

Franklin's anxiety to obtain an Inuit interpreter grew more intense when he was informed of the warlike disposition of the Copper Inuit, as well as the hostility that existed between them and the Yellowknives, who were to be his chief guides and provisioners. Still, he remained optimistic. In a letter of requests and instructions to McVicar, Franklin asked that expedition supplies arriving in the coming weeks be sent on to his winter quarters, adding, "It is not impossible that an Esquimaux interpreter may also arrive here. He must be forwarded direct without delay—direct to the wintering ground, which you will learn at Fort Providence."[15]

On July 29, the expedition was at Fort Providence on the north shore of Slave Lake. Here they met Willard Ferdinand Wentzel, Clerk in Charge of the North West Company post. Like McVicar, Wentzel had instructions to be unstinting in his assistance to Franklin's party. By the time the explorers reached his post, he had already solicited the help of a Yellowknife Chief, Akaitcho, also known by the traders as Big Foot, Gros Pied, or The Leader. Wentzel introduced him to the explorers, and Akaitcho confirmed that his people would act as advisers, guides, and hunters for the expedition. Wentzel himself volunteered to accompany the expedition to the Arctic coast and had another interpreter, Jean Baptiste Adam, waiting with Akaitcho for Franklin's approval. Like St. Germain, Adam had a reputation as an excellent hunter, was thoroughly familiar with the countryside, and spoke the Yellowknife language fluently. His wife, Angelique, was a member of Akaitcho's community.

THE EXPEDITION MEMBERS READY TO JOIN AKAITCHO'S PEOPLE FOR the final push to their winter quarters numbered twenty-five. In addition to the four British naval officers and the seaman John Hepburn, the two interpreters (Pierre St. Germain and Jean Baptiste Adam), and Ferdinand Wentzel, there were seventeen voyageurs: Gabriel Beauparlant, who acted as personal servant to George Back as well as fulfilling his duties as a voyageur; Antonio Vincenza Fontano, an Italian who had served with the de Meurons regiment protecting the Selkirk settlers at Red River; François Semandré, who took on the job of cook during the traverse of the Arctic coast; Michel Teroahauté, a Great Lakes Iroquois; Jean Baptiste Belanger *dit* "le rouge"; Matthew Pelonquin *dit* Crédit; Joseph Peltier; Ignace Perrault; Solomon Belanger *dit* "le gros"; Jean Baptiste Belleau; Joseph Benoit; Emanual Cournoyée; Régiste Vaillant; Jean Baptiste Parent; Joseph Forcier; Pierre Dumas; and Joseph Gagné.[16] Three women—Adam's wife, Angelique, and the wives of two other oarsmen, one of whom was probably St. Germain's wife—were hired to accompany the expedition to its winter quarters, where they would spend their time sewing the leather and fur clothing required by the explorers. Among them they had three children.

Franklin's plan was to get as far north, and as close to the Coppermine River, as possible before winter set in, build a winter camp, and settle down to pass the months until the expedition could head to the Arctic coast in the spring of 1821. Franklin's list of requirements for "the selected place for our winter habitation" included trees of sufficient size to construct a dwelling and various outbuildings for twenty-five people, plus easy access to trees for the winter's firewood. It also had to have access to fresh water, and it had to be in country where supplies of caribou and fish were abundant enough to feed not only the expedition members but also those of Akaitcho's people who would accompany them.

Akaitcho described a lake on the Yellowknife River, at the edge of the barrens, about 550 miles north of Fort Chipewyan and three days' march from the Coppermine River that seemed to meet the expedition's needs. The entire expedition, with Akaitcho's people, set out from Fort Providence on August 2 and spent three difficult weeks struggling up the Yellowknife River.[17]

Toward the headwaters, they found the lake they were looking for and judged it "a fit place for a winter residence." The site was on a "tolerably steep bank on the borders of the river," according to George Back, which "for about four miles on each side was well wooded with pine and a few birch." In a letter to his wife, Richardson dwelt on the scenic beauty of the place the explorers named Winter Lake. "Indeed we could not have selected a more convenient or beautiful spot," he wrote. The word picture he drew could have described almost any south-of-England village or estate: a "country finely varied by hill and dale...interspersed with numerous lakes [and] small streams...a river whose sheltering banks are clothed with wood...an extensive southern prospect...to construct a stately dwelling." It may be that he presented his temporary home as picturesque in order to calm any fears his wife might have had for his comfort and safety. One sentence—"The nakedness of the northern country is hid by a clump of trees on the rising ground in our rear"—hints that he was aware of a dangerous reality and, for the moment at least, did not want to think about it. Like Back, Richardson took note of nearby stands of trees where sufficient wood was available for building winter quarters and keeping them tolerably warm over the winter. Or so he thought.[18]

Franklin, intellectually unprepared for life and travel in such an alien landscape, closed his eyes and his mind to the downside of the Arctic, much as Richardson had done. He focused on the scenery instead of the practicalities of wintering at the northern margins of the boreal forest. "We determined on placing the house on the summit of the bank, which commands a beautiful prospect of the surrounding country. The view in the front is bounded at the distance of three miles, by round-backed hills; to the eastward and westward lie the Winter and Round-Rock lakes, which are connected by the Winter River, whose banks are well-clothed with pines, and ornamented with a profusion of mosses, lichens, and shrubs."[19] As people in alien territory soon learn, "a beautiful prospect" is not the best criterion for choosing a dwelling site. Franklin's choice of a site that reminded him of England's gentle views cost the expedition dearly.

The expedition wasted no time getting set up. Akaitcho and his hunters went immediately to hunt caribou, while the expedition men formed two work parties, "one to cut wood for the buildings," according to Hood, "and the other to bring meat, which we dried for our voyage on the Coppermine River." The four officers believed that the surrounding country would supply all their food and water needs as well as providing sufficient wood for building and for fuel. Within a few days, their belief was reinforced when Akaitcho's hunters brought in about a hundred caribou and a thousand pounds of fat and dried meat and put another eighty caribou in caches at varying distances from the fort. The voyageurs set fishing nets in Winter Lake and put up a small log hut for shelter while they tended them.[20] Franklin chose to call the expedition's winter home Fort Enterprise.

The first unforeseen event occurred almost immediately, when the men sent up a smoke signal to let Akaitcho know they had arrived. Their fire spread to nearby bushes and then to the surrounding woods, burning stands of trees for three days before it was brought under control. By August 23, the fire had destroyed "our fine prospect," as Hood put it. Much more was lost than a scenic view; in destroying Fort Enterprise's potential fuel supply, the fire put the lives of the expedition members at risk. Franklin, Richardson, and Back all failed to recognize the possibility that the loss of available wood resources could have disastrous consequences for the expedition. Only Hood bothered to record the event.[21]

THE BASIC PLAN OF FORT ENTERPRISE WAS SIMILAR TO THE FUR trade posts the party had seen on their long journey from York Factory. The officers' house faced south toward Franklin's "beautiful prospect" and formed the northern side of a quadrangle. It was fifty feet long and twenty-four wide, with a small, square bump-out on the north side. Partitions created a central common room and three bedrooms. Two other buildings, a storehouse and the men's house, flanked the officers' house on the east and west, creating a U-shaped complex. Richardson's description of the officers' living quarters, written on October 6, foreshadowed some of the discomforts to come: "It is…a log-building, the walls and roof are plastered with clay, the floors laid with planks rudely squared by the hatchet, and the windows closed with parchment of rein-deer skin. The clay froze as it was daubed on, and has since cracked in such a manner that the wind rushes in from every quarter. Nevertheless with the aid of warm clothing, and good fires, we expect to get comfortably over the winter." Franklin praised the voyageurs as "excellent cabinet-makers [who] daily added a table, chair, or bedstead, to the comforts of our establishment."[22]

The men of Fort Enterprise kept busy fishing, hunting, and cutting firewood. At Dr. Richardson's insistence, they also engaged in active outdoor sports, sledding and skating. The officers organized evening classes for the men, as well as a variety of entertainments—pantomimes, plays, puppet shows, charades, board games, and contests. The English sailor, John Hepburn, took on some domestic chores and produced handmade soap and candles. Each of the officers busied himself with his special avocations. Franklin kept an inventory of provisions and dealt with Akaitcho and his hunters. Richardson collected specimens of plant and animal life and held regular clinics to check on the health of the expedition and Akaitcho's people. Hood took astronomical readings at every opportunity and turned rough sketches of his travels into finished works. Back made several long journeys to track down supplies that had gone missing en route and to pick up mail and, when he was "at home," worked on his journal, paintings, and maps.

CHAPTER 3

FIRST JOURNEY TO THE WESTERN ARCTIC

1820–1821

WHILE THE MEMBERS OF THE ARCTIC OVERLAND expedition were moving toward their wintering site, events at Churchill were working toward a favourable outcome in the search for an Inuit interpreter. The first northern visitors to reach Churchill in the spring of 1820 were three young men who appeared in the third week of May to announce the imminent arrival of sixteen hunters with their wives and children. The post's accountant, William Ross, gave them "some tobacco for all the gang" and oatmeal and biscuit for the women and children.[1]

It was unusually cold for late May. Chipewyan hunters had already reported that the great flocks of geese that usually provided fresh meat during the season had not appeared, and many inland families were starving. Based on the information the runners had given him, William Ross had every reason to worry about the Inuit. They were on foot, man-hauling their small sleds. The absence of dogs was a sure sign of unusually bad economic times. The dogs either had died from lack of food over the previous winter or had themselves become food for people hard pressed to survive. The presence of women and children in the group was another strong indicator that food supplies in the home territories were inadequate to support them while the hunters were away. A week after the messengers left to rejoin their people, there was still no sign of the group appearing, and Ross worried that they were in trouble.[2]

Finally, on May 28 around suppertime, seven men of the walking party reached the trading post—"among them," Ross wrote, "my old acquaintance Augustine." Augustine confirmed Ross's fears; the villagers had no furs to trade, and they had come "merely for the purpose of killing seals" in order to store oil as an emergency subsistence food. Within a few days, the newcomers—"in all 37 in number," wrote Ross, "men, women & children"—had set up camp.[3]

Ross took Augustine aside and told him about the overland expedition and the need for an interpreter. Anxious to comply with his employer's orders, Ross was prepared to go to considerable lengths to engage Augustine, and Augustine, faced with his own anxieties, agreed. He questioned Ross closely until he had a fairly clear idea of where he was to go, under what conditions, for what purpose, and for how long. Then he negotiated his terms. First, he insisted that a friend of his choosing must accompany him. The companion he chose spoke no English, but no matter, Ross immediately agreed to engage "Hootooreack," a fellow villager of Augustine's and probably a kinsman.[4] Like Augustine eight years earlier, his companion was given a new name, Junius, after the month of his arrival at the post.

Augustine's second requirement was for a credit to his account amounting to one hundred made beaver, and an additional eighty made beaver for his friend.[5] His third condition was that both he and Junius be given all necessary equipment—firearms, ammunition, hunting knives, bedrolls, and cooking utensils. He also asked for a complete set of English clothing for each of them and another complete outfit in the style of the country they were going to, made by a seamstress native to that country. Ross accepted Augustine's terms and assured him that the money and goods would be forthcoming "if they stand to their engagement."[6]

While waiting for Ross to make travel arrangements, Augustine returned to Seal River to join his countrymen in the seal hunt and to arrange for one of Junius's brothers to care for his wife and child during the two years he expected to be away. If Augustine had any doubts about the wisdom of his decision to leave his home and family for parts unknown for a period of two years or more, they may have been set aside by the disappointing results of the hunt. Seals were scarce, even at Churchill, and the more than twenty hunters were able to kill a mere thirty-eight in the first ten days of the hunt. If the previous winter had been a hungry one, the omens foretold that the coming year would be at least as bad. Augustine was very aware that a £25 credit on the company's books would go a long way toward keeping his family alive in the coming years.[7]

In mid-June, Ross was summoned to York Factory and took the opportunity to get Augustine and Junius on their way to the Northwest. On the evening of June 14, he took them to the post's stores and supplied them with the clothing and equipment their contracts called for. Augustine's clothing choices imitated as closely as Churchill's inventory could produce the outward appearance of the British sailors he had first seen on *Brazen* in 1813. Each of the "interpreters" was given a blue serge jacket and a cotton handkerchief. The handkerchiefs were black and large enough to be worn as neckerchiefs in British navy style. Describing the two young men as they set out for York, Ross noted that they had dressed themselves in "English slops."[8]

Determined as Augustine was to ensure that their outward appearance was that of British naval gentlemen, he knew that standard military issue was not sufficient protection against the Arctic climate. He added warm swan-skin vests and red flannel shirts to their wardrobes, and each of them also chose a striped Hudson's Bay blanket, 4¾ yards of "duck,"[9] and half a yard of some other cloth, unspecified in the account book.[10] Ross made up an equipment package to be shared between Augustine and Junius, which included a hatchet, a file, an ice chisel, two pounds of gunpowder, six pounds of shot, and two and a half pounds of tobacco. The entire outfit came to £9/15/1, which included a 6 percent (eleven shillings) handler's fee. To this Ross added two weeks' worth of provisions figured at one shilling per day per man, for a total of £1/8/0. The British Admiralty eventually received the Company's bill for £11/3/1.[11]

During the night of June 14–15, Augustine and Junius, wearing their English slops and backpacking their luggage, left Churchill on foot in company with

William Ross and two Cree guides. Two weeks later, on July 1, they were at York Factory waiting for a canoe brigade that had room for them and their gear and was heading up the Hayes River, on the first leg of their long journey to Fort Enterprise.[12] They made the first long stop of their journey at Norway House, on or about August 5.[13] They were assigned to a brigade led by Paul Boucher, otherwise known by the nickname Lamallice. A second Hudson's Bay Company brigade, led by a man called (but not necessarily named) Magnion, was also being readied for the trip to the northwest.[14] In one of Magnion's canoes was an old acquaintance of Augustine's, Archibald McDonald, who eight years earlier had been in charge of the unfortunate Selkirk settlers during their typhus winter at Churchill, now on his way to Ile à la Crosse to take up his duties as a newly hired clerk-secretary. Also in Magnion's brigade was George Simpson, later HBC's Governor, headed to Fort Wedderburn, the Company's post at Lake Athabasca, for his first winter in fur trade country.[15]

At Norway House the two brigade leaders made repairs to their canoes, and it was August 9 before everything was ready for the Lake Winnipeg crossing—everything, that is, except the guides and oarsmen, who were "in a state of inebriety," a state easy to understand given that they were embarking on two or three months of rough living, short rations, and backbreaking labour. With the return of sobriety the brigades moved out as far as Mossy Point, the jumping-off place for the lake crossing. "Contrary winds" ruffled the notoriously unpredictable waters of Lake Winnipeg, and the two leaders decided to stay in the safety of the Point. The men took advantage of the delay to drink to each other's health, spending the next two days "more or less intoxicated." By the fifteenth, the wind had calmed and the men were sober, and Lamallice moved out with Augustine and Junius safely installed at midships. Two days later, Magnion followed.[16]

The daily routines of voyageurs seldom varied, from brigade to brigade and from year to year. The goal on every river journey was to get people and supplies to their destinations and to return to the starting place with people and furs as quickly as possible. Voyageurs were up and in their canoes every day in the very early hours, often before first light, and stayed at their paddles until late at night. The deciding factor in how long they spent on the river each day was visibility. Brigade leaders took advantage of every ray of natural light. As the brigades moved north, and the daylight hours increased, rest periods became shorter and shorter, and it was not unusual for the workday to extend to twenty hours or more. The wake-up call—"*Levé, levé, levé,* get up, get up, get up"—was given at first light by one of the watchmen who had spent the night guarding his fellow voyageurs as they slept beneath upturned canoes on a gravelly beach or grassy riverbank.

Brigade leaders allowed no time to light a fire or cook a meal. The men went straight from the bedroll to the canoe, with breakfast—pemmican or jerky—eaten while paddling. For the voyageurs, summer journeys were brutally hard work, with little respite, no shelter from the elements, and, often, inadequate food. Augustine and Junius, as passengers, had one advantage over the paddlers: seated in the middle of the canoe, and leaning against bundles of provisions, they could snatch some sleep during the day—if the passage was not too rough, if the portages were not too frequent, and if they were not too frightened by the pace to close their eyes.

The main reason for stops during the day was a leaking canoe. Repairs were effected by gumming small leaks with tree sap or stitching patches over large ones. Severe damage from rocks and deadheads might warrant a stop of an hour or more, and paddlers or passengers took advantage of the pause to get a fire going, boil a kettle, and produce tea or instant soup. The far end of a portage was also a good place for refreshments. On the first crossing, a passenger, or possibly a voyageur who was not fit to make the overland carry repeatedly, remained at the far end to prepare a hot meal. Most fur trade goods and provisions were packed in ninety-pound bundles, which every voyageur was expected to carry. Most did so with ease. With their wide, woven belts supporting their backs, and a tumpline around their foreheads, most canoemen could shoulder at least two such packs. Contests among them were common, and the diaries of travellers recorded many stories of mighty portagers carrying three or even four ninety-pound bundles across mile-long portages.

Magnion demanded extreme efforts from his men. By the time the two brigades were nearing Cumberland House, he had passed Lamallice and was holding a position a few miles ahead. On August 22, Magnion had his canoes in the water by 3:30 a.m. and pushed his men forward for a bone-cracking twenty-one hours, overtaking a North West Company brigade led by Lamallice's brother on the way. At midnight Magnion called a halt for a two-hour rest and then was off again, arriving at Cumberland House at six o'clock on the morning of the twenty-third. Lamallice regained his self-respect as a brigade leader by pushing his men straight through the night of August 23–24 and pulling up at Cumberland House neck and neck with Magnion. Both brigades had unloaded the Cumberland House supplies and were on the river heading north again by two in the afternoon.[17]

BY MOST STANDARDS, MUCH OF THE JOURNEY TO FORT WEDDERBURN was pure misery. In George Simpson's words, the brigades were at the mercy of heavy winds, torrential rains, and "heavy squalls." Their bodies were "drenched with rain" and waves sloshing over canoes that were "old, crazy, and patched up." In the moments between cloudbursts, "myriads of mosquitoes" set upon them, while they worried that mercenaries of the North West Company might be "laying in ambush" at any bend in the river and at every portage. "A scarcity of pemmican" was the norm during the final three weeks. Often the weather was so "boisterous we could not proceed"—while doing the brutally hard work necessary to move goods and people across half a continent in as few days as possible.[18]

Nearly ten weeks after leaving York Factory, and five weeks out of Norway House, Lamallice's brigade carrying Augustine and Junius reached Fort Wedderburn. Ten days later, on September 20, Simpson wrote, "The first frost was severe last night and the air keen today; the country has lost its verdant appearance, which denotes the early approach of winter. Sent off two canoes and ten men for Great Slave Lake with the supplies of that District, [and] passengers two Esquimaux Interpreters for the Northern discovery expedition."[19]

The little northern brigade reached Moose Deer Island at Great Slave Lake on October 7 and was greeted by Robert McVicar of the Hudson's Bay Company. McVicar had neither canoes nor men to spare. His appeal to Edward Smith at the North West Company post for two seats in one of his canoes was refused with a lie. Smith told him that "they had only one canoe going to Fort Providence and that...so very loaded as to render it impossible to embark any more in it." The next morning, to McVicar's disgust, the NWC sent "two half loaded canoes" across Great Slave Lake. Four days later, a third canoe followed with no offer from Smith to take any of the expedition's luggage or the two passengers bound for Fort Enterprise. Augustine and Junius were stranded at Moose Deer Island, more than a thousand miles and many months from home, in an unfamiliar environment and among strangers, none of whom spoke their language.[20]

THE TWO FRIENDS MADE A HOME FOR THEMSELVES IN A WARM, comfortable snowhouse near the trading post and kept busy by giving McVicar a hand with the chores. During the months of October and November, they spent most of their time fishing, once or twice a week bringing their catch to the post for salting and drying, and carrying back supplies of twine and nets. While at the fishing station, they ate primarily their own catch supplemented with biscuit, tea, loaf sugar, and Scottish jam. During their visits to the post they enjoyed a slightly more varied menu, which included cheese, beer, and home cooking. Although the post's daily journals do not mention the presence of women at the post, Robert McVicar, like so many other officers of the Company, was married "in the fashion of the country."[21]

Ten weeks later, on December 10, Augustine and Junius finally made the acquaintance of a member of the expedition with whom they would spend the next year and a half. Midshipman George Back had left Franklin's headquarters on snowshoes on October 18, accompanied by Ferdinand Wentzel, Gabriel Beauparlant, Solomon Belanger, and two Yellowknife hunters, Akaiyazza and Thoolezzeh, with their wives, Little Forehead and Smiling Marten, and their children. Their mission was to find and arrange for the forwarding of supplies, especially food provisions, that had been left behind for lack of space in the canoe brigades. To his great disappointment, Back found that much of the expedition luggage had still not arrived at Fort Resolution and was unlikely to arrive before the party left for the Arctic coast in the spring. He lost no time "in making suitable demands on both parties [HBC and NWC]." McVicar was as generous as he could afford to be. Indeed, he was so generous that he gave Back provisions and equipment he needed for his own men, earning a slap on the wrist from George Simpson for his open-handedness. Edward Smith at the North West Company post was more generous than he had earlier been and pitched in with what supplies he could spare. "I conceive," wrote Back, "that everything was given which could be spared, consistent with their separate interests."[22]

Franklin's frequent requests for supplies from the two fur trade companies were not as heedlessly demanding as they seem at first sight. The expedition officers had little understanding of the realities of climatic conditions and the transportation infrastructure of the northwest, and none of them were aware that the trading posts of Rupert's Land operated on a once-a-year outfitting system. "We never had heard before our departure from York," Midshipman Robert Hood wrote, "that the posts in the interior only received annually, the stores necessary for the consumption of a single year." Somebody somewhere was not paying attention. Either the Hudson's Bay Company's London office had not spelled out this crucial fact of fur trade life or Franklin and his officers could not comprehend what they were told. Supplies being still short of what was needed, Back decided to carry on south to Fort Chipewyan.[23]

Preoccupied with the serious, even life-threatening, problems of outfitting and provisioning the expedition, the 100-mile walk to Fort Chipewyan that lay ahead, and the anticipated 300-mile trek back to Fort Enterprise, Back paid scant attention to the two Keewatin men he met at McVicar's Moose Island post, except to ask that they, along with supplies, be taken to the expedition's winter quarters as soon as conditions allowed. Only after several days did he think to make a diary entry noting his meeting with the two men, "whom I had forgot to state were at the Hudson's Bay house, and had been forwarded from Fort Churchill by Governor Williams. They were short of stature, but broad and well-built, apparently good natured and seemed perfectly acquainted with the purpose for which they were intended."[24]

Augustine and Junius started the last leg of their journey to Fort Enterprise on January 8, 1821, in company with Ferdinand Wentzel and Pierre St. Germain. The men followed the same route up the now frozen Yellowknife River that the explorers had taken five months earlier, arriving at Fort Enterprise on January 27, 1821. Franklin did not take much notice of the Inuit interpreters, although he included in his published narrative some of the ethnographic material gathered by Richardson. The expedition leader thought that Augustine was a chief among his own people and that Junius was his servant. The expedition officers used the name Augustus instead of Augustine. No explanation for the alteration in name appeared in any of their journals.[25]

Dr. Richardson spent considerable time with Augustine (a.k.a. Augustus) over the next few weeks and made detailed notes of their conversations. When time allowed, he turned the ethnographic, linguistic, and geographical data he learned from Augustine into a lengthy essay. After questioning Augustine about snowhouse construction, he was treated to a demonstration. Together the Inuit built a large winter dwelling with an eight-foot ceiling in the main room and several small, attached antechambers for butchering, cooking, storage, and other domestic functions.

To answer Richardson's question about his home village, Augustine explained that "in the spring before the ice quits the shores they kill seal, but during winter they frequent the borders of the large lakes near the coast, where they obtain Rein-deer and Musk-oxen." Augustine also said that he had never been farther north than Marble Island at the mouth of Rankin Inlet, but that "Eskimaux from the Arctic sea [came] overland to trade with his tribe and that canoes [could] go to the country of these strangers by following the sea-coast."[26]

George Back was still on his long search for supplies when Augustine and Junius reached Fort Enterprise, and he did not return until March 17. His impressions of Augustine, recorded on April 4, were mixed and unflattering. "Augustus," wrote Back, "was puffed up with the vanity of being made a great chief and lorded it proudly over the easy disposition of his countryman. He would affect a superiority over our men sometimes....His pride was easily wounded. Still he was very attentive when ordered to do anything, and considered it of the greatest consequence to be allowed to wait at table before strange Indians. He possessed a penetrating and quick discernment in the characters of strangers, and soon perceived their foibles, and being endowed with good natural abilities he made great progress in writing."[27]

Augustine's "progress in writing" was the result of evening classes in reading, writing, and calculating taught by the officers during the long, dark winter evenings at Fort Enterprise. The school was well attended by most of the men. Junius was a less apt student than his compatriot, preferring to spend his evenings smoking and practising with his bow and arrow. During the workday, he willingly carried water and collected wood for the cook. In Back's estimation, Junius was "a perfect model of good nature" and "a great favourite with all."[28]

The expedition's men, including the two Inuit, spent most days doing routine chores. There were fishnets to be attended to, wood to be chopped, and fires to be stoked, ice to be cut and hauled to wooden barrels, knives to be sharpened, and yards to be cleaned. Akaitcho's men hunted, while the women were kept busy making leather boots and winter clothing. The expedition officers edited and recopied their journals, bringing them up to date. George Back finished a series of five drawings, made sketches of Yellowknife men and women, and wrote long descriptions of their customs. Robert Hood conducted studies of northern lights and magnetic variations, as well as working on his journal and drawings. John Richardson held regular clinics to check on the health of expedition members and Akaitcho's people. The rest of his time he spent outdoors collecting rock, plant, and insect specimens and making notes on the habits of local wildlife.

❧

FRANKLIN AND RICHARDSON DID THEIR BEST TO KEEP THE MEN busy during the severe cold that winter, and the evening classes in which Augustine learned to read and write were just one of many structured activities that were more or less compulsory among the men. "By the arrival of Mr Wentzel, who is an excellent musician, and assisted us (*con amore*) in our attempts to amuse the men," Franklin noted, "we were enabled to gratify the whole establishment with an occasional dance. Of this amusement the voyagers [sic] were very fond, and not the less so, as it was now and then accompanied by a dram as long as our rum lasted." Dr. Richardson encouraged outdoor games for all expedition members, as essential exercise for the officers, who, with the exception of Back, tended to be sedentary in their work. For the men, whose daily manual labour kept them in reasonably fit condition, indoor and outdoor games, reading classes, and the occasional musical evening met their needs for friendly social relations.[29]

Dr. Richardson, keeping an eye on the health of his patients, confided to Franklin that he was particularly concerned about Robert Hood's fitness for the journey that lay ahead. The expedition leader noted in his journal, "The exercise was also in a peculiar manner serviceable to Mr Hood. Ever ardent in his pursuits, he had, through close attention to his drawings and other avocations, confined himself too much to the house in winter, and his health was impaired by his sedentary habits."[30]

Another reason for insisting on structured recreational activities and outdoor sports for the men was to keep the Canadians too busy to gossip, among themselves and with Akaitcho's people, about the dangers of the journey they were undertaking. By March, Franklin was having trouble feeding his people and suspected that Akaitcho was deliberately withholding dried meat supplies from the expedition in the hope that the plan to explore the Arctic coast would be abandoned.

Both Franklin and Richardson believed their Canadian voyageurs had been frightened by stories Akaitcho's men told of the dangers that awaited them at the Arctic coast and that the interpreters St. Germain and Adam had played upon the Yellowknives' fear of starvation "with the hope that the want of provision in the spring would put an end to our progress at once." Both senior officers pointed to St. Germain as the most likely agent of rebellion. "An artful man like St Germain, possessing a flow of language…had the means of poisoning the minds of the Indians," wrote Franklin. He also noted that "it is to be remarked that unless Mr. Wentzel had possessed a knowledge of the Copper Indian language, we should not have learned what we did." Franklin threatened the troublemaker with legal action in an English court and thereafter was satisfied that St. Germain was "more circumspect in his conduct."[31]

Following several days in conference with Franklin in March, Akaitcho renewed his commitment to see the expedition safely to the mouth of the Coppermine. He was especially interested, he confided, in a peaceful meeting with the Copper Inuit. His interest extended to the two Inuit at hand. On March 31, when he was ready to return to his own lodge some fifteen miles distant, he invited them to accompany him. Junius returned after a few days when he discovered that Akaitcho's people were living on short rations, but Augustine remained with the Yellowknives for at least a month.[32]

The exact date of Augustine's return to Fort Enterprise is not clear. George Back put it at "the latter end of May." Richardson's journal noted that Akaitcho and Augustine were both at Fort Enterprise on May 24 and, without going into details, described an edgy Akaitcho, who "vented his ill humour in a quarrel with Augustus about a gun." Franklin's diary, reconstructed from memory a year after the events and with the help of Back and Richardson's journals, placed Augustine's return as April 27. A more likely date is May 22, when Akaitcho paid a ceremonial visit to the fort. The Leader was preceded by his standard-bearer and accompanied by a council of elderly men and a bodyguard of young ones. At his insistence, the fort ensign was raised and he was greeted with a gun salute. All the male members of the party, except Akaitcho himself, had painted their faces with vermilion, "the old men having a spot on the right cheek, the young ones on the left."[33]

The purpose of Akaitcho's visit was to argue once more against Franklin's dangerous and, in Akaitcho's opinion, foolish plan. In a long speech to the assembled expedition, The Leader "peremptorily refused to say whether he would continue on with us or not, neither would he give any answer as to what provisions he could provide." Then, saying he did not want the white men to think he and his hunters were lazy, he promised he would keep his word. A day later he reversed himself, hinting that he might withdraw because he had not received the full reward that had been promised to him.[34] The expedition officers had difficulty understanding Akaitcho's wavering commitment. Franklin likened his conduct to "the pettish freaks of a spoiled child" who wanted greater rewards than he had originally agreed to. Richardson thought him greedy and self-serving, with a tendency to sulk when he thought he was not receiving the respect his high position warranted. Back concluded that Akaitcho was "prompted by fear" of the northward journey, specifically of the reputedly warlike Inuit they expected to meet. As they had done in March, the expedition officers sought a scapegoat among their own Yellowknife interpreters.[35]

As Back remembered it, Augustine was called into conference and questioned, "to discover if possible who had been tampering with him." Augustine refused to tell tales on his friends, and as Back noted, "nothing satisfactory was proved." Neither Franklin nor Richardson mentioned questioning Augustine. Richardson's account of Akaitcho's May 22 speech and the negotiations that followed identified St. Germain as the interpreter most likely to have undermined Akaitcho's confidence. Franklin also suspected St. Germain, "the most intelligent of our two interpreters, and the one who had most influence with the Indians," and openly blamed the defection on St. Germain's "unguarded conversations." St. Germain acknowledged his guilt and "exerted himself much...in bringing about a change in their sentiments, and with some success."[36]

None of the expedition officers apparently understood what Akaitcho's objections truly were, although Back came close. The one explanation they would not consider was The Leader's own statement that the proposed voyage along the seacoast would inevitably lead to the death of some, if not all, members of the expedition. His reluctance sprang from a long and intimate familiarity with the environment and its frequent scarcity of resources. Akaitcho had observed the expedition officers in action long enough to know that they were largely ignorant of the dangers they faced and ill equipped to deal with them. His indecision can best be explained as a result of the conflict between his conviction that the expedition was already doomed and his desire to protect the strangers who depended on him. In the end, Akaitcho's fears proved to have been well founded.

WITHOUT REGARD TO AKAITCHO'S WARNINGS, FRANKLIN ISSUED the men their Arctic clothing and gear on May 25. Augustine and Junius were provided with "laced dresses," to the indescribable joy of the latter. The "dress" was an outer garment, similar to a cloak but usually with sleeves, and "lace" was ornamental gold or silver braid on the collar and front closing. Given Augustine's insistence on clothing that emulated the naval officers he had seen in 1813, he might well have been pleased with the new uniforms as indicators of his and Junius's status in the expedition. Franklin was particularly struck by Junius's reaction. "The happy little fellow burst into ecstatic laughter, as he surveyed the different articles of his gay habiliments," he wrote.[37]

On June 4, Dr. Richardson left with an advance party of fifteen men transporting the bulk of the expedition's equipment. Two of Akaitcho's hunters, Basil and Bald-head, and the latter's wife, accompanied them. Three of the voyageurs were in charge of dog teams and sleds, while the others man-hauled small sledges or carried backpacks of expedition equipment, each weighing about eighty pounds, as well as his own personal items. The sleds were, in Richardson's words, "doubly loaded": each carried two bags of pemmican and five bags of fat, at about eighty pounds per bag, as well as an eighty-pound bundle of dried meat, a cask of portable soup, a box of arrowroot, more than sixty pounds of gunpowder, and another bundle of shot and ball weighing close to seventy pounds. Seven nets, line, sails, tents, and canoe equipment, along with presents for the Inuit, including generous numbers of ice chisels, hatchets, and other iron items, completed the loads. The party set up camp at Point Lake on June 10, and Richardson sent all the women and children back to Fort Enterprise. A day later he sent most of the men back, except for the interpreter Jean Baptiste Adam, the voyageur Jean Baptiste Parent, and the Yellowknife guide Bald-head.[38]

The main body of the expedition set out on June 14—Commander John Franklin, Midshipmen George Back and Robert Hood, Royal Navy mariner John Hepburn, the two Keewatin Inuit, the Yellowknife interpreter

Pierre St. Germain, and fifteen voyageurs: Gabriel Beauparlant; Jean Baptiste Belanger ("le rouge"); Solomon Belanger ("le gros"); Joseph Benoit; Pierre Dumas; Antonio Vincenza Fontano; Joseph Forcier; Joseph Gagné; Jean Baptiste Parent; Matthew Pelonquin; Joseph Peltier; Ignace Perrault; François Semandré; Michel Teroahauté; and Régiste Vaillant. The officers carried some of their personal property, "at least 20 lbs," wrote Back, and possibly more figuring the weight of books, boots, blankets, knapsack, and rifle. The others bore greater burdens, between sixty and eighty pounds each according to Back. Ferdinand Wentzel and several of Akaitcho's hunters, with wives and children, went with them.[39]

Three sleds, or "trains," had been built to transport the expedition's canoes, each weighing about three hundred pounds and each dragged by four men and two dogs. They travelled on the ice, where hauling was easier. The others, including the officers, Hepburn, Augustine, Junius, and three Canadians, slogged through swampy, sometimes flooded terrain, with meltwater frequently up to their knees. Mosquitoes, daily becoming more troublesome, added to their discomforts. They passed the nights, often sleepless, in the open with no more protection than a single blanket per man. On the second day, many of the men found it easier to drag their burdens on crude sleds jerry-built out of sticks and antlers they found as they walked.[40]

Within two days, the provisions the men carried with them were gone and wolverines had destroyed the meat previously cached for them by Akaitcho's men. The Yellowknife hunters, daily scouring the countryside, managed to keep everyone fed, but just barely. Dunkings in icy water were common. George Back tried to use a piece of floating ice as a raft in crossing one of the many small lakes, but "my frail friend glided from under my feet, [and] I got a sound ducking." Junius got his "ducking" on the fourth day of the march when lake ice cracked beneath his feet and he plummeted into deep water. After five days, they were all experiencing "rheumatic pains and swellings in the joints…so that it was with the utmost difficulty they could place one leg before the other." Franklin and Back went in search of trees to build a fire at night and ease the men's miseries but were unsuccessful. By the twenty-fifth the already slow advance became a snail's pace, not to be wondered at, according to Back, given the heavy loads each one carried and "that the majority of the men were either lame, or not recovered from their recent fatigue." Dr. Richardson diagnosed "erythematous inflammation on the insides of the thighs" and warned Franklin that they would only grow worse unless they were allowed some rest.[41]

Franklin reduced the men's burdens by abandoning one of the canoes and reassigning the three men and two dogs who had been hauling it to the other two sledges. Heavy rain during the night of June 27–28 turned the river ice into "innumerable spikes which not only gave excessive pain but actually penetrated the feet." The dogs were also suffering. One of them simply lay down on the ice and died. The others left bloody tracks as they walked. With dried provisions gone and very little fresh meat at hand, the discovery that a packet of meat had been left behind by mistake was serious. Richardson and Augustine made a twelve-mile round trip to retrieve it.[42]

On July 2, the party reached more or less open water on the Coppermine River and happily got the canoes afloat. The men's lacerated feet and swollen joints began to heal as they spent more time seated in the canoes or walked with lighter burdens. Akaitcho's hunters kept them adequately, if not sumptuously, fed, which went a long way toward improving their physical health. Meat not immediately consumed was sliced and dried. The supply was augmented on July 9 when the hunters brought down six muskoxen. In relief at finding his pantry unexpectedly overflowing—"Our whole stock of provision, calculated for preservation, was sufficient for fourteen days, without any diminution of the ordinary allowance of three pounds to each man per day"—Franklin declared a day off from travelling to smoke and dry the meat.[43]

༄

BY THE EVENING OF JULY 12, ON THE LOWER REACHES OF THE Coppermine, the expedition was within ten miles of Inuit country and needed to exercise extreme caution against the traditional enemies of the Yellowknives. Augustine and Junius were assigned the task they had been hired to do: locate any Inuit who happened to be near the river and arrange for a peaceful meeting between them and the expedition. Franklin provided gifts—metal knives, mirrors, beads, pieces of iron—to be given to any Inuit they might meet or to be left at places that showed signs of recent use by the residents of the country. As they prepared to set out the following morning, Augustine and Junius dressed in skin suits similar to those they had worn in their own country but altered by the women of Akaitcho's band to make them more like those worn by the Copper Inuit. Each of them tucked a small pistol inside his shirt. Junius, Dr. Richardson noted, showed his excitement at the possibility of meeting with his own countrymen, strangers though they might be, more enthusiastically than did the more solemn Augustine. But both were eager to get on with the job and confident that they would not only find their Copper Inuit fellow countrymen but establish friendly relations with ease. Augustine was so sure of a warm welcome and traditional Inuit hospitality that he did not bother to take any provisions.[44]

Early on the morning of July 13, under strict instructions to return by "nightfall" no matter what happened, the two men began their search. After a long day's march—at least fifteen miles—along the west bank of the river, they spotted four Inuit tents on a small island immediately below a waterfall. As the light faded, which at that latitude in mid-July was shortly after midnight, the adventurers judged that the inhabitants of the tents had gone to bed and decided to hide among the rocks and wait until they showed themselves in the "morning." Morning in this particular place was, of course, a movable event. The sun reappeared on the horizon about an hour after setting. Even during that brief "night," enough twilight remained that the watchers could see the tents below their hiding place.

When a man emerged from one of the tents several hours later, Augustine immediately called out to him. After some standard greetings, he asked the man to cross to the west bank in his kayak with a second kayak in tow so that they could return to the island together. The man seemed to agree at first but had second thoughts as he approached the west bank; he paused a few yards from shore and began to ask questions. Augustine assured him of his good intentions and told him that white men were coming down the river in a spirit of friendship and goodwill. The stranger inquired about the number of canoes the white men had and cautioned Augustine not to let them try to shoot the cascade. Despite not coming into close contact with any of the villagers, the two interpreters were sure they had opened the way for friendly relations.

During the course of the day, Augustine and Junius observed the inhabitants and activities of the small Copper Inuit community. There were four men—two of them unusually tall, in Augustine's opinion—and four women. Their summer residence was like the small villages the two Keewatin men were familiar with. Around the tents was all the usual camp paraphernalia—fishing poles, stone kettles, hatchets, piles of skins—indicating some degree of permanence. Ten dogs were tied safely away from an outdoor kitchen where a stage held dried salmon and mice and a number of animal and bird skins.

As the day wore on, Augustine and Junius began to regret not having brought any provisions with them. Close to thirty hours had passed since their last meal and nothing was offered by their cautious countrymen. They decided that Junius should return upriver for some dried meat or pemmican, while Augustine stayed to keep track of the villagers.

MEANWHILE, WITH STILL NO SIGN OF THE TWO AMBASSADORS reporting in, Franklin grew more and more concerned for their safety. Officers and men took turns watching for them from the summit of a nearby hill, in "considerable anxiety," as both Richardson and Back said, hoping to catch sight of their young companions returning to the camp. After a night of worry, the entire expedition, including Akaitcho and his people, resumed its progress downriver.[45]

Junius did not have far to go—about three miles—before he met his fellow explorers proceeding downriver and was able to report what he and Augustine had seen. His description of the waterfall where he had left Augustine was recognized by the officers as Bloody Fall, the site of the Chipewyan attack on the Copper Inuit reputedly witnessed by Samuel Hearne nearly fifty years earlier. Here the men set up camp, while Junius had a quick meal, packed some provisions for Augustine, and, accompanied by John Hepburn, started again for Bloody Fall.

Still nervous about a possible meeting with hostile Inuit, Akaitcho and his people refused to wait out of sight, and by the morning of the fifteenth, they had inched their way to Franklin's campsite. At noon, with the anxious Yellowknives following, the expedition reached Hepburn, who was patiently standing guard on a hill about a mile above Bloody Fall from which he could see the ice-covered ocean in the distance.

By the time the main body of the expedition reached the fall, the four Copper Inuit hunters and their wives had abandoned their dogs and belongings and disappeared from the rocky little island. Augustine and Junius spent the morning of July 16 searching for them, but without success. With Franklin and Richardson, they hurried to examine the abandoned camp—ten or twelve sleds of meat, a number of dogs, and three canoes—and found, behind a rock, an elderly man, lame and unable to run with his countrymen. Determined, as Back wrote, "to sell his life as dear as possible," the man tried to stab Augustine with his short, copper-pointed spear, until he realized that Augustine was speaking to him in his own language.[46]

Calming himself, the old man allowed Augustine to sit down beside him, listened to Augustine's explanation of what was happening, and accepted the gifts presented to him. Augustine also took care of the introductions, assuming that the naming of people was as important to his new friend as it was to his fellow villagers back on Hudson Bay. The old man identified himself as Tiriganniaq (White Fox) and his people as Nagjuktormiut, People of the Antler. Like two of the men Augustine and Junius had observed on the rocky island, Tiriganniaq was unusually tall, about five feet ten inches, Richardson thought. Augustine and Junius helped him get his tent set up and settled in to spend the night with him. During the half hour or so of darkness that night, Tiriganniaq's wife came from her hiding place among the rocks and joined them.[47]

Over the next twenty-four hours, Augustine and Junius gathered as much information as they could about the country the expedition was heading toward, and they called Richardson to visit the elderly couple in their tent. In spite of the reliance Franklin put on Tiriganniaq's observations, much of what the old man told them sounded more like warnings than good news. "Deer may be killed sparingly on the coast all the year," he told them, and "musk-ox is found only on the banks of the river near the straggling woods and they [his fellow villagers] do not hunt them in the winter." Richardson thought that "respecting the country to the eastward, [Tiriganniaq] was…extremely ignorant." The old man tried to persuade Augustine to stay with him, and even offered one of his daughters as a wife, an offer Augustine refused.[48]

The last night on the Coppermine River, the voyageurs saw the ocean with its burden of floating ice for the first time and were "terrified at the idea of a voyage through an icy sea in bark canoes." Augustine and Junius, accustomed to travel on Hudson Bay in skin boats, expressed their own fear of the fragile canoes and "made many urgent requests to be allowed to return with Mr Wentzel." The officers brushed aside the concerns of their canoemen and interpreters, and on July 19, the expedition men said their goodbyes to their companions of the past several months. Ferdinand Wentzel, with four voyageurs, left to return to Fort Chipewyan. He took Richardson's rock samples for shipment to Edinburgh and promised to take all the records, sketches, maps, and journals from Fort Enterprise for forwarding to England. Akaitcho's people followed Wentzel upriver and headed for their usual summer hunting territories.[49]

The twenty men of the Arctic overland expedition watched as Wentzel and the Yellowknife guides and hunters disappeared around a curve in the river, then pitched their tents and hoisted the Union Jack on a high bluff overlooking the Arctic sea.

CHAPTER 4

DEATH AND SURVIVAL

1821–1822

ON JULY 20, 1821, IN SPITE OF A STRONG NORTHEAST GALE and continuous thunderstorms, Franklin judged the expedition ready to begin the journey eastward along the coast. The expedition officers were worried about the inadequate state of their provisions. Franklin assessed the supply at "only to fifteen days' consumption." Back thought that even on a diet of short rations the provisions on hand were "barely sufficient for three weeks." The canoe men also had doubts and were preparing for the worst by secretly setting aside ammunition. Richardson believed they wanted to be able to "procure ducks and geese privately...to avoid the necessity of sharing them with the officers."[1]

Another concern quickly came to light as the expedition headed east. The hunters, spending most of each day on the land looking for food, saw no signs that Inuit had used the area recently. Contrary to Tiriganniaq's information, there were no inhabited Inuit villages where they could purchase provisions or get geographical information.[2] Barely a week after leaving the Coppermine River, the officers were alarmed to discover that not only were the dried provisions running out but what remained of the pemmican was turning mouldy in the damp air, and the beef "had been so badly cured, as to be scarcely eatable."[3]

Augustine and Junius spent most of their days on land searching for deer. Each of the little barren-ground caribou provided a single meal for twenty people, and not a particularly generous meal at that for men who were fighting heavy ice in wind, rain, and turbulent water for sixteen or more hours a day. Between July 21 and July 31, Richardson recorded the number of caribou killed each day: on July 21, a fat male; on July 23, one caribou; and on the thirtieth, "a young rein-deer." The fresh game total for the first ten days on the ocean was 405 pounds, including the three caribou, supplemented by 30 pounds of fish, and 10 pounds of "other" meat. Four hundred eighty pounds of dried meat was used from the emergency stores.[4] Both the number and the weight of the meat are important to understand how many calories the men were consuming. The officers began to understand that when Tiriganniaq had said that "deer may be killed sparingly," he had meant barely any at all.

The state of the provisions made it, in Richardson's words, "a matter of first importance to receive a supply, on which account we have for some time been very anxious to discover some parties of Eskimaux." Still hoping that Tiriganniaq's information would turn out to be accurate after all, Franklin sent Augustine, Junius, and John Hepburn up the Hood River on July 30, with a supply of presents, to search for local inhabitants and arrange for the purchase of provisions and leather to make shoes. The three ambassadors were back a few days later having found no Inuit and no signs that anyone had been there in recent months. During their absence, the other hunters managed to bring in a brown bear and six small caribou yearlings, all "too lean to have been eaten by any but persons who had no choice." Meals were more satisfying in the first two weeks of August in Bathurst Inlet, mostly due to 600 pounds of nutritious bear meat. Even so, the roughly 1,450 pounds of fresh meat had to be supplemented with 480 pounds of dried meat.[5]

Aside from the problems of provisioning, travel conditions were more difficult than anticipated. No one was prepared for the violence of ocean travel and the large amount of floating ice. As the two canoes moved eastward, they were more and more pressed by heavy ice. "Frequently," wrote Back, "the bowsmen were obliged to leap from piece to piece [of floating ice]...to prevent the bark from being split." Franklin added that "both the canoes were in imminent danger of being crushed by the ice, which was now tossed about by the waves that the gale had excited." When Back inspected the canoes after battling through the "heavy rolling sea" of Melville Sound on August 15, he found that one of them had at least fifteen broken ribs and the second was loose in its frame and in immediate danger of its bark separating from the gunwales.[6]

Suffering the effects of malnutrition, brutally hard labour, and unrelenting raw cold, officers and men began to despair of reaching the expedition's goal. Time after time as the coastline trended southward, they hoped they had finally found the passage they sought, and time after time they found themselves dead-ended in an inlet, facing the unwelcome prospect of making their way north again to the coast proper. Franklin accepted the bitter fact that "the time spent in exploring Arctic and Melville Sounds, and Bathurst's Inlet had precluded the hope of reaching Repulse Bay."[7] The canoemen and hunters, worried about provisions and resenting the loss of the meagre comforts of dry clothes, warm meals, and hot drinks, came close to mutiny.

Franklin recognized that it was time to call a halt. As summarized by George Back, the officers were worried about "the want of food—the badness of the canoes—the advanced state of the season—the impossibility of succeeding—and the long journey...through the barren lands—and to this may be added the dissatisfaction of the men." To this list may also be added the absence of local Inuit who might have eased their situation and the physical and mental traumas of the human body when it begins to break down and of the human mind when despair replaces hope. Franklin informed his officers that the moment to turn back would be the point where the coast took a definite eastward trend without any sign of a southward passage heading in the direction of Repulse Bay, where they had hoped to be met by Captain Parry. The plan was to retreat west to Arctic Sound, head up Hood River, and then make a dash on foot across the barrens to Fort Providence.[8]

With the decision made, the party struggled on fighting heavy rain and a gale that continued with "unabated violence" on August 16 and 17. On the eighteenth, the storm made it impossible to launch the canoes, and Franklin sent out all the hunters to look for animals. Hepburn brought in a white fox, which was boiled with some geese and provided "excellent eating." But while the meal allowed them to ignore the spectre of starvation for the moment, their daily caloric intake was inadequate. The men began to lose all sense of the compass points, circling the campsite, tripping on willow roots, and losing their footing on slippery stones. Jean Baptiste Belanger and Michel Teroahauté lost their bearings while hunting with Junius and were forced to spend the night on the barrens, where they suffered from the cold, "one of them having his thighs frozen." The same day, Franklin, Richardson, and Back walked about ten miles to the east and saw the omen they had been expecting: a coastline bearing sharply north-northeast. Four days later, on August 22, while out hunting, Augustine walked a few miles farther east than the officers had done and, on arriving back at the camp, drew a detailed map that confirmed the officers' opinion. They named the place Point Turnagain.[9]

IN SPITE OF HUNGER, FATIGUE, AND COLD, THE VOYAGEURS WERE SO "cheered by the prospect of returning" that on August 23, they rose at two in the morning and launched the frail canoes into a heavy sea and strong wind. At the end of the day, having covered about fifteen miles, they pulled up on the beach for a meal—a handful of mouldering pemmican and some berries found growing beyond the tide line. On the twenty-fourth, they were on the west shore of Bathurst Inlet, cold and soaked to the skin, but safe on a sandy beach with a small herd of caribou browsing nearby; a few hours later, one was being roasted for breakfast and two more were in the larder. August 25 was another good day, as "plentiful" caribou were spotted on shore. The hunters were landed and brought in two more, one a large male. After a breakfast of steaks garnished with newly picked berries, they were on the water again, and by sunset—around eight o'clock, much earlier now as the season grew late—they entered the Hood River, where, in Back's words, "the men began to sing and be merry, not a little rejoiced at having escaped from the Mer du Nord."[10]

While noting that the voyageurs "could not restrain their expressions of joy on quitting" the sea, Richardson was aware that "the most painful and certainly the most hazardous part of the journey was to come." George Back prepared for whatever lay ahead by changing his underwear, the last change into anything like clean linen he was to make for the next three months.[11]

The journey up Hood River began auspiciously enough. Berries were plentiful and on August 26, Matthew Pelonquin killed a small deer, which "furnished a delightful repast, and the nets yielded ten white fish and trout." The first unwelcome surprise came on the second day of the ascent, when they reached two magnificent falls pouring from the upland interior through a narrow chasm. Back and Richardson agreed that "the whole descent of the river" exceeded 250 feet. Franklin named the "stupendous torrent" Wilberforce Falls.[12]

It was obvious that the men would not be able to carry or track the canoes up the falls. Franklin ordered that they be taken apart and their materials used to make two smaller vessels, just big enough for three people to make a river crossing. For four days, nearly everyone worked on the canoes. Junius hunted, providing the camp with the meat of a caribou and a muskox on his first day out and, with St. Germain, bringing down two more muskoxen a day or so later.[13]

On the last day of August, the expedition prepared to turn inland. Ammunition, nets, hatchets, ice chisels, astronomical instruments, blankets, and three kettles were portioned out to the men, whose backpacks, weighing about ninety pounds each, also held their small personal effects. Each man took some dried skins to make or repair shoes, along with two pairs of flannel socks and a share of whatever articles of warm clothing remained. Books, guns, and stores not absolutely necessary were put in boxes and left in a cache. About midnight on their last night on the coast, heavy rain turned into a violent squall and blew down the officers' tent. In the morning, the ground was white with the first snow of the season.[14]

THE LONG TREK ACROSS THE BARRENS BEGAN AT DAWN ON September 1. Weather and terrain were against them. The rocky ground, wet and slippery from snow, caused frequent falls and painful injuries to feet protected only by moosehide moccasins. The men took turns carrying the two small canoes strapped to their backs diagonally, Chipewyan-style, and were pushed to the ground by every gust of wind that caught the boats side on. By evening one of the canoes had split into two pieces, the other into three, and the march stopped while repairs were made. Most of the men had, by then, thrown away their personal belongings, such as they were, to lighten their loads.[15]

By September 4 they were in woodless territory, with no prospects of a fire and nothing to cook even if they had found wood. A raging snowstorm mixed with heavy rain kept them in their comfortless beds without food for three days while snow piled up around the frozen canvas tents to a depth of three feet. Once on the way again, the party had to navigate through frozen swamps and suffered frequent, bruising falls through thin ice. The canoe-carriers were repeatedly knocked down from violent gusts, until one of the boats was completely destroyed on the rocks and had to be abandoned.[16]

Back described the surrounding country as an "uninterrupted mass of snow, sterile and cold, without the most distant prospect of anything like food." Supper that night, their first meal in three days, was a few sips of portable soup thickened with arrowroot, and for the first time, *tripe de roche* soup, made from lichen steeped in barely warmed water, made its appearance on the menu.[17]

Straggling and on wounded feet, the party reached Cracroft River on September 8. The one remaining small canoe was by then useless for want of gumming. The unattractive alternative—wading through the icy water using rocks some two or three feet below the surface as stepping stones—had to be undertaken. With no wood to make a fire and the need to hurry on, they kept up the march, feeling their clothes freeze around their bodies as they walked. Augustine, Pelonquin, St. Germain, and Adam were the first to cross and immediately went ahead to hunt, leaving the bulk of the party to follow.[18] Junius, who had gone a little farther upriver to look for an easier crossing place, did not reappear during the day. No one was particularly concerned. "As we did not all cross at one place," Back wrote, "it was found that Junius was missing on our arrival at the appropriate side—but nothing doubting that he would soon follow us, we continued our journey."[19]

THE MAIN BODY OF THE EXPEDITION CAUGHT UP WITH THE FOUR hunters the following morning, September 9, on the eastern bank of the Burnside River. The width of the river, some 150 yards, gave them no choice but to glue the broken canoe together using the watery sap of low-lying willow as gum. With St. Germain, Adam, and Peltier at the paddles, the men were ferried across, one passenger at a time lying flat in the bottom of the canoe.[20] About five in the afternoon, after sixteen round trips, everyone was safely across, including Junius, who had returned with about four pounds of meat cut from the carcass of a caribou brought down and half eaten by wolves. Supper was two young hares and the carrion Junius had brought.[21]

At noon the next day, the sight of several muskoxen raised everyone's hopes, and after two hours stalking the animals, the hunters brought down a large cow. In a few minutes the animal was skinned and cut up, and "the contents of its stomach were devoured upon the spot." Even the raw intestines were "pronounced by the most delicate amongst us to be excellent." Hunger slightly curbed, the men grubbed up enough willow to make a fire and cooked some of the meat, which they "devoured with avidity." It was their first filling meal in six days.[22]

Almost from the first week on the ocean, the men had experienced physical ailments from brutally hard labour, malnutrition, exposure to damp and cold, and the lack of any hygienic facilities. By mid-September, new, more painful, and more serious ills arose, caused by meals of raw, undercooked, rotten, and sometimes parasitic meat and carrion. Rockweed, now a staple in their diet, proved to be indigestible. Robert Hood was the first sufferer, experiencing intense pain from "griping" (severe diarrhea), which led to even greater debilitation and dangerous dehydration. Pelonquin and Vaillant were soon feeling the same effects and were barely able to walk. Hoping to increase their speed of travel, Franklin decided to abandon everything except ammunition, clothing, the one remaining canoe, and the navigational instruments they needed to find their way to Great Slave Lake.[23]

On September 13, four days after crossing the Burnside River, they were forced to cross it again. Without a map or knowlegeable guides, the officers did not know that the river drained from Contwoyto Lake in a northeast direction and then made a sharp turn to the southeast before emptying into Bathurst Inlet. They camped that night at the juncture of river and lake and prepared for a crossing that they knew to be dangerous, using the one damaged canoe they still carried. Before they started the next day, Pierre St. Germain, skilled as a boatbuilder as well as a hunter and interpreter, brought each of the officers a small piece of meat, which he had saved from his ration. "Such an act of self-denial and kindness...filled our eyes with tears," wrote Richardson.[24]

FRANKLIN, ST. GERMAIN, AND SOLOMON BELANGER ("LE GROS") were the first to try crossing the river. The swirling water overturned the tiny, unstable craft, and the three men ended up in the rapids. St. Germain managed to right the canoe and get Franklin to the west bank so he could leap out. Junius dragged the unconscious Belanger, who had collapsed on a large rock in the rapids, to the east bank, where Dr. Richardson stripped him, rolled him in all available blankets, and ordered two men to lie on either side of his nearly lifeless body, using their own heat, such as it was, to impart some warmth to him. St. Germain, benumbed from cold, was carried over the rapid with the canoe, and came to rest on the eastern bank.[25]

While Franklin, alone on the west bank, paced back and forth helplessly in rapidly freezing clothes, and Richardson worked over the half-frozen Belanger, the men managed a hasty gumming job on the canoe. Augustine somehow got himself and the birchrind wreck across the river with Franklin's bedroll and helped his commander start a fire. This "hazardous service," wrote Franklin, "he performed with the greatest coolness and judgment." What Augustine's quick action meant for Franklin personally was fully understood by the expedition leader. "Separated as I was from my companions, without gun, ammunition, hatchet, or the means of making a fire, and in wet clothes, my doom would have been speedily sealed," he wrote. In a second act of calm thinking, Augustine had tied one end of a rope to a rock on the west bank. What Augustine's instant reaction in retrieving the canoe and rigging a line across the rapids meant for the expedition was also clear to Franklin. "My companions too, [if] driven to the necessity of coasting the lake, must have sunk under the fatigue of rounding its innumerable arms and bays." By mid-afternoon the next day, the damaged canoe had been repaired and the entire party was across the river. The same day, Ignace Perrault killed a caribou, a "fine male." All hands were "in good spirits," wrote Franklin, because of "the safe landing of all hands, and having fresh meat for the next day."[26] The loss that day was Franklin's portfolio containing his journal and sketchbooks with his astronomical and meteorological observations.

Back's journal entries tracked the course of starvation and exposure. "We were generally shivering all the time, for the blood runs coldly through the veins of a starving man half worn out with fatigue." On most days, mosses and lichens were the only available food, if food they can be called. By September 20, men and officers were plagued by great weakness and had difficulty moving through the new-fallen snow, which "added to the severity of our sufferings." On the twenty-first they were "in a sad state...all meagre and faint," and the next day "greatly dejected and very weak." Richardson's journal from September 18 on, like Back's, contained numerous comments on the men's condition. On the nineteenth he wrote, "Men faint from hunger"; on the twentieth, "Men dispirited and exhausted"; and a day later, "The men much dispirited." Franklin noted that Robert Hood was "particularly weak."[27]

September 23 was a day of disappointments. As the party stumbled blindly through a thick fog, they heard the sound of running water. Augustine went to determine if it could be the Coppermine River but lost his way and did not report in until midnight. When he reappeared, his news was discouraging—the body of water was not the hoped-for river but another unknown lake. Peltier and Vaillant, taking turns at carrying the remaining small canoe, fell behind the main group and, when they caught up, explained that a nasty fall had damaged it beyond repair and they had thrown it away. Supper that night was a meal of old shoes and a few scraps of leather. Next day—the eleventh without meat—St. Germain and Adam killed five small caribou. "The people," wrote Back, "ran to the animals—and some even ate the contents of the stomach. This unforeseen and most fortunate circumstance induced us to remain where we were for the day—when many repasts were made—but the pain and sufferings were shocking after so long a privation and brought on a weakness that was irresistible and for a short time prevented one from even moving. I could scarcely stand—the same time nothing would remain on the stomach—it was truly painful." Franklin allowed a day of rest, and by night a third of the meat had been eaten.[28]

༄

THE BATTERED EXPEDITION REACHED THE COPPERMINE RIVER ON September 26. In spite of the assurances of the officers, the men refused to believe they were within forty miles of Fort Enterprise. "So much had they bewildered themselves in the march that some of them asserted that it was the River on which we had built the small canoes (Hood's River) and others that it was (Tree River).... Their despondency had arrived at its height and they all despaired of ever seeing Fort Enterprise again."[29]

The problem they had to solve was how to cross a river of the Coppermine's size without a boat. St. Germain doubted that he could build a vessel with willow branches, but there was no other way forward. The willow raft, tried out on September 29, proved so unmanageable that even Solomon Belanger, the best paddler, could not control it. Richardson volunteered to swim across with a line and then haul the raft across with one passenger at a time. He would have known that any attempt to swim across was an invitation to hypothermia; what he could not have known was that on entering the river he would step on an old dagger and suffer a severe gash to his ankle bone. At mid-river he sank as the cold leached the strength from his legs. The anxious men on shore pulled him back and landed him safely. Rolled in blankets and settled by a good fire, he slowly recovered. Because of the loss of feeling in his numbed legs, he did not react to the heat of the fire on one side, and more damage, this time from burns, resulted. It was a full year before he was able to walk without pronounced weakness in the damaged leg.

St. Germain, as a last resort, undertook to build a boat fashioned like a coracle with a willow frame and a covering of oiled tent-canvas scraps.[30] The work proceeded slowly, but by October 4 he had accomplished a miracle and the makeshift vessel was as ready as he could make it. The entire party gathered on the riverbank to watch its maiden voyage. With great dexterity, St. Germain paddled across the river, carrying a double line, which he anchored solidly. The conveyance was then hauled back and the next person crossed. One by one, uncomfortable and at considerable risk, nineteen expedition members out of the twenty who had left the mouth of the Coppermine River together in July began to cross the river. Only Junius was missing.

Midway through the crossing, two expedition members set out on new searches. Augustine left to search for Junius or for signs indicating where his friend might have been. He returned a day and a half later, without success. While reporting to Franklin, he noted that Junius was well supplied with ammunition, blankets, a knife, and other necessities and voiced his opinion that Junius would probably have gone to the west end of Point Lake and followed the river until he "fell in with some of the Eskimaux who frequent its mouth."[31] George Back watched while the officers and about half the men safely crossed the river to the west bank, only forty miles from Fort Enterprise. Following Franklin's orders and accompanied by Solomon Belanger, Pierre St. Germain, and Gabriel Beauparlant, Back struck out in the direction of the fort. Franklin's intention and hope was that Back and his small party would reach Akaitcho in time to save the men of the expedition, who were caught in the dreadful situation that the Yellowknife leader had foreseen.[32]

FOR FIVE AND A HALF DAYS, BACK AND HIS THREE COMPANIONS slogged and stumbled their way across the forty miles that separated the main body of the expedition from its winter quarters. Their menus between October 4 and October 8 consisted of "a partridge each," "an old pair of burnt leather trousers," and "a gun cover and a pair of shoes." On the sixth day, October 9, they reached the fort, which was "in the most desolate and neglected state," Back wrote. "The doors and window of that room in which we expected to find provision—had been thrown down—and carelessly left so—and the wild animals of the woods had resorted there as a place of shelter or retreat." Worst of all, there was no note from Wentzel with directions on where to find Akaitcho's people. St. Germain suggested that the best they could do was follow deer tracks and hope the Yellowknife hunters were doing the same. They spent one day, October 10, digging under the snow for scraps of meat, bones, and deerskin, no matter how small. Back used some of the skins to make mittens, while Belanger burned bones to break them down and made "an excellent meal."[33]

They left Fort Enterprise the next day. Still hopeful that the main party would find its way to the house, Back left a note to inform Franklin that he and his companions had gone in search of Akaitcho's people and that, if they did not find them within a few days, they would head south to Fort Providence. After three difficult days of fruitless searching, they made camp at Roundrock Lake, less than five miles from Fort Enterprise.[34] On October 14, Back wrote another note to Franklin and sent Solomon Belanger back to the house to deliver it to anyone who was there or to leave it for anyone who might come later.[35]

Two days after Belanger left, the other three men began to move southward along the west shore of Roundrock Lake, stopping for a brief rest within sight of a small clump of pines near the edge of the lake. Beauparlant, barely able to walk, decided to rest a bit longer while Back and St. Germain moved on to set up camp for the night. As they neared the pines, they noticed crows in large numbers fussing about something on the sandy beach. St. Germain went to investigate and shouted the news of a great discovery—the head and shoulders of a caribou, killed by wolves and frozen halfway into the sand. Some gristly scraps of meat were visible on the shoulder of the carcass, as was the whole of its brain. Then, most wonderful of all, looking ahead some hundred paces to where more birds were creating a racket, they saw another six caribou heads sticking up. "An expression of Oh! merciful God! we are saved broke from us both," wrote Back, "and with feelings more easily imagined than described we shook hands—not knowing what to say for joy."[36]

Back started hauling caribou heads out of the ice while St. Germain cut wood and started a fire for roasting them. Nothing remained to be done, Back wrote in his diary, except to wait for Beauparlant. The voyageur was, however, unable to catch up. Increasingly heavy fog had him pinned down and he could not see his way. Back and St. Germain fired a few rounds, and on hearing Beauparlant's gun in reply, they exchanged shouted goodnights. Back was not unduly worried—Beauparlant had everything he needed to start a fire and Back's blanket as well as his own.[37]

The next morning, October 16, Back and St. Germain collected more firewood and cut more frozen caribou heads out of the snow, but Beauparlant did not appear. St. Germain went to check on him and returned about four in the afternoon carrying Back's blanket. "Well, was he asleep?" Back asked. "Ah, Monsieur, il est mort," answered St. Germain. "He is dead." The news plunged George Back into despair. He wept for Gabriel Beauparlant and imagined not only that all his companions of the last year were also dead but that he and St. Germain were only a few hours from their own deaths.[38]

A DAY AFTER THE COPPERMINE RIVER CROSSING, ON OCTOBER 5, Franklin with the main body of the expedition set out for Fort Enterprise. Dr. Richardson noted that Matthew Pelonquin "was so exhausted, that when he reached the encampment he was unable to stand." He was, like Régiste Vaillant and Robert Hood, unable to stomach rockweed and was "among the greatest sufferers."[39]

Pelonquin and Vaillant were the first to die. By midday on October 6, they had fallen far behind. Richardson, in considerable pain from the wound and burns of his injured legs, retraced his path and found them more than a mile behind and in the last stages of starvation. Both died where they lay in deep snow. The doctor's next concern was Hood, "who was very feeble." He suggested to Franklin that they should establish a camp for themselves at a place where there was sufficient firewood to last ten days and wait there for rescue, both knowing that they "had no hope whatever of human aid."[40]

The next morning, Richardson and Hood prepared to settle down in a thicket of small willows. John Hepburn insisted on remaining with them. After seeing the three of them settled, the commander led his men in prayer, said "very affectionate" farewells, and resumed his journey. With the greatest of efforts, he was able to shoulder a single blanket and the officers' journals. Everything else he abandoned to the barrens.[41]

A day later, October 7, after a night of bitter cold and gale-force winds, Jean Baptiste Belanger ("le rouge") and Michel Teroahauté asked permission to return to Richardson's camp. Franklin agreed and wrote a note to Richardson letting him know that scarcely a mile and a quarter ahead there was a fine stand of pines that would offer better shelter and firewood than the willow thicket where they were camped.[42]

By the next morning, both Ignace Perrault and Antonio Fontano were suffering "symptoms of extreme debility" and fits of dizziness. Franklin tried to revive their bodies with cups of Labrador tea and their spirits with assurances that Fort Enterprise lay only a few days' journey ahead. Fontano was willing to keep trying, but Perrault could not walk without fainting, and, still only a quarter of a mile from their recent camping place, it was obvious that he was incapable of proceeding. He, like Jean Baptiste Belanger and Michel Teroahauté, asked permission to return to Richardson's camp. Of the three, only Michel arrived at the willow thicket. Sometime during the night, Augustine slipped away from his companions unnoticed.[43]

With Perrault, Fontano, and Michel on their way to Richardson's camp, and Augustine off on an errand of his own, Franklin, Adam, Peltier, Benoit, and Semandré left the deep snow for the frozen surface of a lake that blocked their passage. The crossing left Fontano exhausted, faint, and dizzy. Overwhelmed with grief, he begged his companions to leave him, they being too weak to carry him and their well-being further imperilled by delays as they tried to urge him on. Once more the men watched one of their number walk to his death after "having bid us farewell in the tenderest manner." Franklin's anguish over this latest tragedy was all the greater as the Italian soldier had, that very morning, talked to him about his father and "had begged, that should he survive, I would take him with me to England, and put him in the way of reaching home."[44]

The next day's walk started out well. Everyone felt better after some sleep, a few morsels of leather, and warm Labrador tea. They camped after about five miles at the edge of a solidly frozen lake that lay straight across to Fort Enterprise. Being once more in familiar territory did much to enliven the men's spirits, but on reaching the house on October 11, they faced the same disappointment as Back and his men had two days earlier. The men broke down and cried, "not so much for our own fate," wrote Franklin, "as for that of our friends in the rear, whose lives depended entirely on our sending immediate relief from this place." Augustine was still missing, but Franklin was not alarmed, supposing that his interpreter would easily find Richardson's tent if necessary.[45]

Franklin derived some comfort at finding the note left by George Back, with the information that he, with St. Germain, Solomon Belanger, and Beauparlant, had reached the house two days earlier, taken a day's rest, and then set out in search of Akaitcho's lodges. Franklin and his party of four scoured the yard for bones and rockweed, ripped up some of the floorboards for a fire, and soon had snow melting in a kettle ready to receive burnt bones and lichens for soup. While they were singeing old deerskins to add to their supper, they "were rejoiced" by the appearance of Augustine at the door. "He had followed quite a different course from ours," Franklin later wrote, "and the circumstance of his having found his way through a part of the country he had never been in before, must be considered a remarkable proof of sagacity." Franklin did not describe Augustine's condition but remarked that on the next day while trying to fish, his interpreter saw two caribou but "had not the strength to follow them."[46]

Solomon Belanger reached Fort Enterprise on the afternoon of October 14. Covered with ice from a recent fall into the river, he was at first unable to speak. His companions got him into dry clothes, rubbed his frostbitten limbs, and managed to feed him some small sips of warm bone soup. By the eighteenth he felt strong enough to leave the house and by day's end rejoined Back and St. Germain at Roundrock Lake. Back and St. Germain were salvaging scraps of meat from the frozen caribou, planning to dry it for the anticipated long walk to Fort Providence. As Belanger came into view, he was "scarcely moving" and Back ran to help him, crying, "Are they alive? Is any one at the fort?" The news was better than Back had hoped: "Five with the captain are at the house" was Belanger's reply.[47]

AT FORT ENTERPRISE AFTER HEARING SOLOMON BELANGER'S STORY, Franklin decided that his own best course of action was to head for Fort Providence as soon as the men were sufficiently recovered. For the next few days, the five men still at Fort Enterprise with the commander—Augustine, Adam, Peltier, Semandré, and Benoit—planned their last desperate journey. In the midst of the preparations, Adam revealed that he was suffering from several "edematous" swellings so large it was obvious he would be unable to walk. Peltier and Semandré, also considerably less fit than the others, volunteered to stay at the fort with the stricken man.[48]

Six hours after starting on October 20, the three scouts—Franklin, Augustine, and Benoit—had covered four miles and were forced to camp at Roundrock Lake. Augustine tried to fish but with no success, so they dined on deerskins and tea. On the way again next morning, Franklin fell and broke his snowshoes, making it impossible for him to keep up with his two companions. The only solution was for the two stronger men to carry on alone while Franklin undertook the eight-hour slog through deep snow without snowshoes back to Fort Enterprise. At the house, he found Adam and Semandré too ill to manage the daily chores of gathering wood, rummaging through the snow for rotten scraps of deerskin for food, and preparing two meals a day. Franklin took over the cooking, while Peltier, also weak and easily exhausted, did what he could to help. Adam and Semandré kept to their beds, and both suffered long bouts of uncontrolled weeping. Day by day the four men felt their strength ebbing.[49]

During a storm on October 26, Adam, in his bed, and the other three, unable to get out of their seats, calculated that if things had gone well, Augustine and Benoit might on that very day be arriving at one of Akaitcho's lodges. Their hopes were too optimistic by about eight days. After Franklin left them to return to Fort Enterprise, Augustine and Benoit had spent several days searching for Akaitcho or any signs of his people and finding no one. About the time their companions were imagining them safe in one of Akaitcho's lodges, they too were close to starvation. Then, as their strength waned, they stumbled upon a herd of caribou. Augustine kept a steady hand and killed four. He insisted that he and Benoit had to rest and eat small meals slowly and at regular intervals. His prescription was right for the circumstances; their tortured bodies began to digest food without the agonies of distention and bowel distress that afflicted those who ate too much too quickly. For five days, they kept to a sensible routine, making sure to rest between their sparse meals, and they lived.[50]

Meanwhile at Fort Enterprise, everything that could possibly serve as fuel was gone by October 29. Death from freezing was then more likely than death from starvation. That evening, as they huddled close to their miserably small fire, they were astonished to see Richardson and Hepburn walk in. Pleasure at the sight of two friends was mixed with shock and grief when they realized that Hood, Michel, Perrault, Belanger ("le rouge"), and Fontano must all be dead. The following evening, Richardson told Franklin the horrible tale of their last days at the pine tree campsite.[51]

AT RICHARDSON'S WILLOW THICKET CAMP AFTER FRANKLIN AND his party of ten had left the Coppermine River, Richardson, Hepburn, and Hood spent two days wrapped in their blankets, reading religious tracts and praying, sustaining their physical bodies with Labrador tea. On October 9, Michel Teroahauté joined them. He brought Franklin's note and the welcome gift of a hare and a partridge. Asked about Belanger ("le rouge"), the Iroquois explained that his companion had started for Richardson's camp very early that morning and must have gone astray. The next morning, Richardson judged it possible that with Michel's help they could shift their camp to the stand of pine trees mentioned by Franklin. They moved the ammunition and other heavy articles first, and while the doctor and Hepburn rested briefly by the fire, Michel went to retrieve a gun and ammunition that he said he had left not too far away. Richardson and Hepburn returned to Hood at their tent in the evening, with the understanding that Michel would spend the night at the new camp and join them in the morning.⁵²

The following morning, after a fruitless wait for Michel, the three naval men set out for the pines. Hood was "much affected with dimness of sight, giddiness, and other symptoms of extreme debility" and needed help just to stay on his feet. Michel did not appear during the march and was not at the new campsite when they arrived, causing considerable alarm among the others. Hepburn made a second trip to the willow thicket camp to fetch the tent and arrived back at the pines exhausted. Within minutes Michel also arrived, carrying some pieces of meat that he said were from a dead wolf he had found on the tundra.⁵³

For a full week, from the tenth to the nineteenth, Richardson and Hepburn cut wood, gathered rockweed, tried unsuccessfully to snare or shoot partridges, and looked after the rapidly declining Hood. Michel refused to do any camp chores. He left camp on several occasions, ostensibly to hunt, and asked to borrow Hepburn's axe on one of the nights he did not return to the camp. Richardson later wondered about that axe, which Michel took with him saying he would hunt, although a knife would have been adequate to skin and butcher a caribou or any smaller animal. On the sixteenth, Michel declared his intention to set out for Fort Enterprise on his own, but he did not act on the decision.⁵⁴

On the twentieth, Richardson and Hepburn went to gather rockweed, leaving Hood wrapped in his buffalo-skin robe sitting by the fire, just outside the tent, and Michel with him. On hearing the report of a gun, Hepburn rushed to the tent and called out "in a voice of great alarm" to Richardson. Beside the fire, Hood lay lifeless with a bullet hole in his forehead. Michel claimed that he too had heard the gunshot, while he was in the tent searching for a gun at Hood's request. The doctor, on examining Hood's body, found "that the shot had entered the back part of the head, and passed out at the forehead, and that the muzzle of the gun had been applied so close as to set fire to the night-cap behind." It was obvious to Richardson that Hood could not have shot himself in the back of the head, but Michel, always hovering close by, prevented him from speaking privately to Hepburn. While Richardson and Hepburn were careful to hide their suspicion that Michel was guilty of Hood's death, Michel himself "repeatedly protested" his innocence.[55]

Michel's behaviour became more and more alarming. He constantly muttered, sometimes in a scarcely audible voice and sometimes loudly, that he did not want to go to the fort. He tried repeatedly to convince the doctor that they should head due south and support themselves all winter by killing caribou. He accused Hepburn of having spread rumours about him and threatened to kill him, all the while expressing a general hatred for all white people, who, he claimed, had killed and eaten his uncle. He became increasingly disrespectful of Richardson, giving the doctor the distinct impression that he believed himself to have complete power over the lives and deaths of the other two. He kept so close to either Richardson or Hepburn that they never had a chance to speak privately to each other, and whenever Hepburn spoke, Michel asked if he was being accused of murder.

On October 23, Hepburn loaded a small pistol for Richardson and himself carried a gun, as did Michel.[56] Finally, during the afternoon, Michel went to gather rockweed, and for the first time Richardson heard Hepburn's account of Hood's death. Hepburn, cutting down a tree a short distance from the tent, had been close enough to see events there immediately before and after he heard the gunshot. He told the doctor that he had seen and heard "Mr Hood and Michel...speaking to each other in an elevated angry tone," and moments later "on hearing the report [of the gun] he looked up, and saw Michel rising up from before the tent-door, or just behind where Mr. Hood was seated, and then going into the tent." Convinced that Hood could not possibly have committed suicide, given the entry point of the ball, the two Englishmen concluded that Michel had murdered Hood and that their own lives were on the line. Taking "the whole responsibility upon myself," wrote Richardson, "and immediately upon Michel's coming up, I put an end to his life by shooting him through the head with a pistol."[57]

For two days after the execution of Michel, Richardson and Hepburn were trapped at their campsite by thick falling snow that obscured the trail. Neither of them was concerned about starvation for the moment. The doctor, knowledgeable botanist that he was, experimented with a lichen that they found to be quite tasty when moistened and toasted over the fire. Their food stores also contained "a good many pieces" of singed hide cut from Hood's buffalo robe. Cold weather and deep snow were greater problems than food supply. On the third day, as they made their painful way forward, Richardson believed he would have died from cold and weakness and his injured leg, which caused him to fall "upwards of twenty times," had it not been for Hepburn, who "exerted himself far beyond his strength, and speedily made the encampment and kindled a fire." The fourth day, in the late afternoon of October 29, they reached Fort Enterprise.[58]

IN SPITE OF THE HORRORS RICHARDSON AND HEPBURN HAD LIVED through, they arrived at Fort Enterprise in better physical condition than their companions at the house. Adam, Peltier, and Semandré could scarcely leave their beds. The doctor and the faithful sailor took over as many chores as they could, while Franklin, by then very weak, struggled to do his share, digging old skins out from under the snow. Once again, Richardson proved his value as a travelling companion by checking the skins for those that contained the larvae of warble flies, which he knew to be high in protein, and adding them to the daily diet. He also treated Adam's agonizing swellings by cutting small incisions in his abdomen, scrotum, and legs to allow excess water to drain away. He was not able to save Peltier and Semandré. During the night of October 31–November 1, both men died. No one was strong enough to move the bodies, so they were left in the room they had been living in. By November 3, John Hepburn had begun to show signs of distress, with swollen limbs and rapidly declining strength. By November 6, they were all in a state of confusion, such that Hepburn wondered if, in the event that any of them lived, they would ever recover their intellectual competence.[59]

Help was closer than Hepburn dared hope. Augustine and Benoit, having eaten judiciously and rested for five days after killing four caribou, took up their search for Akaitcho's camp, and on November 1 they found a trail well beaten by Yellowknife snowshoes. On the morning of November 3 they reached the Yellowknife lodges. Their first act was to communicate to Akaitcho, in a mix of English, French, and the Athapascan dialect, that they had left four members of the expedition—Franklin, Adam, Peltier, and Semandré—alive and in need of help at Fort Enterprise. No written record has been found describing what steps Akaitcho took on hearing the news. Out of real concern for the welfare of the strangers in his country, he may have been so convinced that no one there could yet remain alive that he devoted all his resources to helping the two desperate men who had just stumbled into his village.

The same day that Augustine and Benoit found tracks, November 1, George Back, Pierre St. Germain, and Solomon Belanger were strong enough to resume their southward trek in search of help. On the third day they also found fresh footprints in the snow, recognized them as the marks of Yellowknife snowshoes, and cried out to one another, "Footsteps of Indians." St. Germain set off at once to follow them to their origin. At the moment of realizing that salvation was at hand, Back came near to collapsing altogether. "Previous to seeing the tracks of the Indians, I managed though in miserable pain to go forward, as the only way to save my life, but scarcely was the cry uttered, than feeling as one escaped from a lingering sickness approaching to death my whole frame became so debilitated that I fell upon the train [sled]."[60] St. Germain reached Akaitcho's winter village at sunset on November 3 and was reunited with Augustine and Benoit. Like his two friends, St. Germain gave news of companions still alive—Back and Solomon Belanger—and asked for Akaitcho's help.

This time Akaitcho did not hesitate. Before full darkness fell, a boy from one of the Yellowknife villages appeared at Back's camp with meat, fat, and a few deers' tongues. To Back's joy, the boy also brought the note Franklin had written on October 21, the day a broken snowshoe had forced him to withdraw from his attempt to reach Akaitcho, faithfully delivered by Augustine.

In the morning, having taken care not to eat more than their half-starved bodies could handle, Back and Belanger started for Akaitcho's lodge. In the afternoon they met Benoit, coming to meet them, and a half hour later Akaitcho himself joined them to smoke a ceremonial pipe in thanksgiving. By the next morning,

November 5, the Yellowknife hunters Crooked-foot, Rat, and Boudelkell were speeding toward Fort Enterprise with a small load of provisions.

&

AT FORT ENTERPRISE, ADAM, AFTER HAVING A PREMONITION OF approaching death, sank so low that he could no longer speak out loud. Franklin lay beside him in an effort to warm and cheer him while Richardson and Hepburn went, as usual, to cut wood. As they struggled to manipulate their broken axe with frostbitten fingers, they were amazed to hear the report of a musket and glimpse the approaching rescuers. Richardson hurried into the house with "the joyful intelligence" that three of Akaitcho's men had arrived with a small quantity of deer's meat, fat, and tongues. Finding the four still alive, Boudelkell immediately returned to the village to expedite more relief. After their first meal of real food, Adam began to feel better, but the three Englishmen suffered from "distention," the result of having eaten more than their shrunken stomachs could handle. "We were perfectly aware of the danger," wrote Franklin, "and Dr Richardson repeatedly cautioned us to be moderate; but he was himself unable to practise the caution he so judiciously recommended." For seven more days, rescued and rescuers waited for the arrival of a larger party of Akaitcho's people who were delayed by stormy weather.[61]

Crooked-foot and Rat took over the housekeeping that the Fort Enterprise men had been unable to deal with. Their first act was to remove the bodies of Peltier and Semandré, placing them outside and covering them with snow.[62] They cleared out all the dirt, including the fragments of pounded bone created when Richardson and Hepburn made bone soup, and brought vast quantities of firewood up the hill from the riverbank to keep a fire blazing. "These kind creatures," wrote Franklin in appreciation, "next turned their attention to our personal appearance, and prevailed upon us to shave and wash ourselves," providing plenty of hot water for the job. Sleep came more easily after nourishment and personal hygiene were tended to, and their caretakers "were so very careful in covering us up, and in keeping a good fire," that it seemed almost as if the weather had suddenly become milder.[63]

On the thirteenth the two hunters left, suddenly and without explanation, causing some alarm to the Englishmen. Then, on the fifteenth, Hepburn hurried into the house from hauling wood to announce that Benoit, Crooked-foot, Rat, Thoveeyorre, and Fop, with two women dragging trains loaded with provisions, had arrived. They brought news that George Back, Pierre St. Germain, and Solomon Belanger had recovered enough that they were starting for Fort Providence and began getting the survivors ready to go to Akaitcho's lodge, where caribou were more abundant. Although the physical health of the expedition members had improved enormously, they were still weak and needed the care their rescuers showed them. They were treated "with the utmost tenderness," wrote Richardson. "[They] gave us their snow shoes and walked without themselves, keeping by our sides that they might lift us when we fell.... [They] cooked for us and fed us as if we had been children." Adam recovered his spirits and physical strength more rapidly than the officers did. On the morning of their departure from Fort Enterprise, Adam "evinced unusual activity," Franklin noted, "dressed himself in clean clothes, and appeared quite an altered man."[64]

Their journey took a full ten days. On November 26, at Akaitcho's village, they were greeted by a large assembly in The Leader's tent, "with looks of compassion, and profound silence, which lasted about a quarter of an hour, and by which they meant to express their condolence for our sufferings." Akaitcho paid them the very great courtesy of cooking some meat for them with his own hands. In the course of their reception, they were reunited with Augustine, who had found comfortable accommodation with a family in the village.[65]

John Hepburn, always solicitous for the comfort of his officers, prepared a campsite for them, and on November 28 they left Akaitcho's lodge for a temporary home of their own. Franklin, once more suffering from indigestion from overeating, was dosed with a brew of rockweed, fish soup, and blood, prepared for him and administered by Akaitcho. To Dr. Richardson's great interest, the commander received some relief from it.[66]

All were accounted for, except one. The last occupants of Fort Enterprise were safely with Akaitcho's people; Back, St. Germain, and Solomon Belanger had gone on toward Fort Providence in good spirits and good health, with warm clothes and bedding and plenty of provisions; and those who remained on the tundra were all known to be dead. Only Junius's fate was unknown. None of the traders in the area and no one at any of the Yellowknife lodges ever saw or heard of him again.

※

AKAITCHO'S ENTIRE VILLAGE, ACCOMPANIED BY THE EXPEDITION survivors, set off toward Fort Providence on November 30 and December 1. They travelled, and sometimes camped, in separate groups, with Adam, now the strongest walker among them, acting as runner to keep the different parties in touch with one another. Meanwhile, Back, St. Germain, and Belanger ("le gros") had reached Fort Providence, and Belanger was on his way back with a dog team driver and two dog teams. They met on the trail on December 6. George Back had sent spirits and tobacco for the Yellowknives, along with clean clothing, tea, sugar, and letters from England for the rest of the party. It was with great satisfaction that Richardson donned a clean shirt and threw away the one he had worn night and day for ninety-eight days since leaving the Arctic coast on the last day of August. Franklin noted the improvement in personal hygiene with wry understatement: "We received…a change of linen & some clothing which we much required."[67]

For ease of provisioning, Adam and Benoit stayed with Akaitcho's people, whose plan was to follow the caribou herd south, hunting as they went. Franklin, Richardson, Hepburn, Augustine, and Belanger, with one of Akaitcho's dog team drivers, hoped to travel more quickly. On starting, the two sleds drawn by dogs were heavily loaded with provisions; Augustine and Hepburn together hauled a small sled with bedding; and Franklin and Richardson walked. Because of the explorers' "enormous" appetites, the heavily loaded sleds grew lighter quickly, and the bedding was transferred to them, relieving Augustine and Hepburn of their burdens. Further consumption of provisions made room on the large sleds for both Franklin and Richardson, the slowest walkers in the group. On December 11, at two in the afternoon, they were greeted by Mr. Weekes, the Clerk in Charge of the Fort Providence Hudson's Bay Company post. George Back had already crossed Great Slave Lake to Fort Resolution and sent back more presents for Akaitcho and his people.[68]

Akaitcho caught up with Franklin's party on December 14 and received his presents along with promises of more to come and the sincere gratitude of all the expedition survivors. Adam, thinking it unlikely that he would find employment with future fur traders and explorers, asked to be discharged from Franklin's service so that he could rejoin his wife and family and with them become members of Akaitcho's band. Mr. Weekes provided two drivers and teams, each with a carriole for the comfort of Franklin and Richardson, for the trip to Moose Deer Island, while Belanger ("le gros") drove a sledge loaded with bedding and drawn by a team of two. Augustine, Hepburn, and Benoit walked. On December 19, they reached Robert McVicar, HBC chief trader at Moose Deer Island, where Back and St. Germain had been since late November. Here Back learned of the deaths of his expedition companions, including that of his fellow midshipman Robert Hood.[69]

The officers' journals had nothing to say about how they spent Christmas of 1821, but Back noted that the Canadians had "a rejoicing day" on January 1, 1822, firing volleys of musketry and drinking rum. St. Germain's contract provided for him to leave the expedition's service at Fort Chipewyan on February 1. He left Moose Deer Island for the journey south on January 7 with Benoit, whose business at Athabasca was to buy and expedite provisions for the expedition survivors who planned to stay at Moose Deer until spring. Franklin and McVicar amused themselves by betting on the date the two men would arrive—Franklin bet on January 19, McVicar chose January 20 or later. The wager was for six bottles of the best port wine procurable at York Factory. McVicar won; Benoit and St. Germain arrived on January 21.[70]

Benoit filled Franklin's shopping list with provisions the expedition survivors would need until they were able to leave Moose Deer Island in the spring. The commander left with four dog trains for Slave Lake on February 8 with flour, tea, sugar, and Jamaica rum. Driving the teams were four voyageurs, Ignace Perrault, Pierre Dumas, Joseph Forcier, and Joseph Gagné, who had spent the winter of 1820–21 at Fort Enterprise and accompanied the expedition only as far as the mouth of the Coppermine River.[71]

Cared for by Robert McVicar, his clerk Auley McAuley, and McVicar's country wife, Margaret, the survivors regained health and strength steadily. Hepburn was an invalid longer than any of the others, suffering from a severe bout of rheumatism that kept him bedridden for several weeks. Richardson continued to limp from the effects of his ordeal in the Coppermine River. With the first signs of spring, the party began preparations to return to York Factory, while Franklin worried that he had not done enough for Akaitcho. On May 26, to the commander's great pleasure, a canoe arrived from Fort Chipewyan loaded with the goods promised to Akaitcho and his people. Franklin added a "considerable present" of ammunition for each of the hunters who had been attached to the expedition.[72]

Late in the afternoon of the same day, Franklin, Richardson, Back, Augustine, Hepburn, Belanger, and Benoit left for Fort Chipewyan with McVicar, McAuley, and sixteen paddlers, in two canoes. Two other canoes joined their brigade, with seven men in each, carrying the year's trade in furs, castoreum, and dressed caribou skins. A fifth canoe carried seven men, three women, and eight children, all belonging to local families. They reached Fort Chipewyan on June 2 and were briefly reunited with Ferdinand Wentzel and the four voyageurs who had returned from the mouth of the Coppermine with him in July the previous year. The officers and McVicar were invited to a small celebration at the trading post, and wine was served. But, wrote the Fort Chipewyan journalist, "No excesses."[73]

At Fort Chipewyan, Edward Smith supplied them with a canoe and bowman, and on June 5 they were on the river, in the last canoe to leave for Hudson Bay that year. Three weeks later they were at Cumberland House, where they stopped on June 28 for two days before proceeding to Norway House, which they reached on July 4. At Norway House, Belanger and Benoit took leave of their companions of the previous two years and found passage in a canoe returning to Montreal by the Winnipeg River route. "We carried Augustus down to York Factory," wrote Franklin, "where we arrived on the 14 of July, and were received with every mark of attention and kindness by Mr. Simpson,...Mr. M'Tavish, and, indeed, by all the officers of the United

Companies. And thus terminated our long, fatiguing, and disastrous travels in North America, having journeyed by water and by land...five thousand five hundred and fifty miles."[74]

INTERLUDE 2

REORGANIZING AND RETRENCHING THE COMPANY

1822–1824

IN 1812, WHEN AUGUSTINE BEGAN HIS LIFE AMONG FUR TRADERS and explorers, the Hudson's Bay Company was on the brink of bankruptcy. For more than thirty years it had been dealing with financial disasters resulting from competition, the loss of its client base, disease, climate disasters, and wars.

From the early 1780s, the Company had met with serious competition from a number of Hudson River Valley fur traders, who had left the newly established United States at the end of the American War of Independence and set up small partnerships in Montreal. By 1799, these traders had merged to form the North West Company. As they pushed west via rivers south of the HBC's Hudson Bay and James Bay posts, the Northwesters blocked the English traders from expanding into the prairies and the fur-rich Athapascan northwest and, at the same time, prevented the prairie First Nations traders from making yearly trips to trade at York Factory. HBC's London Committee had to find a way not only to expand its territory but also to counter the slow erosion of its customer base.

Disease contributed to the loss of the Company's Indigenous clients while causing unthinkable human and social damage among them. No reliable counts of deaths during the smallpox epidemic of 1782 exist, but eyewitnesses estimated the toll: Samuel Hearne believed that among Chipewyan west and northwest of Churchill, the death rate might have been as high as 90 percent of the population. David Thompson, travelling from York Factory to the Rocky Mountains, concluded that "far more than half [of the Indigenous people] had died...it appeared that three fifths had perished." The journal keeper at York Factory wrote that "not one in fifty of those tribes are still living."[1] After the waning of the epidemic, the Athapascan people of the boreal forest and the Cree people living between York Factory and Churchill had to deal with years of grief for the loss of family members and of Chiefs and leaders.

The onset of the four-decade Dalton Minimum (1790–1830) added another problem that reduced the Company's clients. Communities in the boreal forest and the southern tundra suffered from hunger or starvation when the caribou herds changed their routes or disappeared completely. Inuit living on the west coast of the bay did not experience the epidemic but, like their First Nations neighbours, they suffered from exposure and severe food privation as the caribou and seal populations disappeared, and many died.

On a broader geographical scale, the Company lost access to the European market during the Napoleonic Wars in countries whose governments had been overthrown by Bonaparte's armies and those that feared French invasion.[2] In Britain, under threat of invasion from France and its satellite nations, taxes rose and strikes and riots in urban areas were frequent and destructive of property. Men were recruited or forced into military service, often leaving their families without regular incomes. Officers of the Company saw their salaries and bonuses drop when the shares normally given to them lagged behind the European inflation rate. The Company's labourers did not get the higher salary that was usually given when they finished a three-year stint and signed on for a second one. In some years, the Company's shareholders did not receive any returns on their investments.

In 1806 and 1807, Napoleon declared blockades against Britain aimed at preventing foreign vessels from delivering merchandise to, or buying merchandise from, Britain. A complicating factor was that the Hudson's Bay Company's 1670 charter required its Rupert's Land posts to deliver its furs and other goods to England, and nowhere else, whether they were transported by the Company's ships or by hired vessels.[3] The North West Company was not under any similar restrictions and was free to send furs directly from Rupert's Land to ports in China, the Baltic Sea, and the U.S. market at Astoria, Oregon.[4] By 1809, the Hudson's Bay Company was in serious financial trouble.

A solution that ultimately saved the Company was presented to the London Committee in 1809 as a result of a visit to Scotland by Thomas Douglas, 5th Earl of Selkirk, twenty years earlier. Selkirk had been appalled by the poverty and suffering he saw among the peasant herders and small farmers who depended on shared communal land to feed their animals and grow their fruits and vegetables. Their miserable condition was the result of the Enclosure Movement, which originated in mainland Europe and over time had spread to Britain. The government welcomed the movement as a way to increase Britain's wool production, to keep up with the growing wool industry in Europe. It encouraged members of the aristocracy who could afford to buy large tracts of land to privatize them with fences or hedges, leaving the lesser classes with no shared pasture or agricultural land.

Selkirk believed that relocating the Scottish peasantry to places where land was ample and free, or almost so, was the solution. His choice of venue was Canada. In 1808 he began buying shares in the Hudson's Bay Company, and within a year, two of his cousins, who were also his brothers-in-law, Andrew Wedderburn Colvile and John Wedderburn Halkett, had invested in the Company and were among the most important of its shareholders. Their plan, submitted to the London Committee in 1810, was the solution to the Company's financial problems and, at the same time, laid the groundwork for Selkirk's humanitarian dream of a Scottish colony in Canada. In 1811, the HBC granted Selkirk 116,000 square miles of land at the juncture of the Red and Assiniboine Rivers. As Selkirk's Red River Colony became a reality, it served as a wall that would prevent, or at least slow down, the North West Company's push into the prairies and Athapasca.

The Selkirk-Halkett-Wedderburn plan did not end with acquiring land. It included the creation of two new jurisdictions of the Company in Rupert's

Land, a Northern Department and a Southern Department. The Northern Department consisted of all posts west and south of Hudson Bay, which consisted of the newly named Fort Churchill District and its outposts, a Winnipeg and Saskatchewan District and its outposts, and York Factory as the administrative centre while it continued to be a merchandise depot and trading post. William Auld was appointed Northern Department Superintendent. The Southern Department consisted of the James Bay posts—Fort Albany, Eastmain Factory, and Moose Factory—and all of their outposts. The Superintendent of Southern Factories from 1810 to 1814, Thomas Thomas, was promoted to Governor of the Northern Department in 1814.[5] The departments were agreed upon by the Company's shareholders in 1810 but not all of the managerial and financial changes and restrictions were fully effective until 1815, and some not until years later.

Colvile and Halkett realized that to survive, the Company needed to expand into the northwest interior and also recognized that the Churchill River was not the route that would get it there. Fort Churchill was reduced to an outpost answerable to York Factory. The maximum number of servants at outposts under retrenchment was to be limited to one senior officer and six labourers. In the trading year 1810–11, there had been a workforce of sixty-four; in 1812–13, Augustine's first year with the Company, there were thirty. In 1813–14, the Men's House was occupied by fifty-five servants, eighteen of whom were wintering inlanders, men who manned and maintained Churchill's upriver outposts during the summer months.[6]

The "retrenching" business model included plans to lower the Company's subsistence allowances. It specified that provisions supplied by London would be reduced, and posts were encouraged to rely more on country food; building materials sent to posts and outposts were of lower quality than they had earlier been; luxuries such as European wines and English cheeses for senior officers were rationed; boats and bateaux were not replaced until they were close to being unseaworthy; fewer labourers and low-level tradesmen were recruited; and even metal stoves were seen as luxuries rather than necessary household furnishings. The plan included firing, or not renewing the contracts of, European employees.

Although the reorganization of the Company was decided on in 1810 and was intended to be in effect by 1815, Augustine probably did not know about the changes until 1822, having been absent from the post during 1814–15 and between 1816 and 1822. On his return from his first journey to the northwest, he probably realized that he was no longer needed as an interpreter at Churchill. During his absence, a new Clerk had been assigned to Churchill. Nineteen-year-old Robert Harding was hired in 1819; he had served as Clerk in the Swan River district until 1821, when he was transferred to Churchill, where he remained until he retired in 1845. By 1822, Harding was able to speak and understand basic fur trade Inuktitut. Augustine's work at the post was in jeopardy.

CHAPTER 5

THE "ENGAGED SERVANT"
1822–1824

AT YORK FACTORY IN THE SUMMER OF 1822, WHILE THE naval men of the Arctic overland expedition were waiting for transportation to England, Augustine was reunited with old friends. Thomas Topping, who had agreed to let the young man stay at Churchill in 1812 and assumed the role of foster father to the young Inuk, was there, as was Adam Snodie, who had sent him back to his village in the terrible summer of 1816. Topping, heading home on furlough that year, and Snodie, who was retiring, were on the passenger list of *Prince of Wales* for the Atlantic crossing. George Simpson, whose canoe brigade on the long river trip to the Northwest in 1820 had kept pace with the brigade in which Augustine and Junius travelled, was also there.

A new acquaintance was the Reverend John West, a Church of England minister newly appointed as chaplain to the Hudson's Bay Company in Rupert's Land. From 1820 to 1823, West visited his new parish and learned of Simpson's still tentative plans to establish posts in Inuit country, an expansion of the fur trade that West saw as an exciting opportunity to spread the Christian gospel to the Inuit. In the summer of 1822 at York Factory, he sought out Augustine for information on the people of the Keewatin coast and recorded the young man's descriptions of his people. West described the young Inuk, whose name he spelled "Tetaneuch," as a "very intelligent and interesting character" who had learned to read and write while on the expedition.[1]

In a letter to his sister, Emma West Atkinson, the chaplain noted that the young man was "almost always in my room. He is a very interesting fellow. He wants me to send White men to teach his tribe, who traverse the shore about Churchill Factory in Hudson's Bay. Capt Franklin of the Northern Land Expedition feels quite interested about the Esquimaux on this shore, and we are talking over a plan to establish a school for them if practicable." He enclosed a sample of Augustine's handwriting, as a souvenir gift to his sister.[2]

Augustine waited at York Factory for almost a month for passage to Churchill on a Company schooner under the command of Adam Snodie. Snodie's orders were to carry Churchill's outfit for the coming year north, unload it, take on board the previous year's trade, and be back at York before *Prince of Wales* sailed for London.[3] In Snodie's luggage was a letter from Governor Simpson to Hugh Leslie, Churchill's accountant, with instructions for an exploration party to go to Wager Bay in 1823 to open trading relations with Inuit living north of Rankin Inlet. In addition, wrote Simpson, "Augustus...who accompanied Capt Franklin's party now takes his passage to Churchill.... If you can prevail on him to accompany the party [to Wager Bay] it might be well to engage him on moderate terms." In the same letter, Simpson informed Leslie that he was being promoted to Master at Churchill. As it happened, Snodie did not make it to Churchill, Simpson's letter was undelivered, and Augustine was shipwrecked.[4]

Heading north from York Factory, the schooner grounded against a mudbank at the mouth of the Owl River, and no amount of effort could free it. Snodie, Augustine, and their crew had no choice but to walk more than sixty miles back to the Factory. A second schooner was hastily loaded with supplies to replace some of what had been lost, but Augustine was not on board. At Franklin's request, he was allowed to stay at York with his four English friends—Franklin, Richardson, Back, and Hepburn—until they sailed. On September 7, he was on the riverbank to say a second farewell to them, and to Thomas Topping and Adam Snodie when they boarded *Prince of Wales* for the homeward passage.[5]

Augustine was reunited with yet another old friend, Hugh Leslie, when the second schooner arrived from Churchill on August 29. Leslie had disappointing news for Augustine. His brother Astanik, Leslie told him, had been at Churchill early in July and refused to join the whale hunt, because he could "kill no whales for grief for the absence of his brother." Had Augustine reached Churchill on the first attempt, around the middle of August when the last of his countrymen left the post, he might have been able to return to his own village that season. As it was, he knew he would have to spend almost another full year at Churchill before being reunited with his family. What Astanik did not tell Leslie was that his grief was not just a matter of missing his absent brother. Astanik knew that when Augustine returned to Churchill he would face men among his own people who planned to kill him.[6]

Leslie, Augustine, and their crew left York on September 14 with the last of the outfit for Churchill. At Owl River two days later, they began to salvage what goods they could from the half-sunken schooner and, on the twentieth, set sails to take them out of the mouth of Owl River and into Hudson Bay. Weather and tide were against them, and the overloaded boat came to rest on a mud flat. Knowing it would be several days before the tide was again high enough to float the vessel, Leslie decided to leave his four men to bring the schooner north when they could and, with Augustine, set off for Churchill on foot. On September 28, eighty miles and eight days later, Augustine and Leslie were on the east bank of the Churchill River, just across from the post, and sent up a smoke to alert Robert Harding, Churchill's second-in-command, of their presence.[7]

AUGUSTINE HAD ONLY A FEW HOURS TO GREET HIS OLD FRIENDS and say hello to men new at the post before he and young James Dunning were sent across the river to watch for the schooner from Owl River. For five days the two of them camped together and, while keeping an eye on the eastern horizon, Augustine told Dunning of his adventures in the northwest, and Dunning brought Augustine up to date on the new men at the post. Dunning, of course, had already heard through the moccasin telegraph a general account of Augustine's journey. Word had passed from post to post that Augustine had survived his long journey but that Junius had disappeared on the barrenlands and was presumed dead. The first Inuit to check in at Churchill in the spring of 1822 had also heard the news and passed it along to the coastal villages north of the trading post.

By November, life at Churchill had settled into its usual winter routines. Augustine went with Dunning and his family to Goose Lake to hunt partridges. In their packs they carried rations for the week of November 2. The one-day ration for the day's walk to their tent was five pounds of venison and two pounds of biscuit. Rations for the following week, prepared by Mrs. Dunning, consisted of seven pounds of flour to be mixed with water for bannock or pancakes, ten pounds of oatmeal for porridge, dried meat in the amount of a "half piece of pork," six pounds of venison, and eight brined geese. If they wanted to add raisins, sugar, tea, or jam to liven the menu, they bought them at the Company's store. Leslie also gave them a quart of rum, which may have brightened their bleak meals somewhat.[8]

On the sixth of November, Augustine walked back to the House to report a general absence of partridges and was introduced to two Inuit who had arrived the previous day with thirteen Chipewyan men and youths. The Chipewyan "had spent the summer on the plains," and the two Inuit had "been among [them] now 2 years." On the seventh, the visitors left the post. Late that night, one of them returned to the House, "the Northern Indians having left him."[9] Feeling responsible for the abandoned man, who appeared to be well into middle age, Leslie took him to Churchill Creek the following day, "as I think he will be able to angle as many jack-fish there as keep himself." A week later Leslie had proof that the newcomer could do much more than "keep himself" when his first catch—forty-three jackfish weighing in at 150 pounds—was delivered to the House. While Augustine and Dunning continued to report that both caribou and partridge were in very short supply, the recent arrival sent in another sled loaded with forty jackfish weighing 140 pounds, which he had taken by angling through the ice, an especially disagreeable job considering the temperatures he worked in. Leslie decided the newcomer would be an asset to the post and declared that "for the future [he will] be called Moses."[10]

The winter of 1822–23 was unusually cold. On November 26, Leslie recorded "the coldest day this season at 35 below." By the end of the first week of December, he described the weather as "in general very cold, more so than I have seen so early of the winter, but the snow on the ground is not nearly so much as this time last year." The temperature continued to drop, and on December 10, it was 45° below zero. In cold severe enough to freeze the mercury in the thermometers, and with the sun barely visible through the overcast for a mere six hours out of the twenty-four, Augustine and Dunning chopped holes in the river ice and lowered nets filled with geese into the frigid water below to cleanse them of salt before stacking them in the ice house.[11]

Early in January of 1823, Robert Harding and James Dunning took the "York Road" overland to York Factory, while work at Churchill continued as usual in severe cold and semi-darkness. In January and February, Moses's name appeared frequently in the post journal. He not only "kept himself in provisions except 3 lbs of oatmeal once a week which he receives from us" but made significant contributions of fish to the post pantry. He also turned out to be useful in the kitchen on the days he brought in his catch, and when the cook needed firewood, Moses was handy with a cross saw. Besides the constant search for food supplies, the main occupations of the next few months were outdoor activities in breath-freezing semi-darkness: cutting and hauling firewood, soaking geese in the river in preparation for salting them into casks, and sledging in boards from the "Sawing Tent."[12]

In spite of the reappearance of the sun and steadily lengthening days in February, the weather stayed "exceedingly cold…It doesn't thaw, even at noon," complained Leslie in his journal. When they were not hunting, fishing, or cutting and hauling wood, Augustine and Dunning spent more unpleasant days at the miserable task of soaking geese under the ice of the thickly frozen river. Moses laboured at clearing the snow out of the yard to prevent the cellars and ground floors from flooding, although, as Leslie noted, there was, even in the middle of April, no sign of thawing or dripping.[13]

The usually abundant seal population at Churchill's Back Bay was almost non-existent that spring. In the first half of May, Augustine and Moses found only six seals on the ice. They blamed the cold weather, saying "it prevents the seals from coming on the ice." A stranger, possibly Inuit, who was living with a Chipewyan family near James Dunning's tent at North Point joined them on May 25, but by June 1 the three men had still managed to take only eighteen animals. On the sixth, in temperatures that even the seals found too severe to venture out in, the three walked the five miles to the House and again "complained of the cold." Leslie noted that "the other men [at the House were] also complaining of unusually cold weather." Of the eighteen seals that had so far been killed, fifteen were still not processed, "for want of women."[14]

When the usual spring party of Inuit had not shown up by June 8, Leslie despaired of a successful spring seal hunt. "I have now given up all hopes of any [Inuit] making their appearance until they can paddle [here]," he wrote.[15] Sixteen hunters from the north had, in fact, reached Seal River by June 3, but none of them brought anything of value to trade, and did not send runners to the post. Their shopping lists were mostly for utilitarian items: knives, saws, chisels, flints, powder, axes, and kettles. To pay for the imported goods, all sixteen of the hunters joined the seal hunt and six also hunted whales. While Inuit trading at Churchill had been using metal knives, awls, kettles, and spearheads for over a century, Inuit use and adaptation of European clothing was also well underway by the 1820s. Eleven families purchased yard goods, four bought checkered or red flannel shirts, three got coats and jackets, and three went home with new capotes. Their choice of fabric patterns and colours may have had a significance beyond simple body coverings, in a way similar to the skin designs the women so carefully crafted. Beads, bells, mirrors, and coins were not frivolous decorations. Inuit saw them as utilitarian items for communicating with the spirit world and with human communities.[16]

Writing to George Simpson again on June 13, Leslie had bad news: four men had drowned, including the cooper; spring was very late; the river showed no signs of breaking up; temperatures were unusually low; and with no signs of Inuit there was no hope of a spring whale hunt.[17] Ten days later Leslie wrote to Simpson again: "I was expecting to get a good deal of information from the Esquemaux concerning the coast this spring as they were apprised of our intentions last summer and consequently would be mentioning it to their farther away neighbours but none of them have made their appearance and I don't expect them now until they can come in their canoes."[18]

The hunters stayed at Seal River hunting seals and whales for a month, from June 4 to July 3. The first hunter to leave the whale hunt was Pingnahewak. On June 24, he brought his chit marked with the number of whales he had killed or helped kill and was rewarded with a six-button white capote. Atahoona picked up his whaling bonus—a striped blanket—on June 26. On the twenty-seventh, Naeukghahie received a 3½ ell capote for three weeks of whaling. Pingnahewak's brother Utuck earned a striped duffel blanket when he claimed his whaling credit on July 1, as did Atongana two days later. Alecamik, who stayed until July 18, a full two weeks longer than any of the others, left the post with a 3½ ell capote.[19]

The ell, a length equal to thirty-seven and a half inches in Scottish usage, and forty inches in English usage, was a common measure of cloth in the nineteenth century. Using those figures, a 3½ ell capote would translate to a coat somewhere between eight feet and twelve feet long—both unlikely lengths. Another measuring system, however, yields more realistic figures. The very old system in which an ell was a somewhat flexible measure, roughly the distance from elbow to fingertips, or about fifteen inches, makes sense in the context of clothing. Using this as a measure, a 3½ ell capote would have been about fifty-two inches from the top of the hood to the bottom hem. Assuming that Augustine, at five feet one inch, was representative of his countrymen, a fifty-two-inch (or 3½ ell) coat with a slightly pointed hood would be a reasonable size.

Finally, early in July, runners from the North reached the tent where Augustine and Moses were hunting seals and announced that a large party was "on the road." Augustine went with them to the House, where they explained to Leslie that "starvation during the winter was the cause of their failure in coming to the seal hunt." Leslie gave Augustine two pounds of powder and some shot, plus tobacco for himself and the runners, and sent powder, shot, and tobacco to more than a dozen hunters with their wives and families, who, by the time Augustine reached them, were already settled into their tents and had begun hunting at Seal River.[20] "To their wives," Leslie sent beads, biscuit, oatmeal, powder, and shot.[21] There were now women enough to process any number of skins.

❧

THE CHOICE OF GIFTS FOR THE WOMEN REQUIRES SOME EXPLANAtion. All Company traders would have understood that oatmeal and biscuit were welcome as food—cooked oatmeal is soft, and rock-hard ship's biscuit is easily softened by soaking in water or oil for the toothless young and the toothless old. Powder and shot, as gifts for the women, seem more problematic. Aside from the Company's men on the spot, many Europeans, including members of the London Committee who were concerned with income and outgo at its posts, assumed that hunting was men's work. Women, however, were active in netting and snaring birds and small animals, and many of them ran traplines and traded fox, ground squirrel, lemming, and other skins of their own taking. Some were competent in handling rifles and could shoot as well as their husbands and brothers. The frequency with which the traders gave powder and shot as gifts to women might be interpreted as evidence that they were fully aware that women did, indeed, use firearms in hunting. While there are no eyewitness accounts of women using bows and arrows in the nineteenth century, there is nothing to indicate that they did not.

Misconceptions about the intent behind giving beads as gifts to Inuit women were common among eighteenth- and nineteenth-century missionaries and explorers and are also common today. The glass and ceramic beads given to Inuit by the traders were not strings of beads to be worn as necklaces or bracelets for personal adornment. They were individual beads in a variety of colours and sizes and came in small glass vials or paper envelopes. Women were the usual recipients because they were the seamstresses. The fur traders, who knew the people, understood what decorative trade goods such as beads, gartering, buttons, medals, brass rings, bells, and small mirrors meant in Inuit thought.

Inuit cosmology described the universe as filled with unseen spirits and persons-other-than-human, whose assistance was necessary to successful living, whether in obtaining food, finding a good travel route, bringing a woman safely through childbirth, locating essential resources, completing a successful journey, or any number of other life events. Communication with other-than-human personalities was achieved through visual symbols. The symbols could be part of the human body (tattoos and hairstyles), items worn on the human body (earrings, finger rings, nose rings, and combs), or objects attached to clothing (brooches, small bells, tiny mirrors, and fringes). They could also be patterns sewn into the fabric of a parka, pants, mittens, or boots. The designs told unseen powers who the wearer was and what she or he wanted and intended. They conveyed the same information to other human beings as well, an obvious example being the parka with an *amaut*, the roomy back for carrying babies and young children. A young girl might let her community know that she was ready to get married by making herself an *amautik*, a parka with an *amaut*.

Sewing the appropriate designs into clothing was an enormous job for the family seamstress. Different kinds of skins, some with hair still on and some tanned, had to be cut into a variety of shapes and dyed the correct colours through soaking in a brew of seeds, flower petals, grasses, or mosses, or by immersion in human urine, animal blood, or animal bile. Once cut and coloured, the designs had to be sewn onto the front and back panels of items of clothing, or, in an even more difficult kind of sewing, incorporated into clothing by cutting an appropriate shape in the basic skin and then stitching the inserts into place. Pebbles, shells, and bits of bone or animal tooth might all be part of a design. A single mistake could be misinterpreted by a person-other-than-human and bring disaster on a hunter or his community. The only remedy for a mistake was to start over, cutting a whole new basic garment if hides were available and making new, correctly coloured shapes. Beads were perfect substitutes for the intricately sewn skin designs. They came in a variety of colours, shapes, and sizes, with a hole ready drilled, and were a major labour-saving device. The work of threading them onto a sinew or sturdy thread with a steel needle and sewing them to a garment in the required patterns was quick, easy, and almost foolproof. A mistake could be corrected simply by removing the beads and redoing the design. Inuit women had been asking for and buying beads since the first Company vessel had visited the coastal camps in 1719.[22]

Awls and various sizes of screwdrivers were also much-wanted tools for the use of the seamstresses and tailors. A needle made of bird bone was easily broken when pushed with too much force through an animal skin, and even steel needles were hard to push through pelts, especially those with hair still on them. It was much easier to sew two pieces of animal skin together, as all Inuit knew, when an awl, a screwdriver, or a nail made a small hole beforehand.

MORE INUIT, SEVENTEEN IN ALL AND APPARENTLY ALL MEN, arrived "very late" on July 11. Fourteen of them stopped at Seal River to kill whales, while the other three carried on to the post to explain that their people had been suffering from starvation during the winter. They traded their country products and by noon on the twelfth had gone to join their fellow countrymen at Seal River.

The unseasonable weather, as well as causing starvation during the 1822–23 winter and affecting seal populations at the Churchill and Seal Rivers, was responsible for the abandonment of the Company's plan to send a coasting vessel to Wager Bay in the summer of 1823. The lack of an interpreter may also have been a factor: Augustine had already made plans to return to his own community in the summer and to spend the following year in the North.

Orders from Chief Factor John George McTavish to Leslie were to "dispense with the services of as many officers and men as are not absolutely required." Leslie had the unenviable job of picking those he "suppose[d] to be supernumerary." McTavish was blunt concerning Robert Harding's dismissal. Harding was not popular among his fellow officers, who made him the butt of many fur trade jokes about his air of self-importance and his "dainty" manners. Over and over in the letters of his superior officers he was described as "diminutive." Chief Factor McTavish assumed Harding would go home when his contract expired, but to make sure, he instructed Leslie to "order him to accompany the boat to this place." Leslie was told to leave George Barnston in charge of the post and to accompany the boat to York Factory. Along with the letter was a pistol lock belonging to Augustine. It may have been forgotten when Augustine set out for Churchill the previous fall, or he may have left it there for the armourer to repair.[23]

McTavish's letter was delivered by the Reverend John West, who reached Churchill on July 20 according to his journal, or on July 21 by Leslie's reckoning. Leslie sent Augustine across the river to pick up and ferry his missionary acquaintance and two Cree guides to the post. Augustine made a great occasion out of the event by dressing himself in "all his gay [expedition] clothes, and armed with sword and pistols."[24]

The Reverend West recorded that Augustine "expressed much delight at my coming to see his tribe, who were expected to arrive at the factory any day." He noted that every morning, Augustine's first act was to climb to a lookout where he could survey the coast, to watch for the hunters from his community coming south in their "seal skin canoes." Augustine confided to West that when his fellow villagers returned to their homes, he intended to go with them, "to his wife and children, laden with presents." How many children Augustine had in 1823 is not clear. In a letter to the Company's Council at York Factory, West wrote that Augustine had a wife and child, but in his journal he mentioned "children."[25]

On the twenty-third, runners announced the imminent arrival of "a large party of their countrymen," thirty-five hunters with their families.[26] Augustine knew several of the families and spent most of the day greeting them and inquiring about his own fellow villagers, who had still not arrived. From one couple, Ackshanook and his wife, who were camped below the rocks at Back Bay, he received news that caused him to hurry back to the House "much agitated." When Leslie asked him about his state of mind, Augustine confided that his people believed he had unlawfully caused a man's death and that his own life was in danger from a group of men who were even then on their way to the post.

There are two versions of events, both attributable to John West. One is a report by John Franklin of a conversation he had with West in London late in 1823, which he passed on to John Richardson in a letter dated December 15, 1823. As Franklin understood it, or at least as he recorded it, Augustine had "lent" his wife to one of Junius's brothers before leaving Churchill to join the Arctic overland expedition. When the brother "unfortunately died," the rest of the community "imagined that Augustus had conjured him, and his relations wished to revenge his loss on him."[27] West's book, published in 1824, tells a rather more detailed story, which he claims to have heard from Ackshanook and his wife.[28] In this version, after Augustine and Junius left Churchill, one of Junius's brothers "took his [Augustine's] wife." The brother then had second thoughts about the correctness of his action and began to think that Augustine "possessed the art of conjuring" and thus not only would have been aware of the misdeed but would also have been so "displeased" as to have laid a curse on the man who had taken his wife. The belief that Augustine "had determined upon his death...so preyed upon his spirits as to terminate his existence," wrote West. Yet another one of Junius's brothers, Itiviana, was so sure that he had lost two brothers through Augustine's actions that he threatened to avenge himself and his family by killing the returning interpreter. Itiviana had, of course, known for at least a year that Junius was not among the survivors, just as Augustine's brother Astanik knew that Augustine was.[29]

West went on to say that having heard Ackshanook's warning, Augustine "loaded his musket, and fixed his bayonet" before going to the lookout on the rocks every morning.[30] Leslie and Harding, aware of the threat to Augustine's life, paid close attention to new groups arriving from the north. Fourteen or so men and half a dozen boys approaching the post in kayaks on July 31 caused no alarm to the anxious watchers when they were identified as coming from Aughlinatook, a village at Knapp's Bay. The next morning, the sight of fifteen of the "farther away Esquemaux" created some tension around the post until it was determined that they were not Augustine's fellow villagers. Hard on their heels came five more hunters, who had left eleven of their companions at Seal River killing whales. Leslie and Harding traded with the new arrivals and agreed to meet them at the whaling grounds in about a week to pay them their whaling bonuses."[31]

Amid the flurry and scurry of so many visitors to the post, Augustine went to a distracted Leslie and "requested a brace of pistols." On August 2, according to West, Augustine came "running to the Fort with the information that his countrymen had been spotted coming along in their canoes. He waited till he ascertained that Junius's brother Itiviana was not among them before going to meet them." The main group consisted of between thirty-five and forty men, and they were followed by "a small party that came soon afterwards." Augustine's brother Astanik and nephew Annagyniak were in the main group. West indulged his curiosity by taking a close look at their products for trade and noticed "the horn of a sea unicorn about six feet long." The narwhal tusk does not appear in Leslie's detailed inventory of items purchased from Inuit by the Company, but West collected a number of items as mementos of Inuit life and may have bought the tusk from Astanik himself.[32]

West recorded nothing more of the encounter in his published journal, but Franklin's impression of how events played out, based on his conversation with West in December of 1823, expanded the clergyman's role in the affair. Augustine, wrote Franklin in his retelling of what West had told him, "went among them totally armed with his pistols when they first arrived, and defended himself against the charge, and the matter was amicably settled in the presence of West." Neither Leslie nor West mentioned Itiviana by name during the relevant time period. If Franklin's version of West's story is correct, and Augustine "went among them," meaning among Junius's relatives, the dispute may have been settled either with or without Itiviana's presence.

Both accounts are probably accurate to some degree. The missionary's role in the amicable settlement of the whole affair might well be an embellishment, but it makes no difference to the final outcome. One way or another, Augustine was reconciled to Junius's brother Itiviana, his family, and the community, and he reclaimed his wife and child, or perhaps children, as West thought. What is relevant is how the dead brother of Junius and Itiviana came to be involved with Augustine's wife in the first place. West's use of the phrase "took his wife" in his journal and the word "lent" as reported by Franklin are misleading. In trying to explain in English what had happened, Augustine may well have used either word, or he may have used another word or phrase, such as "gave her to him temporarily," but West and Augustine—one thinking in English and the other thinking in Inuktitut while trying to explain in English—could have attached quite different meanings to the word or words.

In the social system of Augustine's people, correct behaviour did not allow for a husband to abandon his wife and children or to leave them without means of support during an absence. Given what we know of Augustine's character—his sense of loyalty and responsibility—and the apparent ease with which he was received back into his community, we can safely assume that Augustine made careful arrangements for the support of his family during his absence. The chosen protector would have been a capable provider, able to absorb additional people into his household without putting his own immediate family at risk.

Inuit kinship included (then and now) both biological and social relatives, as do most European (and other) societies. All the signs point to Augustine and Junius having been somehow related, either biologically, as cousins, or fictively, as in-laws or because they shared an attribute such as the same birthday or had killed their first seal in the same hunt. Leaving his wife and child under the protection of Junius's brother does not imply that she and he entered into a conjugal relationship, although they may have. Such a relationship would not have been seen as infidelity by the community; it would have been seen as natural and acceptable, as well as beneficial. Any child born of such a union would have been recognized by the community as a member of both families, with two fathers, two mothers, and double the usual number of grandparents, aunts, uncles, and cousins. It is unlikely that Augustine's wife had conceived or borne a child during Augustine's absence on the first journey with Franklin. We know from Reverend West's letters that they had two children, a son and a daughter, both born before 1820, and that they had a third child, a son, after 1826.

In his journal and in his conversation with Franklin, West used the word "conjuring." Again, there is the problem of what word or words Augustine actually used in describing the charges against him to West and how the missionary interpreted them. Belief in the power of thought to affect events in the material world, whether it is called conjuring, witchcraft, positive thinking, visualization, or prayer, is common, or has been common, to all societies, and Inuit society is no exception.

Among the Mackenzie Delta Inuit, "hostile sorcery...was practiced against people who had caused offense in cases where direct reprisal was impossible." A similar practice existed among the Netsilik people of Boothia Peninsula. Called *ilisiniq*, it was "a merely mechanical activity," requiring no particular training or spiritual preparation, a "malevolent mental wish that could be performed by anyone."[33] Beliefs and practices adhered to by one Inuit community, such as the Mackenzie Delta or Netsilik people, were not necessarily part of the belief systems of other groups, although they may have been, in the whole or in part.

Another bit of the story was recorded by Franklin as told to him by West but not mentioned in West's own published journal. According to Franklin, "There was also some doubt as to whom the things sent for Junius should be delivered, which Mr West kindly settled by giving them to his brother as they were directed. Augustus faithfully retained them until the decision was made."[34] What things were sent for Junius, which Augustine faithfully retained, remains a puzzle. There was, of course, the matter of Junius's wages, amounting to a credit worth eighty made beaver, but this would not have been in Augustine's keeping. It also seems unlikely that "the things" were Junius's personal effects, which he was said to have had with him when he disappeared into the wilderness. It is possible that he had left some small possessions at the men's house at Fort Enterprise and that Augustine had carried these home with him.

Franklin's account of his meeting with West also reported that Augustine had expressed a deep desire "to accompany him to England to see [Richardson] and me whom he says he likes properly, but our friend B[ack] only a little."[35] Augustine's use of the word "properly" in connection with liking and loving expresses a deeply Inuit concept—that liking and loving are not merely abstract feelings but also require a commitment to take care of the person or thing that is loved.[36] At York Factory the previous summer, Augustine had revealed to West that he had learned something of reading and writing during the spring of 1822 at Fort Enterprise and had given the missionary a sample of his handwriting as a gift to West's sister, Emma Atkinson. At Churchill in 1823, he wrote another sample, apparently dictated by West, which read "White man him love properly." By using the word "properly" in his written sentence, Augustine was saying that he believed that Franklin and Richardson, and probably other white men as well, by sharing with him and providing for him, were showing that their affection for him was genuine.

By August 3, nearly all of the 1823 summer visitors were gone, the "farthest away" Inuit to their homes at Chesterfield Inlet and the Knapp's Bay people and Augustine's community to Seal River to kill whales. Only Astanik and two others, whose names were not recorded by either Leslie or West, were still at the post with Augustine. One of the unidentified men was probably Annagyniak, Astanik's stepson. The three men had "remained behind for the purpose of assisting him," suggesting that the quantity of gifts Augustine took to his family and community was more than he could carry on his own. The four men left Churchill for their home village on August 6, 1823.[37]

INTERLUDE 3

THE SECOND ARCTIC OVERLAND EXPEDITION

1824–1825

THE THREE SURVIVING OFFICERS OF THE ARCTIC OVERLAND EXPEdition arrived safely back in England in October of 1822. They had spent much of the Atlantic crossing planning a second overland expedition to the western Arctic coast of North America. Franklin's first step was to seek the support of the Hudson's Bay Company and, within the Company, the most likely among England's powerful elite to advocate for a new expedition. He chose George Back, his socially acceptable and persuasively charming former midshipman, to meet with them. "He [Back] is going to call on Berens and Garry and propose the Expedition down the Mackenzies River," Franklin informed Richardson. The two men Back was to woo were Joseph Berens Jr., a former Governor of the Hudson's Bay Company and member of the London Committee, and Nicholas Garry, the Company's current Deputy Governor. Both were powerful men who had the ears of the British Admiralty and the Colonial Office. On July 24, 1823, Franklin wrote to Richardson again. "I introduced him [Back] to Garry with whom we dined, and this meeting led to another dinner at which we are to see each other tomorrow."[1]

The plan, as set out to the two Hudson's Bay Company men, made a favourable impression. Berens and Garry declared themselves "most desirous to have this survey undertaken, and have faithfully promised to lend every possible aid towards the prosecution of an Expedition to that quarter." The promised support included the establishment of a winter headquarters for the explorers at any place of Franklin's choosing, its full provisioning, and the utmost cooperation of all Chief Factors and Traders.[2]

Franklin also undertook to sound out the top men in the British Admiralty before submitting a formal proposal. The Admiralty's initially cool reception was, in part, related to the death of Michel Teroahauté at Richardson's hands in 1821. At an informal meeting with John Barrow, Second Secretary of the Admiralty, late in July 1823, Franklin learned that "a few persons" were not sufficiently clear that Michel had actually killed Robert Hood. Barrow, who had read a pre-publication copy of Franklin's *Narrative of a Journey to the Shores of the Polar Sea*, suggested that Richardson's chapter describing the "murder" of Hood and the "execution" of Michel be rewritten to make events clearer. No early draft of Richardson's report has survived for comparison, but presumably the doctor, with the help of the expedition commander, did as Barrow suggested.[3]

John Barrow was Franklin's strongest advocate within the Admiralty and a persuasive voice in its deliberations. He had a direct line to Britain's ruling class through his friend John Murray, publisher of *The Quarterly Review*, Britains' most influential Tory periodical. Every year from 1818 to 1848, Murray published several articles by Barrow, all of which carried Barrow's message of an open polar sea, a navigable northwest passage, and the ease by which both could be attained. Barrow was committed to the extension of empire and national glory and feared a Russian attempt to gain sovereignty in some part of North America. As early as 1817 he had written, "It would be somewhat mortifying if a naval power but of yesterday should complete a discovery in the nineteenth century, which was so happily commenced by the English in the sixteenth."[4]

In this he had the full support of the British reading public. While the men of the first Arctic overland expedition were starving and dying on the barrenlands in the autumn of 1821, Russia's Tsar Alexander I had declared all of the western North American Arctic Russian territory and ordered exploration parties into the Alaskan interior. In the summer of 1823, while Franklin was being lionized as a great explorer and his book was rolling off John Murray's presses to the acclaim of all its readers, a Russian naval captain ordered his men to board and search an American fur trade vessel, *Pearl*, in an attempt to enforce Russia's ban against non-Russian ships entering Alaskan, or even Pacific, waters. The British Colonial Office recognized a threat to its claims of sovereignty in the northern half of the American continent.[5]

Having cleared up the matters of "murder" and "execution" to the satisfaction of the Admiralty, Franklin carried on his long lobby for a new expedition. He appealed to Barrow's raw patriotism. "The objects to be attained," he wrote, "are important at once to the naval character and Commercial interests of Great Britain." He raised the spectre of commercial disadvantage from the encroachment and eventual establishment of a hostile Russia. "It is plain...that the exertions of Russia are directed to the increase of her fur trade and the extension of her dominions in the northern part of America." Nor did Franklin forget to engage Barrow in the matter of national superiority. "It belongs to the high character which Great Britain has always maintained not to allow herself to be anticipated by any other nation in an object which she had thought it worth her while to contend." Finally, he made sure the Second Secretary understood that a new expedition would have the full support of that powerful force in British overseas commerce and colonial government, the Hudson's Bay Company, whose directors were so "desirous of the prosecution of the enquiry."[6]

Barrow forwarded the letter to Lord Bathurst, Secretary for War and the Colonies, four days later, with his full endorsement. The following day, December 2, 1823, in an interesting concurrence of events, U.S. President James Monroe's annual message to Congress spelled out what has since become known as the Monroe Doctrine, a policy that barred European nations from establishing new colonies in the Americas. The implications of the president's announcement for British territories in North America were not lost on Franklin or Barrow. In less than two weeks, Barrow reported to Franklin that

Lord Bathurst thought the plan for a new expedition was "practicable," and "the answer looks well."⁷

While waiting to hear Bathurst's final yes or no, Franklin and Richardson passed a few pleasant hours designing uniforms for their proposed expedition. "It did not perhaps occur to you," Franklin wrote on receiving the doctor's suggestions, "that green and red are the uniform of the Russians, and that by being so clothed, the Indians westward of Mackenzie's River might not be able to distinguish the subjects of the different nation. I was thinking that sky blue, red and silver, would be equally shewy, at the same time it would be very distinct from any dress the Indians have seen. Red Capotes faced with green would however be equally good." Franklin's bride of three months, the poet Eleanor Anne Porden, was, according to her husband, "much amused" at the two naval officers designing uniforms and declared that the doctor "would make an excellent dress maker if all other trades should fail."⁸

FRANKLIN IDENTIFIED TOO MUCH HASTE AND TOO LITTLE PREPAration as major flaws of the 1821 disaster. For the new expedition, he wanted winter quarters built before the arrival of the main party, and Yellowknife and Loucheux hunters and guides at the ready. Beyond that, he wanted all necessary equipment and provisions in place well in advance of taking up residence at the northern headquarters. By March 1824, a mere three months after the expedition received the blessing and backing of the Admiralty, Franklin and Richardson had ordered everything they thought necessary and useful, organized the expedition logistics, and hired most of its personnel.

Franklin also recognized that the best advice he had been given in 1821–22 had come from fur traders like Ferdinand Wentzel and Robert McVicar who lived in fur trade country, knew the weather patterns and the problems of travel and transportation, and had friendly business relations with the local people. Franklin asked the Hudson's Bay Company to lend him a man who had similar knowledge and experience to take charge of building the winter residence, hiring local hunters, and expediting the movement of supplies from Fort

Chipewyan to the northern base. The Company appointed Chief Trader Peter Warren Dease, a solidly practical man who, in the event, fit the bill exactly.

Dease chose to build at the western end of Great Bear Lake. The site had several advantages critical to the success of the expedition: it was close to a fishery known to be abundant and reliable; it was near the winter homes of Akaitcho's Yellowknife hunters, who would supply meat through two winters; and it was within easy reach of the Arctic coast. Franklin planned to name his headquarters Fort Reliance.[9]

Instead of canoes, which had proved too fragile and unmanageable for ocean work, Franklin determined that the new expedition should have sturdy boats, built by master craftsmen in England. They had to be small enough and light enough to be carried by their crews, strong enough to withstand ocean ice, waves, and shale beaches, manageable in fast tides and storms, and with a shallow draft so as not to ground in shoal rivers. He took his suggestions to the Woolwich Ship Yard, where he consulted with the master boatbuilder, Mr. John Cow. Between them they designed three boats that met all the requirements. The largest, *Lion*, measured twenty-six feet long and five feet eight inches in the beam. With a capacity of about three tons, it could be carried by six men and crewed by six oarsmen and a steersman. The other two boats, *Dolphin* and *Union*, each two feet shorter and ten inches narrower than *Lion*, could be manned by five oarsmen and a steersman. Each could carry two and a half tons of cargo.

Mindful of the disasters attendant on river crossings on the earlier expedition, Franklin was delighted with a fourth little vessel, the *Walnut-Shell*, designed and built by an interested friend, Lieutenant-Colonel Charles William Pasley of the navy's Royal Engineers. Oval in shape, nine feet long, and four feet four inches wide, its ash-wood frame was held together by thongs rather than pegs and nails and had a waterproof canvas cover. It could be dismantled in less than twenty minutes into five or six bundles weighing no more than eighty-five pounds in all. Like the three larger boats, it performed beautifully in trials on the Thames River.

No longer ignorant about travel conditions in the northwest, as he had been five years earlier, Franklin was reluctant to trust all of the expedition's equipment and provisions to a single canoe brigade. Instead, he arranged for a series of shipments, all well in advance. The first lot of supplies left England in the care of Robert McVicar, chief trader at Fort Resolution. McVicar had been on furlough in Britain in 1823–24 and was ready to return to Rupert's Land by way of New York in March 1824. He took charge of the expedition's freight at New York and saw it safely by stagecoach to Canada and by boat to Norway House. The Company agreed to add three north canoes to its first brigade of the 1824 season, load the supplies that McVicar brought with him, and start them on the long journey to the Northwest as soon as the rivers were open.

The plan worked, and the boats were at Norway House on July 17, 1824. A day later, McVicar married Christy McBeath, daughter of a Selkirk settler and sister-in-law of the Norway House Clerk in Charge, Donald Ross.[10] Honeymooning in tent and canoe, they shepherded the supplies to Lake Athabasca and delivered them to Peter Warren Dease before winter set in. A second shipment of equipment and supplies was entrusted to the HBC's *Prince of Wales*, along with the three boats from the Woolwich Ship Yard and little *Walnut-Shell*, and off-loaded at York Factory in the fall of 1824. The supply ship also brought two carpenters, a contingent of English marines, Scottish boatmen, and plentiful bales and boxes of foodstuffs. Dr. Richardson, in charge of ordering provisions, had chosen highly nutritious foods packed for maximum preservation and at the same time light enough to be carried on the backs of voyageurs. He also stocked up on medical supplies and the most effective remedies of the day. Included with the English goods were guns with specially tempered locks, made by the reputable firm of Barnet and Son, Gunsmiths. Franklin was determined that firearms for the new expedition would be serviceable even in the coldest winter.[11]

The expedition uniforms and winter clothing, including long underwear and knee-length stockings, were in the second shipment, along with something new and exciting. In the midst of marriage, first fatherhood, and expedition preparations, Franklin found time to take notice of a new discovery that promised to contribute to the safety and comfort of his men. When he began ordering bedding and clothing for the party, he remembered hearing about a new product, still in first production at the Glasgow chemical works of Charles Mackintosh. Glasgow's first gasworks, opened in 1818, produced a waste product—coal-tar naphtha—that Mackintosh thought might be recycled into something useful. He discovered, after nearly five years of experimenting, that the smelly waste product dissolved Indian rubber, which could then be poured into thin sheets. When he glued a layer of fabric between two layers of the rubber sheeting, he had material that was heavy and inclined to stiffen in the cold but waterproof. When Franklin sent in his order, he asked if whole suits consisting of pants, jacket, and hat could be made up. Mackintosh was willing to try and successfully produced two such outfits for each member of the expedition. Franklin also recognized the usefulness of the rubberized material for other things and added waterproof tents, boat covers, and packing cases to his order.[12]

All the heavy and cumbersome materials for building a winter residence and setting up its fishery were ordered from the merchants of Montreal, along with goods for paying the hunters Dease would later hire to provide meat for two winters at Fort Reliance. The Hudson's Bay Company undertook to ship the materials as far inland as possible in 1824 and have them on Dease's doorstep in the summer of 1825.[13]

Franklin shopped for and procured the necessary meteorological, astronomical, and navigational instruments in England. They were sent to Montreal and forwarded through the Hudson's Bay Company's river transport system to the Royal Navy Depot at Penetanguishene on Lake Huron. There, they were stored under the watchful eyes of the Royal Navy's quartermasters to await the arrival of the expedition officers on their way west in 1825.[14]

THE DISASTER OF THE FIRST ARCTIC OVERLAND EXPEDITION showed Franklin that, among other things, not only were canoes inadequate for coasting in Arctic waters but so were the rivermen who lacked familiarity with ocean ice and salt sea tides. When the time came to choose the members of the new expedition, Franklin appealed to the Admiralty for British sailors. The Admiralty gave permission for him to ask for volunteers among enlisted seamen and agreed to make up the required numbers with a small contingent of marines whose principal job would be protecting the party in case natives of the country anywhere along the way proved hostile. In spite of the disasters of 1821, there was no shortage of volunteers, both naval and civilian, when the call went out. First to apply was Neil McDonald, a former HBC employee who had served in the Severn and Athabasca districts between 1818 and 1823. On board *Prince of Wales* bound for home at the close of his contract, he had shared quarters and mess with Franklin, Richardson, and Back. When plans for a new venture into the Arctic became public, he volunteered.

Robert Spinks and William Duncan were also no strangers to Arctic waters, or to Franklin; both had sailed with him (and George Back) on *Trent* in the unsuccessful attempt to reach Spitsbergen Island in 1818. Both had since then served under Edward Parry on two Arctic voyages. Thomas Gillet, another experienced seaman with seventeen years' service in the Royal Navy, came well recommended by his superiors. The last two were Thomas Matthews and Thomas Fuller, both boatbuilders on the payroll of the Woolwich Ship Yard until they heard the famous Arctic explorer was in their midst ordering custom-built boats. They unhesitatingly deserted Mr. Cow in favour of an adventure to the wilds of North America.[15]

Six Scottish volunteers from the Isle of Islay, all experienced in manning ocean life-saving craft, joined *Prince of Wales* at Stromness when the ship stopped to take on water and provisions before its Atlantic crossing in 1824. Franklin wrote to John Rae Sr., the Company's agent there, requesting that he advance them a half year's wages so they could leave money to sustain their families during their absence. From his appended list, we know the names of five of the men. John Macduffie, Archibald Carmichael, Alexander Macarthur, William McLellan, and Alexander Currie were all middlemen, which meant that they were sturdy young men with strong backs for portaging and hands calloused from pulling oars. A sixth man, John McEachern, was not on Agent Rae's list, but Franklin's Fort Chipewyan entry identified him as a native of Islay.[16]

To make up the full complement of men needed, Chief Factor McTavish chose six York Factory men and a seventh man from Red River—"the most experienced and able boatmen who happened to be on the ground," he wrote to Franklin—and assigned them to expedition service. Among them, the York Factory men supplied the skills and experience the English and Scots lacked. John McLennan was an experienced bowman, John McLea a steersman, and Charles McKenzie could take over either job when necessary. James Spence, Gustavus Aird, and Archibald Stewart, a former soldier, were all hefty middlemen. John Hodgson, a Red River man who was an experienced steersman, was particularly valuable for his additional skills as a boat carpenter.[17]

To get the men to the winter quarters by the early summer of 1824, Franklin and Richardson arranged for the twelve men hired in Britain to board *Prince of Wales* at Stromness in June, along with the expedition's boats, *Lion*, *Union*, *Dolphin*, and *Walnut-Shell*, safely stowed in the hold. Governor Simpson instructed the Chief Factor at York to be ready for them with enough additional men to man the three boats and get them started inland before winter.

CHOOSING THE JUNIOR OFFICERS WAS NOT EASY. ONE OBVIOUS CANdidate should have been George Back. But personal feelings simmered below the surface. Although Franklin had sent Back to present the expedition plan to Berens and Garry of the Hudson's Bay Company, it was by no means certain that the young midshipman, recently promoted to lieutenant, would accompany them in 1825. In his long letter to Richardson on December 30, 1823, Franklin made some surprising comments: "I am very happy to tell you that it is quite decided Back is not to be of the party though I made the offer of taking him, and so far I have done my duty towards him and his friends." Franklin's explanation, or excuse, for eliminating Back from his list of possible juniors was that Back's recall and assignment to Arctic duty would endanger his rise to the next rung of the naval ladder.[18]

Eight months later, in August of 1824, when John Barrow joined John and Eleanor Franklin for a few days' holiday at their new house in Tunbridge Wells, the matter was still undecided. Barrow sounded Franklin out about Back. "I could not," Franklin wrote to Richardson, "without entirely injuring his professional prospects, mention my reasons for declining his service.... An explanation on this point would only lead further into the snare." Franklin's and Richardson's reluctance to have George Back with them on the second expedition is, on the face of it, puzzling. In 1819, a year after Franklin and Back had served together on *Trent* in the unsuccessful Spitsbergen attempt, Franklin was pleased to have Midshipman Back assigned to the first Arctic overland expedition. In the spring of 1823, Back still had Franklin's confidence, to the extent that the captain sent him to win the cooperation of the Hudson's Bay Company's directors. Yet, by 1824, Franklin was unwilling to have the younger man on the new expedition.[19]

Franklin's next letter to Richardson began with happy domestic news: a furnished bedroom was ready for a visit from the Richardsons, and Eleanor Isabella, at almost four months old, was "getting fat and heavy." Moving quickly on to what was troubling him, Franklin gloomily confided to Richardson his fears that "the vacancy will be kept open for Back.... This however is mere conjecture on my part, and I hope will prove fallacious." One possible reason, and a fairly weak one at that, for Franklin's and Richardson's dislike and suspicion of Back was the younger man's readiness to criticize his superiors. Another possibility is that Back's off-the-record comments to Wentzel about cannibalism in the first expedition had been leaked into the HBC's gossip pool. John West might have heard the rumours during his 1822 visit to Rupert's Land and passed them on to Franklin when the two men met in London in December of 1823.[20]

With the matter of an experienced junior officer still hanging, the Admiralty appointed Edward Nicholas Kendall as surveyor to the expedition in early winter of 1824. Like most of his colleagues, Kendall had joined the navy when barely fourteen years old and, as Back and Hood had done, trained in survey work and drawing during his midshipman years. In the summer of 1824, he served under Captain George Francis Lyon on *Griper* in an attempt to determine if Repulse Bay was the entrance to the much-sought northwest passage. Severe ice conditions thwarted their advance, and Kendall was back in England on November 10, 1824, available for a new posting. Lyon's report to the Admiralty spoke highly of his surveyor-artist, and the twenty-four-year-old was assigned to the new expedition with the rank of Admiralty Mate.[21]

By December, Barrow had had enough of teasing Franklin over the appointment of the last officer and, apparently without further consultation, made the final decision. He offered the position to George Back, just home from Lisbon where he had been serving on *Superb*. Franklin put a good face on what was an unwelcome circumstance. "Mr Barrow offered the appointment to my friend and former companion Lieut Back," he wrote, "and on *Christmas Day* I had the gratification of seeing him in London, ready to join the party."[22]

The two expedition leaders booked passages for themselves, the junior officers, and a contingent of Royal Marines to New York in the spring of 1825. From New York, they planned an overland trek to York (now Toronto) by stagecoach, and from there by horseback, canal barge, and canoe to the Penetanguishene naval depot. Franklin and Richardson intended to go ahead at full speed in a light canoe, overtaking the York Factory party somewhere along the route, while the two junior officers waited for a brigade of voyageurs to arrive from Montreal.

AUGUSTINE'S WAS THE ONLY NAME EVER CONSIDERED FOR THE position of Inuit interpreter on the new expedition. His competence, uncomplaining good nature, courage, and initiative were so well appreciated by the two leaders that they had no hesitation about engaging him a second time and meeting whatever terms he might put forth as conditions of his employment. Among the many practical and logistical arrangements on Franklin's mind at the time, locating, hiring, and dispatching Augustine was a high priority. In his February 27, 1824, letter to George Simpson, the Hudson's Bay Company's Overseas Governor, Franklin made a specific request for Augustine's services. "It will be important," he wrote, "to send at once to Churchill, to secure Augustus the Esquimaux interpreter, or he may be absent with his tribe when his services are required." But he could not leave it at that. He interrupted a sentence dealing with the transport of provisions and equipment to repeat how necessary Augustine was to the expedition. "I shall thank you to dispatch the [provisions and equipment] into the Interior as soon as you can, so that I may be certain of finding them *and Augustus* either at Fort Chipewyan in the summer of 1825, or some place on the line of march between Canada and the Athabasca." In closing, the anxious commander, determined that nothing should go wrong with his carefully thought-out plan, asked for a reply confirming "what steps have been taken respecting procuring the provisions for us, as well as how and when the boats and stores will be forwarded to Fort Chipewyan" and *"whether Augustus has been sent to join us."*[23]

CHAPTER 6

SECOND JOURNEY TO THE WESTERN ARCTIC

1824–1826

AUGUSTINE RETURNED TO CHURCHILL IN MAY OF 1824 after a winter among his own people. He walked into the post to announce that ten families were on their way, including his own wife and children, who were still about five days from the post. They were on foot, with a few sleds and some dogs carrying hunting equipment, provisions, and household utensils in saddle bags, and could go no faster than the slowest of the children and elderly walking beside the sleds. Biting winds and flying snow from the south made the long walk especially difficult. The weather—"cold for this season of the year," Hugh Leslie thought—offered one advantage for the travellers: the firm frozen crust on the snow prevented them from sinking ankle-deep with every step. Augustine and his companion, a young man named Ullebuk, were given the usual welcoming gifts—"a small piece of tobacco and a few charges of ammunition for each man in the party"— and hurried back to join their countrymen.[1]

The hunters spent June at Seal River with Augustine in charge of the tally book. They killed more than 260 seals, which Baikie Sinclair weighed and started boiling down at month's end, June 28. They were also busy building new kayaks and one or two umiaks, women's boats, that could carry a dozen or so people and considerable cargo. June 29 was a very good day: the river was full of drift ice, the seal hunt was productive, and whales were beginning to feed nearby. In the long summer twilight, after a day of sealing, the Inuit took three small whales, to Leslie's evident pleasure. The weather had finally turned warm, which "will do good to our gardens after the late rains," Leslie wrote. Augustine and Ullebuk were back at the post with Augustine's list of each hunter's seal catch by the end of the month.[2]

Thick fog shut the post in for most of July 6, and no one noticed a smoke across the river till evening, when Augustine and Ullebuk were able to make their way across the mud flats and bring back two York Factory Cree with a packet from Governor Simpson. The following morning, Leslie sent for Augustine. After their talk, Leslie wrote in the daily journal: "Having been desired by Governor Simpson I have this day [July 7, 1824] engaged two Esquimaux for the purpose of accompanying Captn Franklin. One of them is the same who accompanied him on his last Expedition. The other has never been employed by Europeans before. The former is engaged at the rate of 60 Made Beaver plus provisions and the latter at 50 exclusive of equipment."[3] Simpson relayed the good news to Franklin and assured him that while Augustine's companion, Ullebuk, did not speak more than a few words of English, he was "a fine stout active fellow."[4]

Augustine accepted the new appointment "with delight." His pleasure certainly had something to do with his affection for Franklin and Richardson—he had told the Reverend West how much he wished to see them again—but he may have had a second motive for welcoming an offer of employment. Two years earlier, when he prepared for a winter in his home village after his years with Franklin's first overland expedition, he found how useful his earnings could be to his family and community. He also learned that he could not take it for granted that he had a job at Churchill Post. Chief Factor McTavish's instructions in 1823 not to renew Robert Harding's contract were rescinded when the economy-minded Governor Simpson discovered that Harding's language skills would relieve Churchill Post of the wages and perks that earlier had gone to Augustine.[5] He found himself in the same kind of uncertain economic straits as his countrymen whose lives depended entirely on the fickle resources of the land. Service with Franklin offered some economic security for his family and his community, at least for a few more years. In spite of the misery and tragedies of his first employment with Franklin, Augustine was willing to take a serious risk in order to secure some economic advantage for his family and community.[6]

As he had done in 1820, Augustine arranged for the security of his family during his absence. Following Inuit tradition, he chose a protector for his wife and children from among his close kin and watched them leave when the seal hunt ended on August 13. He and Ullebuk then moved into the Men's House to wait for transportation to York Factory. On the sixteenth they stowed their small trunks, bedrolls, and gun cases on the Company's sloop *Churchill* and began the first leg of their long trip northwest to join the second Arctic overland expedition. They were beset by heavy fog from the beginning and spent several anxious days with all hands on the lookout for floating ice and shoal water. The fog banks cleared just as they approached the Hayes River, and on the evening of August 28, in "fine weather," they came to anchor at York Factory.[7]

At York Factory, the two interpreters were assigned spaces in the bachelors' quarters. Governor Simpson had earlier promised Franklin that over the winter "every pains will be taken to improve Augustus' English, and teach his companion a little," and that in the spring he would see them off to the northwest "with the boats." As things worked out, their stay was considerably shorter than Simpson had in mind, a mere two days. *Prince of Wales* had reached the factory a few days earlier, carrying three expedition boats and the man Franklin had chosen to command them, Neil McDonald. Chief Factor McTavish assigned the two northerners to one of the expedition boats and added their names to the list of passengers on McDonald's bill of lading.[8]

Augustine and Ullebuk would take their orders from Neil McDonald on the first leg of their long journey to the northwest. McDonald was no stranger to Augustine. He had been in the brigade that Augustine and Junius had been assigned to on their journey to Athabasca in 1820. Another old friend at the factory was Chief Factor John Charles, who was headed to a new posting at Nelson River District, along with his wife, Jane Auld, and their four young children. On the spur of the moment, Augustine decided to travel with his former boss as far as Split Lake. Chief Factor McTavish and Neil McDonald were amenable and, in accordance with Franklin's wishes, supplied Augustine with "one of the summer dresses and a pair of Indian stockings and…a gun from Crate #36, and the necessary ammunition." They took care that Ullebuk was similarly fitted out, with the exception of a gun and ammunition. At eight o'clock on the morning of August 31, taking advantage of the continuing "fine weather," the Charles family, with Augustine and Ullebuk, left York Factory in a light canoe.[9]

The three expedition boats followed on September 2. Each boat carried nineteen pieces of essential cargo in bales weighing between eighty and ninety pounds, including bundles of canvas, clothing, chocolate, arrowroot, sugar, tea, flour, macaroni, dried soup, coffee, tools, nets, rope, varnish, guns, ball, powder, flints, medicine, stationary, kegs of Demerara rum, and a roll of twist tobacco. The twentieth piece on each boat was one of the expedition's portable canvas and lath boats.[10]

Neil McDonald was in charge of Boat 1 and also took on the job of steersman. His crew consisted of Charles McKenzie as bowman and James Spence, John Macduffie, and Robert Spinks as middlemen, with two seats at midships for Augustine and Ullebuk when they joined the boat at Split Lake. John Hodgson had charge of Boat 2, with John McLennan as bowman, Alexander Currie, John McEachern, and Archibald Stewart as middlemen, and Thomas Fuller, one of the boat carpenters, in the passenger seat. Boat 3 was commanded by steersman John McLea, with four middlemen: William McLellan, Gustavus Aird, William Duncan, and Thomas Gillet. A midship seat was reserved for the second boat carpenter, Thomas Matthews.[11]

Each boat also carried the personal luggage of its crew. Remembering the suffering of the first expedition's inadequately clothed voyageurs, Franklin had not left the matter of civilian dress to the expedition members. He anticipated that the men would need winter clothing before they reached Great Bear Lake.

> I do not wish them to be scantily supplied, but to have every thing that you may consider necessary, especially in the articles of warm clothing, Indian

shoes and mittens, and each to have a fur cap at their winter quarters. In the bales of clothing which I have sent out, marked No 27 and 28, there are winter and summer suits for each man, as well as Indian stockings, all made of the prepared waterproof cloth. The winter capote I shall reserve for them at Bear Lake, but I shall be obliged by your issuing from these bales a summer frock [a lightweight naval uniform] and pair of Indian stockings to each person, and from [bales] No. 32 & 33 prepared canvas sufficient for each man to sleep and also to make a bag for his clothes.[12]

There were as well two sets of waterproof shirts and leggings for each man, made by Mackintosh of Glasgow, and "an equipment with a scarlet belt."[13]

MCDONALD BROUGHT HIS BRIGADE SAFELY TO CUMBERLAND HOUSE late in the evening of October 18, 1824. Chief Factor James Leith was not glad to see them. Nineteen new mouths to house and feed through a long, cold winter was not something any Chief Factor would have welcomed. Leith told the new arrivals that they would have to earn their keep. The "old hands engaged at York Factory" were agreeable, understanding that most posts could not feed large numbers of extra people, but the Scottish volunteers refused outright, claiming that "their engagement and promises from Capt Franklin exempted them from going farther." Leith sat them down and "held an explanation with them." He told them, first, that eleven of them would ship out the following day for Carlton House, where they would be employed making pemmican, and second, that they had to obey orders, whether they liked it or not. In the face of a simmering rebellion, Leith let it go for the moment, on the grounds that he had "no right to use coercive measures to enforce obedience, not having their engagements, nor having the honor of being one of His Majesty's commissioned officers." He assigned the men to a house, issued them the same daily rations as the Company's people got, and bided his time for five days before ordering them to provide their own firewood.[14]

After a month at the post, although by no means happy with their lot, the expedition men were more inclined to cooperate with the Chief Factor and his clerk, Thomas Isbister. At noon on Sunday, November 21, Neil McDonald took seven of his men, fifteen days' provisions, and three trains of dogs, along with the Company's Hugh Gibson as guide, to Carlton House. Augustine and Ullebuk remained at Cumberland House and opted to avoid the unpleasantries of communal living by supporting themselves hunting deer in their own camp across the lake. Taking responsibility for their own upkeep relieved them of any duty to supply the post or their expedition colleagues with meat or fish, while at the same time keeping them near enough to the House to get help if they needed it.[15]

Chief Factor John Stuart at Carlton House had not been alerted ahead of time to expect eight guests for the winter and, like Leith, did not welcome them with enthusiasm. "They could not come at a worse time," he wrote, "with but our own people…we could barely subsist and these people will soon eat us out of house and home." Nevertheless, he assigned them a house and puzzled over where Neil McDonald fit within the hierarchy.

In Stuart's view, McDonald was neither fish nor fowl: not an officer of the Company or the expedition, not a naval officer, and not of the same social class as a Chief Factor. But he was no mere labourer either. Captain Franklin and the Admiralty had put him in command of the expedition's men and boats, empowered him to enforce naval discipline, and given him responsibility for the expedition's material goods. A further troubling fact was that the Chief Factors at York Factory and Cumberland House had given McDonald bed and board in the officers' precincts. Stuart decided to ignore his class-conscious first instincts and treat McDonald as an almost-equal. "Not that he is…strictly entitled to it," Stuart wrote, "but he has had the command of the others from York to Cumberland and being admitted as a messmate at both these places it would not appear well was I to class him with the others." Besides, Stuart continued, "He always bore a good character and Mr Leith writes [that he] is unassuming."[16]

Stuart found, as Leith had, that the expedition men were "very dilatory," in Stuart's opinion. They "seemed to think that our people should do everything," he wrote. Stuart, however, took a sterner line than Leith had done, telling them "once [and] for all that if they were lazy to work I should take care they should be lazy to eat also"—a threat that, to his satisfaction, "had the desired effect."[17]

As the expedition men were settling in for the winter, worrying news filtered down to them from the Company's officers at the western prairie posts. Chief Factor Leith was informed on October 17 that Cree had recently attacked a Blackfoot camp near Fort Edmonton. The attack took place while the Blackfoot men were away hunting, and "the women and children to the amount it is supposed of four Hundred were all massacred excepting about twenty whom they reserved as Slaves."[18] Hugh Gibson, returning to Cumberland House on December 21, reported that the long-standing hostilities between the tribes had spread to the Assiniboine Valley. "The tribes in the Saskatchwan" were on the "war path again," he wrote, "and a good many of the Slave Indians," as the Cree called the Blackfoot, had already been killed.[19] The following year, the Edmonton House journal entry for October 9 noted that the Blackfoot "[inform] us that they had a Battle with the Beaver Hills Crees & destroyed about 16 tents of them."[20] As alarming as this was to the Company's officers, it was also cause for concern to Neil McDonald, who was responsible for the safety of the expedition's people and property, and added to the unrest already growing within the expedition's ranks.

ON CHRISTMAS EVE OF 1824, AUGUSTINE AND ULLEBUK, STILL LIVing at their hunting camp, showed up at the House in time to get their Christmas rations: "15 lbs dry meat, 1 gallon Indian corn, 6 lbs grease, 1 piece pork, 1 fresh goose, 2 gallons ground wheat, 3 ditto of barley, 1½ bushels potatoes & 15 white fish." Early on Christmas morning, each man in the establishment received "two drams" of rum and, as soon as breakfast was done, "half a pint of spirits."[21]

The New Year's menu was much the same as the Christmas one: "18 lb dry meat, 8 lb grease, 6 qts of Indian corn, 2 geese, 2 gall[ons] ground wheat, 4 ditto of ground barley, 18 white fish and 1 bushel of potatoes." Thomas Isbister duly recorded, as he had done on Christmas Day, "Gave the very same to the men of the expedition." New Year's morning each of the men got two drams of shrub and after breakfast half a pint of Demerara spirits. Isbister did not note how the men spent the day, but in the evening they livened themselves with a dance and shared another two gallons of shrub.[22]

At Carlton House, Christmas was not an occasion for special celebrations, but in true Scots fashion, the new year was ushered in with style. The Company's men began by firing a musketry salute at the door of the communal hall and wishing their senior officers a good year to come. The officers in turn invited them and the local people at the post to enjoy generous portions of shrub, rum, and cake. The "ladies" of the post arrived next, for kisses all round, "*a la mode de pays*," and received their share of food and drink. Breakfast was eight pounds of meat, a quart of wheat, a quart of barley, and a portion of grease and potatoes for each man, half that for each woman, and half that again for each child. By ten o'clock the officers were alone in their quarters, and the post population passed the day "variously as suited the people's fancy." At four thirty, all hands, including the expedition men, were invited back for "the best dinner we could provide": two kinds of *ragouts* (stews), two courses of *boulets* (meatballs), and roasted ribs and bosses (bison humps), all "in abundance," followed by currant pies and plum pudding. Thirty-two people sat down for the "best repast," and "though from various countries they all behaved themselves decently." Songs in French, English, and Gaelic followed until eight o'clock, when everyone withdrew briefly to get ready for a dance. Midnight ushered in the Sabbath, a day when dancing and merry-making were unseemly, so Stuart thanked his guests, gave them four gallons of rum to share, and wished them goodnight.[23]

OVER THE NEXT FEW MONTHS, THE EXPEDITION MEN WORKED AT doing what they were good at or what they found interesting. Augustine and Ullebuk could not quite get the hang of hunting in country where trees got in their way, so they moved their camp to the post fishery at a nearby lake. There they were so productive that Leith brought all but one of his fishermen back to the House and left the Inuit to it. The two Woolwich Ship Yard carpenters, Matthews and Fuller, went to help cut and square timber of elmwood on the banks of the Saskatchewan River. By January 29 they were busy building a snow trail so the dog trains could haul the timbers to the House. The same evening, Isbister "got the beer a-barming."[24]

The rest of the expedition men were called on for more menial stay-at-home chores: shovelling snow, laying a winter road, and cleaning the stables. At the end of January, they hauled timber to the building shed, where Matthews and Fuller began ripping and planing the logs. By the middle of April, they had finished two new boats. To the satisfaction of the men of both post and expedition, Isbister's batch of beer, all seventy-two gallons of it, "having done working," was put into kegs, allowed to sit through a second quick "working," and then "bunged up and put in the cellar."[25]

April 29 was the day set for the return of Franklin's men to Cumberland House. Only John Hodgson stayed on at Carlton, at Stuart's invitation, he being "the only one who could, and in fact has, rendered any service here." In anticipation of being released from Stuart's close supervision, the men celebrated in their cups, and their host, for his part, fretted at the difficulty he had getting them up and on their way. "It was no easy matter to get them off, there being not a sober man among them but Mr McDonald, and though countrymen of mine I was glad to see them off." They were back at Cumberland House on May 5, where Isbister kept them busy planting potatoes and grooming the gardens until the end of the month.[26]

❧

WHILE THE EXPEDITION MEN INLAND WERE DEALING WITH THE rigours of winter at Cumberland and Carlton, the expedition officers were ready to start their travels overseas. Franklin, Richardson, Kendall, and Back, with four marines—Corporal Robert Hallcom, Shadrach Tysoe, William Money, and George Wilson—left Liverpool in the American packet *Columbia*, under Captain Lee, on February 16, 1825, bound for the port of New York.[27]

The British Consul in New York, James Buchanan, joined them for the journey north. They travelled by coach to Albany and Rochester, entered British territory at Niagara Falls, and crossed Lake Ontario to the Upper Canada capital city of York. Two days in "carts and other conveyances" brought them to Lake Simcoe, where they transferred to "canoes and boats" for the lake crossing, covered the nine miles to the Nottawasaga River on foot, stowed their luggage in another boat, and reached the Royal Navy Depot at Penetanguishene on Lake Huron in mid-April.[28]

Two large canoes, *canôts de maître*, ordered more than a year in advance, were ready, and for eight days, while waiting for the arrival of hired voyageurs from Montreal, officers and men loaded their personal luggage and the expedition's meteorological and astronomical equipment. The two dozen or so expected voyageurs arrived in two boats, on April 20 and April 22. Three of the Montreal men were Iroquois. While still on Lake Superior, one of them, Charlois Arohauté, revealed that he was the brother of Michel Teroahauté, the alleged murderer of Robert Hood. As soon as the party reached Fort William, Franklin paid him off, along with his two companions.[29] Other Montreal men were more welcome. Twelve were hired to go as far as the expedition's winter quarters in the summer of 1825 and return south the same year. Two others, Alexis Vivier and François Felix, were the only voyageurs to winter at Great Bear Lake. A twelfth man, George Munro, signed on at Red River.[30]

The Montreal brigade carried mail from England, and Franklin's letters brought "the distressing intelligence of the most severe domestic affliction, the death of my dearest wife, which had occurred exactly two months before"— barely a week after Franklin's departure from England.[31] The augmented party set out for Fort William, which they reached on May 10. There they exchanged the big *canôts de maître* for four smaller *canôts du Nord*, better suited to river travel. Franklin and Richardson moved their gear into one of the light canoes, taking only essential provisions and equipment, and struck out for Cumberland House at maximum speed and by the fastest route: Rainy Lake, Lake of the Woods, Lake Winnipeg, and the Saskatchewan River. George Back, with Admiralty Mate Edward Kendall as his second, was left to follow more slowly with the main party in three heavily laden canoes.[32]

AS FRANKLIN'S PARTY OF OFFICERS AND VOYAGEURS WORKED THEIR way inland, winter at Cumberland House was finally over. In late May, the days were warm, with a full seventeen hours of daylight. On the pleasant afternoon of June 1, the day before they were to set out for the northwest, the expedition men arranged for a football match. Already in high spirits and caught up in the game, two of the men, Thomas Matthews and John McLennan, ran full tilt into each other, "striking with such force at the ball that both fell." Poor Matthews was unable to get up. His companions carried him to his bunk, where the officers examined his leg. One of them, Mr. Ross, who had some knowledge of medical procedures, diagnosed a broken bone. He dealt with it by wrestling the two pieces back into position and immobilizing the leg with splints.[33]

In spite of their sympathy for their fallen comrade, the expedition had to move on without him if they were to reach their destination before freeze-up. Chief Factor Leith appointed one of his junior officers, Paul Fraser, to guide the expedition and assigned one of his labourers, George Harcus, to take Matthews's place in the boat. The provisions brought in by McDonald's brigade in October 1824 were loaded into the boats for the next stage of the journey; for each man there were fifteen bags of pemmican, fifty pounds of pease meal, three hundred pounds of barley meal, ten pounds of flour, fourteen pounds of loaf sugar, one pound of tea, a gallon of shrub, and half a gallon of Leeward Island rum.[34] The three expedition boats followed the chosen route from Cumberland House to the English River and then made the difficult ascent through a series of lakes to Ile à la Crosse Lake.

FRANKLIN AND RICHARDSON REACHED CUMBERLAND HOUSE ON June 15, two weeks after the main party in the expedition's three boats had left Cumberland House. Dr. Richardson's first act was to examine Thomas Matthews's splinted leg. He declared that the broken fibula would heal and that the patient would be able to travel in two months. Leith agreed to see to it that Matthews got a seat in one of the Company's canoes heading to Fort Chipewyan and the Mackenzie River in due course, and Franklin took care to formalize the agreement by writing it out and putting it in the packet to be delivered to George Simpson by the next party heading to the bay.³⁵

At Buffalo Lake (now Peter Pond Lake) at about six in the morning of June 29, Franklin and Richardson caught up with the expedition boats at the mouth of the Methye River. At the sound of loud hulloos coming across the lake, the expedition men looked back to see their two officers skimming toward them in their light canoe. Augustine was among the first to greet his commander—"none more warmly," said Franklin—and introduced Ullebuk, "whom he had brought from Churchill as his companion." The rest of the men welcomed their officers "with cheerful, delighted countenance," wrote their commander. After Franklin had checked the boats and stores, and found everything in good order, Paul Fraser cooked breakfast, and the men took an hour's rest to read the letters the officers had brought with them from England.³⁶

The forty-mile haul up the La Loche River took five days. Up to their knees in mud, and driven to distraction by mosquitoes, the men dragged the boats upstream. When a violent gust of wind during a thunderstorm overturned their tents on June 30, Franklin saw the bright side. "The musquitoes which had been incessant in their torment the whole day immediately disappeared," he wrote, "and we enjoyed the evening refreshment of a cool breeze and the pleasure of relief from their attacks."³⁷

They began "the most laborious part of the journey," the eleven-mile Methye Portage, on July 4. The bone-crushing business of shifting the expedition's 116 bales of stores and equipment left many of the men lame and unable to continue under their weighty burdens. Augustine and Ullebuk, having worked too enthusiastically during the ascent, were among the worst of the injured. Franklin assigned them the job of hauling *Lion* on its wheeled truck and made the haul with them, partly to make sure *Lion* came to no harm and partly to make sure they did themselves no further damage. At the end of the portage, the Company's pemmican bateau was dismantled and, along with its oars, was stowed safely at the southern end of the portage for the convenience of the next party of traders heading south and east. At the northern end of the portage, another boat was waiting to carry the pemmican on to Fort Chipewyan.³⁸

Franklin and Richardson, with a small crew, went ahead in the light canoe on July 12 and pulled into Fort Chipewyan on July 15. The heavily burdened boats caught up three days later, and Franklin declared a day off for the crews. The holiday turned into a grand occasion when a party of Yellowknives arrived, "very opportunely," with fresh meat. A feast was immediately arranged, and the guests who spent the day examining the expedition boats had a lot to say about the decorative real and mythical animals painted on them.[39] Although he could not understand their comments, Franklin thought that "judging from the bursts of laughter, some curious remarks were made on them." The expedition commander took equal pleasure in examining the "elegantly shaped" Athapascan canoes. On the twentieth, Richardson took command of the three expedition boats and went ahead to Lake Athabasca.[40]

GEORGE BACK AND EDWARD KENDALL ARRIVED SAFELY ON JULY 23. Franklin discharged a number of the Canadians, as their contracts specified, and gave them a canoe for the long voyage home. Paul Fraser, on loan from Chief Factor Leith, returned to his regular duties at Cumberland House at the same time. Franklin, Back, and Kendall embarked in light canoes after supper on July 25 and spent the long northern evening following the route taken earlier by the boats. By evening of the twenty-ninth they were at Fort Resolution. With no more portages between them and Great Bear Lake, the Canadian canoemen celebrated with a dance, causing Franklin to wonder at their stamina: "they had been paddling for thirty-six out of the thirty-nine preceding hours, [but] kept up their favourite amusement until daylight, to the music of bagpipes," played by George Wilson, one of the marines, "relieved occasionally by the Jews' harp." The officers passed up the revelry in order to settle themselves "once more under the roof of our hospitable friend, Mr Robert McVicar."[41]

Other old friends were also at Fort Resolution to greet them, although not Akaitcho, who was hunting so he could present the expedition with a full pantry when it arrived, which he was sure could not be before the middle of August. Akaitcho's older brother, Keskarrah, was there, however, along with

Humpy, the third brother. Keskarrah filled in some of the details of a recent, deadly war between the Yellowknives and the Dogribs and confirmed that many of the hunters who had been at Fort Enterprise during the first expedition were dead. Keskarrah repeated what Akaitcho had told Dease: "We will not go to those parts where the bones of our murdered brethren lie." Franklin gave the Yellowknife leaders liberal presents, as well as a silver royal medal to be delivered to Akaitcho.[42]

The last expedition brigade to reach Fort Simpson was welcomed by Chief Factor Edward Smith on the evening of August 4. Smith had worrisome news. The Inuit who occupied the Mackenzie River Delta were as yet unaware that a party of substantial size, consisting entirely of armed men, intended to visit their country within a few weeks. More cheerful news was that construction was well underway on the necessary buildings and that Dease had hired local hunters to stock the headquarters' pantries.[43]

At Fort Norman, HBC clerk Charles Brisbois noted in the post journal that an unusual influx of travellers had appeared on his doorstep: "Ce matin...á dix ou onze, M. Capitaine Franklin accompangie de deus officiers dans deux canots sont arrive. Les hommes sont en nombre quarante-deux, tout Canadiens... [et] Anglais."[44]

With Charles Brisbois, Franklin found Augustine, the large boat *Lion*, and a crew of six English mariners, left there by Richardson when he passed through on his way to the winter headquarters. Franklin's basic plan, endorsed by the Admiralty, was to map the Arctic coast both west and east of the Mackenzie River, which meant there had to be two exploration parties in the summer of 1826. "Being now only four days' journey from Bear lake, and there remaining yet five or six weeks of open season," wrote Franklin, "I resolved on following up a plan of a voyage to the sea, which I had cherished ever since leaving England, without imparting it to my companions, until our departure from Fort Chipewyan."

The first part of the plan was for Franklin, with Admiralty Mate Kendall and Augustine, to follow the Mackenzie to the sea, gathering as much information as possible from their own observations and from whatever the Loucheux could tell them of ice conditions and the availability of food resources during the summer and autumn months. The second part, suggested by Dr. Richardson, was that he himself and a small work crew would familiarize themselves with the countryside and identify a well-wooded site at the northeasternmost part of the lake where men from the winter quarters, fully provisioned, would wait for Richardson's party to return from the Coppermine River in 1826 and see that they got safely back to headquarters. The third part of the plan was for George Back to supervise the men and events at the wintering quarters and, with the assistance of Dease, establish a fishing station and hire local hunters. "Accordingly," wrote Franklin, "Dr Richardson, on his quitting this place two days previous to our arrival, had left the largest of the boats, the *Lion*, for my use, and a well-selected crew of six Englishmen, and Augustus."[45]

THE NORTHWARD-BOUND PARTY LEFT FORT NORMAN ON AUGUST 8. At the entrance to Bear Lake River, George Back—with three canoes and one of the small boats, with crews numbering fifteen—headed upriver toward the wintering house, which none of them had yet seen. Franklin, with Augustine, Kendall, and a crew of six, continued north in *Lion* for a first look at the Mackenzie River Delta and the Arctic coast. Shortly past noon, they spotted a group of Hare on the beach and called them out for a visit. The Hare, after a brief hesitation, launched their canoes, bringing a supply of fresh venison to trade. Although Franklin gave them tobacco and ammunition in return, they seemed to take more delight in his boat, with its unfamiliar shape and gaudy decorations, than with the trade items. The expedition men returned the compliments by admiring the Hare canoes.[46]

Late on August 10, the reconnaissance party completed the last of the 312 miles between Fort Norman and Fort Good Hope and knocked on the door of Post Master Charles Dease, causing "great astonishment to the few inmates of this dreary dwelling." Poor Dease took a few minutes to recover from his surprise, by which time his visitors had found seats for themselves. Pulling himself together, Dease "put everyone in motion" to prepare a meal for the hungry explorers, who thoroughly enjoyed the midnight snack, not having eaten since "eight in the morning." The conversation eventually turned to the state of relations between the Loucheux people and the Inuit living just to the north of them. Franklin and Augustine were relieved to hear that the two nations, formerly bitter enemies, had lately met to make a peace agreement.[47]

On leaving Fort Good Hope the following morning, the expedition was accompanied by Baptiste, Charles Dease's Loucheux interpreter. Late in the day, the party came upon a village, where, Baptiste warned, there was much sickness. To avoid "the hazard of contagion" from too close contact, Franklin did not put ashore, but the Loucheux had already heard the news that an Inuit from far to the east was soon to arrive in their country. They launched their canoes and followed the boat to have a look at Augustine, "the principal object of attraction." One after the other, the Loucheux canoes pressed up to the boat so that every man could shake Augustine's hand. Two of them, who knew some words of Inuktitut, managed to convey the welcome information that the Inuit at the mouth of the river, "though they were a treacherous people," would meet them without violence as long as Augustine was with them. Five miles past the village, the expedition put ashore for supper and then returned to the boat to sleep—all, that is, except Augustine, who "spread his blankets on the beach before the fire, and allowed four of the Loucheux, who had followed us from the tents, to share them with him."[48]

A meeting with the people of another Loucheux village the next day was less friendly. The villagers were apprehensive—the women and children ran to hide, and the men stood "in a state of defence, evidently with much distrust"—until one adventurous youth paddled toward them and "discovered Augustus, whom he knew by his countenance to be an Esquimaux." At that the Loucheux youth "threw up his hands for joy" and called his companions to come at once. The villagers made a great display of removing the iron heads and barbs from their arrows in a gesture of friendship and "each person that had a gun discharging its contents." Franklin ordered a landing for breakfast, during which Baptiste found the local dialect impossible to understand. The Loucheux switched to a simplified version of Inuktitut, which Augustine, "with difficulty," made out. Although Franklin and Kendall were gaudily dressed in their expedition uniforms and handing out presents to everyone, Augustine was the centre of attention. The Loucheux "caressed" him and "danced and played around him." Franklin noted that he and Kendall "could not help admiring the demeanour of our excellent little companion under such unusual and extravagant marks of attention," while Augustine refused to be distracted from his usual chore of preparing the officers' breakfasts. When he was ready for his own breakfast, he divided it scrupulously among his admirers.[49]

Just before ten o'clock on the sixteenth, *Lion* reached salt water and was pulled onto the beach of a small island, which Franklin named Garry Island. Franklin and Kendall hurried to clamber to the "most elevated part of the island, about two hundred and fifty feet high," while there was still light from the setting sun and to the north saw "the sea...in all its majesty, entirely free from ice." On the beach, where the men had already set up the tent and were preparing supper, Franklin took from his luggage the silk Union Jack his wife had made as her parting gift "under the express injunction that it was not to be unfurled before the Expedition reached the sea." Eleanor Anne Franklin's flag was hoisted, and spirits were handed round to three cheers for King George and a toast to the success of the expedition.[50]

As Franklin was struggling to put his personal feelings aside, a muddle created by the unwilling passenger, Baptiste, relieved the tension. In his excitement at actually reaching the northern ocean, Baptiste "stuck his feathers in his hat," declared himself one of the "*Gens de la mer*," and in great excitement brought Franklin and Kendall a cup of water to dilute their brandy. What he set before them, however, proved to be salt water, which they added to their "intended draught" before the mistake was noticed. Their toast was made "in the more classical form" by being poured upon the ground. Tests of the streams pouring down the cliffs of Garry Island showed them all to be as salty as the sea, and it was only after considerable searching that the ever-practical Augustine discovered a small lake of potable water.[51]

For two days, the explorers surveyed and charted the several mouths of the river, identifying channels best suited for departures to both east and west. On

August 18 they started back up the river, pausing at each of the empty Inuit villages to leave presents—kettles, knives, hatchets, files, ice chisels, beads, and pieces of red and blue cloth. As they ascended the river the weather turned colder, with daytime temperatures between 37° and 40° Fahrenheit, and low enough at night to freeze the water in their kettles. Thick, wet fog gave way to snow and sleet, and strong northwest winds pushed *Lion* at a rapid pace before turning contrary from the southeast and obliging the party to attach tow lines and haul the boat. One by one they passed the Loucheux lodges they had visited earlier. Through Baptiste, they learned that most of the people believed the explorers had met their deaths at the hands of the Inuit and had reported the dire news to Charles Dease at Fort Good Hope. Another week, Franklin thought, and the story "would have gained entire credence, and, in all probability, spread throughout the country."[52]

Charles Dease, more than half convinced by the rumours, was relieved to see them alive and well. True to his promise to get in a supply of provisions for the next summer's voyage, he had, during their absence, emptied one of his outbuildings and stowed the expedition's five bags of pemmican and some extra stores. For four days after leaving Fort Good Hope, ascent of the river was possible only by tracking, and the men began to suffer from dysentery, which Franklin believed was "brought on by previous fatigue, exposure to wet, and by their having lived for some time on dried provision."[53]

On the fifth day after leaving Dease's post, Augustine, "being tired of tracking," in Franklin's words, wandered away to explore a large sandbank just downstream from the upper rapids, both of which had been barely visible in the high-water conditions of the descent. Now, with rapids boiling on either side of the exposed shoal, Augustine suddenly found himself stranded. With darkness coming on and the boat out of reach at the top of the rapids, he waded as far as a pile of driftwood projecting from the sandbar. The watchers in the boat recognized the impossibility of getting to him but spotted the smoke of a fire on the riverbank and rowed toward it hoping to borrow a canoe to effect a rescue, all the while gesturing to Augustine to return to the sandbar. To the men's disappointment, only one old woman occupied the small campsite, and she did not have a canoe. Admiralty Mate Kendall took matters into his own hands, ordering his commander and most of the oarsmen out of the boat, throwing the cargo on shore, running *Lion* with the current to the upstream edge of the sandbank, striking ground twice on the way, and managing to get the incorrigible wanderer on board. Having proved his excellent seamanship, Kendall brought the boat through the "whirling" current to safety.[54]

In his *Narrative of a Second Expedition*, Franklin expressed sympathy for "the poor fellow"—that is, Augustine—but in his private journal he recorded sterner feelings: "I was rejoiced to see them returning, and not displeased when Augustus was once more among us, that he had received such a lesson as to the impropriety of straying away from the party." Augustine's tendency to wander had caused his companions considerable concern on more than one occasion, and it was, of course, this same kind of "impropriety" that had led to the disappearance and probable death of Junius on the barren lands during the first expedition. Augustine remained calm through the whole affair. As he explained to Franklin, he had seen the fire on the riverbank and was not "as we supposed under any apprehension that we intended to leave him, when he saw the boat pull from him."[55]

Lion's ascent of Bear Lake River on September 2 was marred by an accident in a fifteen-mile stretch of rapids. The boat had to be emptied of its cargo and its crew, except for two steersmen and a bailer, while it was being towed through the rapids. As the men were hauling around a rock point, the tow line broke, and *Lion* was carried some distance from shore into deep water and smashed into a large rock. The men on the riverbank watched as the boat's broadside was exposed to the current and smashed again and again into the great rock. Gustavus Aird waded into the near-freezing water, managed to catch a tow line thrown from the boat, and got back to the riverbank. When *Lion* was pulled to safety, part of its keel was gone and the lowest planks were loose. Thomas Fuller spent a day making what repairs he could with the materials at hand, and by nightfall the boat was ready to launch.[56]

The next day's tow path was both "tedious" and "hazardous," with the narrow ledge at the base of a steep cliff slippery from the night's rain. Augustine and two local boys went ahead by land to let the party at the House know of their arrival. At daylight on September 5, after a few hours of sleep in "raw fog...very cold and comfortless," they started again, bailing steadily to keep the wounded vessel afloat through the last of the river ascent and into Great Bear Lake. At seven in the evening, they reached the House. All expedition members were now together for the first time and spent most of the night bringing one another up to date on their various adventures.[57]

CONSTRUCTION OF THE WINTER QUARTERS HAD BEGUN THE PREVIous July with the arrival of Peter Warren Dease, his wife, and their four children, along with fifteen Canadians, four Chipewyan hunters, and the Chipewyan interpreter François Beaulieu, believed to be a brother-in-law of Akaitcho, the Yellowknife leader. In choosing a building site, Dease gave priority to food resources rather than easy access to wood for building and for fuel. He opted to build on the site of a long abandoned North West Company fort on a clifftop about twenty-five feet above Great Bear Lake. Just below was a reliable fishery that would be the expedition's chief source of food during two winters. To supplement the fish diet, Dease hired Dogrib hunters to start building up a supply of dried meat for winter use and sent messengers to tell the Hare community that a small fort was being built on the site of the old NWC post, and any meat they might bring for sale during the fall and winter months would be welcome.[58]

By the time Franklin and his northern recon party arrived, Dease had built an officers' house, measuring forty-four feet by twenty-four, with internal partitions that created a central hall, four bedrooms, and a kitchen. It was flanked by the men's three-room thirty-six-by-twenty-three-foot house on one side and François Beaulieu's house and a storage shed on the other, forming three sides of a square. The whole was surrounded by the stockading of the original fort. In the next weeks, Dease and his builders added a smithy and a meat store. The compound faced south and was to some degree sheltered from the north winds by a hill half a mile or so distant. Richardson and Back had already named their new home Fort Franklin, and the expedition leader "felt a grateful pleasure in retaining their desire," though his own choice had been Fort Reliance. Completion of the last building was celebrated on September 23 with the hoisting and salute to the flag, followed by a parade around the compound to the music of the bagpipes played by the marine George Wilson. The day ended with a dance in the hall with fiddle and bagpipes, which did not end till the sun came up at around five thirty the next morning.[59]

Fifty people were more or less permanent residents of Fort Franklin: four Royal Navy officers; nineteen British seamen, marines, and labourers; nine Canadian voyageurs; two Inuit interpreters; François Beaulieu, his wife, and their two children; Peter Warren Dease, his wife, Elizabeth Chouinard Dease, and their four children; four Chipewyan hunters; one unattached local woman; and one lad. In addition, there were "a few infirm Indians, who required temporary support." In spite of Dease's care in choosing to build close to the lake, it was immediately obvious that a single fishery could not supply that many mouths. To remedy the lack, he set up two more fisheries, at four miles and seven miles from the fort, and dispatched twenty people to live at them from time to time.[60]

At the end of September a heavy snowfall announced the change of seasons. A delegation of Dogribs brought in "the produce of their autumnal hunt, which was very inconsiderable," Franklin wrote, but he was happy to see them anyway because they "rendered a good service to us by taking away with them several of their relations, who had been subsisting on our bounty for some time." Dr. Richardson kept one family at the fort in a leather isolation tent, having diagnosed the husband with rheumatic fever. The only interruption to a quiet life at Fort Franklin was the arrival on October 14 of couriers from Fort Norman bringing letters and the welcome news that Thomas Matthews—by now able to walk, although with difficulty—had reached Fort Norman in the last canoe brigade from the south.[61]

Productive occupation to ensure healthy bodies and healthy minds was the order of the day at Fort Franklin during the winter of 1825–26. Occasional recreations were encouraged, and sometimes even ordered, for the sake of the men's emotional well-being. The men's spiritual needs were met at Divine

Service twice every Sunday, in the morning according to the Church of England liturgy and in the evening in the Scottish tradition of prayers and hymns. All meals were prefaced by a short blessing by one of the officers. The men's intellectual needs were met by two hours of "school" three days a week when the officers gave instructions in reading, writing, and arithmetic. On evenings when there was no school, the men had the run of the officers' hall "to play any game they might choose" and were often joined by the officers. "The officers made thermometrical, magnetical, and atmospherical observations at hourly intervals from eight in the morning to midnight." They each also had a particular responsibility and an avocation to pursue: George Back supervised the men and worked on his drawings; John Richardson held daily medical clinics, undertook geological surveys, and collected animal, mineral, and vegetable specimens, all of which had to be written up; John Franklin recalculated navigational observations; and Edward Kendall drew up charts and maps based on them and experimented with sound velocity. Peter Warren Dease maintained the physical plant, found and issued provisions, and took charge of everything having to do with the Canadians and Yellowknives. Pascal Coté, one of the Canadians, supervised the main fishery and, for the next several months, managed a daily yield of between three hundred and eight hundred salmon, as well as a few trout, carp, and tittameg.[62]

Four Dogrib men, hired to hunt, proved inadequate to the job, and Augustine and Ullebuk, also assigned to hunting, were no better "from not being accustomed to hunt in a woody country," said Franklin. Providing wood for fuel required three teams of workers: one to cut down the trees, one to haul the logs home, and a third to split and stack them. Another team of labourers had the job of picking up meat when the hunters were successful. Two men most efficient on snowshoes were constantly on the trail to and from the Mackenzie River posts to pick up supplies and deliver letters.[63]

A great storm on the night of October 20–21 put an end to the skating and games but deposited enough snow for winter travel by sledge. The wood haulers found their work easier when they could use sledges to bring in firewood and the cut timbers Thomas Fuller needed for building a new boat. When

Fuller could spare a sledge, the work detail hitched up the dogs and picked up fifteen caribou carcasses from the caches in a single trip. As soon as a sled and team were free on November 9, the couriers mushed away to Fort Norman and returned on the eighteenth with Thomas Matthews, still on crutches and unable to walk any distance, but growing stronger and happy to be reunited with his mates.[64]

In sharp contrast to the Fort Enterprise experience, there was food enough and to spare. Besides the caribou meat brought now and then by the hunters, the records for the main fishery show a total of 17,370 "salmon herring" and 1,843 trout netted between July and October. If the catches from the two auxiliary fisheries had been included, the number would have been well over 25,000 in these two species alone. When an old man and woman from Fort Norman, where provisions were scarce, came for a long visit, the officers who remembered starving at Winter Lake were happy to share with them. Another cause for satisfaction came on December 20 with couriers from Fort Good Hope. The letter they brought from Charles Dease, ultimately of great interest to Augustine, advised that word had come from the Loucheux that they had seen the Mackenzie River Inuit. The Inuit had found the presents left for them by the reconnaissance party and were ready to welcome the white people when they came again in the spring.[65]

Hungry for light in dark mid-winter days—daylight lasted no more than about three and half hours—officers and men planned Christmas festivities with brightness in mind. In preparation for a party to which all the local people had been invited, the men replastered the entire officers' house and whitewashed and repainted all the rooms. Lieutenant Back decorated the walls with paintings of deer heads, flags, and a crown and anchor, while Matthews, still not up to strenuous outdoor work, made a cut paper chandelier and a variety of paper ornaments.[66]

When the hunters, with their wives and children, arrived at the hall on Christmas Eve, it was to a game of snapdragon, which was "to them an entire novelty." No doubt! The game, also known as flapdragon, involved snatching raisins from a bowl of blazing brandy in an otherwise darkened room and tossing them into one's mouth still aflame. "It would be as difficult to describe the delight which the sport afforded them after they recovered their first surprise, as to convey the full effect of the scene," wrote Franklin. "When the candles were extinguished, the blue flame of the burning spirits shone [on our companions], in whose countenances were portrayed the eager desire of possessing the fruit, and the fear of the penalty."[67]

Christmas Day itself was quiet. Because it fell on a Sunday, celebrations were limited to a feast. The usual Christmas dance took place the following day. Sixty people entered into a great community sing-along in English, Gaelic, and French, joining in flings and reels to the music of a fiddle, Wilson's bagpipes, and the Jew's harps owned by most of the men. New Year's Day celebrations were limited to a general round of congratulations and best wishes, followed by Divine Service. On January 2, the new year was welcomed in by "similar festivities...to those at Christmas."[68]

AS THE NEW YEAR, 1826, BEGAN, THE MAIN TOPIC OF CONVERSATION at Fort Franklin was the mystery of the vanishing fish. A small team of dogs that had been trained to haul each day's catch from the fishery to the house without a driver was starting its trek with a full sled and arriving with a diminished load. Augustine and Ullebuk spent four cold January days hunting down the culprit, a fish-stealing she-wolf who had become adept at helping herself from the sledge. The she-wolf was bold to the point of stopping to kill a fox in full sight of the two Inuit stalking it. On the fifth day, an exasperated Augustine set his gun in the snow and shot the thief as she tracked the fish sled.[69]

February was the most anxious period of the winter. A considerable drop in the number of fish taken daily put the establishment on short rations. Dease sent three dog trains to Fort Norman to retrieve some of the pemmican, arrowroot, and portable soup set aside for the northern voyage.[70]

In the lengthening days of March, the expedition officers and men became more active and spent longer periods outdoors. Richardson hiked north to check out some interesting geological formations in mid-March and was gone two days. Franklin and Back together made an excursion of nine miles out and nine miles back just to enjoy the view from the highest hill in the neighbourhood. William Duncan and the blacksmith discovered that the local trees did not produce coal cinders when fired and made a trip to Fort Norman to produce charcoal clinkers from the plentiful birch trees there. On April 10, Kendall and Richardson set off on snowshoes to complete the survey of Great Bear Lake, covering 380 miles in three weeks.[71]

On May 23, the ice had broken away from the shore below the House, after being solidly frozen for eight months less three days, and on the twenty-fourth, the mosquitoes appeared as if on cue, "feeble at first, but, after a few days... vigorous and tormenting." Thomas Matthews, with his leg strong once more, worked with Thomas Fuller to complete a new boat by May 24. It was similar to *Lion* in construction but with a fuller bow, twenty-six feet long and five feet eight inches in breadth. The boat carpenters substituted strips of Mackintosh's waterproof canvas for tar and made their own paint from pine resin and grease. In christening the new boat, Franklin was finally able to use the name he had originally intended for the fort, *Reliance*. The other three boats were in need of considerable repairs, *Lion* as a result of the accident in Bear Lake River, and *Union* and *Dolphin*, which were showing signs of sponginess from having been repaired with elm wood at Cumberland House. The carpenters set them to rights by replacing all the elm with white spruce. Trials on Great Bear Lake confirmed that all boats were seaworthy and ready to go.[72]

AT THE BEGINNING OF JUNE, PREPARATIONS FOR THE NORTHERN explorations were complete. Franklin handed command of Fort Franklin over to Peter Warren Dease with a reminder of the procedure to be followed to support Richardson's returning eastern detachment after August 6. Franklin's longer-term orders were for Dease and his men to keep the fort well maintained, provisioned, and inhabited until the spring of 1828 in case the western party— Franklin, Back, and Augustine, with their crews—had to spend two winters on the Arctic coast. With the fort in Dease's capable hands, and arrangements for the relief of Richardson's eastern detachment clearly understood by Beaulieu and the Canadians, the expedition was ready to head north.[73]

The officers issued the men their sky-blue waterproof uniforms, feathers, and warm clothing and assigned them places in the boats. A week before the planned departure date, all hands readied the boats and packed them with extra bedding, provisions, navigational equipment, and presents for the Inuit. In the evening they gathered together for a tot of rum and a "merry dance in which all joined with great glee in their working dresses." On the following Sunday, June 18, officers and men assembled for Divine Service in their new uniforms and prayed for "the special protection of Providence...on the enterprise." They spent Monday cleaning their guns and stowing them in the arms chests, specially made to fit the boats, and on Tuesday and Wednesday they packed clothes and toiletries for the voyage and crated the personal possessions they were leaving at Fort Franklin to await their return, or to be sent on to their families if there was no return. Late Wednesday evening, June 21, the men pushed off in the boats, while the officers finished packing charts, drawings, and other documents to be left at the fort. The next morning, accompanied by Peter Warren Dease, they left in canoes to catch up with the boats. "Old Coté," a local fisherman, remained alone to await Dease's return from Fort Norman.[74]

CHAPTER 7

JOURNEY TO THE POLAR SEA
1826–1827

NO ONE AMONG THE EXPEDITION EXPECTED TO FIND large masses of churning ice flowing from Great Bear Lake into Great Bear River in late June. But the fact was, as Franklin noted, that the ice was moving "with such rapidity as to render embarkation unsafe." A delay where the lake spilled into the river was one of a very few circumstances the officers had not prepared for. The boats carried adequate rations for "an uninterrupted passage" to Fort Norman, where a new supply of provisions awaited them, but nothing beyond that. Franklin had to send couriers back to the winter quarters for provisions to get them through two days of anxious waiting.[1]

When open water appeared around breaking ice on the morning of the June 24, the HBC bateau, stowed with the heavy stores, began the descent from Great Bear Lake. The four expedition boats followed at a safe distance. Twelve hours later the small fleet entered the Mackenzie River, and the men began the brutal work of tracking upstream through riverbanks liquefied by melting ice, up to their knees in slippery mud at every step. Exhausting as the going was, the worst problem of the day was the "ceaseless torment of the musquitoes." Darkness, falling about half an hour before midnight and lasting a mere hour and a half, brought no relief. Twenty-eight hours after leaving Great Bear Lake, at noon on the twenty-fifth, they reached Fort Norman.[2]

Much work remained to be done. The first job was checking the condition of all provisions and equipment stored in the fort's warehouses, including the ironwork, knives, and beads intended as gifts for the Inuit. The oarsmen spent a day making pemmican, while the naval men made a large foresail for *Reliance*. Finally, on June 27, five vessels—*Lion, Reliance, Dolphin, Union*, and the HBC bateau—with ensigns and pennants flying, pulled away from the beach amid the cheers and waves of Peter Warren Dease, the Canadian rivermen, and HBC trader Charles Brisbois.[3]

A favourable current and a perfect wind moved the party downriver at a good pace through the short summer night. By full light they had reached the sandbank, now six feet under water, where Augustine had been stranded during the return of the reconnaissance crew the previous fall. On July 1, they were at Fort Good Hope, where the new Post Master, John Bell, was busy trading with a party of Loucheux.[4]

Franklin and Augustine were eager to meet the two Loucheux who had been hired as interpreters, but the meeting was disappointing. Augustine quickly found out that the two guides spoke the Inuit language so imperfectly as to be almost unintelligible. Questioning others among the visitors, Augustine learned that the Loucheux had recently been at a trade meeting with "sixty canoes" of Inuit at (Mackenzie's) Red River,[5] a number considerably higher than anyone had thought possible. When he probed for details, the Loucheux told him about a serious quarrel that had broken out between the two groups.[6] Augustine advised the officers that the appearance of Loucheux in Inuit territory could spark a new confrontation, and they paid off the two hired guides. Franklin ordered his men to check that their firearms were in good working order, "just in case," and added to the stock of gifts set aside for the Inuit. Augustine also alerted the officers that among the goods the Loucheux had traded from the delta Inuit were five large knives, one of them with handle inlays in brass and copper. Careful examination indicated that they were of German manufacture and could only have come from the West, where the Russian American Company had regular contacts with native Alaskans.[7]

The first day back on the river, they camped at the edge of Inuit territory. The following morning, July 3, the officers checked again that each man had a dagger, a gun, and ammunition, because, as Franklin wrote, "vigilance and precaution are never to be omitted in intercourse with strange tribes." A few hours' rowing in the afternoon brought them to the fork of the eastern and western channels, where they stopped to camp for the last time before the two parties separated. Provisions carried by the HBC bateau were redistributed—bags of pemmican, arrowroot, macaroni, flour, and portable soup for each boat, sufficient for eighty days at full rations and for a hundred days at two-thirds rations. The bateau was stowed on the west bank of the river along with several bags of pemmican in case the western detachment had to return to Fort Franklin for another winter.[8]

The two detachments spent their last evening together "in the most cordial and cheerful manner." The cooks set out "the best supper our means afforded" and "a bowl of punch crowned the parting feast," all to the lively sounds of George Wilson's bagpipes. One final auspicious event occurred before bedtime. An elderly Loucheux man presented himself at the campsite and was able to give a better account of the routes to the sea through the eastern and western channels than they had previously heard.[9]

At six o'clock on the morning of July 4, the boats were ready. The western party left first, at Richardson's suggestion, and pulled away to the sound of hearty cheers from the eastward-bound boats. Franklin, in *Lion*, sat facing toward the unknown ocean, with his thoughts on the many differences between this expedition and the disastrous 1822 exploration. "Instead of a frail bark canoe and a scanty supply of food," he wrote, "we were now about to commence the sea voyage in excellent boats, stored with three months' provisions." Augustine positioned himself to keep the other boats in view as long as possible. Franklin thought his interpreter was feeling "low" due to "his parting with Ullebuk his only Countryman and about to proceed he knew not whither."[10]

THE EASTERN DETACHMENT UNDER THE COMMAND OF DR. JOHN Richardson headed upriver in search of a passage to the east. Two hours at the oars fighting a strong current brought *Dolphin* and *Union* to the entrance of the Middle Channel, where they turned and worked their way downstream to an east-flowing branch that Richardson thought would take them to the sea. As they settled down for the first night, they established a routine to be followed at every campsite thereafter: Richardson and Kendall took astronomical readings, the men unloaded the boats and set up the tents, all firearms were checked, and a night watch was set to prevent visitors coming upon them undetected. Richardson announced a new daily schedule: the breakfast stop was to be at noon each day, "in order to economize time, as it was necessary to land [at noon anyway] to obtain the meridian observation of sun."[11]

For four days *Dolphin* and *Union* moved slowly toward the sea, while the crews looked for signs of recent Inuit occupation. At the second night's campsite, Richardson created a lobstick by hanging "a small kettle, a hatchet, an ice-chisel, and a few strings of beads" on the branch stubs. Admiralty Mate Kendall prepared a message in hieroglyphs to be left with the trade goods, showing twelve men—two in naval uniform, one in a traditional Inuit parka, and nine in voyageurs' work clothes with backpacks—facing five people in Inuit clothing across a body of water on which floated two boats. Between the two groups of people, superimposed on water symbols, were pictures of a kettle, a hatchet, and a string of beads.[12]

Early on the morning of July 7, they found the first inhabited Inuit camp—four or five tents and several kayaks and umiaks. Richardson and Ullebuk had already worked out a procedure to be followed in all contact situations. Only the two of them were to go ashore, Kendall was to remain with the boats, ready for any eventuality, and the men were to ensure their muskets were loaded and handy but out of sight. They had almost no time to take in the sight of the Inuit village before two women on shore spotted the boats and raised the alarm, at which the men of the community rushed out of the tents, bows and arrows in hand. Ullebuk and Richardson both called out to them and stepped onto the beach holding some files, knives, and strings of beads at arm's length in front of them, at which the men stopped, put their bows aside and tucked their knives up their sleeves. An old woman, catching on quickly, picked up some dried fish and handed it to the doctor, who gave her a string of beads in exchange. As more people emerged from the tents, trading became brisk, until Ullebuk and Richardson ran out of goods, a circumstance that did not sit well with their hosts. They became noisier and began to make threatening gestures. Ullebuk reacted by picking the doctor up, piggyback-style, and heading back to the boats, muttering about "very bad people." Richardson named the place Point Encounter.[13]

The men of the community, twenty-one in all, followed in their kayaks as the expedition boats pulled away, and within fifteen minutes, the women had taken down their tents, packed children, dogs, and luggage into umiaks, and were in pursuit. When they caught up, they surrounded *Dolphin* and *Union*, and the whole became a floating market, as beads, fire-steels, flints, files, knives, hatchets, and kettles were exchanged for fish, spears, and arrows.[14]

Ullebuk found himself translating several conversations at once. First, the Inuit wanted to know the name of every person in the boats. With their curiosity on that important point satisfied, they insisted on examining the construction of the boats and inquired about the use of everything they saw within them. Ullebuk caused some excitement when he lit his pipe and started puffing smoke from his mouth. His audience seemed satisfied with his less than enlightening explanation: "*Poo-yoo-al-letchee-raw-mah* [*pujuletsirama*], I'm smoking a pipe." They questioned the purpose of the small book of Inuktitut vocabulary that Richardson took out of his pocket. Ullebuk told them the book "spoke" to the doctor, at which they asked him to put it away. They understood at once what the telescope was for and identified it as "*eetee-yawgah* [*itiviga*]" ("far eyes"). Richardson noted that Ullebuk had no trouble communicating with them, in a dialect that Ullebuk said was similar to the dialect of his own people.[15]

Over the course of the morning, *Dolphin* and *Union* passed several more camps. At each, the occupants "embarked bag and baggage" and followed the expedition boats as they headed toward the sea. The followers, numbering at least forty kayaks, became bolder, pulling their kayaks to the sides of the boats and slipping under the raised oars to reach the bales and packages. "One fellow would lay hold of the boat with both his hands," wrote Richardson, "and while the coxswain and I were disengaging them, his comrade on the other side would make the best use of his time in transferring some of our property into his canoe." The doctor resolved the problem, but only temporarily, with humour. Whenever some item was removed, he put on a jolly face and demanded that the culprit return it at once, which they always did "with the most perfect good humour." The doctor joined them in their hearty laughter. His goal in turning it all into a joke was to gain "the natives by kindness and forbearance, the more especially as our ignorance of the state of the ice rendered it doubtful whether we might not be under the necessity of encamping for some time in their neighbourhood."[16]

By "breakfast time"—noon on Richardson's revised daily schedule—the crews were tiring and "faint from want of food." A stop was imperative, unwilling as the officers were to go ashore while so many people remained deeply interested in the contents of the boats. But stop they did, close to a high riverbank, and "breakfasted in the boats," while their followers watched from the middle of the channel.[17]

After their meal, Richardson looked for a deep-water passage through the dozens of small islands and accepted the Inuit's offer of guidance. "But," he wrote, "whether by accident or design, they led us...into a shallow channel, where we grounded on a sand-bank." For an hour, with "much difficulty," they pushed against the current to get back to where they had started. Before the men had time to catch their breath, *Dolphin* was under assault. Three kayaks pulled up close to the boat, their owners laid their paddles across its gunwales to form a platform, and a fourth jumped to the improvised gangway. "The dexterity with which he leaped from his kaiyack was remarkable," wrote Richardson. "He ran with velocity and sprang upon the stern seat," and was "immediately tumbled out again." The doctor came up with another stratagem for defusing the situation. He asked if he could buy their bows, and when the men of the little convoy understood that he would not trade for anything else, they handed over their "most powerful weapons."[18]

For the rest of the afternoon, the kayakers demonstrated their seamanship, delighted when they outpaced and outmanoeuvred the boats. The women's umiaks went ahead as evening approached, and Richardson and Kendall, thinking they had chosen the best route, followed them. It was a mistake; the new channel was too shallow. The last of the sandbanks neatly grounded *Union*. Seizing the moment, seven or eight of the escorting Inuit jumped into the water, grabbed *Union*'s bow, and started dragging it ashore, while more than thirty other kayaks stood a few yards off. Richardson gave Kendall permission to fire "if necessary." Kendall stood and pointed his fowling-piece directly at three of the assailants who had hold of the sweep-oar. His crew, in the water trying to budge their boat, jumped back on board, and snatched up their muskets. "Happily," Richardson wrote, there was no need to fire a shot; the Inuit were fully aware of what firearms could do, having seen them used by their Athapascan neighbours.[19]

Union broke free when a fresh breeze sprang up and, under a raised sail, managed to get away. Some time after midnight, the crews beached the boats in a small inlet, which they named Refuge Cove. Here they pitched a tent and lay down in their wet clothes, leaving Kendall and one crew member on *Union*, "to be ready in case of accident."[20]

The accident happened: *Union* broke loose. Kendall and his companion used their oars against the tide, and the rest of the party pushed off in *Dolphin* and effected a rescue. As the "benumbed" men, still in their wet clothes, tried to get some sleep, they were more thoroughly drenched by their tent falling in on them. Over the next hour or so they unloaded the boats, dried the cargo, drew the boats up on the beach, and used the baggage to create a three-sided breastwork as a retreat, in case the Inuit paid them "a hostile visit."[21]

Behind their makeshift bulwarks, they "slept quietly" until ten in the morning of June 8, or at least some of them did. The two officers were awake, dealing with a potentially fatal problem. Sometime during the night's ups and downs, Kendall had fallen against a tent pole, and the force of his fall had driven the sheathed knife he wore on a rope around his neck into his chest, "exactly in the region of the heart." Richardson, assuming his physician's role, determined that the point of the blade had been deflected by one of Kendall's ribs, which prevented any "fatal consequences," and over the course of the next few days, the wound healed.[22]

THE WESTERN DETACHMENT, AFTER LEAVING RICHARDSON'S PARTY, searched for a suitable channel to the sea. They were beyond the treeline well before noon on Wednesday, July 5, and on Friday the seventh paused at a sandbar that blocked their access to the sea. They stopped to lighten the boats, pulled across the barrier, and began reloading. Franklin hiked toward the river mouth and unexpectedly found himself near an island occupied by "a crowd of tents" and many Inuit.[23]

Withdrawing unseen, he gathered the men around him and explained that his reading of the "narratives of different navigators" had convinced him that in encounters with strangers most native groups mistook "noise and violent gestures for decided hostility." It was, therefore, imperative that the men sit quietly in the boats, with their firearms ready but on no account to be used unless he fired first or Lieutenant Back gave the order.[24]

With ensigns flying so as to give some advance warning of their approach, *Lion* and *Reliance* pulled up in mid-channel in sight of the village. Augustine thought it prudent that only he and Franklin go ashore together for the first encounter. Franklin agreed, but shallow water kept the boats about a mile from the beach and prevented a landing on foot. Some discreet beckoning on the part of Franklin and Augustine brought three kayaks into the water, then seven more, followed by even larger groups, as well as some umiaks, until the "whole space between the island and the boats was covered by them." The men's count reached seventy-three kayaks and five umiaks before they lost track as more and more skin boats were launched into the already crowded river channel. Three elderly men in kayaks drew up close to *Lion* and listened as Augustine assured them of the visitors' friendly intentions and explained the purpose of their visit.

Franklin noted with pleasure that they "testified their joy by tossing their hands aloft, and raising the most deafening shout of applause."[25]

Excitement was even greater after the presentation of gifts. Between 250 and 300 people pressed up to the boats and offered bows, arrows, and spears, which until then had been concealed inside their kayaks, in exchange for knives and other metal items. The advice they gave when Augustine inquired about the quickest route to the coast was loud and contradictory. Franklin and Back decided to turn the boats and pull away from the crowd, but luck and the river were against them. *Lion* went aground. The villagers, under the direction of two of the elderly "chiefs," came to the rescue. Or so it seemed. With the tide ebbing fast, the "helpers" managed to get both boats mired in the shoal. In the midst of the chaos, one of *Lion*'s oars flipped a kayak upside down and plunged its owner headfirst into the mud, where he appeared likely to drown. *Lion*'s crew pulled him to safety in the boat, and Augustine wrapped the shivering man in his own great coat. In the process, the man spotted the many bales in the bottom of the boat and called out to his countrymen to come and share in the treasures. Several of the younger men among them tried to do just that and began clambering aboard.[26]

Augustine appealed to the elderly "chiefs" to control their young men, which for a short period they seemed to do. *Reliance* broke free of the mud, but *Lion* could not be budged even when Back managed to rope the boats together and attempted a tow. As the tide went out, and the water sank below knee level, younger Inuit began wading out to the boats. The expedition men started to find their possessions in the wrong hands. Augustine's fire bag disappeared from his seat in the boat, as did William Duncan's. The man whose kayak had been upset was discovered to have Back's pistol tucked under his shirt and was still wearing Augustine's great coat when he jumped into the water and waded toward the beach. Another short, sharp speech from Augustine to the chiefs brought a second respite, followed almost immediately by a full-on attack.[27]

Several of the villagers brought their kayaks across the bows of the two expedition boats, blocking any possibility of forward movement. Snatching up the ropes Back had used in the attempt to tow *Lion*, they began pulling the boats toward the shore. As soon as both boats were mired in the tide flats, the whole of the community began a systematic pillaging of *Reliance*. Boarders stripped every article they could find out of the boats and handed them to the women, who scurried out of sight with them. Poor Alexis Vivier suffered the indignity of having his knife snatched out of its sheath and used to cut the buttons off his coat. An assault on Back's buttons was foiled by one young man who drove the assailants away, wrested from them a writing desk and a cloak they had snatched up, and seated himself on Back's knee, apparently with the intent of defending the lieutenant, or perhaps just the lieutenant's possessions.[28]

Augustine reacted to the assault on *Reliance* by leaping into the water and wading ashore, all the while shouting accusations of treachery at his out-of-control compatriots until he was hoarse. Hard on his heels, Franklin started to follow but was called back by Duncan when the excited pillagers formed a "bucket brigade" and began bearing away *Lion*'s cargo. *Lion*'s crew, still in their seats, concentrated on protecting the most important cargo—oars, masts, firearms, and navigational instruments.[29]

The struggle continued for several hours. When three of the Inuit tried to take Franklin's pistol and dagger, Back somehow persuaded his own protector, still sitting on his lap, to go to the commander's aid. Back's champion was successful in driving Franklin's attackers away, and the commander, on rising from his seat of imprisonment, saw, to his horror, that George Wilson at the front of the boat was about to fire his musket at one of the marauders. Just as Franklin reached his piper and forced the musket down, the attackers began to flee, taking cover behind the driftwood and kayaks piled on the beach. In the sudden calm, the beleaguered party realized that the tide had come in, *Reliance* was afloat, and Back had his men ranged with levelled muskets. In a few moments, *Lion* was also able to push off from the beach. A few Inuit, not yet ready to lose the source of so many precious goods, put their kayaks in the water and started to follow the retreating boats. Augustine put a stop to their plan by shouting out that the first man who came in range of a musket would be shot.[30]

Less than a quarter of a mile beyond the place the expedition men dubbed Pillage Point, the boats grounded again. The crews roped the boats together, side by side, and began to take inventory of their losses. As it turned out, the losses were not as great as they had feared. Canteens and kettles, one tent, a bale of blankets and shoes, one of the men's bags, and the jib-sails were missing. Except for the jib-sails and the personal baggage, most of the missing items had been intended as gifts anyway.[31]

Seven or eight men from the village, including the "young chief" who had protected Back, appeared on the beach shortly afterwards and invited Augustine to go ashore. Franklin reluctantly gave permission on Augustine's assurances that all would be well—and then regretted it as the numbers on the beach grew to around forty, even before Augustine had waded ashore. The watchers in the boats heard nothing but saw what seemed to be an animated conversation, with Augustine doing most of the talking. According to his subsequent report, Augustine first delivered a good scolding, shaming the delta people with the observation that no other Inuit had ever been known to act with such rudeness. He then warned that their conduct might well result in the white people refusing ever to come near them again, thus depriving them of many benefits. He also delivered an even more frightening warning: "It is entirely owing to their humanity that many of you were not killed today," he announced, "for they have all guns, with which they can destroy you either when near or at a distance. I also have a gun, and can assure you that if a white man had fallen, I would have been the first to have revenged his death."[32]

Greatly impressed by Augustine's courage in going ashore and haranguing forty armed men, Franklin suggested putting their sincerity to the test, calling out to Augustine to request the return of one of the large kettles and the tent. Augustine no sooner relayed the message than the items were handed over. Delivering them to the crews in the boats, Augustine asked permission to rejoin the people for a small celebration, during which he hoped to get some information about tides and an easy passage to the sea. Permission granted, he spent an hour "dancing and singing with all his might in the midst of a company who were all armed with knives, or bows and arrows." To Augustine's delight, the words of the songs and the steps of the dances were "precisely similar to those used in his own country when a friendly meeting took place with strangers." Slowly the celebrants on the beach went off to bed, and when only a few remained around the fire, two of *Lion*'s crew went ashore with the proper utensils "to prepare chocolate for the refreshment of the party." They, along with Augustine, were back in the boats before midnight, when, as Augustine had learned, the tide began to flow. An hour and a half later, around 1:30 a.m. on Saturday, July 8, both boats were in deep water. An approaching storm forced them to pull up on another beach and batten down.[33]

Secure in their new position and with two guards posted, the men, one by one, reported their experiences at Pillage Point. Only then did Franklin and Back learn that *Lion*'s bowman, Gustavus Aird, and three of the *Reliance* crew had narrowly escaped injury in a series of knife attacks that shredded their outer clothing. George Wilson revealed a slight scratch from a deflected knife. William Duncan, after several times rescuing the box with the astronomical instruments, had tied it to his leg, "determined that they should drag him away also if they took it."[34]

The thoroughly exhausted men got close to six hours' sleep after their twenty-five-hour day of fighting the river and the Inuit. Their first job on waking around noon on Saturday, July 8, was to repair the sails and rigging damaged in the fight. As they settled to work with their canvas and needles, "the whole body" of the Inuit fleet of kayaks and umiaks was seen paddling toward them. All hands set to work tossing the baggage into the boats and launching them through the surf to deep water. At that moment, the lead kayaks came up within speaking distance, and one of the paddlers held out a kettle, shouting to Augustine that he wanted to return it and that the umiak some distance behind carried the rest of the purloined items. The expedition party saw no reason to believe the story, and Augustine shouted to them to be off. When they continued to advance, Franklin pulled his pistol and shot ahead of the leading kayak, which had the desired effect.[35]

THE EASTERN DETACHMENT PULLED OUT OF REFUGE COVE AT NINE o'clock on the evening of July 8, the same day that the western detachment was battling the people of Pillage Point. By four the next morning, "a stream of ice" forced Richardson to order both boats to the beach to avoid being crushed. At the new landing, they were disappointed in finding fresh water that was "too hard to make tea" but grateful that there was plenty of driftwood for a fire. After a day's sleep, they had "an agreeable change of diet," dining on a caribou brought down by Ullebuk. Richardson read the Sunday prayers before the assembled company, and all but the watch slept again till nearly five on Monday morning.[36]

Richardson took a relaxed approach to their progress. When rough water made rowing especially difficult, he decided not to fatigue the crews, settling them in a sandy bay. High winds kept them at their moorage for two tedious days. On several occasions, the crews spotted Inuit watching them from a distance but contact with them was very low on Richardson's list of priorities, and he decided that the crews would stay in the boats offshore, land only to cook, and go ashore only in the company of one of the officers. The good news was that the bay was full of happy omens: the water was brackish, the beach was strewn with saltwater seaweed, and white whales sported themselves just to the north. To celebrate their progress toward the coast, Richardson handed out a glass of grog to each man.[37]

On the evening of July 12, two "elderly" Inuit came to visit. Their spokesman, "Eetkooyak" (*Itqujaq*, "sea urchin," Inuinnaqtun dialect), gladly accepted a present of ironwork, traded some dried fish for beads, and invited the crews to visit his tents the next day. The visitors had seen Ullebuk bring down a caribou with his awesome weapon a few days earlier, they said, and had made a quick trip to Point Encounter to find out who the men in the big boats were. The Point Encounter people had assured them that the strangers were "well-disposed." Of the attempt against *Union*, the local Inuit could only repeat that the people at the river mouth were "bad people" but they themselves were "good-hearted men."[38]

Early the next morning, Itqujaq was back with eight other men, the younger ones showing every sign that they wanted the strangers to be on their way. Richardson declined Itqujaq's repeated invitation to visit his tent, and the boats moved off. They anchored at an island around five o'clock, after an easy day at sea. A day later in heavy fog, Ullebuk spotted a long line of floating seaweed and announced that they were near the mouth of a river. By sounding their way with great care, they reached a "snug" harbour where they passed a peaceful night. At the oars again at three o'clock on the morning of the fifteenth, they rounded a small cape, stopped at a substantial piece of ice for their noon breakfast, and crossed the inlet that now lay before them to a larger cape, which they named Cape Dalhousie.[39]

The social isolation they had enjoyed for five days after leaving Itqujaq's band ended on the eighteenth. Just as the explorers sighted twelve tents on the beach, they were themselves spotted by a woman who gave the alarm. A dozen or more men rushed forth at her shouts, waving knives and calling out warnings not to land. The doctor tried an earlier stratagem, shouting "*noowoerlook* [*niuvirpuq*]" ("trades, buys, sells"), which had the desired effect. Soon eleven smiling men in kayaks surrounded the boats, and the usual trade items were being exchanged.[40]

While trading, the local people had, as usual, inquired about the names of their visitors and identified themselves one by one. Ullebuk reported that although they had heard about white people, they had never seen pale-skinned people before. When Richardson traded some caribou meat for fish, some of the men wanted to know how the white men had managed to kill the animal. Ullebuk showed them his gun, warned them not to be alarmed, and fired it into the distance. The report echoing from the floating ice made them think the ball had hit the shore more than a mile distant, and in a few minutes all of the escorting craft made a hasty departure.[41]

IN THE CALM THAT FOLLOWED, ULLEBUK HAD GOOD NEWS TO report. The recent visitors had confirmed that the shore on their right was the mainland and that they were very near a passage that led to the open sea. Getting the boats across a mud barrier and into the predicted passage required "much labour" at the oars, but the instant they were over the bar, the water was clear green, "perfectly salt," and, best of all, the white whales and a few large black ones they saw indicated that the water was of considerable depth.[42]

In the week after they escaped from the delta, July 18 to July 25, they found the coast to be a series of bays and inlets separated by headlands. Richardson named the first of the major headlands Cape Bathurst. Eastward from Cape Bathurst, the coastline "appeared to run in a straight direction for Coppermine River," causing considerable "joy" among the men. For three days they rowed south "with high hopes," while a relaxed Richardson spent the days on shore indulging his interest in geology and wildlife and making copious notes on the habits of nesting birds, soil types, and varieties of seaweed. On the fourth day, they saw the coast trending north again. "No pleasant sight to us," Richardson admitted, when he realized they had been lured to the bottom of a large bay, which he named after Captain Franklin.[43]

At the northernmost point of Franklin Bay's eastern shore on July 23, they pulled up on the beach so the officers and some of the men could climb a hill, estimated at about seven hundred feet above sea level. The view from the summit confirmed that they were near the northern cape of another peninsula, which Richardson named Cape Parry, and that in rounding it they would enter yet another bay, which would take them south and then north to yet another headland.[44]

They erected a cairn and left a letter addressed to Captain Edward Parry in case he found a passage through from Hudson Bay. On July 25, after rounding Cape Parry they crossed directly to the second peninsula, which Richardson named Cape Lyon. Heavy weather kept them there for three days. The officers used the time to draw a series of maps of the coast, while Ullebuk brought in a goodly supply of caribou meat. At the highest point of land on the east side of Cape Lyon, they built another cairn and deposited a second letter for Parry, with copies of their updated maps of the coast to the west as far as the Mackenzie Delta.[45]

At midnight on July 26, the sun touched the horizon for the first time in several weeks, a warning that darkness and winter were ahead. For the rest of July, ice, both new and old, made navigation difficult and dangerous. *Union* came close to being crushed by pans of ice coming together "with violence." Four days later— days in which the men could move the boats forward only "by the constant use of the hatchet and ice-chisel"—*Dolphin* narrowly escaped a crushing between two fast-moving ice floes. Late on the afternoon of August 3, a lane of open water appeared at exactly the right time for the boats to cross yet another bay (Stapylton Bay) in safety, again to the "joy" of officers and oarsmen. Reckoning showed them to be once more in the longitude of the Coppermine mouth, about seventy miles north of it. Again, on the night of August 3–4, their hopes seemed premature when Richardson walked seven or eight miles across the headland, in "hopes of beholding the sea on the opposite side." Instead of the south-trending coast they hoped for, the doctor caught a glimpse of land to the northeast.[46]

While the crews worked the boats through closely packed ice, Kendall went in search of high ground. He was back two hours later with "cheering intelligence." The "continuous line of land" to the north was not an impassable obstacle between them and their goal: it was the highland of an island separated from the North American mainland by a narrow stretch of ocean. The continental coast, as far as Kendall could see, inclined southeast, and the ocean was almost ice free. "On the strait," the doctor wrote, "I bestowed the names of our excellent little boats," *Dolphin* and *Union*.[47]

❧

A DAY AFTER ESCAPING THE PILLAGE POINT KAYAKS, ON SUNDAY, July 9, Franklin's party pulled up on a small unoccupied island. Here, the crews were left in peace to mend sails and snatch an hour or two of sleep. At three in the morning, they went forward and, four hours later, reached salt water to find the ice just breaking up and no way through to the westward. Disappointing as the new setback was, they took comfort in knowing they had ample provisions to allow for a few days' delay. The men, still recovering from the recent battle, had just settled into their sleeping bags at about eight in the morning when the watchmen raised the alarm, and all hands tumbled forth, fully armed, to see three Inuit near the tents about to discharge their arrows.[48]

Augustine stepped forward, gave his usual speech, and calmed everyone's fears. He arranged for an exchange of gifts with "tact and judgment." The newly met men pointed to their tents some two miles away and asked that Augustine go with them to invite the rest of their community to visit the white men and see the large boats. Augustine accepted the invitation, but before leaving, he implemented some safety precautions. At his bidding, the sailors set up markers 150 yards from the expedition tents, and Augustine explained to the visitors that they marked neutral territory where they would exchange greetings and conduct trade and beyond which neither they nor the expedition people would go. Augustine then made it clear to his fellow countrymen what destructive power was within his party's guns, telling them that any of them who passed the markers toward the tents or the boats would be shot.[49]

He was back about five hours later, with twenty unarmed men and two elderly women. He lined them up at the boundary markers and then talked Franklin and Back through the ritual of greeting, which the officers followed to the letter. They approached the boundary slowly, shook hands solemnly with each of the visitors, and presented each with a gift of fish hooks and awls. Then the interpreter-diplomat called the rest of the men to approach, and each of them presented the visitors with a string of beads. The two women made their selections from among the beads, pins, and needles laid out before them and at once began to attach earrings and thimbles to their clothes. Satisfied that his ambassadorial arrangements were going well, Augustine withdrew to his tent briefly and reappeared in his dress uniform displaying all his medals.[50]

For half an hour, the Inuit examined his clothes, paying special attention to his buttons with their embossed anchors. A conference of officers and elders followed, and Augustine gathered much useful information on the configuration of the seacoast, the positions of safe and unsafe channels, and ice conditions to the west. The elders among the visitors warned that as soon as the nights were dark enough to show starlight, unfavourable winds would blow the pack ice against the shore, crushing any boats that happened to be in the way. The officers were not much inclined to take the warning seriously after they learned that the local people seldom travelled to the west and might not have had first-hand experience of the dangerous wind.[51]

Augustine accompanied the twenty-two emissaries to their lodges in the evening. He was back next morning with a mixed crowd of forty-eight villagers, men, women, and children. All those who had not been in the previous delegation received gifts, with Augustine and Robert Spinks representing the expedition in the mild trading that followed. Hatchets, files, ice chisels, fire-steels, awls, and fish hooks changed hands for eleven pairs of sealskin boots, some pieces of tanned sealskin, and a few lengths of twisted deerskin cording. The visiting men asked for metal blades, but Franklin, having noted that each of them already had a knife, decided to keep his stock for possible meetings with other villages. At day's end as the visitors prepared to return to their homes, Augustine disappeared again into the men's tent, to emerge fully decked out in George Wilson's Royal Marines uniform with three great plumes in his hat. He went off to spend a second night with the visitors and was safely back in the morning, having seen the villagers on their way to a favourite fishing spot.[52]

A strong wind was opening a lead in the ice as Augustine reported in, and the boats pushed through the breaking ice for about a mile and half before they were forced to pull up and unload at the site of the now deserted village where Augustine had spent the last two nights. From the top of a nearby hill, the officers looked down on an impenetrable barrier of ice to the westward. Uncomfortable as living in dripping tents was, the entire party welcomed the heavy rain that began about three the next morning when they saw that the downpour was rapidly eating away the already candled ice. By eight on the evening of July 12, a passage was open, but no advance could be undertaken because Augustine had once again slipped away from the group.[53]

George Back's navigational protractor had gone missing, a loss that could be disastrous for the expedition, and Augustine had set out in pouring rain to overtake the villagers on their way upriver. At midnight he was still not back. Just as his bunkmates were organizing a search party, at about three in the morning, he reappeared, "greatly fatigued," with the protractor in his pocket. Three of his countrymen accompanied him, bringing a gift of white fish and some samples of crystal from the nearby mountains as a means of making up for the misdemeanour. They explained, through Augustine, that the light-fingered woman who had taken the protractor had done so in "ignorance of its utility" to the expedition. Franklin insisted on paying for the fish and the crystals as a reward for their thoughtfulness in not letting Augustine return alone.[54]

※

HEAVY RAIN, THICK FOG, AND FLOATING ICE MADE PROGRESS UNPREdictable. Augustine made the most of the enforced stops to visit every Inuit village and camp within walking distance. His first objective at each encounter was to gather information on tides, ice conditions, the locations of reefs and sandbars, and the number and size of communities that lay ahead. As the expedition neared Herschel Island, he spoke with one young couple who told him that it was unlikely the ice would clear enough for the expedition boats to get there. Augustine and William Duncan made a two-hour walk across the ice for a closer look at conditions around the island and discovered some open water and a channel leading to it. *Lion* and *Reliance* were loaded, were launched, and reached Herschel Island before the lead closed, passing a village on the way. While the men were setting up camp, Augustine went back to the village and returned with a dozen people, each bringing a piece of dried meat or fish for the explorers. By evening the visitors numbered about two dozen. Augustine gave his usual speech and arranged a receiving line and gift exchange. As so often happened where Augustine was concerned, the greater part of the night was spent in singing and dancing.[55]

Augustine by this time had a finely tuned understanding of the kind of ethnological information that interested his officers. He asked every new acquaintance along their route where they got iron, knives, beads, and especially firearms. The Herschel Island Inuit explained that they met with people "at a regular spring trade fair" who lived "a great distance to the westward." The westerners, they said, spoke a "dialect so different from theirs, that…they had great difficulty in understanding them." The informants had heard that the source of the metal goods and beads they traded for were white people "who reside far to the west." Franklin and Back were certain none of the articles they saw were of British manufacture or of the same style as those sold by the Hudson's Bay Company. They concluded the items must have come from Russian fur traders.

Two of the informants, who appeared to be "middle-aged," told Augustine that the first meeting with the far western white people had taken place about the time they reached adult status, which Franklin and Back recognized as coinciding with the Russian push into the Alaskan interior and along the north Alaskan coast after 1799.[56]

On July 30, the sun passed below the southern horizon for the first time since mid-May, a reminder that time was passing and the chance of reaching Icy Cape before freeze-up was becoming ever more unlikely. All hands were even more aware that their time on Arctic waters was running out when the last day of July was crossed off the calendar. The Admiralty had left no doubt in anyone's mind that they were under orders to retreat on August 20. On Thursday, August 3, with less than three weeks left for exploring westward, commander, officers, and men agreed to go forward through the night. At shortly after three in the morning, passing Barter Island, the lookout spotted tents, kayaks, umiaks, and dogs on the beach, the first signs of human habitation in two weeks. Augustine hailed the camp, and in a few minutes the entire beach was crowded with over fifty completely naked people just roused from sleep, all armed with bows, arrows, and knives. Augustine refused an invitation to go ashore after Franklin pointed out that they did not have enough gifts for everyone in the village.[57]

West of Barter Island after close to thirty hours of sleepless travel, Franklin called a halt just before noon on August 4. As the exhausted men lay on the gravel beach or leaned against piled rocks, the lookout alerted Augustine that two kayaks were approaching from the west. The young man in the leading kayak unhesitatingly accepted Augustine's invitation to land. The other kayak was "driving with the wind and tide" while its owner slept. Augustine's loud bellow woke him, and he scrambled to join his companion on the beach. The two young men, on their way back to Herschel Island from a hunting trip, reported that a narrow strip of coast for some distance to the west was free of ice. Like the young men at Barter Island, they had no information about the coast farther to the west, but they had been told by the Alaskan people they traded with that it was low and protected by a series of reefs that were dangerous to umiaks and best avoided. Their description was apt. For nearly three days, the expedition sought a way west, sometimes finding open water close to the reefs, where *Lion* and *Reliance* suffered serious scraping, and sometimes having to seek deeper water where floating ice pans presented another kind of danger to the boats.[58]

At Flaxman Island on August 6, *Lion* was "very leaky," but with constant bailing the men kept it afloat, and the officers decided not to stop for repairs. The final decision, however, was not theirs. As they made for the mainland some three miles distant, the combination of sun in their eyes, a heavy wind signalling an approaching storm, and misinterpretation of foaming surf as tide ripple brought *Lion* up on a reef. Although the "exertions of the crew" easily freed it from the reef, the boat took on so much water that repairs were unavoidable. Anxiously scanning a nearby island and the mainland shore for a sheltered anchorage, the lookouts spotted a series of posts set up by the Inuit. The posts, which Augustine recognized as typical Inuit landmarks, indicated an "approachable part of the coast." They managed to get the boats into a sheltered cove on the little island, which, for good reason, the men dubbed "Foggy Island."[59]

For three days the party waited out the storm, which "continued violent," while carpenter Thomas Matthews struggled to plug the holes in *Lion*'s bottom. Augustine made good use of the delay by bringing down a caribou to enliven the monotonous menu of pemmican and dried meat. Freezing, impenetrable fog set in as the storm moved to the east, and an attempt to get away was thwarted by arm's-length visibility and floating ice. "Heartily tired of our late encampment," the men tried to move camp but could make no headway around the shoals. On returning to their small cove, which they now declared to be cursed, they spent two hours getting the boats through the mud, in 40° water and 41° air temperature. The hours in the mud produced painfully swollen, inflamed legs by evening, and Franklin resolved to avoid the risk of more serious consequences by remaining where they were until they had better visibility and a calmer sea. A dreary nine days later, the western detachment was still there. Their tents, saturated from fog and rain, were "comfortless abodes"; there was no relief to be had from hunting, as the caribou were wary after Augustine's kill a few days earlier; and there was barely enough driftwood left for one cooking fire a day.[60]

ON THE SECOND DAY OF AUGUST, RICHARDSON'S EASTBOUND CONtingent entered a narrow strait filled with closely packed ice except for a few lanes of open water. The two helmsmen, Thomas Gillet in *Dolphin* and John McLea in *Union*, zigzagged their vessels through twenty-five miles of floating ice before making a landing ten miles as the crow flies from their previous night's campsite. On August 5 and 6, all hands worked "with their spirits pleasantly excited" and progressed "with a rapidity to which they had lately been unaccustomed." Only one small setback delayed them. About noon on August 6, an ice floe pushed *Dolphin* out of the water and onto a piece of grounded ice, breaking a timber and several planks, which Thomas Fuller was able to put to rights while supper was being cooked. After supper, with the air temperature at a balmy 60° Fahrenheit, the officers walked along the shore fully confident that nothing could now prevent them from reaching their goal and crossing the barren lands to Great Bear Lake before cold weather set in.[61]

At sea again on August 7 they were out of Dolphin and Union Strait and into Coronation Gulf, thus connecting their survey of the coast with the more easterly survey made during the first Arctic overland expedition. None of the expedition men yet understood what they had accomplished. On August 8, with the mouth of the Coppermine River only a few miles distant, the "gratifying intelligence" was shared, and the men responded with "heartfelt expressions of gratitude to the Divine Being." Richardson named a small headland Cape Kendall and the magnificent bay just south of it Back Inlet. Rounding one more small headland, the men pulled up on the beach at the Coppermine mouth and pitched their tents within a hundred yards of the first expedition's 1821 campsite.[62]

THE WESTERN DETACHMENT FINALLY ESCAPED THE "DETESTABLE island," a week after Richardson's party reached the Coppermine River. Only four days were left before they had to turn back in accordance with the Admiralty's instructions. A clear day and a flowing tide put the party "all in the highest spirits" as they launched into a fair wind with set sails and steered west. The holiday spirit did not last. Within a few hours the wind freshened, the fog returned, the ice drifted in, and the reefs reappeared, creating such a swell that they had to seek a safe harbour. Low water and high waves foiled two attempts at landing at Point Heald and entering Prudhoe Bay. In the face of an increasingly violent gale and ever-denser fog, the officers decided their best hope was to head out to sea and tether to a large piece of ice. Searching for a channel away from shore, they quite unexpectedly ran over a shoal into smooth water and grounded. A brief lift in the fog revealed their campsite to be a gravel reef about five hundred yards in circumference, surrounded by low banks and protected to seaward by grounded ice, but with no fresh water and only enough driftwood for one fire. The noticeable lengthening of night—by August 16 lasting close to four hours and lengthening perceptibly—was another reminder that the long-sought goal was out of reach.[63]

Past experience, present situation, and future prospects of the western detachment suggested nothing was to be gained by pressing forward, and much could be lost. Augustine's informants had warned of the inhospitable terrain of Alaska's north slope; temperature and hours of daylight were dropping perceptibly day by day; caribou herds were disappearing; and there were no known villages along the way. As well, there was the matter of obedience to the Admiralty's instructions to retreat no later than August 20. "It was with no ordinary pain that I could now bring myself even to think of relinquishing the great object of my ambition," wrote Franklin, but "we had reached that point beyond which perseverance would be rashness, and our best efforts must be fruitless."[64]

That night, August 16, Franklin announced the detachment's imminent retreat, but no escape was possible until the eighteenth. Their passage back to Foggy Island was short; by three in the afternoon, they were setting up camp, and the "detestable island" was no longer cursed. "We now enjoyed the comforts of a good fire and a warm meal." Before bed that night, the men put up a square pile of driftwood on the island's highest part facing toward the sea and under it placed a tin box with a silver medal, a ha'penny, and a letter addressed to

Captain Edward Parry, in the distant hope that his ships had found a northwest passage and made their way through. Another letter was left unsealed and addressed to the Russian fur traders in the hope that some passing Inuit might take it to them. For the Inuit who might come by, they left an ice chisel, a knife, a file, and a hatchet attached to the outside of the pile and then topped the pile with a red flag.[65]

GALE-FORCE WINDS HELD THEM UP FOR THE NEXT TWO DAYS, AND the place became again "this ill-omened island," but when they put to sea on the twenty-first, they were rested, warm, and dry. The first night out they camped within sight of Flaxman Island, followed by nineteen hours at the oars to reach Barter Island after dark on the twenty-second. Anticipating that their next stop would be near where they had seen more than fifty adult Inuit in one camp, they cleaned their guns and set a supply of ammunition handy to each of them. As it happened, the large community they were wary of meeting had dispersed or moved on, and only two families remained. They seemed happy to have a second visit with Augustine, who sat up most of the night talking with them. In the morning he reported to Franklin that a day's journey would bring them within sight of a family of four tents, and contact with them would be unwise. The inhabitants had recently lost both their parents and in their state of mourning might "do some injury" to unexpected visitors. Franklin took the warning seriously and agreed to let *Lion* come in close enough for Augustine to call out to them, but nothing more.[66]

At sunrise on August 26, high winds cleared the ice out of the path of the boats and filled their sails, bringing them within sight of Herschel Island in two hours. They rested for an hour and ran before the wind for the next eight, to within a day's sail of the Mackenzie Delta. About six o'clock, the gale became a violent squall, the sea turned white with foam, and spray and waves breaking over the two boats threatened to sink them. Faced with a choice of letting the boats founder under the weight of the water washing into them or staving them in an attempt to land on a rocky beach, Franklin chose the second alternative and "providentially took the ground in a favourable spot." They were then just a few hours' sail from Pillage Point.[67]

Heavy surf ruled out all thoughts of departure next day, and the men spent their time drying bedding, clothes, and pemmican and cleaning their guns. The always sociable Augustine passed the day visiting nearby Inuit tents. When he brought the neighbours to meet his travel companions the next morning, the women good-naturedly agreed to sew sealskin to the soles of the men's worn moccasins. Their families had recently been to Pillage Point and told Augustine that the people there had been thinking about destroying the party of explorers entirely.[68]

As Franklin recorded the story, the first thought of the Pillage Point people on seeing the expedition boats approach was to welcome the newcomers in a friendly manner. When the man whose kayak was upset reported that the large boat was filled with desirable items, they began to rethink their situation. A short conference among the elderly chiefs concluded that the goods were theirs for the taking if the visitors could be overwhelmed and all of them killed. Cooler heads suggested it might be a mistake to kill Augustine, reasoning that if his life was spared, he could be sent back upriver "with a story which we shall invent" and bring more white people with valuable articles to them. After their evening of singing and dancing on the beach with Augustine, they regretted having let the treasure-laden boats escape and decided to make another, more organized attack, during which their goal would be to kill all members of the white men's party and seize not only the boats' cargoes but the boats themselves. Augustine was included among the doomed in the new plan, because his talks with them during the dancing party had convinced them he would never become their willing ally.[69]

As the expedition approached the Mackenzie on August 28, the boats again started to take on water. Franklin ordered a stop on a gravel reef to make repairs. During the course of the day, three Inuit who saw the English tents from a distance came for a visit. Augustine recognized one who had been active in the Pillage Point attack. From him Augustine heard the story of the July 7 battle again, exactly as he had heard it the day before. The young man assured him that the inhabitants of the Pillage Point village had moved to the eastern side of the delta, but, in case any should still be around, he knew of another way of entering the river without passing Pillage Point, which he explained to Augustine. The expedition set off again in the late afternoon and camped a mile and a half beyond the Inuit tents, with a view of Garry Island on the eastern side of the Mackenzie Delta.[70]

Blustery weather continued overnight, and again the expedition remained in camp. So many Inuit came calling that Augustine drew a line around the tents, marking the boundary between a public space where the Inuit were welcome and a private space that was out of bounds to the visitors. Augustine spent a glorious day visiting with his fellow countrymen, especially an elderly man to whom he gave a knife on behalf of the expedition.[71]

The visitors also had news of Dr. Richardson and his eastern detachment. Just before clearing the eastern channel, they told Augustine, Richardson's party was attacked by a band of warriors wishing to plunder them. The boats had managed to get out of harm's way and a few miles farther on had stopped to give some kettles to three men in kayaks before disappearing along the coast to the east. Hearing of an attempt to plunder the doctor's boats greatly alarmed the western detachment, who worried that on returning by the same route, Richardson's people might once again be assaulted. Their fears were all the greater because of other recent news that large numbers of Inuit regularly gathered near the eastern channel at the close of summer, among them the people of Pillage Point.[72]

Scarcely had the bearers of the bad news left when two young Inuit were seen "running in breathless haste and crying out that a large party of Indians had come down from the mountains with the express purpose of attacking the boats and killing every man of the party." In urging the expedition to get on the way to some place of safety, they added that the war party was angry because the white men had traded with their ancient enemies. Franklin refused to move until Robert Spinks returned from hunting. At hearing this, the two young Inuit climbed to the top of an old lodge to look for him. Seeing him on his way back, they urged him on with all their might. At the same time, they gave

Augustine detailed instructions on the course that would take them round the reef and into a western outlet of the Mackenzie. Franklin thanked them with gifts of iron, which they accepted, insisting all the while that their main concern was for Augustine's safety.[73]

With Spinks back on board, the expedition made good its escape, overnighting in a sheltered inlet. When the sun rose on August 30, *Lion* and *Reliance* were under sail heading for the Mackenzie West Channel. By ten o'clock they had passed Pillage Point and were scudding easily before a light gale. During the run, Augustine regaled *Lion*'s crew with more of what he had recently heard from the two young men so determined to save his life. Seven Mountain Indians, he said, had been to Herschel Island to trade with Inuit there and had seen a number of items left by the expedition on the way west. They had long since heard about the Pillage Point episode and were inclined to follow a similar strategy, namely, to watch until the expedition crews were fully occupied hauling the boats over the sandbanks, at which time three or four of them would go out and offer assistance and, once near the boats, stove them. The rest of their party was then to rush forth and join the assault. The potential assailants, so the two young visitors told Augustine, had planned to go to the mouth of the Mackenzie River and support themselves fishing and hunting while waiting for the return of the expedition boats. On catching sight of the expedition tents and the armed watchmen on duty, however, the seven would-be attackers realized that they were outnumbered and under-armed and began to rethink their strategy. To beef up their numbers, they stopped at a small Inuit camp in an attempt to recruit reinforcements. Their conversation with possible recruits was overheard by an elderly man, the same man to whom Augustine had given a knife on behalf of the expedition, who took steps to thwart them by sending the two young men to warn Augustine.[74]

For three weeks after starting up the Mackenzie on August 31, the expedition had easy passage, with no complaints except against sand flies and mosquitoes. At Point Separation, where they had last seen the eastern detachment, they looked for a mark that Richardson's party had returned by way of the eastern channel. Finding nothing, they left a bag of pemmican and a letter in case he came along later. Near Arctic Red River, they met Barbue, a Loucheux Chief, who tried to pass on the rumours that were spreading from village to village along the Mackenzie, saying that an important man, a leader, had died by violence somewhere on the coast. Language difficulties prevented clear communication, and the western party pressed on upriver in considerable anxiety. They reached Fort Good Hope on the seventh of September, where Post Master John Bell had already heard stories that Franklin, or Richardson, or both, had been killed. Franklin asked Bell to send two Loucheux to the eastern mouth of the river as soon as possible to inquire among the Inuit there for anything they might know or have heard about the eastern detachment.[75]

THE EASTERN PARTY'S RETURN TO FORT FRANKLIN TOOK TWENTY-one days. The men left *Dolphin* and *Union* eleven miles upstream at Bloody Fall on the Coppermine River, along with everything not absolutely necessary for the long walk ahead. They left the tents standing and securely pegged, and in them placed all that remained of the presents intended for the Inuit: "fish hooks, lines, hatchets, knives, files, fire-steels, kettles, combs, awls, needles, thread, blue and red cloth, gartering, and beads." They hoisted a Union Jack over the tents, and to prevent an accident involving gunpowder, they threw what they no longer needed into the river.[76]

On leaving their campsite, each man carried a portion of the provisions, some of the astronomical tables and charts, fishing nets, plant and rock samples, kettles, hatchets, blankets, spare shoes, guns, ammunition, and *Walnut-Shell*, in its five small packages. Alert to the tendency of the men to overestimate their strength, Richardson warned them not to load themselves down with too many souvenirs and promised that after the first leg of the march, he would inspect their bundles for superfluous items. By the time they reached the summit of the first hill, many small articles lay on the trail below them, and the doctor was satisfied each bundle was manageable.[77]

During the breakfast stop, the men assembled *Walnut-Shell* and loaded it with all the baggage, but when they came to tow it, they found that its shape, so "admirably adapted" for calm river crossings, allowed it to take on water in the rapids. The doctor decided it had to be abandoned and, by leaving five muskets and a half bag of arrowroot behind with it, reduced the loads by about fifteen pounds per man. Kendall took the lead and set a steady pace, with a five-minute rest every half hour, which allowed stragglers to catch up. By the end of the second day, they had covered eighteen miles, and two meals a day had reduced each man's load to about fifty-two pounds. The thermometer continued to register in the sixties during the day.[78]

At noon on the fourth day, they left the Coppermine to follow a direct route to the northeast arm of Great Bear Lake. When they set out at five on the morning of the fourteenth, it was through country entirely without trees, and their pace was "pretty brisk." Although the absence of tree cover meant they would have to do without a fire and hot tea, it also made the partridges easy to see, and the men managed to kill several by throwing stones. They marched late in order to find firewood to cook the partridges along with some meat from a caribou that John McLea brought down.[79]

They reached the height of land separating the Coppermine River and Great Bear Lake at mid-afternoon on August 15 and could see a well-wooded country beyond. A gathering storm put an end to their hopes for a comfortable night. Instead of sheltering from the impending downpour in a lean-to made of branches and warmed by a wood fire, they laid out their blanket rolls in a crude shelter built by propping chunks of sandstone against each other. A moss fire barely warmed the remains of McLea's caribou.[80]

At the makeshift camp, with most of the men already in their bedrolls, Kendall saw three Hare—two adult hunters and a lad—coming toward them. To attract their attention, the officers threw more moss on the fire and hoisted St. George's ensign on the end of a musket. The new arrivals were wary. The hunters hid the boy in a ravine and crept cautiously forward, one holding his bow and quiver at the ready, the other with his gun cocked. When Richardson and Kendall stepped out to meet them unarmed, they recognized Richardson in the uniform he had worn in his survey of the lake during the previous fall. Through signs and what little each knew of the others' language, the officers gathered that the two hunters, on the advice of their chief, Itchinnah, had been hunting in the neighbourhood in the hope of meeting the returning eastern detachment.[81]

In the morning, Itchinnah's emissaries pointed out the best route down to Great Bear Lake and left to pick up provisions in a cache a short distance away. Richardson halted his men in the early afternoon to wait for them and set fire to a tree to inform them of their stopping place. That evening they "revelled in abundance," enjoying two deer that McLea had brought in and a goodly supply of tongues, fat, and half-dried meat delivered by the Hare hunters. After a short march, they breakfasted the following noon at a small stream where whortleberries grew in profusion and enhanced their meal of cold meat. As they neared Great Bear Lake and Itchinnah's lodge, Richardson continued to set fire to isolated trees to signal their position to the chief.[82]

Their guides left them on the lakeshore about a mile from Dease River, where Richardson expected to find François Beaulieu and his voyageurs. As there was no sign of the welcoming party, and an examination of the provisions revealed only two day's allowance remaining, the men dispersed, with some heading to Dease River to make a raft and set their fishnets and others off to look for traces of Beaulieu. A week later, as Richardson's men were settling down for the night, they heard voices among the trees. Firing a musket to attract the newcomers' attention, Richardson and Kendall met Beaulieu's party of four Canadians, four Chipewyan hunters, and ten Dogribs with their wives and children, thirty in all.[83]

Richardson left Beaulieu in charge of mustering the men from the fishing camp and headed for expedition headquarters with Kendall and ten men. "We arrived [at Fort Franklin] on Friday, the 1st of September," the doctor wrote matter-of-factly, "and received a warm welcome from Mr Dease, after an absence of seventy-one days, during which period we had travelled by land and water one thousand seven hundred and nine geographical, or nineteen hundred and eighty statute, miles."[84]

Richardson's eastern detachment journal closed with high praise for Ullebuk. "Our good-natured and faithful Esquimaux friend, Ooligbuck, carried with him to his native lands the warmest wishes and esteem of the whole party. His attachment to us was never doubtful, even when we were surrounded by a tribe of his own nation." After a few days at Fort Franklin writing up his collections and his personal diary, the doctor set out for Fort Resolution with a small complement of men. By September 28, he was with the McVicars, where he stayed until Christmas Day. In the next six weeks he walked 900 miles on snowshoes to reach Carlton House on February 12, 1827. He collected botanical, animal, and insect specimens on his own until April 5, when naturalist Thomas Drummond joined him. Richardson and Drummond prepared their collections for shipment and carried on to Cumberland House, arriving on May 21, and settled in to await the first of the 1827 brigades to York Factory.[85]

THE WESTERN DETACHMENT REACHED FORT FRANKLIN ON September 21, to find all the winterers well and the eastern detachment with them, except for Dr. Richardson and his travelling companions. The second winter at Great Bear Lake was, overall, colder than the first winter had been. A succession of storms blanketed the winter quarters in snow much deeper than in the previous year. Short rations were a concern relieved only marginally when Kendall made a trip to Fort Norman in October to pick up food and warm clothing, "as much…as his canoe would carry." By mid-November the fisheries were "sufficiently productive," and a second trip to Fort Norman brought more provisions, but the fish were out of season, the menu was uninteresting, and stomach complaints were common. Weather, winter darkness, minor health problems, and, perhaps, boredom all contributed to a general feeling of depression and homesickness at the little fort. Franklin several times described life as "gloomy" and did not bother to give details of daily life, noting only that "the same occupations, amusements, and exercise, were followed by the officers and men as in the former residence; and the occurrences were so similar, that particular mention of them is unnecessary." News from Fort Norman that one of the expedition's Dogrib hunters had murdered his wife's seducer sparked an investigation, and the man's dismissal, adding to the general "melancholy."[86]

The appearance on the last two nights of November of a comet, which by December 1 was "brilliant," brought some excitement, and the prospect of festivities at Christmas and New Year's raised everyone's spirit. Charles Brisbois made a Christmas visit, giving the two artists, George Back and Edward Kendall, a "chance to display their ingenuity" in the production of stage scenery to backdrop a "comic piece" Back had written. The play "afforded such general amusement" that the men insisted on repeat performances over three evenings. Brisbois left after the New Year's dance, and occupations again became "ordinary."[87]

The new year, 1827, brought more extremely cold weather—minus 52° on January 4—and more snow. Franklin's plan to start south with dog teams via the Mackenzie River as soon as the survey maps and scientific tables were finished had to be shelved when word came that the river ice was too rough for travel. On the seventh, the mercury fell to minus 58°. The sled dogs were the chief sufferers, three of them with frostbitten feet and all of them "much thinner." The men built "warm houses" for them but, try as they might, could not get the animals to sleep under any kind of shelter.[88]

AUGUSTINE, ULLEBUK, AND TWO DOGRIB GUIDES LEFT FORT Franklin on February 16 to lay out a trail of food caches and were followed four days later by five men, including John McLea, and Franklin in his carriole. George Back's orders were to stay at the winter quarters until breakup and then proceed to Norway House with the rest of the British expedition men and the Canadian voyageurs. At Norway House he was to arrange for the Canadians to get to Montreal by the Winnipeg River route, continue on to York Factory with Augustine and Ullebuk and see them safely on their way to Churchill, and then take the Company's supply ship to England with the British recruits.[89]

The sled dogs were still too weak to pull a fully loaded sled, so Franklin hired two local guides to carry some of the pemmican. On the second night out, to Franklin's disgust, the guides disappeared, taking the pemmican with them, but the sight of Augustine and Ullebuk waiting at the appointed place brightened his mood, and the party reached Fort Simpson on March 8, in "fine weather." Edward Smith recorded their arrival: "At 9 a.m. we were cheered by the arrival of Captain Franklin accompanied by three of his men, two Indians, and the indefatigable Augustus...[on] their 17th day from Fort Franklin." They stayed for a week to allow the dogs to "recruit their strength" and to replace the missing pemmican with a new supply. On March 15, they could wait no longer, but one of the dogs being still "unfit for the journey," Smith generously gave them his best dog for the carriole and they took to the trail again. "We were sorry to be deprived of Captain Franklin's cheerful company," Smith noted in the journal, "who at 1 p.m. took his departure for Stair Lake accompanied by his four men and Augustus."[90]

The McVicars welcomed the party to Fort Resolution on March 26, and McVicar reported on the good health of "this gallant and enterprising officer,...two Canadians, 2 Englishmen, and Augustus." With Robert and Christy McVicar, and their three-month-old son, John Richardson McVicar, the party continued on to Fort Chipewyan, where they were welcomed by an "agreeably surprised" Chief Factor Alexander Stewart on April 12. On May 23, while waiting for a brigade to take his party to York Factory, Franklin performed a marriage service for Stewart's daughter Katherine and William McGillivray, which, as a naval captain, he had the authority to do. Five days later, he conducted a "ceremonial marriage" for the McVicars. Neither McVicar's journal nor the captain's *Narrative* made note of the event or of the presence of the McVicars' baby son.[91]

ON MAY 26, AT FORT CHIPEWYAN, AUGUSTINE WATCHED THE FIRST canoes of the year arrive from Slave Lake. Among them were some of his fellow adventurers to the Arctic: François Beaulieu, interpreter for Peter Warren Dease for four years at Great Bear Lake, and several of the expedition's men. Close behind them came Robert McVicar with his men in two canoes bringing the year's returns from Fort Resolution.[92] Augustine checked the destinations of each of the brigades and went to Franklin with a plan. Was there any reason why he and Ullebuk could not go ahead to Cumberland House, and if necessary to Carlton House, to spend a few extra days with Dr. Richardson? Franklin had no objections, and the two Keewatin men, along with two other expedition members, loaded their small bundles into the next passing canoe on the route to Cumberland. Franklin, McVicar, and Fort Chipewyan's post manager Alexander Stewart followed in light canoes on May 31.

At Cumberland House, Augustine and Ullebuk found Dr. Richardson happily busy collecting plant specimens, while the post's men prepared their year's returns for shipment to York Factory. On June 18, they greeted Franklin, who had travelled from Fort Chipewyan with Robert McVicar and Alexander Stewart. Chief Factor John Charles joined the brigade at Ile à la Crosse. As soon as the Cumberland House brigade was ready, Augustine, Ullebuk, Franklin, and Stewart settled themselves as passengers among the baggage, while Richardson, Charles, and McVicar followed in light canoes.[93]

The next stage of their journey "was nowise expeditious," Alex Stewart later recorded, due to "much bad weather." For three weeks the brigade fought its way through high winds and heavy rain to reach Norway House on June 24. Richardson's canoe caught up three days later. The expedition party remained together at Norway House for two weeks, while transportation to Red River was arranged for Franklin and Richardson. Parting from them was a sad occasion for Augustine and Ullebuk. Augustine wept and stressed his "very strong desire" to accompany them on any future expedition, for which, he said, he and Ullebuk would "be ready at any time to quit their families and their country." Six years later, Augustine kept his promise and answered a call for help from one of his explorer friends.[94]

Augustine and Ullebuk remained at Norway House until George Back and Edward Kendall arrived with the men who were returning to England on the Company's supply ship. They left Norway House for York Factory on July 7.

CHAPTER 8

AUGUSTINE, ULLEBUK, AND MOSES

1827–1830

T HE LAST OF THE EXPEDITION'S PEOPLE REACHED YORK Factory on September 1, 1827, after a two-week passage down the Hayes River. The junior officers, Back and Kendall, settled into York Factory's officers' quarters, and the marines and canoe men joined Augustine and Ullebuk in the Men's House. George Back had one final duty to perform, spelled out for him in a letter of instruction that Franklin had given him the day before the commander left Fort Franklin for the last time with Augustine and Ullebuk. "On your arrival at York Factory," the instruction read, "Augustus is to be furnished with such goods from the HBC store as you may suppose will prove most useful to him to the amount of £33 sterling in part payment of his wages, and Ulligbughk to the amount of £30." Back did not count the pennies when he accompanied his two friends to the York Factory General Shop. Augustine's choices totalled £37/9/6, and Ullebuk's came to £32/19/3. Exactly how the two men were to get the rest of their wages was still uncertain, or so Franklin thought. "The remainder of their Monies," he wrote, "will be reserved until the pleasure of Earl Bathurst be known as to its amount and disposal."[1]

That there was any question of the amount would have come as a surprise to both Augustine and Ullebuk. Their contract with Hugh Leslie promised wages at 60 and 50 made beaver respectively, with equipment and living at the Admiralty's expense. Earl Bathurst's pleasure, it turned out, was to reward them handsomely, and beyond what they had originally contracted for. The news reached Franklin in London as his *Narrative of a Second Expedition* was going to press, and he was just in time to add a short footnote: "I have pleasure in mentioning that, by permission of Government, the pay which was due to Augustus and Ooligbuck, has been delivered to the Directors of the Hudson's Bay Company, who have undertaken to distribute it to them annually, in the way suited to their wants.'"[2]

One of Churchill's boats was waiting at York Factory to take Augustine and Ullebuk home. They said their goodbyes and well wishes to their expedition mates and sailed north with a crew of old friends—James Dunning, Moses, William Oman, and Baikie Sinclair. They were in Churchill River by three on the afternoon of September 14 after an easy four days at sea. A low tide kept them well away from the landing dock, but in their haste to be ashore, passengers and crew threw out the anchor and slogged their way across the mud flats on foot.[3]

Their friends had alarming news for the returning men about their home village: a deadly sickness had struck the coastal Inuit communities in the summer of 1825 and lasted well into the winter of 1825–26. The death toll was high. Eight hunters reporting to the post on July 9, 1826, had brought distressing news. "Utuck informs me," wrote George Taylor, second-in-command at Churchill, "that before the commencement of the thaw, he received a visit from one of the subjects of his neighbour, whose lands being contiguous to his, who reported to him the mortality with which they had been visited with the last summer and in the fall [of 1825]. Utuck himself has had the misfortune to lose part of his tribe. I could not distinctly make out the number of deaths in each respective tribe, but of the two the numbers amount to 34, of which 22 were men, 10 women, and 2 children. The deaths were not caused by starvation, as they were at that time living in affluence." Augustine's brother Astanik and his nephew Annagyniak survived. Junius's brother Itiviana may not have; he was not among the seal hunters who came from Augustine's community for the annual seal hunt in 1828 or later.[4]

The returning explorers were also brought up to date with less distressing news: renovations planned by Chief Factor Colin Robertson during his brief tenure at Fort Churchill in Outfit 1824–25 were underway. Building and rebuilding at Churchill in the summer was almost a yearly ritual. In 1814, a new Men's House big enough to accommodate sixty or more men replaced the one that had burned down during the visit of four Selkirk colonists the previous year. Also in 1814, Churchill was downgraded from a factory to an outpost to be manned by a half dozen or so servants and the unnecessary new Men's House became a vastly under-occupied white elephant. In 1815, a three-room two-storey officers' house was built, and the following year the stockade was reduced by moving the palisade closer to the buildings, so that employees could prevent their Indigenous clients from walking around out of sight. In 1818 the palisade was moved outwards again so that visitors could not take away building materials for their own use without being seen.[5]

In 1825, Robertson had the old launch house pulled down and used part of it to make a kitchen for the officers' house and another part as an annex to the still house. When Robert Harding was promoted to Clerk in Charge in 1826, he inherited Robertson's ambitious plans to rebuild Fort Churchill's physical plant. Workshops and storage spaces were, after ten years of neglect, being dismantled and rebuilt to serve more practical needs.[6]

Harding's purpose in rebuilding most of Churchill Post may not have been quite what Robertson had in mind when planning its renovations. By 1820 James Dunning Jr. and William Oman, sons of British men and First Nations mothers (Chipewyan and Cree, respectively), were married to Indigenous women and starting families of their own. Both men had large families of in-laws—parents, grandparents, siblings, aunts, uncles, cousins, and all of their in-laws who lived nearby. Family reunions at Churchill were frequent as family and in-laws came to visit their kin, shared the rations given to post employees, spent nights in the Men's House with their relatives, and moved freely in and out of all the Company's buildings.

In the daily journal for March 22, 1827, Harding expressed some of his frustration at managing Churchill's clients. "Bad day snowing blowing and drifting hard from NW," he wrote. "Mallette unable to work outdoors consequently men employed making some alterations in the Men's house by taking down the partition between it and the 2 back rooms which hitherto have been places where Indians have had liberty to enter without any leave from the Person in charge on the frivolous excuse of Relationship."[7] At its core, his difficulty was in dealing with conflict between cultures. For him, his job getting the Company's goals met on time and within budget was paramount. As the "person in charge," he had no personal relationship with anyone at the post and held himself to the standards of the Company, which were not the same as those of the growing number of bicultural employees at the post. From the other point of view, family was more important than organizing chores, eating, sleeping, and working in accord with the clock, and keeping buildings and yards in peak condition.

WHILE THE HOMECOMING TRAVELLERS WERE TAKING NOTE OF new arrangements at Churchill, Robert Harding went through the mail packet from York. The next day, September 15, he engaged Augustine and Ullebuk "as Men for the winter, [having] received instructions from Mr McTavish to that effect."[8] As they settled down to the familiar work of the trading post, they were given a predictable assignment. "Dunning, Augustine, Oman, and Ullebuk start to cut wood," Harding wrote, of a quite ordinary and routine assignment. But, he continued, "The 2 former took a tent with them and are to remain there constantly. The 2 latter men will sleep at the House and go and come from there morning and evening, the distance being only about one and half miles from this."[9]

The four woodcutters were productive, putting up eighty-one piles of wood in two weeks, although both teams complained that they had to spend too much time restacking the piles that the autumn winds were constantly blowing down. On October 4, when Moses finished digging the turnips out of the freezing soil and stowing them in the vegetable shed, Harding assigned him to the woodcutting force as well and was specific that his station should be "at some distance from the other men." Four days later, Harding was even more precise in spelling out once more how he wanted the men to be deployed. Moses was to work with Oman and Ullebuk "together in one place" while "Dunning and Augustine [are] together in another direction," he wrote. "The two parties are to have no connection one with the other." He gave no explanation for his decision that the men be kept apart.[10]

Increasingly as the weeks passed, Harding gave Ullebuk more specialized and demanding jobs than the woodcutting, hunting, and hauling assignments he gave Augustine. Ullebuk was not only living at the post but assigned to indoor work, building sleds, taking down partitions in the newly erected Men's House, and building an outdoor oven with Moses and Oman. As Ullebuk and Oman took on the work of skilled carpenters and mason, Augustine was kept at what John West had called "menial chores."[11]

On January 23, 1828, Harding sent Augustine, James Dunning, and Alex Dunnet to the tents to hunt ptarmigan and told Ullebuk and William Oman to get ready for a trip to York Factory. The two men set out on the twenty-fifth in weather well below zero with two dog trains and a trailer sled. Harding did not record any reason for their trip, but sending them with two sleds, six dogs, and a trailer suggests that they were delivering something, probably furs, to York Factory or that the purpose of their trip was to bring back supplies of some kind, provisions possibly, or merchandise. They were absent long enough for Harding to become uneasy. "Can form no idea," he wrote on February 21, "what can be detaining Oman and Ullebuk so long unless they have been working for York Factory…this is now 28 days since they left here, altho' the trip could have been made with ease in 20 days." Finally, on March 12, "our long looked for men arrived.…They brought letters from Mr McTavish with some garden seeds. [They] have been 8 days on the route owing to the dogs being scarcely able to walk with starvation. 3 of the dogs only returned, one knocked up on the route and the remaining two were detained at YF." He sent the men straight off to look for ptarmigan at Bushy Island.[12]

Satisfying the constant need for food and firewood occupied all Churchill's men in March and April. Oman and Ullebuk went on long, fruitless searches for ptarmigan, while the other men shared the work of cutting wood and building trails through the snow to haul it on. Year by year, Churchill's surrounds were being "logged out," and the men were forced to go farther and farther afield to find wood. Rafting timbers downriver was no longer an option.[13]

In May, seals appeared in the bay behind the Stone Fort, and Augustine and Ullebuk, finally allowed by Harding to work together, set up their tent at Seahorse Gully. Moses, as usual, took charge of the fishing nets. A newcomer to the post, Wacacoo, a Cree hunter, spent his days hunting geese. The journal during the month noted a number of women at the post, weeding the garden, sewing, and doing errands, but Harding did not name or identify any of them. The wives of James Dunning and William Oman were there, of course, as were the wives of Baikie Sinclair and Patrick Cunningham, but the "other" women at the post were the wives of the Chipewyan hunters who came every year for the goose hunt. They took over Moses's usual garden chores during his absence at the fishery. Well weeded by the women, the kitchen garden had two thriving turnip beds, two beds each of radish and lettuce, one of carrots, three "bores" of cabbage, and one of cauliflower. By the end of May, ninety ducks and 1,228 geese, 900 of them salted and pickled, were in the larder, and the Chipewyan were given their usual allotment of grog to celebrate before leaving the post.[14]

ON THE FIRST DAY OF JUNE, HARDING CLOSED THE DAILY JOURNAL and finished his annual district report for Outfit 1827–28. In his Servants' Assessments, he described Ullebuk as "a smart, active, obedient man, and ever ready for any duty required of him. He would be a serviceable hand at the place if willing to engage." Harding's reservations about Moses concerned his physical abilities: "Moses...is a quiet obedient man and altho not the most active is very steady to his duty and ever ready to do any thing required of him. Has been at this place now 6 years, for which services he has been but poorly rewarded and he would be willing to engage if required." Augustine, on the other hand, did not have the high esteem of his immediate boss. "He would I believe wish to engage if required, but doubt he has too great an opinion of himself to make a good man. He appears to have been spoiled on the late Land Arctic Expedition. Hitherto he has done the duty of an engaged servant and behaved himself tolerably well since last September at which time he arrived here from York Factory." In spite of Harding's doubts about Augustine, his superior officers instructed him to offer all three men new contracts, which they accepted.[15]

With the district report thoroughly and neatly done up, Harding prepared to deliver it to York Factory, along with twenty-two kegs of fat and three kegs of cured deer's tongues. He left Alex Dunnet in charge of the post, with William Oman and Baikie Sinclair to assist, and embarked late in the evening of Wednesday, July 2, with George Taylor, Augustine, Moses, Ullebuk, James Dunning, and two Cree as crew. A heavy headwind forced them to drop anchor to keep from being blown into close-packed ice along the shore. On the fifth day, they heard the loud hullooing of a passing Chipewyan hunter, Thulchoke, who was following the coast toward the trading post. "He informed us," wrote Harding, that "within a mile of where we were lying, the ice was in the same state as in the middle of winter, and had not as yet broken in the least. He likewise seemed to think that the navigation would be long in opening." Harding decided to return to the post to wait for better conditions.

They made a second try on July 13 and spent five days fighting through loose ice with strong headwinds. On July 18, the wind went round to the northwest, and they ran under sail all night, through "cold raw weather with thick fog." The next day around four o'clock in the afternoon they judged themselves to be somewhere near Owl River. Less than an hour later, they found, much to their surprise, that they were in fact within sight of one of the Company's beacons. At four in the morning of the twentieth, they raised their sails again and were at York Factory shortly after noon, with their cargo intact.[16]

They remained at York Factory for close to three weeks, while Harding met with his superiors to discuss Churchill's business. Some decisions made then were of no great importance to the operations of the Company but had effects on the lives of Churchill's Inuit employees. In an unusual move, the Company, for whatever reasons, decided to send Ullebuk to work at Lac la Pluie (Rainy Lake, now Fort Frances) and to transfer Augustine to York Factory.

The practice of keeping local labourers at their home posts was well established by the 1820s. Augustine and Ullebuk had no reason to think that signing on as engaged servants would be any different for them than it was for James Dunning or William Oman. They might reasonably have assumed that they too would have their families at the post with them. If either of them voiced an opinion on the unexpected transfers, none of their superiors recorded it.

On their wages as engaged servants at £15 a year and the money from the Arctic overland expedition, Augustine and Ullebuk could afford to outfit themselves with English clothing and bedding, buy tools that they preferred over those that the Company gave them to do their work, and enjoy some luxuries. The three Inuit, Harding, and Taylor all shopped at York Factory's men's emporiums in late July.

1 plain blanket 3½ points	1 pair Mercers' scissors	1 clasp knife
2 cotton shirts	2 yds plain green stroud	1 scalper knife
2 white flannel shirts	½ yards B.B.U. garters	1 cartouche knife
1 quilted vest	3 lifts colored thread	1 8-inch file
1 gray cloth capote	6 yards gartering	1 narrow ice chisel
1 pair fine blue cloth trousers	20 glovers' needles	10 lb gunpowder
2 pr cotton stockings	20 W.C. needles	15 lbs shot
1 wool hat	1 pins	15 ball
1 silk hat cover	½ box beads	20 gunflints
1 cotton shawl	6 pounds white soap	1 tin porringer
1 cotton handkerchief	1 ivory comb	1 iron tinned spoon
1 pr men's grey worsted hose	1 large horn comb	18 lbs loaf sugar
2 plated breast buckles	1 skein #7 twine	½ doz hunters pipes
	1 skein #10 twine	5 carrots tobacco

Figure 1. Augustine's purchases at York Factory, July 26, 1828. (Source: HBCA, Churchill Post Account Books, B.42/d/126 [26 July 1828].)

2 shirts	4 yards ferretting	3 pipes
1 pair trousers	some thread	1 clasp knife
1 cloth capote	needles in quantity	12 cartouche knives
1 swansdown vest	25 needles	32 pounds loaf sugar
1 cotton shawl	some sheeting	1 pound Souchong tea
1 3-point blanket	1 horn comb	2 loaves bread
1 pair hose	1 paper-cased razor	1 pair scarlet worsted cuffs
1 yard blue stroud	3 pounds white soap	cotton handkerchiefs
12 yards gartering	some tobacco	

Figure 2. Ullebuk's purchases at York Factory, July 24, 1828. (Source: HBCA, York Factory Account Books, B.239/d/327 [24 July 1828], transferred to Churchill Men's Debts, B.42/d/126 [13 August 1828].)

Robert Harding and George Taylor shopped among the more expensive, luxurious, gentlemanly goods at the officers' shop. Harding's York Factory purchases included 1⅜ yards of green silk gauze and nine yards of silk ferretting. According to fur trade gossip, Churchill's Clerk in Charge used his supply of luxury fabrics to decorate his utilitarian living quarters. Taylor chose items intended for a lady: one pair of women's scissors, two ivory combs, one roll of hair ribbons, twelve skeins of coloured silk thread, five horn combs, one pair of women's bootees, and two pairs of women's worsted hose. To these boudoir luxuries, he added fifty ounces of tallow for making candles.[17]

Moses had spent almost nothing during the preceding year, other than buying a pound of twist tobacco on June 7, another on June 24, and a third on July 3, each of which cost him a shilling. At York Factory, he spent lavishly, and the bulk of his purchases were for clothing or materials for clothing, some of it decidedly on the dandy-ish side.[18]

Back home in Churchill, Moses had to rein in his spending when Harding told him his indebtedness had mounted to within a few shillings of his wages. He bought a pound of Congou tea a few days after getting back to the northern post, but he could not afford a pair of badly needed new skin shoes. Harding provided them free of charge. On October 11, Moses sold Harding a dressed moose skin for five and a half shillings, which he immediately spent on a pair of scissors at three pence, half a yard of white stroud for one shilling four pence, four army lace garters at a penny each, and a third of a skein of wine-coloured thread for another four pennies. On October 29, he bought another quarter yard of blue stroud and four dozen hunter's pipes.[19]

1 plain blanket 3½ points	3 cotton handkerchiefs	1 ivory comb
1 plain blanket 3 points	1 yard white duffel	1 horn comb
2 white flannel shirts	2 yards plain white stroud	1 clasp knife
2 white cotton shirts	¾ yards plain blue stroud	1 more clasp knife
1 blue cloth jacket	1 yard striped cotton	1 scalper knife
1 pair fine blue trousers	6 yards gartering	8 carrots tobacco
1 grey cloth capote	3 lifts colored thread	12 hunter pipes
1 swansdown vest	10 glovers' needles	3½ pounds loaf sugar
1 scarlet milled cap	10 W.C. needles	1 pound congou tea
1 silk hat cover	1 dozen breast buttons	9 pounds white soap

Figure 3. Moses's purchases at York Factory, July 26, 1828. (Source: HBCA, York Factory Account Books, B.239/d/327 [26 July 1828].)

༄

AUGUSTINE SETTLED INTO THE MEN'S HOUSE AT YORK FACTORY and prepared to take up his duties in his new posting. A month into the work, he filled some gaps in his wardrobe and tool kit at the men's store.

1 striped cotton shirt	1 yard plain duffel	½ skein #1 twine 1
1 white flannel shirt	10 assorted needles	pocket knife
2 cotton handkerchief	1 lift colored threads	1 cartouche knife
1 pair blue trousers	1 yard highland gartering	½ doz hunters pipes
1 pair flannel trousers	1 plain 3-point blanket	1 razor
1 Dutch cap	6 pounds yellow soap	4 carrots tobacco
1 pair hose	1 gilt looking glass	1½ pounds loaf sugar
1 sateen jacket	1 large horn comb	2 pounds Congou tea
⅔ yards white stroud		

Figure 4. Augustine's purchases at York Factory, September 28–29, 1828. (Source: HBCA, Churchill Post Account Books, B.42/d/124 [28–29 September 1828].)

1 4-point blanket	6 army lace garters	1½ pint tin pot
1 blanket capote	¾ yards cloth	2¼ lb covered copper kettle
1 pair of sheeting trousers	2 dozen assorted needles	10 pounds crash sugar
1 swansdown vest	1 small horn comb	2 twists tobacco

Figure 5. Augustine's purchases at York Factory, February 22, 1829. (Source: HBCA, York Factory Account Books, 1828–29, B.239/d/336 [22 February 1829].)

Unfortunately, the York Factory journal for Outfit 1828–29 has not survived in the Company's archives. However, we might assume that at a depot and administrative centre filled with important people and much coming and going, Augustine became one among many labourers whose names seldom appeared in the factory's journals. His daily occupations there would have been noted in the journal only if they had been far above the norms of his fellows or far below them.

In York's highly stratified society, relations between officers and servants were about orders, on the one hand, and obedience, on the other. The emotional and intellectual satisfactions that made Augustine's other separations from home and family bearable—the dependence of expedition officers and men, the respect of Yellowknife chiefs, the admiration of Loucheux and Dogrib people, the adrenalin rush of Pillage Point, the equal-footing exchange of ethnographic information with Richardson and West—were not part of the York Factory experience. If John West was indignant at the servile chores Augustine was assigned to at Churchill—"they make him work at drudgery about the Fort, and send him out daily to fish which seems to go much against the grain, and for which indeed he is not much fitted"—how much more might West and John Franklin have railed on their Inuit friend's behalf over his anonymous lot at York Factory?[20]

On February 4, 1829, Harding, Dunning, Oman, and Jean Baptiste Boisvert, who had been sent to Churchill in the late summer of 1828 to replace Ullebuk, started off to York Factory on foot. In bitter cold, and sixteen hours of darkness out of the twenty-four, they walked for seven days and spent an eighth holed up in a leather tent on the north bank of the Nelson River to wait out particularly nasty weather. Harding thought fit to note, "Nothing strange occurred on the route." When they set out on the 150-mile trek home in the last week of March, Augustine was with them. "Boisvert remained at York," wrote Harding, "and Augustine takes his place."[21]

※

FOR AUGUSTINE, RETURNING TO CHURCHILL MEANT RESUMING old chores with old friends. He spent all of March cutting trees several miles to the southeast of the post, and early in April he and William Oman started hauling the logs home. Harding sent him with Moses to hunt seals on the ice at Back Bay at the beginning of May, where the two men spent a peaceful three weeks together before the Knapp's Bay people began to trickle in.

When visitors were announced by runners on May 6, Augustine generously sent them a welcoming gift of the same items the Company always sent to incoming groups but in more generous supply: five pounds of gunpowder, fifteen pounds of shot, twelve flints, and four pounds of tobacco. Harding recognized Augustine's generosity by making a note in the margin of the Servants' Account Book that the "gifts were sent by Augustine and paid for by him." In mid-June, Harding hired two of the Inuit who had settled in at Seahorse Gully and set them to rafting seal blubber from the mouth of the river to the oil house inside the stockade under Augustine's supervision.[22]

At the end of the month, because "the ice is now all driven to sea," and the seals with it, the hunters moved on to Seal River for whales. More beluga than usual had already been seen in the river mouth and the Inuit were anxious to get to the northern whaling station, where they expected to find even more beluga. Within the week they had killed forty-one and were trying to solve the problem of delivering the blubber to the post. Harding had neither the men nor the boats to help with transportation—"we are unable to render any assistance from the few men here," he wrote—and assigned Augustine to organize "the whole party to bring the two boats they have...laden with blubber...and to make a second trip."[23]

Harding's annual Churchill District Report for 1828–29 was done by June 15. He had few complaints about his permanent staff and offered restrained praise for their work. Thirty-four-year-old cooper Alex Dunnet was "a steady trustworthy servant" who "conducted the trade with the Esquemaux in a satisfactory manner." James Dunning was "a steady servant, but naturally slow in all his motions, can make himself serviceable here and is occasionally employed hunting geese or partridges." William Oman, a veteran of eight years with the Company, was a "steady, obedient, and active servant and very serviceable." Moses was also, in Harding's opinion, "a steady, obedient and willing servant." Baikie Sinclair was "a steady obedient servant, and serviceable as blacksmith," married and with two children.[24]

Of Augustine, Harding noted an improvement in his attitude since his return from York. "Augustus Esquemaux was employed as labourer at York Factory from August [1828] to March [1829] when he arrived here, since which time he has been constantly employed here. He appears to have lost most of that nonsensical pride taught him by the late Expedition Gentry, and not to be above making himself useful in any duty required of him at present, which was far from being the case last year. He likewise was but too fond of spiritous [sic] liquors, which he must have been encouraged to partake of by his late employers as the Esquimaux never received any liquor at this Post. He is not engaged, and will go with his friends this summer, according to his own request."[25]

The Fort Churchill Account Book that accompanied Harding's district report noted that at the end of May 1829, Augustine had asked that fifteen shillings should be transferred from his account to the account of a man named François Doré at York Factory, in payment of a debt. The York Factory Abstract of Servants' Accounts added details of the financial situations of Augustine and Ullebuk. Ullebuk, identified as "C369, middleman, assigned to Lac la Pluie," had a credit balance of £108/14/3 on June 1, 1829, £7 of which was owing in Churchill. On the same end-of-outfit date, Augustine, "C368, Esquimaux Indian, laborer, assigned to YF," had a credit of £94/6/10. Moses owed £4/9/9 to the men's shop at York Factory, where he already had a debt of £14/15/1.[26]

During the last two weeks of June, Augustine made several trips to the men's shop. Between June 15 and 27, his purchases included items he would need as a hunter, and items his wife would use as she made clothes for her family.

1 white cotton shirt	10 glovers' needles	12 lbs ball shot
2 silk bandana handkerchiefs	1 bundle china beads	10 gunflints
3 yards blue stroud	1 bundle blue agate beads	5 gunworms
½ yard plain green stroud	½ lb white enamel beads	1 7-inch hand dag
5 yards army lace garters	⅛ lb round beads	3 roach knives
5 yards M.I.S. garters	5½ lbs twist tobacco	1 clasp knife
5 yards plain garters	1 grafting saw	

Figure 6. Augustine's purchases at Churchill, June 1829. (Source: HBCA, Churchill Account Books, Men's Debts, B.42/d/131 [15–27 June 1829].)

Glovers' needles and bundles of assorted beads—china, blue agate, and white enamel—were suitable gifts for a woman who worked the patterns of power and protection into her family's garments. The clasp and roach knives would have been welcome additions to a nephew's tool bag, and a white cotton shirt with a silk bandana knotted at the neck was appropriate finery for greeting loved ones after a long absence. Augustine frugally reduced his total expense by returning a 5½ gallon tin kettle, an oval tin pan, and a used gun. After deducting the returned goods, Harding charged his account with £2/7/9.[27]

ON JULY 9, RUNNERS ANNOUNCED INCOMING INUIT. WORD SPREAD quickly through the post that the hunters were Augustine's kin and fellow villagers, among them his nephew Annagyniak. As he had done in May, Augustine sent gifts at his own expense: one pound twist tobacco, half a pound of gunpowder, one and half pounds of shot, and one flint per person.[28]

A full week later, two vessels from York Factory, *Endeavour* and *Dogskin*, hove to around suppertime. On board with Dunning and Sinclair, who had taken Harding's district report to York Factory, were five York men as crew and, surprisingly, Ullebuk, who had appeared at the factory sometime after mid-May. No explanation for his recall from Lac la Pluie, or perhaps his own refusal to stay there, appeared in the Churchill journal, although it is most unlikely that Harding simply greeted Ullebuk and let it go at that. As it happened, more pressing events had taken place at Seal River that needed Harding's attention without delay.[29]

Only hours after Ullebuk's unexpected appearance, a party of hunters from Seal River showed up with one boat "laden with blubber" and reported that a contrary wind had driven the other boat and its cargo onto the rocks. Men still at the whaling ground were trying to make repairs before the boat sank. Others made it to Churchill with "some difficulty in saving their lives and saving their cargo" in the watery turmoil created by wind and tide battling each other in opposing directions. Even within the shelter of Churchill River, the whale hunters were unable to force their way upriver. An attempt to land at the Stone Fort failed, and the boat ended up at Cape Merry, five miles downriver from the post on the eastern banks. Harding got its crew into another boat and sent them off to rescue the stranded vessel.[30]

While Harding dealt with a sinking boat and a stranded one, fifteen new arrivals from the north, Augustine's fellow villagers, reached the post late in the evening and wanted to trade at once and be on their way. Harding put them off until the next day, the nineteenth, and, after trading with them, seems to have had a few words with Ullebuk. He did not record what passed between them, but he agreed that instead of going back to York Factory, Ullebuk could stay and work at Churchill. Baikie Sinclair, who had already tendered his resignation and planned to return to Britain on the next supply ship, agreed to stay on with the Company and was willing to replace Ullebuk at the more southern post. Within twenty-four hours, Sinclair and his wife, Elizabeth Swain, had packed up their possessions and their two small children and were on their way to Lac la Pluie with a stopover at York Factory.[31]

Another thirteen men from Augustine's village arrived before July 23 and joined the whale hunters already at Seal River, with Augustine and Dunning tallying their kills in the Eskimo Trading Book for the year. On the twenty-seventh, six men arrived from Seal River with a boat "laden with about 3/4 tun of oil [and] the flesh of two whales for our dogs." Because the whales were leaving, the hunters made plans to start for home. All of them were at Seahorse Gully by the night of the twenty-seventh, and on the twenty-eighth they left in an armada of kayaks with Augustine and Annagyniak among them.[32]

A WEEK AFTER AUGUSTINE LEFT FOR HIS HOME VILLAGE, CREE couriers arrived from York Factory with a letter from Chief Factor McTavish instructing Robert Harding to make his annual trip to York Factory earlier than usual.[33] Harding thought the trip would be a good time for a trial run in "the double Esquemx canoe" recently built by Ullebuk and Moses, and he took the two of them with him. They left Churchill on August 17 and in the first few hours "doubled Cape Merry in safety, altho there was a heavy swell." But their luck did not hold. Early in the afternoon, while they were trying to get ashore to plug some of the leaks in the canoe's fabric, a curling wave swamped them completely and split the little vessel's skin bottom. They spent the rest of the day mending the tear and trying to dry their sodden clothing. On the sea again early the next morning, they made slow progress. Wind and waves were too strong for the delicate craft, and they had to "land up the canoe and commence walking."[34]

They managed about fifteen miles a day on the spongy, lowland hummocks, and nine days later, with wet and swollen feet, aching legs, and faces scarred and bleeding from mosquito attacks, they reached the shelter of the hunting tent near the mouth of the Nelson River. No one was there, so they carried on up the river and "commenced burning the woods, in hopes that some person might see the smoke." Nobody showed up in response to the smoke, until one of the York Factory men, Belonie Gibeault, and two Cree couriers happened to pass their camp headed for Churchill to get some dogs. Harding scribbled a note to let Alex Dunnet know which dogs to send and which to keep. Finally, on the thirtieth, a boat crossed from York Factory and delivered the Churchill men to the dry comfort of the Great House.[35]

When the Churchill men set out for home in *Endeavour* on September 19 with a year's worth of overseas supplies, "principally flour, oatmeal & coals," three new hands were on board along with two York Factory Cree to make up an adequate crew. The new hands were John House (blacksmith), William Driver (cooper), and William Deerness, a sailor new to the service. Deerness was at Churchill less than a year before he was assigned to the Company's new venture to the northeast.[36]

The trip turned out to be one misery after another. A fresh northward wind struck them with enough force to send them desperately looking for a creek where they could lie in safety. In a fast-ebbing tide, they went aground about a mile from the high-water mark. For five days, *Endeavour* lay sideways in the mud. When they finally floated free and made a run for deep water, they were caught again in the unfavourable wind and dropped both anchors. They rode safely for about two hours, until one of the anchor cables broke. The second anchor held in the tossing sea, while the men sat "in constant dread of losing the only anchor" they had. At daylight they saw the line of beach about three miles distant and for the next twenty-four hours fought the wind tacking toward land. In the process of swinging over their own anchor they opened a gaping hole in the hull. *Endeavour* started to sink, "in 4 feet of water," Harding wrote glumly, with casks "actually floating in the boat."[37]

Repairs were impossible. On October 1, Harding gave up, took Ullebuk and one of the York Cree with him, and started for home on foot. The others were left "to finish up stowing" and follow when they could. Twelve days later, when the three foot travellers estimated themselves no more than two days' fast march from Churchill, Harding forged ahead, slept in the open, and reached the east bank of the river the next day.[38]

❧

WHILE HARDING AND ULLEBUK WERE STRUGGLING TOWARD HOME, Governor Simpson was trying to get in touch with Augustine. On October 6, two Cree couriers delivered a letter from Governor Simpson at Moose Factory, dated August 11, 1829, to Chief Trader Robert Miles at York Factory requesting that Augustine be found and sent to Moose Factory for a special assignment, identified only as the "North East Expedition."[39] A copy of the letter was made and Miles entrusted it to William Oman, who was about to leave with the Churchill bateau. Two York Factory couriers went with Oman to bring back Harding's response. "The packet," wrote Harding in reply, "is principally concerning an Esquemaux Interpreter to be sent back immediately with these two Indians to York Factory where two other Indians have expressly come to accompany the Esquemaux to Moose for the Ungava Expedition. Augustine is the person wished by Governor Simpson to be sent but as he is now absent with his friends with no chance of his being found I intend engaging Moses & Ullebuk for the purpose."[40]

Harding spoke to Ullebuk, who was willing to undertake a new expedition but, as Harding foresaw, only if Moses also engaged for the job. Moses, it seemed, was amenable, and both agreed to new contracts. Harding supplied them with snowshoes and "everything required for the trip," while the two men made their own "preparations." Their backpacks contained clothing, bedding, some provisions, and a kettle and spoon dangling from the straps. Their firebags, fastened to their belts beside their sheathed knives, held flints, tinder, dried moss, clay pipes, and tobacco. Guns hung on shoulder straps along with gun cases containing flints, powder, and shot packed into the cases' pockets. Each of them set out on the 150-mile walk south to York with a small bundle of emergency medical supplies.[41]

Just a month earlier, Moses had spent close to £10 at the York Factory emporium and was well supplied with new clothes, work equipment, and sugar. On October 16, Harding added a dressed moose skin, a pair of sealskin boots, and two pounds of twist tobacco to Moses's purchases, free of charge. Harding also credited his account for the return of a corduroy jacket Moses had bought in June and provided free of charge a round-head axe, a gun, and an ice chisel—articles that Harding conceded were "work-related" when the work was being paid for by the governor's office but that were not considered necessary for the jobs the two men did at the post.[42] Ullebuk had also been shopping, on September 18, and spent a total of £6/15/5. His October 16 purchase was limited to a second pair of drab corduroy trousers.[43]

On the morning of October 18, the two Inuit with their York Factory guides crossed the still-open Churchill River in a bateau. Because of new snow, snowshoes were necessary, and once again Harding provided them as items "required for the trip." Fifteen days later, they were at York Factory, and Harding's letter explaining that Augustine was not available, at least for the next eight or nine months, was in Chief Trader Robert Miles's hands. While they waited to be handed over like batons in a relay race to the next pair of guides sent to retrieve them, Moses and Ullebuk settled in, taking advantage of the factory's well-stocked men's shop to outfit themselves and keeping busy with small chores around the post. They also had the interesting experience of watching one of York's cooks slaughter three pigs.[44]

Predictably, Moses was the first to visit the men's shop. All but one item was a ready-to-wear addition to his wardrobe. The cleaned and softened moose skin Harding had given him would have been used for the production of boots and stockings by a local seamstress or tailor.[45] Ullebuk did his shopping a day later, making similar choices, including a dressed moose skin. These items were charged to the Governor's account, according to a note attached to the account book: "The above supplies, being required for Oulibuck's voyage from York Factory to Moose, and valued at the summer sales tariff. Total £3/-/1." No similar gloss appeared next to Moses's name, but he would have been treated in an equal manner.[46]

In the last week of November, two Cree guides arrived from Fort Albany ready to take the two Inuit on the next leg of their journey. Robert Miles introduced the Inuit and their Cree guides to each other, while John Charles interpreted in three languages. Miles made notes on what was said at the meeting that would later be copied into the York Factory journal for November 22, 1829. "[We] explained," he wrote, "the care which they [the guides] are expected to take of the Esquemeaux, both in regards to feeding them the same as themselves, and not to distress them by marching more expeditious than they find convenient. One of the Indians...named Sutherland and understands English assured me that I need be under no apprehension, as he would pay every attention. Indeed, they already appear to be on very friendly terms. Mr Charles had previously given them their supplies for the voyage, but as they expressed a desire for a little more tobacco I ordered them a pound each gratuitous."[47]

As soon as it was light enough for them to see on the morning of November 23, the little travelling party set out, carrying letters to Governor Simpson and

Chief Factor William Christie, who was due to take over the York Factory command in December. Miles's letter to Simpson brought the governor up to date on his desired interpreter for the North East Expedition.

> The day following receipt of your instructions I dispatched two Indians from this place to Churchill for the purpose of procuring Augustus as interpreter. They returned to this place on the 2d instant bringing me a letter from Mr Harding dated 17th Ulto (copy of the same therewith transmit) by which you will learn that Augustus was living with his tribe, in consequence he forwarded Oulibuck and Moses, both or either to be sent, but recommended the latter. They seem however to wish not to be separated, and as by so doing possibly one may not proceed willingly alone, I have thought it advisable to forward them both not doubting but that it will meet with your sanction and that they will make themselves useful to the Expedition.[48]

Ullebuk and Moses were on the trail for fifty-three days, in temperatures near 40° below zero. For Moses, the trip was a nightmare. His legs burned with intense pain from the unaccustomed gait of snowshoeing, and cramping in his swollen feet made it almost impossible for him to walk at times. The party reached Albany on January 14, 1830, where the journal recorded that "we had the pleasure of seeing arrive the two Indians [Cree] who were sent to York on the 20th August. Two Esquimaux have come with them, one accompanied Captain Franklin on his northern expedition, the other is an elderly man. Why he is sent, except to keep company with the other, I have not been informed."[49]

Their stay in Albany was short. Guides were already waiting to escort them to Moose Fort, along with two of the men who would be their close companions for the next three years, William Taylor and George McKay. After a four-day rest, during which Moses nursed his painful legs, they were on the road again, heading for Moose Fort with "six days' provisions and any other thing they may require for the journey." The brief stop had not been enough for Moses. The first day back on the trail, severe pain in his legs crippled him past the point of being able to walk. The Albany guides settled him on their small sled and took turns pulling him. Fortunately, the weather was, by local standards at least, mild and pleasant. They reached Moose Fort five days later and were greeted by George Gladman, Clerk in Charge, on the evening of January 23.[50]

None of the Company's officers noted in their journals and letters that Ullebuk and Moses had been given any explanation of where they were going and what they were intended to do when they reached their unknown destination. Even so, they must have picked up some information along the way. Communications between trading posts were frequent and, considering the transportation technology of the times and the geography and size of Rupert's Land, surprisingly fast. Chief Factors and Clerks, from McTavish to Harding, along with every man in a Company bunkhouse were speculating about Governor Simpson's plans for a northeast expedition.

The facts underlying all the gossip about the North East Expedition were simple enough, at least on paper. Governor Simpson wanted a fort at the bottom of Ungava Bay. A dozen men had been chosen for the project. The senior officer was to be Nicol Finlayson, Clerk in Charge in Albany District; Finlayson's second was to be Erland Erlandson, Clerk in Charge at Eastmain. They were to lead a party of ten men from Richmond Gulf through a network of lakes and rivers to the mouth of the Koksoak River on Ungava Bay. There they were to build a trading post. In addition to the simple facts, rumours were rife: Ungava was a bleak and desolate place; the Inuit were fierce, violent, and constantly at war with the people who lived just south of the Koksoak River; Cree guides were afraid to go there; winters were bitterly cold and summers unbearably hot. The rumours, it turned out, accurately described Ungava.

WHAT ULLEBUK AND MOSES SAW OF THE CHANGING LANDSCAPE ON the way south was considerably more lush than their home country, even in winter. For Ullebuk, much of it was familiar after his journey with Franklin and the six months he had spent at Lac la Pluie. To Moses it was a new world of trees. Balsam fir, quaking aspen, and paper birch that did not exist in his northern home surrounded the travellers as they walked, and the familiar black spruce and tamarack were taller than any trees he had ever seen. At the small Cree villages they passed, he got his first glimpses of bark-covered teepees, insulated with thick layers of moss.

Moose Factory in 1829 was an imposing complex of buildings and fields. Its palisade walls sported tall watchtowers; its buildings, some of them with three storeys, occupied an acre of cleared land and were connected by raised wooden walkways. Another twenty-four acres of cleared land served as natural pasture for cattle and horses. Chief Factor Christie's 1829 annual report for Moose dwelt lovingly on the fort's gardens. Just over five acres—more than two and a half times the size of the entire Churchill establishment—were under cultivation, most in potatoes, the rest in turnips and a few other vegetables. Nearly half an acre of well-sheltered land produced upwards of seven or eight bushels of barley every summer. The vegetable harvest in the previous September, Christie wrote with pride, "amounted to 1000 bushels, which may be considered as exceeding considerably a general average of returns." Although the newcomers were getting their first glimpse of the place in the dead of winter, and could only imagine the gardens in full production, their plates were well stocked with homegrown produce at nearly every meal.[51]

The Company's rules on the separation of officers and labourers were respected and in force at Moose. The Clerk in Charge, George Gladman, lived in the officers' quarters with his wife, Harriet, their children, and his mother-in-law. They had their own dining room and enjoyed the services of a cook-waiter, George Rivers. The factory's usual complement included a tradesman class of three blacksmiths, two boatbuilders, two carpenters, and one cooper, as well as ten labourers and a cowherd. The men had their own dining room and their own cook, Daniel Reed. Among the men, both George Moore and John Saunders are known to have been married, with sons living at the post. Wives and daughters also lived and worked at the post, but their names, and even the fact of their existence, were seldom remarked upon in the journals or correspondence. There was also "one invalid" being cared for at the post.[52]

Gladman assigned the two Inuit to bunks in the men's kitchen. A week later, while Moses was recovering "from the fatigues of the journey," Ullebuk was lending a hand with chores, "doing light jobs such as cleaning away snow, cutting a little wood, and carrying up water." Life in the kitchen with the cook, Daniel Reed, was warm and comfortable, food was abundant, and the work was easy. The furnishings of their quarters included all the cook's equipment as well as their own bunks and small leather kists (trunk lockers) and, on occasion, such unlikely things as a bundle of staves newly cut by the cooper and "put up to dry in the mens' kitchen."[53]

Chores sometimes involved the unexpected. In February the two Churchill men had the rare good luck to observe a bull and a horse yoked together hauling a sledge of timber to the sawpit. On the evening of February 17, the cowherd came up one short in his count of the calves as he herded them into the barn. Moses and Ullebuk were called on to help in an "utmost search...all over the island." After a day of poking into every possible hiding place on the plantation, "no trace of the little animal was found." The searchers concluded that it "must have fallen into the hole [in the river ice] from which the cook draws water and immediately carried under the ice by the current." Having by then carried many pails of water from the river to the kitchens, Ullebuk and Moses were thoroughly familiar with that hole in the ice.[54]

On other days, they were on kitchen duty. Gladman discovered that "from the severity of the weather about the beginning of this month [February]... much of the potatoes in the vault are frozen." Ullebuk and Moses spent four days squatting on a canvas spread with potatoes, assisted by all the boys of the establishment, "picking out such as appeared to be frozen" and covering what was left with hay and "deerskin tentings." The "boys" were the sons of two employees, John Saunders and George Moore, "natives of Hudson Bay," as well as others never named in the journals.[55]

From late March to early June, Ullebuk and Moses continued to earn their keep, mostly by doing domestic chores considered to be light duty. During the week of March 22 to 29, they were cutting wood for the office. In April, as the days lengthened and the snow melted and gathered in pools that threatened to flood the buildings, they took on the more arduous job of making drains. Near the end of May, it was time to get the garden planted; one of

Moose's men, James Davidson, explained the concept of fertilizer to Ullebuk, placed his hands on a wheelbarrow, and set him to carting and spreading cattle manure, while James Morwick, another man assigned to the northeast expedition, hilled seed potatoes.[56]

As the river ice began to thaw, the men's, as well as Gladman's, attention shifted to the anchorage where two coasting vessels, *Beaver* and *Union*, had just been lowered from their winter moorings. All went well with *Union*, which was lowered and safely moored in the channel. *Beaver* was more difficult to deal with. The men managed to lower it a short distance, "which placed her in comparative security," but at the end of the day the vessel was still in danger of tipping over, because, as the journal noted, "much ice is still adhering to her keel." On the twenty-second, over it went, coming to rest on one side "apparently without sustaining any injury," or so Gladman hoped. A task force of six—two sawyers and four labourers—cleared out all the sloop's ballast, "lightened her of all her spans, cable, anchors, &c, and got a chain out in readiness for bearing her off in case of a high tide." As a precaution, they also unloaded all the gunpowder and stowed it in the magazine.[57]

WHILE ULLEBUK AND MOSES WERE AT MOOSE FACTORY SEARCHING for a lost calf and sorting frozen potatoes, their friend Augustine, his wife, and their three children were setting out on a twenty-five-day trek across the barren lands that brought them to Churchill on March 11, 1830. They entered the trading room on March 12 with the products of their winter's work: one white fox, six parchment deerskins, two deers' heads, one deer's head with blood, a skin bag of fat, and a "tooth," probably a walrus tusk. Their trade was meagre in the extreme, a poor showing for eight months' work, and the deers' heads and fat can have been of little use to Harding except perhaps to feed to the dogs, as Augustine would have known.[58]

There are questions here that Harding did not ask, or perhaps he just did not bother to record the answers. Where had Augustine and his family spent the winter that it took them twenty-five days to reach Churchill? Why did they come in March, before seal hunting began? The twenty-five-day journey Augustine and his family had just completed echoes a visit described by George Taylor in 1827. That year, eight men and a boy from Augustine's village came to the post on June 9, having taken seven days to cover the distance between their inland camp and their bayside village and another eighteen days along the shore to reach the post. Comparing the travel times noted on a map drawn for Peter Fidler in 1809 by an Inuit elder named Nayhektillok with the report of the 1827 visitors indicates that they may have wintered along the lower Thelon River or at Baker Lake and from there followed the river to Chesterfield Inlet and thence to Churchill. The coincidence of both journeys having taken twenty-five days is not enough to conclude that Augustine had also wintered at the Thelon, but it is suggestive.[59]

Why Augustine came to the post so early in the year may be answered by Harding's comment that "Augustine is now entirely destitute of actual necessaries...and since he left here last year with a large supply, he has managed to squander it all among his friends." Such poverty, "destitution" as Harding called it, would be motive enough for them to make the trip south in the worst of the winter and early spring. The first part of Harding's statement is probably accurate. Their immediate "necessaries" were for gunpowder and a powder horn; without a functioning gun, the chance of bringing down large game would be almost nothing. Harding's use of the word "squander" is unwarranted. Augustine's poverty is a sure sign that even with the "large supply" he took with him when he left Churchill, his whole community had had a difficult winter, possibly living at the edge of starvation. If, as is likely, he had used some of his money for the good of his community, he was not being reckless. Few, if any, of his people would have thought so. It was his duty to share with his people, and with his wife's, when they were in need. It was also, in the Inuit world view, his pleasure to do so.[60]

Nor does Harding's comment mean that Augustine was destitute in an absolute sense. At the end of Outfit 1827–28, Augustine's credit balance with the Company had been £98/14/10. A year later, the opening credit balance plus wages minus expenditure left a closing balance of £94/6/10. He had spent

£19/8/0 during the outfit, certainly a considerable sum of money but, just as certainly, not his entire fortune. The same account book recorded Ullebuk's credit balance as £101/11/3.[61]

When Augustine left the post, he had told Harding he would return with his friends to hunt seals later in the spring. Harding relayed the information to his superiors at York Factory by letter on May 1. On receiving the letter, Chief Trader Robert Miles was uncertain whether Augustine's services would be required at Ungava in addition to those of Ullebuk and Moses. His response was to tell Harding, "In regard to Augustine, I do not wish that you should engage him at present, but merely detain him in the vicinity of Churchill in event of his yet being required for the Ungava Expedition."[62]

Ten weeks later, Augustine and his family were back at Churchill having "arrived from a party of 10 who are on their route here," according to Harding. He added a sentence he had already used in the annual district report he had just finished. "From all I learn, with the exception of deerskins they have little in the way of trade."[63]

Whatever it was that Augustine had to trade, there was nothing pitiful about what he could afford. His overland expedition money and the country products he brought together amounted to over £100. When he and his wife left the trading room on that visit, Augustine had a new gun, plenty of ball, shot, and gunpowder, a number of essential cutting tools, and a new capote. His wife had gartering, beads, a goodly supply of needles, and brass finger rings for working the identifying patterns into her family's clothing. Three shirts and three large handkerchiefs could have been for any member of the family, but because there were three of each, it is tempting to think they may have been special treats for the couple's three youngsters.[64]

Augustine hunted seals throughout June and July, trading seal blubber and meat for a little tobacco, flints, gunpowder, ball, a small round-head axe, a roach knife, and a new powder horn. By the twentieth of July, Chief Factor Alexander Christie had decided that Augustine was needed at Ungava after all, and he wrote Harding that Ullebuk and Moses had "arrived at Moose Factory in perfect safety and by the last intelligence from thence, they were preparing to depart in company with the intended Expedition for the Ungava District." But, continued Christie's letter, "It will nevertheless be necessary to engage Augustus on moderate terms, say £15 per annum, for three years in which case he should be sent hither by the return of these boats."[65]

Harding followed Christie's instructions and engaged Augustine. On his last day at the seal hunt, July 28, Augustine brought out two white fox skins and agreed to sell his two dogs to the post. Except for his purchases of June 1, everything he bought to July 28 was bartered directly against the products of his seal hunt and entered in the Eskimo Trading Book. He charged a few things on July 29, worth £4/16/8, to be drawn against his Churchill account, and transferred £9/13/4 from his district account held at York Factory.

Harding, typically, made no mention of Augustine's wife and children in his Churchill journal or his letters to York, but later evidence confirms that Augustine's wife and one son, their youngest child, accompanied husband and father to Ungava. The other two children, one son and one daughter, would have been put into the care of a kinsman still hunting seal near the post.[66] Harding assigned the family to one of the boats taking Churchill's returns for the outfit to York Factory. Ten days later, Christie's letter of August 2 reached Harding, confirming Augustine's transfer to the east. "We have retained Augustus," he wrote, "for the purpose of proceeding hence with the vessel which is to deliver the outfit for the Ungava district on her homeward voyage."[67]

While waiting at York Factory for the vessel that would take them to Ungava, the Augustine family did more shopping, stocking up on items they thought might be in short supply at their new home, especially sewing notions for his wife.

INTERLUDE 4

THE NORTHEAST EXPEDITION
1830

AS EARLY AS THE 1740s, THE HUDSON'S BAY COMPANY'S MEN AT Albany and Eastmain were gathering information about The Labrador, the great expanse of land between Hudson Bay and the Atlantic Ocean. They had heard that it was occupied by large numbers of local tribes in the south and Inuit in the north, all potential trading customers for a company committed to expansion. They had also heard from the Cree hunters of the Hudson Bay east coast that the land contained stands of trees sheltering huge herds of caribou and great lakes filled abundantly with fish of many varieties. The London Committee gave instructions to the traders on the eastern shores of Hudson Bay and James Bay to send sloops to the north whenever possible so that ships' captains could learn more.

The traders and sloop captains did not bring back the kind of information the Committee wanted to hear. They reported that the fine forests, reindeer herds, and teeming lakes were less fine and less teeming than the Company had been led to believe, and the woods, wildlife, and waterways they had heard about did not extend north of Richmond Gulf. Beyond the gulf the coast was uninviting, there being neither "wood nor bush nor brake nor hardly one liveing thing." The Company's interest in the area faded except for occasional forays from the James Bay posts to the southern interior.[1]

The interior of the Labrador and Ungava peninsulas north and east of Richmond Gulf was still unknown territory when the Company undertook its major reorganization in 1810. The only European visitors to have taken a close look at the eastern interior were members of the Society for the Furtherance of the Gospel among the Heathen, commonly known as Moravian Brothers. Their missions lay along Labrador's Atlantic coast, a string of tiny settlements from which missionaries alternately preached the gospel and traded with the local people. They had come into the region with the blessing of the British Colonial Office after the transfer of New France and Labrador to Britain at the end of the Seven Years' War. The new territory proved extremely difficult to govern, not least because of Inuit raids against European fishing settlements along the Atlantic coast. The Colonial Office solved its administrative and defence problems in 1771 by giving the Moravian Brothers the exclusive right to settle and govern the area and sweetened the agreement by giving them a monopoly on trade.

In accordance with their mandate to preach the gospel, the Labrador Moravians sent two of their missionaries, Brother Benjamin Kohlmeister and Brother George Kmoch, to explore Ungava Bay in 1811. Accompanied by four Atlantic coast Inuit families, they sailed north from Okak, around the tip of the Labrador Peninsula into Ungava Bay, and as far south as the Koksoak River at the bottom of the bay. Exploring upriver for about twenty-five miles, they identified a site they thought would be appropriate for a mission.

They named the site Pilgrim's Rest and deemed it "a very good place for a Missionary settlement," it being "pleasant, with wood, grassy plains, and gentle hills." They noted that "the timber in the woods hereabouts is not large" but had no concerns about the adequacy of local building materials or fuel because "the woods appeared very thick…[and] the Esquimaux say that higher up, large timber is found." They described the attractions of the place, including "great quantities of sorrel and other European plants" and an abundance of berries, while reindeer tracks led them to conclude that they had come to "a place much frequented by these animals."[2]

The Report of the Moravian Brothers was the only report that expressed a favourable view of northern Labrador. Missionary zeal, a failure to appreciate the practicalities of domestic life, and a tendency to recognize familiar and desirable features within an environment while ignoring its strange and troubling aspects were the rose-coloured glasses through which they saw the place. Few other men familiar with the region in the nineteenth century took survival there for granted. James McKenzie of the North West Company wrote that to live even in the southernmost parts of the tundra required "blood like brandy, the skin of brass and the eyes of glass, not to suffer from the rigours of a Labrador winter."[3]

The Moravian Society, while it had a legal monopoly on trade on the Atlantic side of the height of land, was no threat to the Hudson's Bay Company. It recognized and respected the trading rights of the Company in Rupert's Land and beyond. Although Ungava Bay was not in Rupert's Land, and therefore not legally off limits, the Moravian Society diplomatically requested permission to establish a mission there and to support it through trade with the Indigenous people. Permission was not forthcoming.[4]

While the HBC could be sure that the missionaries would honour its decision and keep its missionary-traders within its assigned territory, Inuit from Ungava Bay and Baffin Island were used to trading at the Society's posts, and the London Committee had no scruples about drawing off their trade for the Company's benefit. There was also a possibility, even a probability, that other traders, not constrained by the ethical position of the religious society, would try to set themselves up in competition with the Hudson's Bay Company. Rumours that the North West Company was setting up posts in the Labrador interior were already circulating by 1810.

To establish its tenuous sovereignty more securely, the Company sent three small expeditions inland from James Bay between 1816 and 1820. George Atkinson Jr. and John Stewart, on a canoe journey of about 375 miles up Great Whale River in 1816, were unimpressed by the country. They saw no signs of beaver—the most desired of trading commodities—and no caribou, ptarmigan, fish, or hare, the essentials of a trader's larder. Just as serious a drawback from a trader's point of view, there was no "appearance of the natives frequenting the interior parts for some years past." In fact, they reported, "It is a most barren country, a very bad river, no fish to be procured, and little or no game to be seen." Atkinson's second exploration, from Richmond Gulf in 1818, did nothing to change his opinion of a barren, inhospitable, and dangerous country.[5]

In 1819–20, another Hudson's Bay Company employee, James Clouston, explored the rivers and countryside along the southwestern coast of Ungava Bay and concluded the area was "by no means a good like country for beaver." Descending the Kaniapiskau River (South River), he reached the juncture of the Kaniapiskau and the Netwakamy (Larch River) where they united to create the Koksoak River. He did not follow the Koksoak to the bay, but what he had seen convinced him that neither resources nor potential clients could be depended upon. "From the partial survey which I have made," he wrote to his superiors, "I cannot venture to recommend the establishing of any new post." Farther inland along the Kaniapiskau and Larch Rivers he noted other drawbacks: "rock in many places, other places sand and gravel"; insufficient birch bark for making canoes; increasing barrenness and absence of trees suitable as firewood toward the north; and rivers so full of rapids as to be unnavigable, with steep, rocky banks where a boat or canoe could not land or be man-hauled from the shore.[6]

The merger of the two fur trade companies in 1821 removed the possibility of competing posts in the Labrador interior, at least for a few decades, and the question of an Ungava trade was set aside during the reorganization. As the 1820s were ending, however, Governor Simpson turned his attention to the region. The severely cold climatic regime that gripped much of the northern hemisphere from about 1790 to 1830 had reduced the numbers of animals available west of Hudson Bay and greatly impeded communities' ability to hunt and trap. Overhunting had also played a part in reducing animal populations in some areas. The Company's shareholders felt the decline in their dividends. The Governor's plan for increasing the trade, submitted to the London Committee in September 1827, reopened the issue of expansion into Ungava Peninsula and Ungava Bay.[7]

Simpson appointed William Hendry to make a new exploration in the summer of 1828. Hendry's second report expressed serious doubts about the feasibility of future trade in the region. He saw no place along the Koksoak River suitable for a trading post and no substantial population of potential new customers in the interior, or prospects for a good trade. He described the country as "barren and rugged, alike destitute of wood...and animals." What was worse, the Cree people he consulted during his exploration warned him that north of the treeline there was a constant danger "of being butchered by the Esquemaux," which, Hendry thought, "would be an insurmountable obstacle."[8]

Simpson chose to ignore the observations of his own officers and men, who reported that the rivers were frozen all winter, potable water was in short supply in the summer, the banks of the Koksoak River were so precipitous that they were unnavigable, freighting goods and personnel by water was not possible, the scattered stands of spindly trees were inadequate for post construction and a post's needs for winter fuel, birch was so sparse that canoe manufacture was problematic if not downright impossible, and the James Bay Cree were unfamiliar with the geography of the country and as a result were unable and unwilling to act as guides, or even enter the area at all, out of fear of the Inuit.

When it came time to lay his reasons for establishing a post in Ungava before the Company's ruling body, Simpson cited Brothers Kohlmeister and Kmoch. "From the report of the Moravian Missionaries who visited those parts a few years ago," he told the London Committee, "we have every reason to hope that a good field for trade will be found." He continued to make his case by declaring that "various sources," which he did not name, indicated that "the means of living are abundant in deer, fish and fowl, likewise that the country produces timber" and "the natives" are "very numerous."[9]

Governor Simpson's mind was made up, and he managed to convince his superiors in London that the country would yield profits to repay the effort of setting up establishments there. "Our original object in settling Ungava," he wrote to Nicol Finlayson, his choice for District Clerk in Charge at Ungava, was "to open a communication with the Esquimaux on the coast...and by degrees to settle the Interior and to open a trade in Furs with the Tribes inhabiting the

Country…behind the Moravian Missions on the Coast. This original object we still have in view, and mean to follow up." Governor Simpson assumed that the construction and maintenance of the physical plant, the conduct of trade, and the serious business of surviving in Ungava would follow patterns similar to those of other trading posts familiar to the men of the fur trade. He refused the notion that building, maintaining, and living at the proposed Ungava post would be more difficult, perhaps impossible, and certainly extremely dangerous to the lives of its people because of Ungava's inhospitable environment.[10]

What made the post on the Koksoak River different, even unique, was its isolation. Six hundred miles of extremely difficult country lay between the post at Eastmain on the eastern shore of Hudson Bay and the small fort that Simpson planned to build on Ungava Bay; 200 miles separated it from the nearest Moravian mission at Okak on Labrador's Atlantic coast. Mail, provisions, trade goods, and medical assistance could not be summoned up at will, nor were recreational and restorative visits in new surroundings possible, as they were in other places. There would be no regular express bringing letters, no dependable ship's visit in late summer, no sloop or whale boat to take the sick or injured to the nearest surgeon.[11]

When Churchill Post ran out of gunpowder, or needed a medical man, no more than two weeks were needed to restock the shelves, and medically trained men could arrive in less than a week. Moving the winter packets of letters and supplies, while it could be dangerous when human beings were ignorant or careless, was relatively safe, frequent, and straightforward in the Company's other territories. Couriers routinely left York Factory for inland posts between freeze-up and the approach of spring and, using a relay system, were able to deliver mail and packages as far as Fort Resolution at Great Slave Lake in ninety days or less.

Not so in Ungava. There would be no one dropping in for Christmas, as Charles Brisbois had done at Fort Franklin; no possibility of sending for medical assistance, as Churchill's Thomas Topping had done during the typhus crisis; no sending to the next post for gunpowder when stocks ran low, as Adam Snodie had dealt with. Even finding guides, such as the men who had delivered

Ullebuk and Moses safely to Moose Fort, was impossible. The Inuit who lived north of Richmond Gulf had a reputation for ferocity and violence, and those from Baffin Island who hunted there in the summer were an unknown quantity—and for that reason all the more frightening. The Cree who were clients of the Company's posts in James Bay and Eastmain, while loyal and steady, were afraid to go into the unknown country, and Nicol Finlayson was well aware, as he reported to Simpson and the London Committee, that "the NE expedition since first it became a subject of conversation was looked upon with terror...by the labouring class."[12]

Every day, the men of Ungava would risk hunger, exposure, accident, and possible death from starvation, freezing, drowning, or an infected wound. Even George Simpson, blindly determined to have a post on the Koksoak, recognized the danger he was sending his men into. In his Character Book for 1830, he wrote opposite Finlayson's name "gone on dangerous service."[13] The doubts that clerks, traders, and factors had about the feasibility of the plan, they kept to themselves. "The duty of the [clerks and traders] is to sit and listen to whatever measures the governor may have determined on," one of them said, "and give their assent thereto, no debating or vetoing being ever thought of; the Governor being absolute, his measures therefore more require obedience than assent."[14]

Governor Simpson somehow failed to recognize that a post on the Koksoak River would face insurmountable problems, especially in the matter of provisioning both food and necessary equipment for building in territory close to void of resources. To get supplies to the new post, he decided that in the first year two vessels would visit: one, the sloop *Beaver*, destined to be permanently moored in the Koksoak River and used for visiting Inuit villages and other communities around Ungava Bay every summer; and the other, a chartered brig that would take building supplies, tools, and other necessary items in the first year, including food, to the new post.

With the agreement of the London Committee, Simpson set his plan in motion, choosing three men of officer rank to lead the founding party: Nicol Finlayson to establish and command the post; Erland Erlandson as Second, to set up outposts and to locate, map, and mark a track where future posts should be built; and William Taylor, formerly a canoeman, interpreter, and steersman in the Albany district, as Master responsible for daily operations at the new post. Instructions were sent to various establishments to alert nine men of lesser rank to prepare themselves for the expedition and to report for duty at Moose Factory before the beginning of June in 1830. Of the nine men, only one was specially hand-picked by Governor Simpson: the interpreter Augustine Tataneuck.

CHAPTER 9

THE UNGAVA ADVENTURE

1830–1833

THE UNGAVA MEN, 1830, OVERLAND

Nicol Finlayson, Clerk in Charge
Erland Erlandson, 2nd in Command
William Taylor, Post Master
George McKay, blacksmith
John Hay, boatbuilder
Frederick Faries, labourer
James Morwick, steersman
Joseph Rocher, steersman

Moses Esquimaux, interpreter
Ullebuk, interpreter
James Slater, labourer
Richard Prince, labourer
Louis Le Fond, canoeman
BY SEA Augustine Tataneuck with his wife and son

BY JUNE 3, 1830, ALL THE UNGAVA ADVENTURERS WERE AT Moose Factory except Erland Erlandson and James Slater, who were at Eastmain, and Augustine, who at that point was not expected to join the expedition. Erlandson had already spent a year preparing for the journey, coming up against one obstacle after another. His mandate was to hire guides and hunters from among the East James Bay Cree, who were presumed to be familiar with the geography, wildlife, and human occupants of the territory. Only two were willing to accept the job: Mascataugan and his brother Payopscum agreed to go, but after Payopscum's death in the winter of 1828–29, Mascataugan's plans were unclear. Just as troublesome was the matter of canoes. Erlandson had hired several men to build a small fleet of birchbark canoes and deliver them before March of 1830. When the canoes were finally delivered in June, they were too small and too few for the expedition's needs. While Erlandson struggled with problems of logistics, the other expedition men were making their way toward Eastmain House.[1]

NICOL FINLAYSON'S SMALL BRIGADE LEFT MOOSE FACTORY ON THE evening of June 10, 1830. Three large canoes belonging to the Hudson's Bay Company and one small canoe owned by two Cree guides paddled into the face of a strong northeast wind. Two of the large canoes were heavily loaded with provisions, tools, and trade goods; the third carried the wives and children of the two Cree guides. Ullebuk was a competent middleman, but Moses, skilled though he was in a kayak, was not familiar with the synchronized rhythms of several oarsmen. As a mere passenger, he was assigned a seat on the luggage bundles in the centre of one of the canoes.[2]

On the first leg of the journey, the party pushed against drifting ice in heavy rain and gale-force winds. Ice, wind, and a roiling sea forced them to camp from June 17 to June 21. Finally, on the thirteenth day at sea, June 22, they started through heavy fog at three in the morning and spent fifteen gruelling hours crossing the mouth of the James Bay. At Eastmain the following morning, they heard Erlandson's discouraging news that of four guides he had managed to hire, only one knew the route to South River (Kaniapiskau). Finlayson solved the problem of too few canoes by hiring four Eastmain men and their canoes to help move the cargo to Whale River. Even then, only about half the outfit could be fitted into the available vessels. Worse was to come. Erlandson had to tell his already anxious new boss that all of the local men, including the four new recruits, had refused to go to Ungava Bay. The reason they gave was "the severity of a winter in that inhospitable country." Finlayson took precautions. "All the provisions except 54 lbs. lard I got packed," he wrote, "but I took twine and ammunition enough to serve for a season, at least to secure our return if we should be obliged to do so."[3]

Erlandson's last task at Eastmain was to hand over the post to his successor. "Accordingly," he wrote in his final Eastmain journal entry, "I immediately delivered over to Mr Andrew Moar the charge of the Honorable Company's Post and Property, and placed myself under Mr Finlayson's command." The next day, Moar made his first entry: "Messrs Finlayson, Erlandson & Taylor and 10 men and 6 Indians, making a party of 10 canoes,...left this post for the South River in Hudson's Straits." As usual in Company documents, neither Erlandson nor Moar mentioned that the newly hired James Bay men were accompanied by their wives and children.[4]

The brigade fought densely packed broken ice and high winds for eleven days after leaving Eastmain House. At Great Whale River they camped for two days so their guides and hunters could make arrangements for the women and children to live with a band of Great Whale Cree while the men were away. "I could not well refuse," wrote Finlayson, who, with some of his men, spent the extra day "drying our cargo and otherwise usefully employed."[5]

Pulling onto the beach at Little Whale River two days later, the guides again found kinsmen and refused to go on until they had feasted together on a newly killed porpoise. The reluctant guides had another excuse for refusing to embark. An old hunter "used all his eloquence to persuade us to return," Finlayson wrote, "saying the country we were going to settle in did not produce so much wood as would boil a kettle; that the natives would kill and eat us; and such like." Finlayson and Erlandson, in response, used all their eloquence, along with taunts of cowardice, to get their guides into the canoes. A few hours of paddling brought them to the narrow strait leading into Richmond Gulf. Here they breakfasted, and by four o'clock in the afternoon they had crossed the gulf and entered the Deer River. Two and half hours upriver they came to the first portage and made camp.[6]

THE FIRST FULL DAY ON DEER RIVER, JULY 14, WAS "VERY SULTRY," wrote Finlayson, "and we feel it the more, the transition from cold to heat being so great and sudden: yesterday along the coast we had to guard against cold, to-day we are scorched by a burning sun." The first day's two portages, plagued by mosquitoes every inch of the way, was a mild introduction to what was still to come.[7]

On the Deer River the travellers were going uphill to the peninsular height of land through a series of lakes connected by rapids like a string of randomly threaded beads. Between July 14 and July 24, Finlayson's men made twenty-five portages and carries, some of them between lakes, some up rapids, and others down falls. At times the crews were hip deep in water guiding the canoes through shallows. More than once, one or more of the men suffered painful injuries carrying canoes and goods over "very bad and broken ground." The Cree guides began to claim that they were "indisposed" and could go no farther. Mosquitoes continued their maddening attacks, except on days of violent rain and heavy winds. The brigade reached the headwaters of Deer River on July 24 and faced three more portages between lakes, "each a stage long."[8] The same day, one of the canoes was stove on a rock, "by the carelessness of the bowman." Finlayson closed the day's entry by remarking, "I never saw mosquitoes so dreadfully numerous as this afternoon."[9]

The descent to Ungava Bay began at the headwaters of the Larch River (Netwakamy), where they made three short, easy portages and shot thirteen rapids, six of which required that the canoes be lightened and the goods, as well as the canoes, carried. As the rapids became steeper and swifter, the travellers had to "hand down the canoes" with ropes. On the twenty-ninth they ran five rapids, and for the second time, one of the canoes was stove. Adding to their misery, clouds of blood-hungry mosquitoes settled on every square inch of exposed skin. Blood smeared the men's faces and dripped from hands clutching slippery paddles.[10]

Besides worrying about the welfare of his men, Finlayson had to deal with his nervous and unhappy guides, who were "under fearful apprehension of the Esquimaux." On July 29, he "put ashore to settle with them," gave them one canoe to go back in, and redistributed his men and baggage to continue downriver. The second strong rapid of the day "broke the head of one of the big canoes nearly off." After running six more "very strong rapids" the next day, the party reached the junction of the Larch River (Netwakamy) and South River (Kaniapiskau), which together become the Koksoak. Here they brought their canoes side by side and let the current carry them toward Ungava Bay, "a thankful respite from our late labour."[11]

Finlayson's goal now was to find a place to build the new post. In the widening river on August 2, he split the brigade into two parties, one to each side of the river, with orders to watch for an "eligible situation to form an establishment." Two things were necessary: first, wood, for building storehouses and dwellings and for fires to heat them, and second, a safe anchorage for *Beaver*, the sloop that had been promised as part of the new post's permanent equipment. Finlayson also kept in mind that *Montcalm*, the supply ship, would need deep water to reach the new site.[12]

A STRONG EBB TIDE CARRIED THEM TO THE MOUTH OF THE KOKSOAK River on August 4. Here the land was desolate, unsuitable even for an overnight stop. The men proceeded back upriver for a second look at Unity Bay, where the river widened and was surrounded by a generous stand of larch trees. Finlayson and Erlandson concluded that the Moravian missionaries, Brothers Kohlmeister and Kmoch, who had recommended the site as a "very good place for a Missionary settlement," had not made a choice based on reality. The presence of trees for building and heating was an attraction, but the river was too shallow to overwinter a ship. "Places that are commodious for the vessel are destitute of wood," Finlayson thought, "and where some wood might be procured is inconvenient in other respects. Loam we did not see in this river." The absence of loam at the site was a serious problem, not least because it was the only effective means of chinking crude log and stick buildings against bitter cold and wind.[13]

The final choice of building site was on the east bank of the river about twenty-seven miles from the sea where the Koksoak is about a mile and a half wide.[14] There was deep water—not a perfect anchorage, but the "most eligible spot we could find...convenient for discharging of vessels...and a safe winter berth for the sloop." The site was "destitute of wood for building, and clay," but a decision had to be made. All hands went to work cutting timber and clearing the ground for their first building's stone foundation. They worked on half-empty stomachs. The poor hunts of three weeks on the river had forced them to go on short rations: "one pint corn [all types of grain] and half-pint flour or oatmeal per diem," Finlayson wrote. "On these miserable rations the people wrought well." In the afternoon, Ullebuk shot a large buck caribou, "for which seasonable supply," he wrote, "we thank kind providence."[15]

Finlayson continued to worry about food, carefully recording each day's catch of fish and the often disappointing results of Ullebuk's hunt. The men cooked, ate, and slept in tents, with no "convenience" other than the scattered low shrubs. When it wasn't raining, the weather was "sultry." On fine days, they were hunted by mosquitoes; on rainy days, they battled wind as they hauled stones, felled timber, and set fishnets. The obvious ploy of hanging nets from floats did not work, because the swift river current and the high tides, even twenty-seven miles upstream, lifted the nets to the surface, trapping few fish. Finlayson fiddled with the nets until he found a way to pin them to the riverbed with stakes. On August 12, the catch was seventeen white fish and one trout. After this success, Finlayson and Erlandson spent a day in the rain changing the rest of the nets.[16]

At the beginning of the second week, all hands went upstream to cut timber, except Ullebuk, who built a fire and began boiling juniper bark to dye fishnets, and Moses, who went hunting. The timber crew was back in two days, rafting home enough wood to build two houses. By the end of the week, they were ready to start building.[17]

On Tuesday of the third week, the foundations for three buildings were in place and a storehouse and dwelling had been framed. The carpenters, Erlandson and William Taylor, had a roofing problem—they had not found grass suitable for thatching and, for good reasons, were reluctant to use the plentiful arctic moss surrounding them. Arctic moss is a highly dangerous construction material. A low water content and rapid drying habit make lichens and mosses particularly susceptible to fire. Mosses contain high levels of flammable ether, as well as lipids composed largely of fat and wax, a deadly combination that ensures a low ignition point and an extremely hot burn. Lichens and mosses also have a far greater surface-to-volume ratio than do vascular plants, which prevents deep burning and facilitates the rapid horizontal spread of flames.[18]

The chances that an unwanted fire could start at the new post were high, in part because of the characteristics of the available firewood and in part because of the nature of the post's cooking and heating arrangements. The most common and most accessible firewood was larch, one of the hardest of the coniferous woods. In its "green" state it produces more smoke than fire, but once dried, it not only has good burning quality due to its high resin content but also has a tendency to spark. Indoors, open, dry stacked stone fireplaces, leaky stoves, and sooty chimneys cannot be counted on to confine sparks and resin flares. The constant drafts swirling from poorly fitted caribou-skin doors and shutters, and through inadequately chinked log walls, too often encourage flames to go where they are not wanted. Outdoor fires are equally dangerous for their tendency to shoot sparks, and at northern trading posts, outdoor fires were common. Ullebuk dyed his fishnets over an outdoor fire, the blacksmith worked outdoors whenever possible, and Moses and Slater burned all the rubbish in the open air year-round. A single stray spark from any source onto a moss roof could destroy a tent or small building within a few minutes. Because all sources of water are frozen for much of the year, it is impossible to douse a fire.

Erlandson and Taylor finally decided, reluctantly, to try one of the local grasses for thatching and set four men to the job of gathering. Moses and Ullebuk went hunting, accompanied by Finlayson's prayers. "I need hardly say how much we want [a deer], if kind providence would make their hunt successful, for the people are working hard and starving." The nets yielded only twenty-five small fish during an entire week, nowhere near enough to satisfy the stomachs of thirteen men doing heavy labour on half rations. To add to the general misery of carrying logs and stone and levelling land, and in spite of "violent rain," the mosquitoes were bad again. At week's end, the men had to give up working in the woods.[19]

WHILE ULLEBUK AND MOSES WERE REASONABLY SAFE ON THE EAST bank of the Koksoak River, at least for the moment, their friend Augustine was starting his journey to Ungava. Travel arrangements were made at York Factory according to Governor Simpson's instructions. The North East Expedition plan called for the sloop *Beaver* to take supplies and provisions to Ungava, and the addition of a late-arriving expedition member or two to the manifest was no problem. But, as had been the case in 1828, *Beaver* was found unfit for the trip and, even after extensive repairs, was in danger of being swamped in high winds during its first attempt to get into Hudson Bay.[20]

The vessel that Simpson planned to send with supplies for the new post was a chartered vessel, *Montcalm*, under Captain Robert Royal. The 215-ton brig had construction problems, with water leaking into the cargo holds and a false keel given to breaking. Three times at York Factory, *Montcalm* "took the ground" and needed repairs. An investigation by the Company's boat carpenters showed "a very bad leak…in her Garbert [garboard] plank." Chief Trader Robert Miles blamed *Montcalm*'s construction—it "being very indifferently fastened"—for problems arising from what would be a harmless "gentle rub" for one of the Company's sturdier vessels.[21] In addition to the problems inherent in *Montcalm*'s construction, any number of hazards lay in wait for the vessel, from the predictable autumn gales of Hudson Bay and its random equinoctial tides to the shallow, uncharted waters of Ungava Bay. There was a good chance that *Montcalm* might never reach the Koksoak River.

Governor Simpson prepared for both success and failure. On August 25, he dictated four letters with instructions on what to do with Augustine in any eventuality. In the event that *Montcalm* made it safely into Ungava Bay, found the Koksoak River, and made contact with the Company's people there, Captain Royal carried a letter for Nicol Finlayson. "We send you Augustus," the governor wrote, "whom we think you will find useful, as he is faithful, attached, intelligent, and can make himself pretty well understood in English."[22]

Simpson's second letter, to Captain Royal, lumped Augustine in with the cargo: "An Esquimaux interpreter, Augustus, is forwarded by you, likewise a boat for the use of the establishment, and a few packages of leather, ironworks, &c." Royal was instructed that if he did not reach the Koksoak, or if he failed to find the Company's people there, he was to sail on to Quebec and deliver a letter, along with Augustine, to the Company's agent, James McKenzie. Simpson's letter to McKenzie dealt with Augustine in a single sentence: "An...interpreter Augustus is on board, whom you will forward to Mr Keith at Lachine." The fourth and final letter, to James Keith, alerted him that "a few articles have also been put on board here, as p[er] Bill of Lading & Invoice, also an...Interpreter Augustus....forward him to the Northern Department by the canoes of next season." Thus was Augustine's welfare assured, assuming that *Montcalm* stayed afloat long enough to make it into the Koksoak or the St. Lawrence. Of Augustine's wife and son, nothing was said.[23]

With the Augustine family's small leather trunk stowed on board, *Montcalm* sailed from York Factory on August 27. Passage was "quick," only seventeen days, but the ship was "buffeted a good deal by the currents" after entering Ungava Bay. For passengers whose stomachs were unused to rolling seas, the journey was decidedly unpleasant.[24]

THE STRESS OF LIFE AT UNGAVA WAS TAKING A TOLL ON FINLAYSON. He worried about food resources, about the men's safety and comfort, about *Montcalm*'s whereabouts, and when or if *Beaver* might arrive. He found some respite in long walks to a rocky mound near the post that he called his chapel. There he sat alone for long periods, watching for any sign of the expected ships. With his anxiety building, on the last day of August he sent Erlandson and James Morwick downriver to map its rocks and shoals, take soundings at both high and low tide, and set up a beacon to mark its mouth. At the same time, he sent Ullebuk and Richard Prince to camp at the river's mouth and watch for the arrival of either ship.[25]

The same day around suppertime, the first Inuit clients arrived in six kayaks and two umiaks. Moses answered their calls by inviting them to come ashore, where a great deal of handshaking took place. Finlayson brought out gifts for everyone and directed them, with Moses's help, to a place where they could pitch their tents. They had nothing to trade except skin boots, which Finlayson stocked up on for the use of his own men. Two days later the Inuit went upriver to hunt deer.[26]

At about ten o'clock on the morning of Monday, September 13, a "joyful circumstance brightened every countenance." Ullebuk and Slater arrived from the coast in Erlandson's canoe, and with them was Augustine.[27] For Finlayson, the arrival of *Montcalm* meant a restocking of the post's pantry. In his first report to Governor Simpson about the state of the North East Expedition, one sentence comes as close to revealing his innermost thoughts as anything he wrote: "We were beginning to look with terror on the barren rocks that surround us, when blessed be the Father of Mercies, the brig appeared in the river and dispelled all our doubts and fears." In relief and thanksgiving, Finlayson called a halt to the day's work and handed out a bag of flour and some pork from his greatly depleted supply of provisions, and the men celebrated with "a hearty and joyful breakfast."[28]

After breakfast, Finlayson headed downriver to join Captain Royal and his crew for the last few miles to the new post. The journey proved hazardous when the captain failed to follow Erlandson's advice on the safest course, and *Montcalm* went aground in shallow water. Within five minutes, the brig was free, but its false keel was once again damaged.[29]

Over the six days following the arrival of *Montcalm*, the post's men worked at bringing cargo ashore. "Boisterous" weather, with high winds, storms, and showers of hail and snow, kept the work at a slow pace, and, what was even worse from Finlayson's point of view, *Montcalm* had only one boat suitable for carrying heavy and bulky items. The post's two large birchbark canoes were called into service to land smaller items, causing Finlayson considerable concern. In a letter to Governor Simpson, he stressed his unhappiness: "When your Honours consider how ill adapted birchrind canoes are for carrying heavy cargo, you will be pleased to [see] that we lost no time in facilitating the brig's departure from this place,…for nothing but mere necessity would oblige me to spoil my canoes which are invaluable to me at this place."[30]

Erlandson piloted the brig out of the river on Tuesday, September 21, "which duty he accomplished much to the satisfaction of Captain Royal," who seems to have been as glad to leave as Finlayson was to see him go.[31]

WINTER SET IN BEFORE THE END OF SEPTEMBER. THE TEMPERAture dropped below zero, and within a few days all the ponds were frozen. Enough snow had fallen to make walking without snowshoes difficult and tiring. Four buildings were completed: a storehouse, two dwellings, and a kitchen. The carpenters built chimneys and an oven, ripped logs for flooring, and made a hatch for the cellar. The labourers had their hands full building and rafting wood. Moses took on the housecleaning work and, despite recurring periods of being "unwell," became assistant cook to James Slater. Ullebuk and Augustine hunted until Ullebuk took a bad fall on slippery rocks and cut his arm seriously enough to keep him idle for several days. With his hunting partner laid up, Augustine scouted for good fishing spots and finally decided to set up a fall fish camp at a lake west of the river. Taylor went with him in order to construct a basket to catch and haul fish, a design so successful that they brought in about seven hundred fish within a few days. The men dubbed the camp Taylor's Basket.[32]

Finlayson finally had to give up his hope that the sloop *Beaver* would arrive that year. The men were no less disappointed. Their luggage was to have come on the sloop, and its failure to appear meant they were deprived of their personal property, including their storage boxes, for at least a year. Only Augustine had his cold weather gear and a few changes of clothing, safely tucked into his small leather trunk. He also had the comfort of family life with his wife and son.[33]

When Morwick closed Taylor's Basket for the season, Augustine and Ullebuk insisted that fish were still to be had at a lake not far from the Basket. Finlayson agreed to let them operate a fishery there until the river was completely frozen. On November 1, in fine weather with a temperature of 20° Fahrenheit, they set out in a small canoe to fight their way through swirling ice to the west bank of the river. The post journal is silent on the subject of Augustine's family, but his wife and son would have been at the new fishery with him, if only because their absence from the post relieved Finlayson of the burden of feeding them.[34]

At the House, the carpenters began making furniture. Frederick Faries turned wood for snowshoe frames and handed them over to Finlayson and Erlandson for netting, a job they could do by firelight as the nights grew longer. Morwick finally had time to work on a "house of convenience."[35]

Six months into the Ungava project, the stress of isolation, work without recreation, inadequate food, crowded quarters, and long, dark nights began to affect the men. A week before Christmas, an argument between Joseph Rocher and James Slater escalated to the fisticuffs stage. Finlayson fined them for "indecent conduct," deducting ten shillings from the former's account and fifteen from the latter's. December 25, according to Finlayson's journal, was kept as a holy day by the men, and on the twenty-seventh, the men were "sleeping out their Christmas gambols." They observed another "holy day" the following Saturday, January 1, 1831, and were back at work on Monday, January 3. Taylor's first business that day was to make a new door for the Men's House, the old deerskin one having somehow been set on fire during the celebrations.[36]

EARLY IN THE NEW YEAR, FINLAYSON BEGAN TO WORRY ABOUT Augustine and Ullebuk, who had been at their fishery since November 8. "All communication between them and us has, with the exception of a day or two, been cut off by floating ice in the river.... I am apprehensive they have starved." He sent Moses and Richard Prince to check on their well-being. Prince was back on January 15 to report that Moses and the two fishermen were on the way but moving slowly, "they having no snow-shoes, and walking without is tiresome."[37]

Finlayson was also concerned that his superiors had no idea of the difficulties he and his party were experiencing. It was, he and Erlandson decided, well past time for a report of the Ungava project to be delivered to the Governor. Erlandson, Prince, and Faries were chosen to go to Moose Factory to deliver news of the new post, its people, its prospects, and its problems to the Company's senior officers.

In preparation for the journey, John Hay and William Taylor built sleds, Augustine and Ullebuk scraped deerskins to make snowshoe netting and harnesses, and Finlayson cut traces for the post's dog. Planning on a forty-five-day journey, Finlayson set aside provisions amounting to one pound of flour and one pound of pork per man per day, adding ammunition in case they saw any game on the road. A load of 120 pounds, the upper limit of what the post's only dog could pull, was lashed onto the sled. The rest was divided into the men's backpacks. On Sunday, February 13, all hands kept the Sabbath and prayed earnestly for the safety of the travellers, and at six thirty on Monday morning the little party left the House.[38]

Erlandson carried with him two letters from Finlayson: one to Governor Simpson and another to Chief Factor John George McTavish. The somewhat terse letter to McTavish contained a brief description of the overland journey to Ungava Bay and a summary of events and conditions at the new post, along with a lament for the promised *Beaver* sloop. "The non-arrival of this vessel," Finlayson wrote, "deprives me of many necessaries and of the means of ascertaining what a coasting voyage might produce....I am for the present at a loss to judge what quantity of goods and provisions I may require for outfit 1833."[39]

After the departure of the travellers, the stay-at-homes got on with their usual jobs in spite of temperatures that swung wildly from a low of minus 35° Fahrenheit to a balmy 27° on the first day of March. Heavy snowfalls kept the hunters from their tents and drove the carpenters indoors when their sawing pit filled with snow. Finlayson worried about the effects of the bad weather on the trail. "The travellers have not been very fortunate in getting good weather in the beginning of their journey," he noted on February 20.[40]

On one of the relatively windless days, Augustine and Ullebuk trekked out to Taylor's Basket for a load of cached fish and found the whole supply rotted as a result of mild weather. At the same time, George McKay and Louis Le Fond reported no deer in the vicinity. Fortunately for the men's stomachs, the mild weather attracted ptarmigan, and the hunters brought in 204 in a single day. Toward the last week of February, the snow-laden clouds disappeared and the strong rays of the sun burst the walrus-gut windowpanes of the Men's House. Three days later, before new window coverings could be fashioned, the mercury plummeted to minus 34° Fahrenheit. When a sudden storm hit during the night of March 21–22, leaving snowdrifts "as high as the houses," Finlayson fretted about Taylor and Ullebuk, who had been sent off the day before to survey False River twenty-five miles from home and were camping in the open.[41]

By the end of March, the first snowbirds had appeared, followed immediately by a day of snow and a day of heavy rain, which caused the houses to "drop at every pore." On the last day of the month, the temperature rose from 32° Fahrenheit in the morning to 50° at noon, and the men left their sawing and timber hauling to clear the snow out of the yard and cover the store and houses with oilcloths.[42]

Temperatures continued to fluctuate during April, from a low of minus 18° Fahrenheit to a high of 32° above. Rainy days were followed by falling and drifting snow, which gave way to bright sunshine, only to turn to overcast and rain once more. The hunters proved unproductive. Fewer than 150 ptarmigan were killed during the entire month, 105 of them brought in by Slater and Ullebuk—both suffering from snow blindness after four days at the hunting tent. Augustine and Moses, long overdue from Taylor's Basket once again, were another source of worry to Finlayson, and on April 12 he sent Slater and Ullebuk to look for them. They returned the next day without having seen any sign of their friends and, just as distressing, without deer. Finlayson blamed the hunters. "Had I one good Indian hunter," he wrote, "I should have more meat in one season than I can have in two years with such miserable hunters as I have at present: not but that they are eager and willing to hunt, but they have no idea of it further than lying in wait in the paths until they happen to see some crossing."[43] Finlayson did not record what, if anything, he said to his hunters, but either their luck or their efforts took a turn for the better, or perhaps it was just the time of year when the caribou were moving. Within a week, tracks of two herds were seen, and the hunters estimated each herd to number at least a hundred animals. Augustine, Slater, and Moses together brought home eighteen deer in eight days. Geese were also in evidence by early May, and Moses and Slater began to dish up more sumptuous meals.[44]

The temperature, rising steadily to 3° above freezing, coupled with the lengthening of the days and more abundant food, put new heart and energy into the men. They reacted with a bout of spring fever, undertaking a thorough housecleaning, crafting tools to make their work easier, and producing chairs, tables, chests, and other articles for their comfort that they had not had time to make during the first ten months at the Koksoak.[45]

Two Inuit families, having made a six-day journey from their wintering site, arrived on May 19 hoping to buy a gun on credit and pay for it after their summer hunt. Finlayson promised them two guns as well as other articles if they would stay by the river and hunt whale. On the twenty-first, the two families headed downriver, accompanied by Moses under orders to check on the welfare of Augustine and Ullebuk, who were out hunting. Moses was back two days later with Ullebuk, who wanted help bringing home nine deer from the hunting tent. Finlayson was characteristically pessimistic: "As the ice is very weak on the river am afraid we shall have trouble before we get them home." Less than a week later, the river was full of heavy, driving ice. Nevertheless, Rocher and Le Fond set off in a small canoe with Ullebuk to fetch the meat, returning safely five days later with Augustine and the meat of nine caribou.[46]

JUNE OF 1831 WAS WARM. TEMPERATURES HOVERED IN THE 40s, AND frost crisped the ground on only six days. Augustine and Ullebuk spent much of the time at the river mouth, hoping to intercept any passing Inuit. Finlayson had instructed them to "prevent any of them who might be inclined to go along the east coast for the purpose of meeting the Esquimaux from the Mission, whom they were in the habit of seeing yearly and barter with them." Moses asked for, and received, time off to go with them in order to get his "kyak sewed by the women." Perhaps he was interested in female companionship for reasons other than having his kayak covered. Both he and Ullebuk had recently bought several chintz shawls, and either or both of them may have had more on their minds than finishing and testing Moses's new kayak. The excursion to the coast kept them absent from the House for six weeks.[47]

The interpreters returned from the bay on July 4, "much reduced in flesh from what they were on leaving here," accompanied by three umiaks and six kayaks of visiting Inuit. The newcomers brought about one hundred foxes, both red and white, small quantities of ivory and whalebone, some pipe oil, and some blubber. Other Inuit had also begun to drop in more frequently than Finlayson liked. He and his men, he wrote, were "much troubled by the frequent visits of the poor inoffensive natives, who seem never satisfied with seeing our customs and manners of life." He discouraged them from dropping by unless they had surplus oil to trade and turned his attention to attracting a more lucrative trade. He sent McKay and Le Fond on a reconnaissance of South River (Kaniapiskau) with instructions to persuade any local people to come to the post. McKay packed an assortment of gifts to hand out if they made contact with possible clients. If they left before meeting any local people, they were instructed to leave marks at conspicuous places to let any passersby know there were traders downriver.[48]

A second party in search of customers, consisting of Taylor, Morwick, Rocher, and Ullebuk, went east to explore the George River. Their instructions, like McKay's, were to seek out possible new clients and collect any information about water depth, topography, and the number of whales and seals in the area, as well as taking a census of any people in the vicinity and noting their manner of killing whales—"in short everything worth communicating." Ullebuk, as the only Inuktitut speaker in the party, was to encourage his countrymen to bring their oil and other country items to the House to trade. If anyone they met had furs, they were to be further encouraged by the giving of gifts.[49]

Just as the George River party was leaving, four kayaks arrived from the coast, three of them loaded with meat. A day later, an umiak and four kayaks pulled in from upriver. Two of the upland men were already known to the traders. One was The Conjuror, who had been at the post the preceding summer. Another was Strait Foot's son, who brought the sad news that his father had died during the winter. They were headed for Hudson Strait to hunt seal in the open sea and then intended to go to an even more distant country to hunt foxes. In the absence of Ullebuk, who had gone to the coast, and Augustine, who was out hunting, the only interpreter on hand was Moses. He interrupted his occupations for the day—brewing beer and working on his kayak—and did a creditable job of interpreting.[50]

The number of visitors continued to grow. On the twenty-eighth, three umiaks and twelve kayaks came in with the afternoon tide. It was fortunate that all three Inuit were home at the time. As Finlayson put it, "The three Esquimaux are busy enough although doing nothing, keeping their countrymen from prying everywhere, their curiosity seems never gratified."[51]

TO THE PLEASURE OF ALL HANDS, AND A YEAR LATE, THE LONG-awaited sloop *Beaver* finally reached the Koksoak River, dropping anchor opposite the House at six o'clock on the morning of Saturday, September 3, 1831. An attempt to sail the sloop to Ungava the previous year had been abandoned because "contrary winds,…snow, sleet and generally boisterous weather" had alarmed shipmaster Thomas Duncan and caused him to lay up for the winter at York Factory. From the perspective of *Beaver*'s crew of six, it was not a good year to be at York Factory. When *Beaver* reached Ungava, four of the crew were already suffering from scurvy and after the month's passage were so ill that they had to be carried off the vessel.[52]

With the arrival of *Beaver*, the post population rose by seven men: the sloop captain Thomas Duncan; Joseph Millette, a cooper from Canada; and five Orcadians: George Flett, George Garson, Thomas Garson, William Deerness, and William Malcolm. Finlayson's journal entry for the day contains no information about the new arrivals, not even their names. It was a Sunday, and he refused to make any notations beyond his usual Sabbath record: "+45. Fine weather." Presumably the newcomers were assigned sleeping places, fetched their gear from the sloop, and settled themselves in. One of them, William Deerness, was already known to Ullebuk and Moses. He had been one of the sailors on *Endeavour* in 1820 carrying freight to Churchill, with passengers Ullebuk, Moses, and Robert Harding. Harding had judged him to be so shortsighted that he could "never be entrusted with the charge or even to steer a boat." He was, in Harding's mind, "both indolent and insolent," unable to "agree with his own associates at any time," and "by no means fit for this place."[53] The post's population also increased by one woman, Betsy Kennedy Finlayson, and one baby, thirteen-month-old Roderick Finlayson.[54]

Within four days, the men had all of *Beaver*'s cargo stored away and the vessel itself in a secure wintering site about two miles from the House. Everyone was back to the usual chores—Moses and Ullebuk hunting; Hay making window frames; and Faries, Morwick, and the newly arrived cooper, Joseph Millette, gathering grass for thatching a new house. The invalids, Flett, Malcolm, and the two Garsons, were improving and "getting round fast."[55]

Erland Erlandson and Frederick Faries had also arrived on *Beaver*. Erlandson had much to tell his boss about his seven-month-long journey to York Factory and his visit to Governor Simpson. Finlayson recorded the barest of bones of Erlandson's story.

> Mr Erlandson and Frederick Faries...with Richard Prince, started from here the 14th of February last for Moose Factory....On their journey thither they endured great hardship by being...ignorant of the route....Eventually they arrived at Moose Factory, on April 27, and as soon as the Moose River became navigable Mr Chief Factor McTavish sent off this party, assisted by two men, in a canoe [down the Michipicoton River to Fort William]...but unfortunately when a short distance from Meshipicoton their canoe upset and R. Prince and one of the Moose men met a watery grave. The rest of the party succeeded in getting ashore but with the loss of everything in the canoes, dispatches and all. Subsequently Mr E. and the other two men reached Meshipicoton [on May 21], and by the advice of Mr Chief Factor George Keith proceeded from thence to [Norway House] and York Factory [arriving on June 27] for the purpose of acquainting verbally Governor Simpson with our prospects etc.[56]

Sometime during the next few days, in the intervals between unloading cargo and settling in new recruits, Erlandson reported that the Northern Department Council had fixed on an official name for the Ungava post. It was to be called Fort Chimo.[57]

AS THE FORT CHIMO MEN BEGAN PREPARING FOR WINTER IN LATE September, all the signs indicated that food would be a major problem. Taylor, Morwick, and Flett set up the fall fishery at Taylor's Basket but were largely unsuccessful. Augustine had little success searching for deer. The upriver Inuit were having no better luck at hunting than Augustine was. Several groups passed the post heading for the coast, afraid that they would starve if they stayed on the river any longer.[58]

Stress began to manifest itself in Finlayson's behaviour. On twenty-one days out of October's thirty-one, he did not make a journal entry, even though it was a mandatory daily duty expected of all senior officers at every post. When he did make an entry, usually a short Saturday summary of the week just past, he wrote about his anxieties: no deer had appeared at the usual river crossings; country food for the month consisted of one caribou, 125 ptarmigan, and 1,300 small fish, not nearly enough for his large establishment; Inuit passing by the post were more and more often "in a starving condition"; the Men's House was overcrowded and uncomfortable. More and more he went to his "chapel" in search of a calmer mind. Ultimately, there was nothing he could do about any of it, except the one thing he did do. He kept all his men occupied and feeling useful.

The November 1831 journal has only nine entries out of a possible thirty. Some old problems were getting worse, and new concerns were rising. When it was time to close down the fisheries, the salted and dried supplies were so inadequate that Finlayson decided to keep Augustine and Ullebuk at Taylor's Basket to bring in what few fish might be available and, if possible, to feed themselves and their families. Three local Inuit families decided to spend the winter at the post, "afraid to leave us as they have nothing in cache," which for Finlayson meant that about ten more people had to be fed. The men began to react to the pressures of isolation, poor nutrition, and weeks of winter darkness. Finlayson's November 12 journal entry reported that George McKay and Joseph Rocher had "kicked up a row in the Esquimaux camp about 2 o'clock in the morning of Sunday [November 6]." The price of their misconduct was a fine of ten shillings for McKay and five pounds ten shillings for Rocher. The difference in punishment reflected a difference in their respective crimes. According to Finlayson, "McKay went merely to fetch the other, for which they quarrelled and ultimately fought, for which each of them was fined ten shillings, and Rocher for his scandalous behaviour at the camp £5 more, despising the regulations I made on my arrival here with regard to the Esquimaux women."[59]

One more food item vanished from Slater and Moses's kitchen after four days of heavy rain and freezing temperatures had coated the woods and willows with ice. Ptarmigan had deserted the post to seek better foraging conditions inland. Relations between Inuit and the "Indians" remained problematic.[60] Four men from one of the Naskapi communities coming in to trade were afraid to pass the Inuit camp. They fired their guns to attract attention and would not approach until Finlayson sent an escort for them. The purpose of their visit was to get rum for themselves and sixteen of their companions who waited out of sight. Finlayson was thankful that all the Inuit were safe at the post at the time, because, he wrote, "had this band [the Nascapi] met with them [the Inuit] at a distance from the fort there is no doubt that they would, through mere levity, have sacrificed them." The four were back a day later with all sixteen of their friends, "some of them roaring and singing as they came along: gave them some more rum to enjoy themselves, and they encamped a gun shot from us."[61]

On December 19, Augustine came to the House from Taylor's Basket with exactly three martens, the whole product of his hunt. When he returned to check on the nets on the twenty-eighth, he found a mere thirteen fish, hardly worth the long walk in weather that had turned "very sharp," with temperatures between 23° and 26° below zero during the whole of Christmas week.[62]

THE WEATHER AND THE SPECTRE OF IMPENDING HUNGER MADE A depressing start to the new year. The only advantage of a drop in the temperature to 35° below zero on January 7, 1832, was that there was enough packed snow to cut blocks for porches around the entrances to the dwellings. In the suddenly much warmer buildings, Erlandson spent a week netting snowshoes, McKay and Millette made drawers for the shop counter, and Taylor "sewed" sleds.[63]

On the last Saturday of January 1832, Finlayson opened one of the oil pipes that Rocher had filled the previous July for "serving out blubber to the three Esquimaux families here, as they had nothing these six weeks except what they picked up about the House; they were very thankful for it, the more so as they did not expect it." Finlayson was following a system of providing relief that the Hudson's Bay Company used for more than two centuries. When local residents had a good (or even adequate) hunt and wanted to trade their surplus at the post, Post Masters paid them for it and stored it. When hard times came, as they inevitably did, the traders had a supply of basic foodstuffs laid by, which they could use for the relief of hungry neighbours. The local people benefited from the assistance when starvation threatened, and the Company benefited by keeping its customers alive to trade another day.[64]

The general depression felt by the Company's people and the Inuit wintering nearby deepened when tragedy befell one of the families on January 20. Finlayson wrote the story in considerable detail.

> One of the three Esquimaux families, consisting of a man, his wife and three children, had made a brush tent last fall and surrounded it outside with blocks of snow. The man was confined to bed since last August by the palsy; the woman was wont to keep a fire in the hut, and on Friday last while she was gathering wood the hut caught fire, and the poor invalid and one of his children then in bed with him were burnt to death before we could render any assistance. We however succeeded in rescuing the bodies before they were much burnt. The poor survivor's lamentations on viewing the bodies was truly great. The men dug a grave for them and they were buried the third day in two large hairy deerskins, which I supplied for that purpose, besides two more I gave to the widow to sleep on: they were very thankful, Cooloolae, an old man, rendering all the assistance in his power. He told me with much apparent sincerity that if it was his lot to see ever a white man lying without the rites of

sepulture, he should perform them as far as in his power. I was much affected with the old man's speech.⁶⁵

In February, Finlayson deployed his people on the land, sending Erlandson, Taylor, Faries, and Malcolm to False River to hunt. The first week they got "a few partridges and a porcupine"; the second week, sixty-four birds. Of the regular hunters, Moses arrived with thirty-nine ptarmigan and a porcupine in the first week and fifteen birds in the second. Le Fond and Rocher had eighty-four ptarmigan to show for a fortnight's work.⁶⁶

March brought no relief. The temperature dropped to new lows, and the men whose work kept them in the open air were able to do "little or nothing" the first week, had "no employment" the second week, and in the third week were back to doing "little or nothing." If the men at the House were largely inactive because of the cold, the hunters, living in tents miles from the post, were working hard for a very small reward—a total of 240 ptarmigan. When Augustine came in from his tent on March 17, he had three trout and a wolverine and reported "nothing to be got except a few fish." By the end of the month, Deerness and Le Fond were ill, two starving Inuit had arrived from the coast, and Moses reported in from his hunting tent, also starving.⁶⁷

In April the weather turned "soft." Food was still a worry, but sunshine and warmth heartened the men. The woodsmen were able to go back to work cutting pickets. Deerness laid the floor in the vault, Millette made small kegs, McKay produced a fur press, some nails, and a number of knives and steels and repaired a damaged pit-saw. As cheering as the bright days and the flurry of activity were, there was no real improvement in living conditions. Augustine and Ullebuk came in from the fishing tent at mid-month with no fish, and along with them came Garton and his brother, two Inuit from the coast who needed help for their families, who were starving. Finlayson gave them eight gallons of oil for their distressed kin. Of the Company's men, Finlayson wrote, "There are five of us infected with the scurvey." By the twenty-eighth, Taylor, Deerness, Le Fond, and Finlayson himself were showing symptoms of the disease. "The scurvey is making rapid strides among us," he wrote. The next time

Moses came home, he reported that the hunters "can get nothing by hunting." He had had a bit of luck, though, and brought back a porcupine.[68]

The first week of May, Moses was back for more provisions. With him was another group of Inuit from the coast, starving because of "having killed nothing this week." McKay, Deerness, Flett, Hay, and the two Garsons were still on their feet, but Millette and Morwick had joined the invalids by May 12, and Taylor was still confined to his bed. Between May 5 and May 26, Ullebuk killed three deer and Faries four—a godsend, but not enough. By the twenty-sixth, McKay was showing symptoms of scurvy and experiencing pain in his foot, which had never properly healed after an accident with an axe on the river. None of the sick showed any sign of improvement, and the general gloom deepened when ten Naskapi who came in to trade a few marten and otter pelts reported starvation all winter and several deaths among their families.[69]

JUNE BEGAN WITH ALL OF THE MEN RECOVERING FROM SCURVY except Morwick, who was not able to get up from his sickbed until the end of the month. Captain Duncan, with help from Malcolm, Flett, and the two Garsons, cut the ice from around *Beaver* and got it out of its winter berth undamaged. Augustine and Ullebuk, having seen no deer for some time, concentrated on fishing, bringing in an average of sixty fish a week, not enough to feed twenty-one company people as well as several Inuit families tenting nearby.[70]

Toward the middle of the month, Erlandson prepared to go inland to establish a new post, the second in the proposed line of posts George Simpson wanted to secure the Company's trading supremacy in the Labrador interior. The two officers had something more pressing in mind than fulfilling Simpson's plan. They hoped that by separating the Company's people into two groups living in different places, they would have at least "a chance of subsisting." On the afternoon of June 23, Erlandson, with seven men, left for the uplands with twenty-seven pieces of luggage in two large canoes and one small one.[71] On July 7, Erlandson sent four men in the two large canoes downriver to get more supplies and deliver his first report. He had by then built a storehouse, set up a fishery, and named the new establishment South River House. He had also spent several days battling a forest fire that threatened the tiny new post.[72]

His men, meanwhile, had reached Fort Chimo. Finlayson, refusing to see that there was no realistic way his people could survive, sent Morwick, "who is convalescent," to manage a fishery at South River House. The two large canoes with the last of the supplies left Chimo on July 17 and were back at South River House on the twenty-second. Morwick reported the full extent of the devastation from the fire, which had destroyed the woods on both banks of the Kaniapiskau.[73]

AT THE BEGINNING OF AUGUST, FINLAYSON ASSIGNED AUGUSTINE as *Beaver*'s interpreter on its first summer voyage into Ungava Bay and Hudson Strait. Finlayson's August 6 letter of instruction to Captain Duncan directed him to proceed along the western coast as far as Hudson Strait looking for Inuit for the purpose of opening trade with them. "As a spur to their future exertions," he wrote, "you may tell them by Augustus that if they exert themselves in hunting foxes and other marketable articles they shall be well paid for them here." Before they sailed at eight on the morning of August 7, Ullebuk brought the ship a bon voyage gift: the meat of half a caribou. The other half he gave to Finlayson.[74]

With the exception of one small deer killed by Moses at the House, it was the last fresh meat Finlayson was to see for two months. Ullebuk was out during the whole of that wet and windy month but was "quite unsuccessful." The fishery was also unproductive, and on September 10, Finlayson sent Malcolm, Moses, and Hay to South River House. They were no more than two hours up the river when they met Faries and Slater bringing Morwick, again seriously ill with scurvy, back to the relatively more comfortable of the two establishments. Erlandson's letter to Finlayson, carried downriver by Faries and Slater, explained the situation more thoroughly, and pessimistically, and ended by telling Finlayson not to send a replacement for Morwick. "If you send the carpenter up here," he continued, "you may if you think proper keep Slater also;

I shall then have five men, which are more than I have employment for, except getting their own living; and it is a matter of doubt with me whether they will be able to find it."[75]

Finlayson's response, carried to South River House by Hay, struck a note of desperation.

> I am much concerned to learn your poor prospects; I had calculated on supporting six of the people in the interior on the produce of the country or I most certainly would have sent the sloop this season for a further supply from York. As it is we must *fight it out the best way we can*, providence assisting.... You are well aware that if partridges and deer are not more numerous this season than last that our stock of pork will be done before it is possible to get a further supply; therefore am confident that you will *leave no stone unturned* in endeavouring to procure provisions for the people that are with you.[76]

Captain Duncan brought *Beaver* into the Fort Chimo anchorage on September 3, having sailed as far north as Bay of Hopes Advance before having to turn back in the face of storms and thickly packed ice. On leaving the vessel, Augustine immediately set about preparing his hunting gear and, with Moses and Ullebuk, went looking for deer. They came back on the twenty-ninth with the quarters of two caribou—small reward for seventeen days' hard work in rain, wind, and frost, and totally inadequate to feed fifteen men, three Company wives, their children, and the elderly and sick Inuit who had come to the post for assistance.[77] In the two weeks from September 22 to October 6, the nets yielded about 250 pounds of fish, which provided the only protein food available and was eaten with flour and oatmeal. To add to the general gloom, a badly undernourished Will Deerness suffered a serious axe wound to his foot, "which will render him unfit for duty at least a month."[78]

AT SOUTH RIVER HOUSE, ERLANDSON'S JOURNAL ENTRIES FOR October and November were almost frantic. "Two of the men came home," he wrote. "They have not caught fish sufficient for their own support....'Tis a wretched country....How we shall subsist during the winter, heaven knows." The next day, "All the fish in store would be sufficient for twenty days only, at a scant ration." Later in the month, "In the evening the men...arrived hungry." And later still, "The four men whom I sent down the river to fish returned: they affirm that while away, they have not caught enough fish to afford them one meal a day; and that sheer hunger compelled them to come home." On November 4 he wrote, "It is literally impossible for us all to subsist here."[79]

Augustine, Ullebuk, Moses, and three of their companions were constantly on walkabout during November, looking for ptarmigan. The efforts of the six of them during the entire month brought home only thirteen ptarmigan and eighteen fish.[80] By November 19, Finlayson faced the hopelessness of the situation and started preparing Faries, Le Fond, and Rocher for an overland journey to Moose Factory to ask for help. At the same time, he sent Malcolm and Flett back to South River House with a letter for Erlandson. "As I cannot support all the people here it becomes absolutely necessary that I should apprise the governor of the state of affairs by a winter packet....We are entirely living on European provisions. There is no partridges. Got no deer in the fall." Augustine, Ullebuk, and Moses also came home, bringing their luggage and fifty small trout, to report a complete absence of deer. The three travellers bound for Moose Factory—Faries, Le Fond, and Rocher—left on December 15, with provisions for fifty-four days, which Finlayson thought would get them as far as Eastmain.[81]

In a letter to Governor Simpson, Finlayson noted briefly that Captain Duncan's voyage along the Ungava coast with Augustine as interpreter had been disappointing. They had seen only two families of Inuit during their search, most of the Inuit having been inland hunting caribou.[82] The rest of the letter dealt with other failures that were of greater concern to Finlayson. In describing Erlandson's venture to the Kaniapiskau River, he dwelt on the treachery of the "Indian guide" and blamed the guide's men, "who failed in their endeavours to make a fall fishing...I cannot but think that the country abounds in fish," he wrote, "the fact is none of his people were good fishermen."

Other than that, he made no reference to the serious food shortages at the two establishments. Much of the letter concerned the subject most likely to catch Simpson's attention: the failure of the local Ungava bands to trade. Finlayson insisted that the failure of Inuit to trade at the fort was "owing to the boisterous state of the weather" and asserted that the "late opposition [the North West Company]" was responsible for having spoiled "a proud, saucy and independent set."[83] He also put his finger on a key fact, one that Simpson probably would not have been happy to hear: the Ungava Naskapi were deer hunters, whose spiritual as well as economic existence was based on their relationship with the caribou herds. They were simply not interested in beaver or in any other kind of trapping.[84]

FINLAYSON MADE ONLY FOUR JOURNAL ENTRIES IN FEBRUARY 1833, noting that the weather was boisterous, sharp, and excessively cold; the fishermen and hunters shot fifty-six partridges and one hare; Augustine and Ullebuk reeled in or speared fifty-six trout; Moses got sixteen white fish from the nets; Morwick took sixteen white fish; and George Garson was well enough for kitchen duty. The last February entry noted that on the twenty-first, Finlayson, Duncan, Malcolm, and Rocher started for South River House but ran out of provisions after being stormbound for three days on the river and were forced to return to the fort.[85]

March brought some relief in the matter of provisions. The Little Captain, a Naskapi, came to the fort to say his band had some meat cached—in fact, had had plenty all winter but had, until then, been afraid to bring it in for fear of meeting "the *Divel* on the road." He wanted help to bring it to the fort. McKay took a work party and came back with 240 pounds of dried meat and two otters. A second trip added another 392 pounds, and a third, 1,368 pounds. Each round trip took a week. Finlayson paid one made beaver per 10 pounds of meat. "You will say that this is dear trading in a country where deer are so numerous. I say so too, but I was glad to get some at any price." He then hired two Naskapi as hunters, hoping to cover a wider territory.[86]

Malcolm and Rocher made a quick trip to South River House and came back with enough horror stories to convince Finlayson that Erlandson and his men were slowly starving. Finlayson wrote immediately to Erlandson. "As I cannot see at present any policy in keeping up your post, you will concert measures to take all your goods and stores down; the boat can take everything."[87]

To add to Finlayson's troubles, three men were on the sick list again by the end of March. Millette, who was assigned to the South River House trip, took sick the first day out and Malcolm had to help him back to the fort; Deerness was still lame; and Augustine was unable to get out of bed on account of an old rupture that had begun to bother him during his last long hunt. He was on his feet again in early April and went off to hunt with Ullebuk and Moses. They were successful to the tune of five deer, "which," wrote Finlayson, "will be a great help to us."[88]

New trouble arose at the beginning of May. Erlandson sent Rocher, accompanied by Slater, to the lower post. "You were probably not aware," he wrote to Finlayson, "of Rocher having ruptured himself a short time before you sent him up to here…: he has been of little service and is now unable to do any duty. I am therefore under the necessity of sending him down, and Slater along with him to take care of him; for, besides the complaint that I mentioned, he is subject to convulsive fits and other fits of sickness, which renders him insensible at intervals." A day after seeing Rocher and Slater on their way, John Hay was ill, "complaining of pain in all the joints of his body." After ten days in bed, Hay was up and working on a new boat. "But," Erlandson wrote, "in consequence of the skin having during his illness peeled off his whole body, his hands are very tender and he is scarcely able to handle a tool."[89]

❧

AMID THE GENERAL MISERY, FINLAYSON PREPARED THE 1832—33 Fort Chimo District Report. His impression of Augustine was not flattering: "A good interpreter, but a drunken sot." Of Moses: "faithful but nearly superannuated." And of Ullebuk: "Faithful and good servant…has agreed for 3 years at 17£ per ano of which he is deserving."[90]

June's soft weather had a cheering effect. Officers and men turned their hands to making improvements around the post. Thomas Duncan planted a flagpole, the men cleared rubbish from the yard, and Millette set a gate in the fence at the back of the post. Regular chores also got done: McKay made harpoon heads to trade and Moses tended the fishnets, while the men boiled oil and filled freshly scrubbed pipes. The sweetness of the Arctic spring made it all the harder for Finlayson to make the only decision that made sense. He knew he could not keep his men alive and healthy through another winter, and he was painfully aware that the poverty of Fort Chimo's trade did not justify the number of men at the post. Six men, perhaps, could survive at the Koksoak River; ten would have to return to York Factory.

In the third week of June, Finlayson sent Taylor and six men in the sloop to South River House with a letter of instruction telling Erlandson to abandon the outpost and come, with all his men, to the fort. To help with packing all Erlandson's store goods and to provide sufficient crew for the inland boat, Finlayson sent "all the efficient men except the three Chimos [the Inuit]. You will lose no time in coming down," he wrote in closing.[91]

During the same week that Finlayson was writing up his district report, Captain Duncan moved *Beaver* from its winter anchorage, did a thorough cleaning, and with the help of William Deerness started rigging sails. Erlandson arrived with all his men in two boats, "one of them a fine batteau Mr E. and the carpenter built this spring," and two canoes loaded with all the goods and equipment from the upper House. By July 30, everything was ready for the voyage through Ungava Bay and Hudson Strait and across Hudson Bay to York Factory. The passengers included Augustine, his wife, and their son, with ten Company men—William Taylor, George McKay, James Morwick, Joseph Rocher, James Slater, William Deerness, George Flett, George Garson, Thomas Garson, and William Malcolm—who were redundant now, at a post too isolated to be profitable and too potentially hazardous to human life to be maintained. Six men remained to run the post: Nicol Finlayson, senior officer; Erland Erlandson, clerk; John Hay, boatbuilder; Joseph Millette, cooper; Ullebuk, hunter; and Moses, fisherman.

CHAPTER 10

"FAITHFUL, DISINTERESTED, KIND-HEARTED CREATURE"

1833–1834

I N THE SAME WEEK THAT AUGUSTINE LEARNED HE WOULD BE returning to York Factory on *Beaver* as soon as ice conditions were favourable to the little vessel getting out of the Koksoak River, George Back was on his way to the Northwest for the third time. On the afternoon of June 17, 1833, Back, now a captain in the Royal Navy, arrived at Norway House from Canada in a light canoe with the flag of the Hudson's Bay Company snapping in a stiff breeze at its stern. The captain's mission was to reach the Boothia Peninsula by way of Great Fish River (also known as Back River) and search for news of the long overdue expedition of Captain John Ross in search of a northwest passage, who had not been heard from since he entered Lancashire Sound in *Victory* in 1828.[1]

Following the example of John Franklin, who had depended heavily on Willard Ferdinand Wentzel and Peter Warren Dease in the first two Arctic overland expeditions, Back wanted a senior officer of the Hudson's Bay Company with him. Governor Simpson agreed to lend him Chief Trader Alexander Roderick McLeod. When Back asked about hiring the rest of the men he needed, the Governor told Back to "go as speedily as possible to Norway

House, where, by intercepting the different brigades of boats on their way to Hudson Bay, [you] might have an opportunity of selecting a choice crew of old hands." Taking this interesting advice at face value, Back did exactly as he was told, and within a week he had his full complement of men. The last crewman hired was the Iroquois Pierre Kanaquassé, who, according to Back, was "an Iroquois belonging to the Company."[2]

During the same week, Back had a chance to talk to three Chief Factors, Alexander Christie, John Rowand, and John Lee Lewes. He asked each of them to find "an Esquimaux interpreter, either in the person of my old friend Augustus, who [is] expected from the Labrador coast, or in that of a lad of the name of Dunning at Churchill, and represented by Governor Simpson as equal to the task." Rowand and Lewes promised to do their best but did not agree with Christie, who expressed his opinion that the Dunning "lad" would not answer Back's need for an Inuit interpreter. As for Augustine, Christie was not sure that he would be available for the new expedition. On September 5, Christie wrote to Back that the *Beaver* sloop from Ungava had not yet arrived at York Factory: "Unless this vessel comes here before the close of the navigation, we will have no means of providing an Esquimeaux interpreter for the Arctic Land Expedition, as the only three persons in the Churchill quarter capable of acting in this capacity are now absent at Ungava District."[3]

BEFORE CHIEF FACTOR CHRISTIE HAD TIME TO SEAL HIS LETTER TO Captain Back, a messenger burst into his office with the welcome news that the annual supply ship, *Prince of Wales*, was bearing toward the anchorage at Five Fathom Hole, and not far behind it, Chimo's coaster *Beaver* was visible to the guard in the watchtower. A day later, Christie confirmed that Augustine was on board.

For twenty-one days after leaving the Fort Chimo anchorage, captain and crew had fought "the great quantity of ice that drove into the bay from the north" before getting *Beaver* safely out of the Koksoak mouth.[4] The fifteen-day passage through Hudson Strait and Hudson Bay was at least as miserable as and considerably more dangerous than Augustine and his family had experienced on *Montcalm* three years earlier. Captain Duncan did not hesitate to let Christie know what he thought of the Company's carelessness in assigning *Beaver* to Ungava, nor did he mince words with that very senior officer. The voyage, he said, was "extremely perilous," and *Beaver* itself was "a frail Bark which in her present defective state is considered unsafe for going to sea." The Chief Factor took Duncan's words to heart and reprimanded the Company in a roundabout way in his circular letter to the Chief Factors and Traders in the Southern Department. That *Beaver* had survived the passage at all was, he wrote, "a most fortunate circumstance."[5]

By the end of the week, Christie had finished his public letter to all Chief Factors, Chief Traders, Clerks, and Post Masters in the Northern Department, reminding them that the Company was responsible for getting Augustine to his destination as expeditiously as possible and instructing them to treat him with the respect due to a member of an important expedition of discovery. "Augustus the Esquimaux Interpreter came here by this vessel (*Beaver*), and is sent hence with this boat for Carlton, thence to be forwarded, so that he may join the Arctic Land Expedition under the Command of Captain Back before the opening of the Navigation next Spring."[6]

With Augustine (and his wife and son) safely on dry land at York, Christie added a postscript to his letter to George Back: "Since writing the foregoing, the Beaver Sloop arrived from Ungava District with Augustus the Esquimeaux Interpreter, passenger, he now departs hence for the purpose of being with you before the opening of the Navigation next spring." Augustine and his family reached Norway House in a brigade of four York Boats on September 21 and waited for the next vessels heading west.[7]

On September 30, the Saskatchewan brigade landed at Jack River, and by noon the next day, under overcast skies and with a fresh southeast wind in its back, one of its large canoes headed west across the lake on its way to Carlton House. Master steersman Paul Boucher *dit* Lamallice, who had led the brigade that carried Augustine and Junius inland in 1820, was in charge. Crammed into the canoe along with the Augustine family and an HBC clerk, John Hutchinson, were six kegs of Red River flour, the packet box in which were Christie's letters to George Back, the Company's current internal correspondence, all the mail that had arrived from Britain on the annual supply ship for the Company's people, and an assortment of the previous year's newspapers and magazines from London.[8] At the oars were fourteen new fur trade recruits from Orkney, whose first job in the service of the Company was to take up the paddles and head inland with all the speed their unaccustomed backs could manage. Augustine missed, by only a few hours, the arrival of three more boats from York, whose passengers included his old friend and mentor, Chief Factor John Charles.[9]

Lamallice brought his boat, cargo, and passengers safely to the Carlton House dock on October 31, exactly a month after departing Norway House. "The Fall boat arrived," wrote Chief Trader John Peter Pruden. "Passengers Mr John Hutchinson, Augustus the asquimeau and his wife and child, and the cargo and packet Box delivered safe."[10]

Life for the HBC's people at Carlton and for their Indigenous neighbours had been particularly difficult that fall. Food was in short supply and, possibly even more unnerving, Cree, Blood, and Stoney people were involved in a series of skirmishes and shifting alliances. Just a week earlier, five Cree hunters had reported to Chief Trader Pruden that they could not find enough animals to support their families and had come to the House with "nothing to eat." They found little to cheer them at Carlton. "We are," wrote Pruden on October 26, "unable to give them any assistance...[because] we are as nearly as ill off as themselves." A messenger from Fort Pitt arrived on the twenty-eighth with bad news of a different kind: war had broken out between the Cree and Blood on the western plains. Cree communities in the vicinity of Carlton, as well as the HBC people at the fort, understood that their own lives could well be under threat within weeks. Fighting of a different sort broke out at Carlton on October 30, when one of the labourers, Pierre Papin, threatened to shoot the Chief Trader in an argument over scarcity of rations.[11]

The weather caused different problems. Although it was "calm, clear, fine," and "mild" day after day throughout October, there was no snow, and dog teams and sleds were out of the question as transport when the ground was bare.

Experienced winterers, knowing that the river could freeze at any moment, would not risk the dangers of river travel. Augustine and Hutchinson had no choice but to wait for better conditions before taking the northerly route to Ile à la Crosse and Fort Chipewyan.[12]

Carlton's carpenter began making sleds in preparation for Augustine and Hutchinson's trek to Great Slave, but the mild weather held and no snow fell during November. The lack of snow cover affected the country's wildlife; game animals were not where they usually were, and reports began filtering in to Pruden of Cree who were "very ill off for living...which prevent[s] them a good deal from hunting." By the last week of the month Cree families were "pitching to the fort in a starving condition." Hutchinson and Augustine, anxious to be on their way, grew more and more frustrated at the delay.[13]

By the middle of December, Augustine was keenly aware that he had to get on his way soon if he hoped to be with Captain Back in time to start for the northern coast in the spring. Hutchinson was eager to move on as well, and with provisions declining daily, and more and more people "pitching in" needing assistance, Pruden was equally anxious to see them off. Augustine and Hutchinson decided to go as far as Green Lake and hope for better travelling weather thereafter.[14] Pruden lent them horses for the first leg of the journey and supplied them with sleds and dogs. He explained the situation in his journal: "The Packet & Mr. Hutchinson has been detained here since the 31st October, first for the want of a guide and after on account of there being no snow to enable sleds to run. The ground is still quite bare of snow and to assist the dogs I have sent 4 horses to accompany them about half way to Green Lake when their traveling will be chiefly on ice when the dogs will be able to travel but too slippery for horses on which account the horses are to return with 2 of the [Green Lake] men."[15]

In spite of "very poor traveling," no snow on the ground, and the journey likely to be difficult in the extreme, Augustine and Hutchinson left Green Lake on foot and reached Ile à la Crosse on New Year's Day, 1834. While they waited for guides, they heard disturbing news. Throughout the year, Chipewyan and Cree had been forced to spend all their time hunting for subsistence and had amassed nothing in the way of pelts for trade. The few animals they were fortunate enough to bring down were barely sufficient to keep their own families alive, and they had nothing to spare for the usual provisions trade with the post. Instead, they came to the post "all starving" and in need of relief, a condition Chief Factor Roderick McKenzie said they blamed on "the country getting poor for all kinds of big animals." McKenzie reluctantly informed the Chief Factors and Traders in his district that they would be unable to send any provisions to Captain Back "unless Mr Chief Trader Pruden will have in his power to give us some assistance," and even if extra rations could be found, he wrote, there was little chance they would "be able to haul the quantity of provisions required…for want of dogs."[16]

Augustine and Hutchinson left Ile à la Crosse on January 7, with two guides, dogs and sleds in case it snowed while they were on the trail, and horses to carry luggage and provisions until they could use the dog trains. Within a day of their departure, the longed-for first snow fell—a mere half inch in all, which proved more of a curse than the blessing they were hoping for when it turned to freezing rain. Sweat on the horses' bodies turned to icy armour, the dogs were unable to get traction on the slick ground, and the men were unable to control the skittering sleds. Eighteen cold, hungry, and miserable days later, they reached John Charles's establishment at Fort Chipewyan.[17]

※

AT CARLTON HOUSE IN LATE FEBRUARY, AUGUSTINE'S WIFE AND SON were better off than they would have been with Augustine on his dangerous northwest journey, but their living conditions were far from comfortable or safe: rations were short, the weather was all wrong for the time of year, new and increasingly ominous rumours of war spread through the House with each new arrival, and strange events were happening on the prairie. Pruden was "desperate" for a buffalo sighting and reported "very little meat in the store [house]." Incredibly, the river had already begun to break up, making it impossible to cross. Large numbers of the Stone tribe stopping at Carlton House to trade reported that "the Slave Indians had killed nine Stone Indians, young men."

In March, a war party of Cree and Stone attacked a camp of "30 tents of Slave Indians and had killed a good many & brought off 96 horses & 6 women of the party." One Stony and four Cree were killed during the battle, which, Pruden noted, "will put a final stop" to any of the tribes bringing in the provisions the House so sorely needed. Also in March, Carlton's people "perceived The Plains to be on Fire in a [southeast] direction and apparently 5 miles distant." A few days later the fire was so close that Pruden set a watch throughout the night. In late April, there was so much smoke hiding the sun to the west that the Carlton people wondered if the tribes had set the whole of the plains on fire to drive the bison away from their starving enemies.[18]

The same distressing and frequently fatal climatic conditions prevailed at Fort Resolution, as well as at Fort Reliance, George Back's expedition headquarters north of Great Slave Lake. At Fort Resolution, William Mcdonnell wrote that he had "seen but very few Indians" during the winter, and the few he did see were from "the Chipewyan lands, they were starving and had nothing." George Back was seeing comparable suffering among the Yellowknives. In October 1833, "starving Indians continued to arrive from every point of the compass, declaring that the animals had left the Barren lands…and that the calamity was not confined to the Yellow Knives, but that the Chipewyans also were as forlorn and destitute as themselves." By February of 1834, Back was writing to Charles that "many Indians have starved to death, and some of our dogs have suffered a similar fate." Day after day through the winter of 1833–34, Back's journal noted starvation and destitution among the Yellowknives and recorded reports they brought him of extreme poverty in neighbouring communities.[19]

WHEN AUGUSTINE AND HUTCHINSON REACHED FORT CHIPEWYAN late in the evening of January 25, 1834, Augustine was pleased to greet his old friend John Charles and dismayed to learn that a further delay in his journey to Fort Reliance was likely. In a letter to George Back on February 2, Charles conveyed the happy news of Augustine's safe arrival and promised to send him north as soon as possible; in the same letter, he warned Back that because "the means of provisions & a guide" might not be readily to hand, "there is a probability some detention may arise therefrom."[20]

Charles was still uncertain what arrangements Back had made for Augustine's northward journey to the expedition's winter quarters. In a letter to William Mcdonnell at Fort Resolution, dated February 2, 1834—the same day he wrote to George Back—Charles suggested that "the most prudent plan [might be] to send him on to you at once with the Expedition Packet, and if there is provisions and an opportunity by Indians, or probably the Iroquois, two of them must be forwarded with Augustus to the Captain." Getting Augustine safely to Fort Reliance was so high on Charles's list of priorities that, in spite of knowing how pressed for food supplies Mcdonnell and his people were, he had Augustine and two guides on the way to Fort Resolution in less than a week. With them they carried Charles's letter to Mcdonnell instructing him to make Augustine's journey his own top priority. "Should provisions be scarce with you at present," Charles had written, "let your first object be to provide sufficient to forward the Esquimaux, the second to send my two men back."[21]

Charles assigned two of his men, Antoine Morin and Pierre Blondin, to take Augustine to Fort Resolution.[22] The three men left Fort Chipewyan on foot on February 3 and almost at once found themselves walking face first into nasty weather. By February 7, it was "snowing thick," and on the ninth it was suddenly "very warm weather." Augustine and his companions had to force their way through slushy cold water during the seven or so hours each day when the sun warmed the snow. Their boots and trousers were soaked through with snow melt, and their shirts with sweat.[23]

After the first few days, a sudden drop in temperature turned the snow's surface to ice that broke under the pressure of every step, tearing through their sodden skin boots to bruise and stab their feet. On the twelfth, Morin, Blondin, and Augustine reached Fort Resolution, where two of Back's men, Pierre Kanaquassé and Charles Boulanger, were waiting to take Augustine the rest of the way to the expedition headquarters. Mcdonnell wrote John Charles that he was able to give "provisions sufficient for them" and on the twentieth saw them off to Fort Reliance on the far eastern arm of Great Slave Lake. On the twenty-fourth, Morin and Blondin were back at Fort Chipewyan. They brought the news that the Fort Resolution post was "favourable respecting subsistence" but that no Chipewyan had yet arrived due to the "strangeness of the weather."[24]

The route that the guides, Kanaquassé and Boulanger, had chosen followed the shore of Great Slave Lake as it trended northeast. The "strangeness of the weather" was noticeable here, as it was at Fort Chipewyan, where the thermometer inched up to an unseasonable 42° Fahrenheit on February 25. After six days, Kanaquassé and Boulanger were lost, and they started to retrace their steps. Augustine protested, first at the halt while the guides conferred and then, more strongly, when he realized they were turning back.[25]

For eight days the guides "explored" their way back to Fort Resolution, uncertain of where they were until the last moments before they stumbled into the post on March 6, without Augustine. Their missing companion, they told Mcdonnell, had "persisted in spite of their entreaties," and when they left him, he was carrying "only ten pounds of pemmican, and [had] neither gun nor bow and arrow." A ten-pound bag of pemmican was nowhere near the "sufficient provisions" that Mcdonnell said he had supplied to Augustine. Why he no longer had his gun or his bow and arrow was never explained in the Company's journals or correspondence or in Back's accounts of the disastrous journey.[26]

On March 8, two days after Kanaquassé and Boulanger returned to the fort, Mcdonnell sent two more expedition men—"Iroquois, with plenty of provision"—on the trail, with "instructions to follow the same track" and, if they found Augustine, to continue forward to Fort Reliance. They too lost their way very quickly. "Like the first [guides]," they explained to Mcdonnell, "they had got bewildered, and having exhausted all their provisions were compelled to explore their way back," reaching Fort Resolution on March 20. Augustine had been missing for over three weeks. Back pointed out what he thought was an odd coincidence: the first two guides, Kanaquassé and Boulanger, took eighteen days to walk back to the fort without Augustine, and on the day of their arrival, Mcdonnell sent two more Iroquois to search for the missing Inuk—"but strange to say, after a similar lapse of time, viz. eighteen days," these two men also made their appearance at the fort.[27]

Mcdonnell dispatched a third search party, an Iroquois and a local Chipewyan, who reached Fort Reliance on March 26 without incident and without seeing any signs of Augustine along the way. They broke the news of Augustine's arrival at Fort Resolution and his disappearance on the trail and handed Back his packet of letters. Back opened Mcdonnell's letter first and "found this account but too true." Unwillingly, he faced the possibility that Augustine might be dead. Depressed and in a pessimistic mood, he pondered on the unfair workings of fate. "The ready zeal with which Augustus had volunteered to partake the hard fortunes of the service, his attachment and generous devotion to myself, and the probability that his recompense had been a shocking and untimely death, impressed me with a melancholy that for some time fixed deeply in my mind."[28]

While Back admitted "there was, indeed, every reason to fear the worst," he took heart from one sentence in Mcdonnell's letter: Kanaquassé and Boulanger "had heard the report of two or three guns in the direction of the place where they had left him." The news, Back wrote, "afforded me a feeble hope that he might have fallen in with some party, and be yet alive." He sent out all his guides to spread the word among the Athapascan peoples that Augustine was missing, offering an "unlimited reward" to anyone "who should find and save him." The Resolution Post Master included one other snippet of information learned from Kanaquassé and Boulanger: they reported that "Augustus was obstinate in repeatedly refusing to turn back & out of humour because he had to drag his own things in the same manner as those who were with him."[29]

A month later, on April 25, another messenger from Fort Resolution knocked sharply on the door of the Fort Reliance dwelling house and walked in to thrust a packet into the hands of the startled expedition leader. "He is returned, sir!" said the messenger. "What! Augustus?—thank God!" Back exclaimed. But, no: "Captain Ross, sir.—Captain Ross is returned." Good news, surely, but not the news Back was hoping for at that moment. It was hard for him to take it in. "Eh! Are you quite sure? Is there no error? Where is the account from?" he asked. The courier pointed to the packet the captain held. "You have it in your hand, sir."[30]

ON MAY 3, MORE THAN TWO MONTHS AFTER AUGUSTINE'S DISAPpearance, three of Back's men left the expedition's service. Two of them arrived safely at Fort Resolution. The third, David Williamson of the Royal Artillery, did not. Alexander McLeod brought the news to Fort Reliance on May 25. Back tried to make sense of the known facts and the circulating rumours. "It appeared," wrote Back, "that [Williamson] had left the fishery with his [two] companions, and two Indians as guides; but, being a slow walker and much encumbered with useless baggage of his own, he had one day set out first, the route being quite straight; while the others, knowing that they could easily overtake him, had loitered in their encampment, perhaps an hour after his departure. Aware of his eccentricity, they were not alarmed at not seeing him for the better part of the day; but as the evening drew in, their fears were excited, and one of his Indian guides retraced his way, in order to be quite sure that he was not behind among the islands. His search was fruitless, and he very properly returned with the information to the Fort Reliance fishery."[31] McLeod made up search parties and promised "a considerable reward" for any information concerning Williamson. Continuing "strange weather" added to the discomforts of the search, as the temperature in the sun rose to 106° Fahrenheit around the middle of May. In such heat, any snow that remained would have disappeared quickly, and on the ice of Great Slave Lake near Rivière à Jean, the searchers found not David Williamson but what remained of Augustine.[32]

Word of Augustine's death spread through fur trade country. By May 22, John Charles at Fort Chipewyan had heard the news. His first response to the description of events given by Kanaquassé and Boulanger was disbelief. In particular, he doubted their story that Augustine was "out of humour because he had to drag his own things." So certain was Charles of Augustine's character that he wrote to Governor Simpson, "The men who were with him report he was obstinate, sullen and ill tempered...but...it may not however be improper to state that when he left this place the man was quite in good spirits."[33]

On June 3, George Back wrote that he had heard from his fishermen that "the Indians had been at Fort Resolution without hearing anything about poor Williamson,...but the remains of Augustus also had been discovered not far from Rivière à Jean." Back went on to write,

> It appeared that the gallant little fellow was retracing his steps to the establishment, when, either exhausted by suffering and privation, or caught in the midst of an open traverse in one of those terrible snow storms which may be almost said to blow through the frame, he had sunk to rise no more. Such was the miserable end of Poor Augustus!—a faithful, disinterested, kind-hearted creature, who had won the regard not of myself only, but I may add of Sir John Franklin and Dr. Richardson also, by qualities, which, wherever found, in the lowest as in the highest forms of social life, are the ornament and charm of humanity.[34]

As he was finishing the annual Athabasca District Report for 1833–34 Charles added a postscript, which he copied into the Fort Chipewyan correspondence book and dated June 3, 1834: "We hear by Indians Report at Great Slave lake, that the Body of the interpreter Esquimaux, was found upon the Ice, the poor Man it appears had laid down upon the Snow, Overcome no Doubt with Fatigue + Misery + fell asleep never to rise again."[35]

In John Charles's mind, George Back was chief mourner, more for the sake of the expedition than for any personal loss. "The services of this man, now no more, would have been of the first importance to the expedition," he wrote. "With this unfortunate summation of the poor fellow..., the impression on my mind is that Captain Back will be obliged to give up further attempts."[36]

CHAPTER II

THE FAMILIES
1834–1863

AUGUSTINE TATANEUCK'S FAMILY

As late as June 1, 1834, the news of Augustine's death had not yet reached Carlton House, where his wife and young son had spent the winter. With food supplies growing more precarious by the day, Chief Trader Pruden sent them back to Cumberland House where, he hoped, food was more plentiful.

They settled in at Cumberland House to wait for Augustine's return from the Arctic, expecting to be there, or back at Carlton, for at least a year. As it happened, it was only a matter of weeks before the first brigade from Athabasca arrived with the news of Augustine's death. Nearly two more months were to pass before there were places for Augustine's widow and son in another Company brigade bound for York Factory. On the day they left, August 14, the post accountant entered a charge of £1/1s for "2 ½ months board for Augustus family" against George Back's Arctic overland expedition.[1]

A month later, the widow and child were at York Factory, and within the week they were aboard one of the HBC's coast boats heading north. On the morning of September 24, the bereaved wife saw Churchill's Stone Fort for the first time in four years. All that day they waited for the evening tide to carry them to Cuckold's Point and then passed the night waiting for the crew to bring the vessel to an anchorage "nearly opposite the House." Robert Harding settled them in somewhere at the post, perhaps with the Dunnings or the Omans, or possibly somewhere in the empty part of the Officers' House.[2]

Like everyone else at Churchill, Augustine's widow drew a weekly ration adequate for subsistence, duly recorded in the post's provisions blotter. On October 4, Robert Harding handed out her first weekly ration: four pounds of flour, two pounds of pemmican, four fresh ducks, and four salted ducks. On October 11 and 18, the issue was exactly the same. On October 25, there were no fresh ducks, and her share of the salted ducks remaining in the post's storehouse amounted to only two. To make up the deficiency, Harding gave her a salted goose and twice the usual ration of pemmican.

By the middle of November, the post's supply of salted fowl was low, the post hunters reported no ducks remaining near any of the hunting tents, and ptarmigan were not yet in evidence. In place of the usual fresh or salted ducks and geese, Harding issued two deer's tongues and six pounds of venison to bulk up the usual four pounds of flour and four pounds of pemmican. Also during that week, Augustine's widow drew a quarter of a gallon of "spirits." Her ration was similar to that of Mrs. James Dunning and her children during the same week: seven pounds of flour, one pound of fat, ten pounds of pemmican, two gallons pease for making pease porridge. Mrs. Dunning also got four salted geese and six salted ducks from the dwindling supply.[3]

Ptarmigan appeared in the last week of November, and week after week Harding handed out the same monotonous ration: four pounds of flour, half a pound of fat, a quarter of a gallon pease, four ptarmigan, and six pounds of "green" (that is, fresh) venison. On January 1, 1835, the week's ration consisted of four pounds of flour and sixteen pounds of deer's meat, and in the second week of the new year, eight pounds of venison. As ptarmigan became more numerous, Harding reduced the amount of meat in the weekly provisions bag to three pounds and raised the number of partridges to eight. In addition to the consistent four pounds of flour and quart of pease, he occasionally added a few pounds of oatmeal.[4]

The flour allotment was for bannock, the fur trade country version of the baking powder biscuit and soda bread common in the northern Scottish and Irish homes of many of the Company's labourers. Men—on the trail, on the river, and at the post—used their supplies of flour, along with some fat and some salt, when they had any, to mix up a soft dough that could be cooked in a frying pan over an open fire, as their mothers and grandmothers had cooked at an open hearth or campfire. Every man's bannock differed from every other man's, as each tried to remember how the women of his family back home had produced the family's daily bread. As each woman's method differed, so every trader and canoeman came up with a distinctive variation on the common theme.

Luxuries like tea, sugar, and molasses were private expenditures for Augustine's widow, as they were for the men at the post. Augustine's financial legacy enabled her to buy more than the absolute necessities of survival, if and when she chose. Her choices did not go much beyond tea and crushed sugar, the food items Augustine most often bought, along with yellow soap, tobacco, and clay pipes.

When ptarmigan were plentiful, Harding assigned the men and their families to tent camps at some distance from the House. In February of 1835, one group of hunters went to the Wooding Camp, several miles upriver, and "the Esquimaux woman likewise." Her job was to cook for the hunters and keep their clothing in good repair. Harding gave her provisions intended to last for three weeks: twelve pounds of flour, ten pounds of pemmican, one and a half pounds of fat, eight pounds of dried meat, and three quarts of round pease.[5]

About the time the Wooding Tent's three-week supply of provisions was due to be replaced, two Inuit from northward came unexpectedly to the post to announce the imminent arrival of a group of their countrymen. The runners said they had been "ten days on their route," indicating that they had come from one of the Knapp's Bay to Whale Cove villages where Augustine and Ullebuk had been born.[6] They would have chosen to travel at night. Between early March and late May, night was the easiest and preferred time to travel. Under a bright sun for twelve hours a day, snow crust broke easily, making every step difficult and even dangerous. Snow crystals cut through skin boots and sometimes into flesh. Sled dogs were particularly susceptible to torn paws, and Inuit on the trail watched for spots of blood on the snow and protected the dogs with seal or walrus paw boots. The lower nighttime temperatures made the snow crust stronger, allowing for safer, quicker travel.

Harding saw their arrival as "a favourable opportunity for the deceased Augustus's wife and child going off [and] prevailed on them to go to the Wooding Tent." It was, on the whole, a good time for her to return to her people. They were apparently living comfortably, perhaps even in affluence, having told Harding they had no need for seal meat, oil, or skins and would therefore not hunt seal at the river mouth that year. Harding sent the runners upriver at noon on March 13, and they were back at the House the next day with their kinswoman and her son. Harding supplied the widow with three pounds of oatmeal, six pounds of biscuit, twelve pounds of pemmican, six pounds of venison, and a quantity of ammunition and saw her off.[7]

TWO YEARS PASSED BEFORE AUGUSTINE'S WIDOW RETURNED TO Churchill. She came on March 18, 1837, "as runner....Her errand is for tobacco and which she will take to them when nigher hand."[8] She was not mentioned in the Company's journals after that date. Four months later, on July 26, six men from Augustine's home village announced that "a great many others" were on their way in. "One of these," wrote Harding sympathetically, "is the brother of the deceased Augustus and this being his first visit here since his brother's death, we must pay him some little attention, more especially as he now has the care of his nephew from Ungava."[9] Harding did not note the name of this man, but the only brother ever mentioned in connection with Augustine was Astanik, so he was probably the guardian of the unnamed "nephew." Even if Augustine's widow had remarried and was still living, the child is likely to have remained in his uncle's household. The older children, one daughter and one son who had not gone to Ungava with their parents, would have been in their very late teens or early twenties by 1837, possibly married and parents themselves.

With Augustine's death, the Company became his executor, as it had been for hundreds of officers and servants over two hundred years. For nearly twenty years after their father's death, Augustine's children continued to visit Churchill Post to make purchases that were charged against their inheritance. The Hudson's Bay Company's journals and account books from the time of Augustine's death to 1863 give an idea of exactly how little they needed or wanted. Augustine's name did not appear in the account books again until 1838, when his heirs made their first withdrawal, amounting to just under three pounds. His name had by then been entered in the "Annuitants and Families of Retired and Deceased Servants" section of the account book, and payments were debited to the account of "Augustus Esquimaux, family of." During the next year, Outfit 1838–39, various members of the family took two pounds in trade goods, and during Outfit 1839–40, they spent £4/8/4. Similar sums were drawn from the estate nearly every year for the next twenty years.[10]

James Hackland, Master at Churchill in the 1850s, summed up how Churchill Post had handled Augustine's legacy. Each of Augustine's children got "a little supplies to the amount of 4£ [a year] among them, as the old man left some money," wrote Hackland, "about 70£ when he died, which his heirs will get by small portions that it may last the longer, and indeed it is very little they want."[11] At York Factory in 1833, Augustine and his wife had made purchases amounting to £6/6/6 before starting inland. At Norway House and Cumberland House, they had spent an additional four and a half pounds.[12] At the end of Outfit 1833–34, the York Factory accountant moved Augustine's name from the list of active servants to the Arctic overland expedition account and charged the expedition £15 for his wages. In the next end-of-outfit accounting, in May 1835, Augustine's widow spent £3/18/2. A comment next to Augustine's name in the ledger read "Died in spring 1834."[13]

In 1858, on July 1, James Hackland reported from Churchill to Chief Factor James Hargrave that "a daughter of Augustus the Interpreter [was] with the seal hunters [this year]. She has been making enquiry if her father left any money, but I did not know. She got a few trifles as a present and was pleased, but was told that she would know after the schooner came about the money."[14]

Hackland closed the letter noting that he was also sending the "Notice of Retirement of William Ouligbuck," the son of the interpreter and explorer.[15]

The following spring, William Ullebuk arrived as runner for a party of four men, three women, and eight children, who reached the post on April 8. Among them was one of Augustine's sons. Hackland traded with three of the men, who left immediately after, while Augustine's son stayed to "wait for his brother," who was still a few days' march away. On April 9, both brothers were in the trading room "to get a little supplies to the amount of 4£ among them."[16]

In 1863, another senior trader at Churchill, who never knew Augustine, Ullebuk, or Moses, reported that "the order sent to the factory for Augustus son was not complied with, poor fellow. He was much disappointed. I am glad I gave him nothing from here."[17]

MOSES ESQUIMAUX

When the Finlayson family left Fort Chimo on June 7, 1836, Moses went with them, in accordance with his superiors' decision that it was time he retired. At Chief Factor George Keith's suggestion, his place of retirement was to be Fort George. A week after embarking with the Finlayson family, to Erlandson's surprise and annoyance, Moses was back, having become ill, or, as Nicol Finlayson thought, "pretended to be ill." Erlandson promptly sent Moses "down the river to his companion Oullibuck," who was camped at a caribou crossing, hunting "for himself and his family."[18]

Moses's "illness" and unexpected return to Fort Chimo may have been because he, like Ullebuk, was married, or had plans to marry. By February of 1837, Erlandson was grumbling to his superiors that half of the meat and fish that the two Keewatin men produced through hunting was used to feed themselves and their families, suggesting that both men were married.[19]

While Finlayson had never complained about his three Keewatin hunters and interpreters, Erlandson's comments in his first post journal and district report were openly hostile toward the two that remained on his staff. With Augustine permanently removed from the picture, Erlandson preferred not to be reminded that Ullebuk and Moses existed. He kept them well out of his sight at the river mouth, hunting to feed themselves.[20] They remained there, living in tents and snowhouses, for most of the winter. When they returned to the House on April 11, 1837, Erlandson was not pleased to be reminded of their existence. "They are two stubborn beings," he wrote, "and by too much indulgence have been induced to consider themselves independent of the person in charge here. I wish that I could get rid of them."[21]

It was not long before he was rid of at least one of them. At the beginning of the travelling season in 1837, Erlandson sent Moses, accompanied by his wife, upriver and overland to Richmond Gulf with two Cree men who were returning to their homes in James Bay. They left Fort Chimo on July 13, 1837.[22]

When Moses arrived at Churchill in 1823, with no apparent family or connections in his own country, Hugh Leslie described him as "well into middle age." In 1830 the Albany journal called him "an elderly man," in 1833 he was, in Nicol Finlayson's opinion, "nearly superannuated," and in 1837 Erlandson noted him suffering "the infirmities of age." Their impressions were a bit wide of the mark. On October 12, 1837, Moses reported to Thomas Corcoran, the senior officer at Fort George, and three days later, he was at work getting the year's hay crop under cover. Corcoran entered Moses's name to the post servants list as an interpreter.[23]

A week later, on October 21, Corcoran moved Moses's name to the list of officially retired pensioners, but "instead of having wages, with which to purchase his few wants, he gets such things gratuitously out of the Honble Company's Store and is of course fed the same as other servants at their [the Company's] costs." Moses did not think retirement implied inactivity and continued to do what he had been doing for the previous fifteen years.

From time to time he had to take to his bed for a few days, but not from the "infirmities of age." On October 26, 1837, a careless step drove a rusty nail through his foot, and he was confined to his tent for a week. On November 6, he was up and "able to do a little about the house, which is enough to show that the poor man is getting better," Corcoran noted. By the thirteenth he was cutting firewood, and for the rest of the month he hunted partridges, kept the post's paths clear of snow, and made himself some snowshoes. At the beginning of 1838, he was busy hauling squared logs until an old problem resurfaced on January 18, possibly as a result of his efforts with the logs. "Old Moses confined to his bed with a complaint, hernia, with which he has been afflicted many years," wrote Corcoran, who saw his superannuated but hard-working employee as an asset. "He cannot do much work of a laborius nature," he wrote sympathetically, "but what he can do, he does it cheerfully; for from the first moment that I saw him until he left here, I never heard him murmur nor never saw him out of temper."[24]

Pensioner though he was in the eyes of head office, Moses undertook a new assignment given him by the Fort George officers. He went to Little Whale and Great Whale Rivers to explain to the Inuit the benefits that would come their way if they made peace with their "Indian neighbours" (probably Cree) and opened themselves to trade with the Company. Moses, in Corcoran's opinion, was well suited for the job because he spoke Cree, "so as to be understood," and could "act the part of a Pacification between the Indians and the Esquimaux: as there are many of our northern Indians, who still look upon [the Inuit] with an evil eye, and in consequence would not scruple much if an opportunity offered to have recourse to acts of violence and blood in retalliation of crimes perpetrated in the days of their fathers." Moses, with three Cree guides, left Fort George on June 14 and returned on August 22, 1838, having gone as far north as Richmond Gulf without making contact with any Inuit.[25]

In 1839, Corcoran tried again, but this time head office was informed. "With respect to Moses Esquimaux, who was sent off with Indians on the 5th April," Corcoran wrote in his District Report, "I have only to say that the poor old man whilst here did all he could to make himself useful and agreeable, but... his services so far have been no great acquisition to Ft Geo. What they may be hereafter in the Character of Esquimaux Interpreter (I hope the poor man is alive and well to act the part of one. I must own that I am somewhat anxious about him, but at the same time I have no more cause to be uneasy about him than what I stated to Mr [Chief Trader] Miles in my official letter of the 30th Ult) time will tell." Because the Inuit living north of Richmond Gulf had a reputation for ferocity, especially in their dealings with the Eastern Cree, Corcoran took the usual step of assigning a Fort George man, Oostineedjue, as Moses's personal bodyguard.[26]

By late February of 1840, Moses had still not returned. The only news of him came from a local man who reported having seen a large group of Inuit north of Richmond Gulf only a week earlier. Corcoran at once sent two of his labourers and a Cree guide to find them and to ask if Moses had been among them. On March 6, Moses himself walked through the gates of Fort George and reported on his journey. Shortly after leaving the post in 1839, he had separated from his guides, joined fifteen or sixteen Inuit families near Richmond Gulf, and spent the next eleven months travelling with them, including a summer visit to Fort Chimo. Corcoran was more than pleased with Moses's "most useful" accomplishment and assigned him to the Fort George sloop on its 1840 trading trip to Great Whale River. In spite of age and infirmity, Moses found time and energy enough to give Inuktitut lessons to one or two of the Company's young lads, act as interpreter for the Fort George missionary, and teach the Inuit at Little Whale River how to build umiaks and use them to hunt whale. For the next ten years he continued to live at Fort George during the winters, sailed with the post's sloop most summers, and, at least once, took his family to pass the winter with the Inuit north of Richmond Gulf.[27]

In 1851, the Company built a post at Little Whale River and appointed Moses as interpreter. During the summer he visited the Belcher Islands with a cargo of goods and conducted a successful trade.[28] He returned to Little Whale River in the spring of 1852 to interpret and mediate among Inuit trading there and, despite his failing eyesight, carried the mail and the furs recently traded—more than five hundred of them—to Fort George. At the recommendation of several of the Company's officers, Governor Simpson agreed to give the "old man" a pension of £10 per year as a reward for his services. Joseph Gladman was of the opinion that Moses should also be given a comfortable life tenancy at whatever post he chose. In the spring of 1853, he was still at Little Whale, and in spite of almost complete loss of sight, he was still serving as interpreter to the Inuit who traded there.[29]

Details of Moses's personal life after 1853 have not been found in the HBC's James Bay journals and correspondence, and there is no mention of his wife or any possible children. One last mention of him occurs in the Churchill correspondence for 1865, suggesting that he may have lived until the early 1860s. "The estate of Esquimaux Moses is now represented by a distant male connection. I was asked last summer whether this person was entitled, and if so, at liberty, to draw on the credit balance. Still due to the Estate of £25/1/2, will you kindly inform me in this matter." No clues have come to light to tell what happened to the £25 that remained in Moses's account at the time of his death.[30]

ULLEBUK'S FAMILY

In 1836, while Moses and Ullebuk were living and working under Erland Erlandson's unfriendly supervision, the Hudson's Bay Company was organizing a new expedition to map the still-uncharted parts of the Arctic coast beyond Franklin's farthest stop east—Point Turnagain on Kent Peninsula—to Hudson Bay. Peter Warren Dease was the Company's chosen commander, with Thomas Simpson as his second responsible for scientific investigations.[31]

John Charles, chief at York Factory in 1836, wrote to Robert Harding in July of that year, wondering who among Churchill's Inuit might be available to serve as interpreter for Dease and Simpson. While waiting for a reply, he assured an anxious Simpson that "if it is not possible to get an interpreter from Churchill, Oulibuck will be sent for from Ungava." The following spring, on April 9, 1837, Charles wrote Harding again to say that he had written to Moose Factory asking that someone be sent to Ungava to get Ullebuk.[32]

Harding's response to Charles's April 9 letter was not helpful in finding an interpreter, but it is interesting for another matter. Simpson and Dease were not the only people who wanted to get hold of Ullebuk. Harding wrote at the end of June that Ullebuk, "on leaving this place [Churchill], had a wife & son with his friends. His wife is since dead and the person who has the care of his son [Donald] is most anxious to see him back." Nothing in the Churchill or Fort Chimo journals and correspondence prior to 1837 suggests that the

Company's officers were aware that Ullebuk was married and a father before he left Churchill in 1830, although Harding, at the very least, must have known.³³

In the meantime, George Keith, Chief at Moose Factory, had written to Erlandson in search of an Inuktitut speaker for the expedition. Keith's letter gave Erlandson what he so ardently wished for: a way to get rid of the other "perfectly useless" and "stubborn" man, Ullebuk. Erlandson provided Ullebuk with a canoe and saw the family off to Eastmain by way of Richmond Gulf. They reported in at Fort George on September 29 and were "forwarded on from thence" on foot the next day.³⁴

Their guides found the family too slow—young William could have been no older than six, and his sister was younger—and left them to plod along as best they could. They reached Rupert's House on November 23, five days after their guides, and were welcomed by Robert Miles. On December 9, Miles judged the weather good enough for the family to travel "with safety" and had them "sent forward...from hence to Moose." To hasten them along the way, Miles provided a dog team "to expedite the children." They were at Moose by December 15 and on the Albany road four days later.³⁵

Along the way, factors, traders, and clerks formed opinions about Ullebuk's character and his potential usefulness to the Company's Arctic expedition. At Moose, Keith blamed Ullebuk for "very dilatory movements" and thought that "he will not, cannot, join that Expedition in time to be of any service." Even so, Keith recognized that Ullebuk was entitled to the Company's protection for himself and his family and wrote to Albany District Chief Factor Jacob Corrigal that "it is necessary, at any rate, to afford him and family all necessary and consistent facilities with a view to their reaching York Factory during this winter or following spring.... [They] may have to winter at Albany," he said, "and proceed summer 1838."³⁶

Corrigal reported the travellers' safe arrival at Albany on December 26 and was willing to house and feed them over the winter. Ullebuk "must of course remain here for the present," Corrigal decided, but he noted that "had [Ullebuk] been an active being, I would have found means of forwarding him on so as to overtake the party destined for York, but he is quite unfit at present for so long a march, even had he been unencumbered with wife & children."[37] The Ullebuks finally left Albany with the boats going to Lac Seul and York Factory via Red River in July of 1838.[38]

Keith's predictions that Ullebuk would not reach Fort Confidence in time to be of any use to the expedition proved wrong. Ullebuk, with his wife and children, reported to Peter Warren Dease and Thomas Simpson at their winter quarters, Fort Confidence, on the eastern tip of the Great Bear Lake Dease Arm, in April 1839. The expedition had already surveyed from Point Barrow in the west to Point Turnagain in the east and had passed a winter at Fort Confidence, but there was more still to do—the coast between Point Turnagain and Back's discoveries at Chantrey Inlet had to be mapped. Keith's and Erlandson's low opinions of Ullebuk's physical strength and willingness to work were also mistaken. Thomas Simpson, unlike Erlandson and Keith, regarded Ullebuk as "an important accession" to the expedition and was grateful for the "extraordinary diligence by Chief Factor Christie, and the Gentlemen along the route," which enabled Ullebuk to make "the whole journey from [Red River] in only three months, less eight days."[39]

The Ullebuks spent four years, 1839 to 1843, in the Mackenzie River district. When the Dease-Simpson survey was finished in late summer of 1839, Ullebuk joined the HBC's John Bell on the 1840–41 exploration of the Peel River. He then chose to stay in the area working at an HBC fishing post until 1843, when he took his family back to York Factory.

Letitia Hargrave, wife of Chief Factor James Hargrave, as so often happened had the gossip and passed it on in a letter to her sister in Scotland. "There is a Huskie man here with his wife, son & daughter. They have just returned from MacKenzies River & have saved £100.... The boy is about 12 & speaks ten languages. He is otherwise a little scamp, but very smart & hideously fat...tho very well dressed. The girl looks better & the father [Ullebuk] told Hargrave the wife was 'pretty pretty.' He went to the North with Franklin as an interpreter, he is going home to Churchill."[40]

Nothing in Finlayson's post journals had ever acknowledged the existence of Augustine's wife and son or noted that Ullebuk had married within a year of arriving at the site of the new post. Erlandson, on the other hand, made it clear that the post suffered because of the need to supply food to the family of a labourer. Who Ullebuk's second wife was is not apparent. However, early in the winter of 1831–32, a few Inuit families had spent the winter near the post. Among them was the family of Ceghannack, well known to the traders as The Big Man, "a giant of a man over six feet tall." In the first years after establishing the Fort Chimo post, Ullebuk spent much of his time hunting with Ceghannack, and it may be that Ullebuk's wife was a member of Ceghannack's family. By 1836 the couple had two children: a boy, William, born in 1832 or 1833, and a younger daughter, who, like her mother, was never named in the Company's documents.[41]

AT HOME AGAIN IN CHURCHILL, ULLEBUK WAS REUNITED WITH Donald, the son of his first wife who had died sometime during the 1820s. The family settled at Churchill in 1844, where Harding assigned Ullebuk and Donald to the dreary tedium of clearing snow, hunting ptarmigan, and rinsing brined geese through holes cut in the ice of the still-frozen river. These mindless chores were soon to be replaced by a more exciting adventure.[42]

The Hudson's Bay Company was preparing to send a new expedition to the Arctic coast to survey the last unmapped stretch, between Fury and Hecla Strait and the Castor and Pollux River. Dr. John Rae, a Company surgeon, was chosen to lead the survey.[43] Ullebuk was Governor Simpson's choice as interpreter for the expedition, a choice Harding accepted without enthusiasm, noting that since there was "no probability of securing the services of a more active intelligent Esquimaux than Ouligbuck," he would have to do. For the time being, it was settled that Ullebuk "with his wife and 2 children from Ungava and with another son [Donald] that he left some time since with his countrymen (a sturdy youth both willing and able to make himself serviceable) will winter here, and he will, I trust, be available for any service the honorable company may require at his hands, altho he remains here on the footing of a labourer at present."[44] Simpson was pleased and passed the word on to James Hargrave: "I am glad to find by Mr Harding's letter that he has already secured the services of Ooligbuck for the discovery expedition…he will of course be liberally paid."[45]

Chief Factor Hargrave assumed that Donald Ullebuk would accompany his father on the expedition and wrote to Harding, "You will be pleased to take measures for getting him instructed in the English Tongue." Rae, however, preferred an interpreter who was already reasonably fluent in English, and in February 1846, he wrote to Governor Simpson: "I prefer the younger lad [William Ullebuk], as in addition to his own language he can speak both Indian and English."[46]

THE RAE EXPEDITION BOATS, *MAGNET* AND *NORTH POLE*, LEFT YORK on June 13, 1846, with ten York Factory men at the oars and a tightly packed cargo of provisions, hunting, fishing, and navigation equipment, and presents and barter items for the local people. They reached Churchill on June 25 and were on the way north on July 5, having "taken on board Ouligbuck and one of his sons [William] as Esquimaux interpreters." On the afternoon of July 25, they reached Gibson Cove at the head of Repulse Bay, closely watched from the beach by four Inuit hunters. Rae immediately leaped out of the boat and, taking William Ullebuk with him, greeted the hunters, explained the reason for the expedition, and gave them some gifts. With friendly relations established, the hunters answered questions on the geography of their country and one of them sketched a map of the route to the salt sea.[47]

Forty-eight hours later, the exploration party was on its way northwest in search of the salt sea that the Inuit had described and that Rae hoped would lead to a northwest passage. All hands spent the morning of July 27 at the gruelling job of man-hauling the heavily loaded *North Pole* up a small, almost dry river to the first of the lakes that formed the route to the sea. Something about Ullebuk caught Rae's medical eye, and when the party set out for the coast, Ullebuk did not go along. Instead, Rae assigned him to return to Gibson Cove with one of the oarsmen, John Folster, to guard the expedition's baggage and the boat *Magnet*. Because local Inuit were in the area, Rae gave Ullebuk the job of maintaining good relations with them. A further task for both Ullebuk and Folster was to gather large stones for building a stone house for the winter, which Rae later named Fort Hope.

Fifteen days later, on August 10, the travelling party was back. Rae had not found a northwest passage; instead, he had crossed the base of Simpson Peninsula to Pelly Bay and was within reach of Lord Mayor's Bay, where John Ross had wintered from 1829 to 1833. He had confirmed what Ross had claimed thirteen years earlier—that Boothia was a peninsula, not an island, and there was no northwest passage through it.[48]

Ullebuk, meanwhile, had laid in a supply of fresh meat and was conducting a war on a pack of hungry wolves who were harassing the camp. He was away hunting when the travellers returned, and Folster reported that he was overdue. Rae was worried enough to record that he "began to feel anxious about him." His concern was even more acute in January of 1847, when Ullebuk, hunting alone on the tundra, was gone for a week. When his interpreter finally reappeared at Fort Hope, Rae confessed his anxiety and relief in his journal: "[I] had given up all hopes of ever seeing him again in life."[49]

RAE'S PLANS FOR THE SPRING OF 1847 INVOLVED TWO OUTWARD treks: one was to retrace the track to Pelly Bay and then overland to what he hoped would be the other side of Boothia Peninsula; the other was to survey the western shore of Melville Peninsula as far north as Fury and Hecla Strait. The departure date for the first journey was set for April, but the plan changed abruptly in the last week of March. Ullebuk returned from a night on the land "very faint from the effects of a severe wound he had received on the arm by falling on a large dagger which he usually carried." After cutting away Ullebuk's clothing to examine the injured arm, the doctor discovered that "the dagger had passed completely through the right arm a couple of inches above the elbow joint." Rae refused to leave Fort Hope until he saw that the "wounded arm [was] in a fair way of recovery." By April 4, Ullebuk was hunting again, and the doctor was satisfied that he could safely leave his patient.[50] The reconnaissance party left on April 5 and returned on May 5 having found the terrain west of Pelly Bay too difficult for winter travel.

The last survey, to Fury and Hecla Strait, was ready to set out on May 14. The travelling party consisted of four expedition men, Corrigal, Folster,

Matheson, and Mineau; a local Inuit named Ivitchuk, with his sledge and dog team; a fatigue party to move the necessary food and other supplies to caches across the isthmus; and Ullebuk as hunter and interpreter.[51] Although confident that Ullebuk's arm was healing well, Rae was deeply concerned about his general health. "Although we had not travelled much more than twenty miles," he wrote, "Ouligbuck was so fatigued that I determined to send him back with those who were to return to Repulse Bay."[52] When the fatigue party went back to Fort Hope, Ullebuk went as well. As Rae explained, "Ouligbuck...from his inability to walk would have been an incumbrance to us."[53]

The team was back at Fort Hope on June 9, having been within a day's walk of Fury and Hecla Strait but prevented by severe ice movement from getting there. The men who had remained at Fort Hope had a lot to say about the behaviour of young William Ullebuk during their absence. "During the few days of his fathers absence," wrote Rae, "he was twice caught with the old man's bale open, eating sugar; some tobacco was also taken, and the trousers of most of the men were completely cleared of buttons by the same hands."[54]

Having done everything they could to fulfill their goals, the expedition left Repulse Bay on August 12. Ullebuk and young William took leave of their expedition companions at Churchill on August 31 and remained at Churchill. Ullebuk and William continued working for the Company for another year. In June of 1848, the whole family went north to Ullebuk's home community.[55]

In early winter of 1852, word reached Churchill that Ullebuk had died. The HBC Abstracts of Servants' Accounts continued to list Ullebuk as a pensioner until 1857, when it noted a balance owing of £10/16/0 and closed the entry with the word "Deceased."[56]

WILLIAM ULLEBUK

William Ullebuk, "a full grown youth of about 20 years of age," travelled once more with John Rae, in 1853–54, to map the last uncharted stretch of the Arctic coast, from Bellot Strait to the Castor and Pollux River.[57] In his search for an interpreter, Rae remembered William Ullebuk's pilfering and mischief-making habits at Fort Hope in 1847 and refused to consider him as a member of the new expedition. "To Oulibuck I have no particular objection," he wrote, "but the boy (his son) that I had with me formerly is one of the greatest rascals unhung."[58] While at Churchill on the way north, however, Rae met William Oman, who had known Augustine and Ullebuk since they were all teenagers thirty years earlier. As a close friend of the Ullebuks after they settled at Churchill in 1844, Oman also knew William very well. His assurances that a more mature William was reliable and hard-working convinced Rae to give him a second chance. His change of mind did not solve the immediate problem of an interpreter, however; William was out of reach, somewhere to the north hunting seal, and was not eager to travel with John Rae again, partly because he was newly married. Rae still needed an interpreter and hired an eager young man named Munro, whose grasp of English was rudimentary at best and who spoke neither Chipewyan nor Cree. The expedition party left Churchill on July 13, 1853.[59] As luck would have it, William Ullebuk was conducting a seal hunt much closer to hand than anyone at Churchill thought. "We have just met a number of Esquimaux and among them young Ouligbuck," wrote Rae to Governor Simpson. "[He] has agreed to accompany me." The letter's dateline read "Coast about 50 Miles North of Churchill 13th July 1853."[60]

After a failed attempt to reach Back's Great Fish River through Chesterfield Inlet, the expedition continued north to Repulse Bay, where the party wintered. On the last day of March 1854, with four men and William Ullebuk, Rae began to retrace his 1847 route. On April 17, they reached Pelly Bay. In order to avoid the rough terrain that lay between them and the Castor and Pollux River to the southwest, Rae decided to head as straight west as possible toward the magnetic north pole. The route brought them into Netsilik country, where they found seventeen Inuit, a few of whom had been at Repulse Bay in 1847 and recognized Rae and William. The rest were "forward and troublesome," Rae thought, and "would give us no information…none of them would consent to accompany us for a day or two." The few who had met Rae on his earlier explorations warned him that the Netsilik were involved in a "war" against their neighbours to the west. The violence, they said, was widespread. Strangers in particular were in danger.[61]

On April 21, two local men came looking for the white men that they had heard were in the area. Both were friendly and did not hesitate to answer Rae's questions about the best route to salt water in the west. They were also more than willing to answer Rae's usual question on whether they had ever met with white men. It turned out that they had. They spoke of "a party of Kabloonans, [who] had died of starvation...beyond a large River." Rae and his men heard many details about ships being crushed by ice and men like skeletons hauling sledges, as well as thirty corpses along with some graves at a place later called Starvation Cove, and another five dead bodies on an island later known as Montreal Island. "Some of the bodies were in a tent or tents," Rae recorded. "Others were under the boat...and some lay scattered about in different directions."[62]

The visitors left Rae's party on April 22. Following their instructions, Rae and his men reached the Castor and Pollux River five days later, thus fulfilling the primary goal of the expedition. They were back at Repulse Bay on May 26 and were forced to remain there due to an unusually cold summer. Rae made good use of the delay and of his "good interpreter," William Ullebuk, to "question the Esquimaux regarding the information which I had already obtained of the party of whites who had perished of starvation, and of eliciting the particulars connected with that sad event." Many of his informants were willing to sell him articles they had bought from the people of Boothia Peninsula and Chantrey Inlet, and the doctor made a careful list, which included more than a dozen pieces of silver cutlery, several watches, a silver tube, and a surgeon's knife, many of them marked with family crests and initials.[63]

They were back at Churchill on August 28, 1854. "My good interpreter Wm. Ouligbuck was landed," Rae wrote, and he performed one last, sad duty. "Before bidding him farewell, I presented him with a very handsomely mounted hunting knife, intrusted to me by Captain Sir George Back, for his former travelling Companion Ouligbuck; but as the old man was dead, I took the liberty of giving it to his Son."[64]

The importance of the information gathered from the Boothia Inuit on the fate of the Franklin expedition, along with articles they had found or bought from the local people, was recognized by the Admiralty. In 1856, Rae was informed that he and his companions were entitled to a reward of £10,000. The Admiralty set aside £8,000 for Rae and deposited the remaining £2,000 with the Hudson's Bay Company to be divided among the other expedition members. William Ullebuk's share, £210, was deposited to his personal account, along with £40 pounds owed to him for his services as interpreter on the expedition.[65]

William spent the winter of 1854–55 at Churchill as a labourer and the following year accepted a three-year contract as a middleman and interpreter at £17 a year. At not quite thirty years old, he gave his notice of retirement in the spring of 1859 but changed his mind when the Company offered him the job of interpreter for £20 a year.[66] When his contract was finished, his account showed a healthy credit of £143/16/10. He invested a portion of it in a schooner and went into the business of carrying freight and passengers along the coast north of Churchill.[67]

In 1872, William was back at Churchill as interpreter and harpooner, and in 1875 he began a three-year stint with the HBC's whaling fleet at Marble Island. For the next twenty years, he alternated between living in his home community and working at Churchill, where his yearly wage rose to $116.80 in Canadian dollars in 1882. During the 1870s and 1880s, he became a jack-of-all-trades. George Simpson McTavish enumerated William's talents: "He could do blacksmith work…was tinsmith, carpenter, sledmaker, hunter, trapper, boatman, could splice a rope and make a net [and] was respectiful, and could be a 'white' man with the dignity of a trained mind. And yet he was Esquimaux, could eat raw meat…and forget the luxuries of the forts when in his native state."[68] In 1894 William Ullebuk retired for the last time, and he died, aged about sixty-five, in the winter of 1895–96.[69]

EPILOGUE

We should ourselves be sorry to think that posterity should judge us by a patchwork of our letters,...preserved by chance,...independent of their context,...written perhaps in a fit of despondency or irritation,...divorced, above all, from the myriad little strings which colour and compose our peculiar existence, and which in their multiplicity, their variety and their triviality, are vivid to ourselves alone, uncommunicable even to those dearest to us, sharing our daily life....Still, within our limitations it is necessary to arrive at some conclusions, and certain facts do emerge.

—*Vita Sackville-West*[1]

The only thing is to know and realize that Vita has got blanks in herself, and those blanks are blank. If I find a blank, I get a plank and bridge it, and I don't look down, lest I get vertigo.

—*Edwin Lutyens*[2]

Some facts of Augustine's life *do emerge*: He was born somewhere near Whale Cove around 1800; he had at least one brother (Astanik) and at least one nephew (Annagyniak); he married sometime between 1816 and 1819 and was the father of two sons and one daughter. His Euro-Canadian companions described him as intelligent, loyal, generous, helpful, honest, and having a pleasant temperament. His survival skills in the Arctic wilderness were finely honed and he was always willing to take on the hard labour of subsistence and Arctic travel. He was a competent hunter who understood the geography and wildlife of the territory he lived in, and he had a basic knowledge of neighbouring territories as well. He was linguistically competent in at least two languages. Nothing in these facts sets him apart from other Inuit at the beginning of the nineteenth century as far as we know, or from many other Indigenous people who lived near trading posts.

Yet Augustine's life was unusual among Inuit, because he had opportunities that no other Inuk could have had at the time. Foremost among them was that his community was the first Inuit group to have had a recurring relationship with a trading post. In the 1700s there was, in fact, no other trading post positioned so that Inuit could or would have been seen as potential clients. Inuit from the western Arctic coast had moved to the west coast of Hudson Bay north of Churchill and south of Rankin Inlet about two generations before Churchill was established in 1717. Until 1790, contact between the British traders and the migrant community, now known as the Kivallirmiut, was sporadic and at arm's length. Inuit and European traders gathered knowledge about each other slowly between 1717 and 1800, and their rare meetings were nearly always friendly. By 1812, Augustine's father trusted the British traders enough to leave his son in their care.

Detailed eyewitness testimonies, some archived by the Hudson's Bay Company and some recorded in the published memoirs of British naval officers, bring Augustine's extraordinary history to life. Without these documents we would know very little, perhaps nothing, about Augustine Tataneuck today. The documents tell us that he lived, comfortably and successfully, in the world of his Kivallirmiut kin and in the commercial and political world of Europeans. How he perceived the ideologies and traditions of two cultural worlds and behaved within them are "blanks" that may be at least partially understood by looking at the "planks" that surrounded him. The most influential "plank" was Churchill's work and cultural environment.

CHURCHILL RIVER TRADING POST

The Hudson's Bay Company's goals for its newly established trading post at Churchill River in 1717 were to find a navigable northwest passage from Hudson Bay to the Pacific Ocean, track down a rumoured copper mine on the central Arctic coast, establish a profitable black whale fishery at the mouth of the river, and develop a thriving fur trade with Inuit and Athapascan communities in the north and northwest.[3]

All four projects failed. Efforts to find a northwest passage were, by 1764, seen by the HBC's London Committee as showing "no promise of being either a benefit to the nation or an extension of the trade of the Company." The dream of a profitable copper mining operation died in 1771 when Samuel Hearne reached the mouth of the Coppermine River and realized, first, that sea-going ships designed to carry mined copper out of the Arctic would not be able to navigate the river's shoals and rapids and, second, that the supposed "mine" was a "jumble of rocks and gravel" containing only small numbers of useless copper flakes. In 1772, the Company was forced to shut down the black whale fishery at the mouth of the Churchill River because black whales had "proved elusive," and the fishery itself was "a costly experiment" that over about fifty years had cost more than £20,000 and yielded no profits.[4] As for establishing a profitable trade northward, the coastal Inuit showed little or no interest in trekking to Churchill every year to trade or to work at whaling.[5] By 1790 the annual sloop trade had cost the Company more than it had gained, and its shareholders ended the practice. Also in 1790, the London Committee realized that its decision to trust the Chipewyan "with ever more and more debt," which was seldom or never repaid, was another financial disaster.[6] And, anyway, by then the northwestern Athapascan people were happily dealing with the Canadians from Montreal nearer to their own territories, and they, like the Hudson Bay Inuit, saw little reason to make the difficult overland journey to Churchill.[7]

By 1800 it was clear that Churchill Post was of very little value to the Hudson's Bay Company. With the exception of the senior officer, who remained at the House to deal with visiting Chipewyan and Inuit during the short spring and summer, junior officers, tradesmen, and labourers spent most of the year at hunting and wooding camps, usually called "tents," outside the stockade, anywhere from four to twenty-five miles distant. Status markers such as separate living and dining arrangements for officers and men lost their meaning when all ranks shared living quarters in the Men's House, including wives and children. In most years, the post's only cookstove was not used in the summer so that wood could be saved for winter use. For about four months every year, the post's cook, Thomas Spence, was assigned to other chores around the post or at a tent.

The London Committee's vision of a status-based society eroded as all hands, including Chief Trader John Charles, dug through the ashes and debris side by side with Augustine, Shenandoah, and low-ranking employees after the Men's House fire in 1813. Everyone, officers and labourers alike, did whatever was necessary. Many officers over the years noted the loss of occupational rigidity, identifying themselves as "jacks of all trade" as they built furniture and mended leaky roofs.[8]

The post was beset by a number of other problems. In 1796, Chief Factor Thomas Stayner complained that "lack of discipline among the men" was the reason efforts to establish an inland post upriver from Churchill failed.[9] By the early 1800s it had become difficult to recruit Orkney men for service at Churchill. District Superintendent William Auld, on a trip to Orkney to hire labourers in 1805, was "faced with something of a conspiracy" because of Churchill's "reputation for inadequate food."[10] Twenty years later, in 1824, Colin Robertson was appointed chief at Churchill, "which was deemed a suitable sinecure for [him] because no other post required less effort."[11] Churchill was stripped of its high status as a factory in 1810, although it was five years before it was fully operational as an outpost of York Factory.[12]

As the post became less important to the Company, and its officers grew more despondent, Churchill's work and social environments veered farther from the London Committee's ideal. In the absence of officer-class leadership, two men hired by the Company as mariners in the early 1780s—William Oman from Sandwick, Orkney, and James Dunning from Stockton-on-Tees, England—became mentors to the post's many short-term labourers.[13] They settled comfortably into Churchill's relaxed and unregulated lifestyle, married Indigenous women, raised large families, and spent their working lives and retirements at the post. They created a business and social life lived in multiple languages—English, Cree, Chipewyan, and Orcadian. By the time Augustine arrived in 1812, the sons of Oman Sr. and Dunning Sr. were second-generation labourers, and by the early 1820s the third generation was emerging. Happily settled in Churchill, they spent their official work time on their own schedules while hunting and trapping for their own benefit. Later generations of labourers followed their example.[14]

INUTTITUT (THE INUIT WAY)

Augustine's arrival at Churchill in 1812 was not typical of the way Inuit youngsters had spent a winter or two at the post. Between 1750 and 1790, captains in the sloop trade had *invited* one or two youngsters to spend a winter at the post most years. The practice led to friendly relations between Company and Inuit but did not result in a settled Inuit Homeguard near the post.[15]

Unlike the sloop youngsters, Augustine was not at Churchill by the Company's invitation. He was there at the request of his father, or perhaps his own wish relayed by his father. Over the next two decades, he tended to make decisions about his life and tell the Company's officers what he was planning or had already done, *after the fact*. In 1814, for instance, after nearly two years at Churchill, he joined a group of Inuit who had been seal hunting nearby and announced that he was leaving within a few hours in search of a wife.[16] Ten months later, in May of 1815, he returned to Churchill, still unmarried. Taking for granted that he would be welcomed back, he settled his belongings in the kitchen with John Leask and cook Thomas Spence, without asking permission or being told to settle in. Only then did he seek out John Charles to explain his plans for the future—not at all the kind of behaviour the London Committee expected from its low-status servants.

The same independence was obvious during the Admiralty's overland explorations. In 1821, during the first Franklin expedition, Augustine left the main body of men on the retreat across the barren lands to Winter Lake against orders and kept himself and his companions alive while half of the expedition's men died from starvation. In 1824 he opted out of Franklin's plan that he and Ullebuk travel northwest with Neil McDonald's brigade and instead joined John Charles's party headed for Split Lake. This is not to say that he failed to do the work he was assigned to do, at the post or on the expeditions, but it does suggest that he saw his relationship with his "superiors" in a specifically Inuit way. In Inuit society, claiming agency over one's own life would have been seen as normal for a young person approaching maturity.

Formalizing close relationships with chosen others through fictive kinship would also have been seen as normal by Inuit. Life was never easy in the Arctic: drownings were common, food resources were often scarce, deadly infections occurred after minor injuries, death from exposure and hypothermia was frequent. The only help in disastrous situations came from community and involved an ideology of sharing and a system for creating kinship beyond shared DNA and in-laws. Members of the nuclear family among Inuit are the obvious first responders in times of trouble, as they are in many other cultural traditions. Depending on how serious the situation was, sharing may have been limited to the nuclear family, or it may have included members of the extended family and in-laws. In the Inuit world of small, isolated communities, the number of blood relatives and in-laws who could be called upon for help was small, so Inuit created a system of fictive kinship that broadened the circle of who counted as "family" beyond genetic relationships. Hunting and fishing partners, midwives, healers, and drummers were, by joint agreement, often recognized as kin. Fictive kinships were insurance against hard times for adults and for children. Once agreed on, the arrangements were as binding as blood relationships.

Before starting out on the first Franklin expedition, Augustine arranged for his wife and child (or children) to be cared for by Junius's brother. When Ullebuk Sr. went to Ungava, he made arrangements for his son Donald to be looked after by a household in their village.[17] The caregivers in each case would have been, or would have become, "family." Augustine, as usual, did it his way and took his wife and son to Ungava and later to Cumberland House when he set out to join George Back in the search for John Ross.[18] We can safely assume that he made appropriate arrangements for his two older children.

How the Churchill traders dealt with Augustine in 1812 was similar to the way Inuit themselves would have treated a newcomer, especially a youngster on the verge of manhood. Without hesitation the traders provided him with a warm place to live, food on the table, and friendly efforts at communication. In English we separate the concept of loving and the concept of taking care of someone or something. Among some (but not all) Inuit groups, loving and taking care of are always linked. People who love are morally bound to take care of the loved one, and taking care of another person implies loving. Having understood the concept from early childhood, Augustine would have seen Churchill's traders as parents because when they provided him with the basics of shelter, food, clothing, and companionship, and protected him from the typhus danger, they were doing what his biological parents would have done. He, in return, would have behaved toward the traders as a son, doing what they asked of him without question or complaint. Being singled out by Superintendent William Auld on a Sunday afternoon as a hunting companion, and then being taken along on an exciting trip to York Factory, may have been perceived by Augustine as a perquisite of kinship.

As for why the traders took him under their wings so readily, and on his own terms, Augustine may have been a diversion from the boring and repetitive life of the post or have filled the emotional needs of men far from home and family. It is not unreasonable that officers and men simply grew fond of him.

AUGUSTINE'S EXCEPTIONALISM

When the Lords of the British Admiralty decided to expand the search for a northwest passage by sending explorers overland to the Arctic northwest, they and the naval officers chosen to lead the expedition realized that an interpreter who spoke both English and Inuktitut would have to be part of the team. The path to finding an interpreter was straight and simple. In the early 1800s, only the Hudson's Bay Company had any accurate information about Inuit within

British territory. The Admiralty took the obvious step and asked the London Committee for advice. In 1819, Churchill was the only trading post within range of any Inuit. Augustine was the only Inuk who actually lived, or had ever lived, at Churchill, and he was the only Inuk on the planet who spoke both languages. He was the right person in the right place at the right time.

What the Admiralty and the Company did *not* know was that Augustine's people were descended from Inuit who had moved from the northwestern coast to Hudson Bay only a century and a half earlier. No distant European would have known that there were multiple, often mutually unintelligible, dialects within Inuktitut, a fact that the Churchill traders may not have clearly understood either. Augustine's ability to understand and speak the dialect of coastal Coppermine Inuit was a happy and unforseen coincidence.

Augustine's bilingualism, however, made him exceptional for more than just translating. Linguistic scientists have determined that *how* people learn languages has psychological side effects, which may have played a role in how Augustine lectured, shamed, threatened, and ultimately subdued the Mackenzie Inuit at Pillage Point. Babies in all cultures learn their first language by *acquisition*—they hear, understand, and over time begin to think and speak. Older people who learn a second language are more likely to do so through *learning*, which involves teachers, classrooms, lessons, and memorizing vocabulary. In spite of being well past babyhood, Augustine learned to speak English through *acquisition*, much the same way he had learned his first language.[19]

The ability to speak more than one language leads to psychic changes in the speaker. A bilingual or multilingual person goes back and forth between languages easily and rapidly, often without thinking about it—a phenomenon called code-switching—which creates and reinforces cognitive flexibility when multi-tasking and when making judgments or decisions.[20] Linguists tell us that "bilingual children are consistently better at task-switching than monolingual children."[21] Linguistics research has also shown that, generally speaking, a first language shows stronger *emotional* responses than second *learned* languages do, but even in later life, emotion is stronger *if* the second language is *acquired* rather than *learned*.[22]

If I am correct that Augustine was around twelve years old when he first arrived at Churchill, his age may not have been ideal for acquiring a second language, but acquire it he did, through compulsory immersion. By the time of the second Franklin expedition, he was proficient in English and capable of switching quickly between languages. His behaviour at Pillage Point in the Mackenzie Delta and again along the coast to Alaska shows a new side to his personality, possibly the psychic change that linguistics experts have seen in their research. In assuming authority over the expedition officers and men as well as the local people, he acted in a European way that would not have been normal in an Inuit community.

I do not see Augustine as a "marginal man" shifting uneasily between ethnic and corporate communities. He was at home with his multiple identities, remaining *Inuttitut* (behaving in the style of the Inuit) when he left Franklin's straggling, undisciplined crew of dying men to make his own way to the safety of Akaitcho's camp, and in doing so saved himself and Joseph Benoit from starvation. A few years later, he rejected his village's traditions, breaking with the Inuit practice of leaving his family in the care of kinsmen in his home community, opting instead to take his wife and youngest child to his new posting at Fort Chimo. On his last journey, to the northwest to join Captain George Back, the Company apparently had no problem letting Augustine's wife and child go with him as far as Cumberland House and supporting them there and at Carlton House to wait for his return. The Company's apparent acceptance and support of his decisions suggests that the local traders and the London Committee held him in high esteem.

I do not believe that Augustine was unique. He was just the first young Inuk to spend most of his life in a society that was in many ways different from the kindred-based polity he was born into. His community had for at least fifty years been observing the *Qabluna* traders who had brought trade goods to the coastal summer villages and had learned a great deal from their observations and from the young, probably teenaged, Inuit who spent a winter at Churchill. They knew that the foreigners had good intentions and were not a threat to them, as well as realizing that there were benefits to be had within the relationship.

Augustine Tataneuck never became a household name, in Canada or anywhere else. Aside from comments in the Hudson's Bay Company's records and in the diaries of three officers of the British navy, he remains unknown. He is, however, worthy of being recognized. It was because of his understanding of Inuit and ice that John Franklin's second expedition (1825–27) was able to survey and map about 1,200 miles of the western coast between the Mackenzie River Delta and Point Beechey.

Perhaps more importantly, Augustine saved lives. Without his generosity in using his wealth to benefit his extended family community, many of them would have died. Without him in control of relations between the explorers and the coastal Inuit of the Mackenzie River Delta, the men of the second Franklin overland expedition are unlikely to have survived the Pillage Point attacks or the several ambushes planned by local communities along the ocean coast to the west and again when they returned to the Mackenzie Delta.

The success of the second expedition had no effect on the final geopolitical status of the far western Arctic. As it happened, the expedition reached its farthest point west a year too late. The boundary between Russian Alaska and Yukon was agreed upon in 1825, a year before the expedition people left Fort Franklin to return to their homes.

Perhaps Augustine's most remarkable characteristic was his tolerance. For him there seems to have been no boundary between peoples. He was completely at home among Europeans and at the same time lived *Inuttitut* all his life.

MEMORIALS

The Geographical Names Board of Canada has recognized the civic services and sacrifices of five men who served on the overland expedition by naming a lake in the Mackenzie District of the Northwest Territories after each of them.

- Augustine Tataneuck (Augustus Lake)
- Junius Hiutiruk (Junius Lake)
- Ullebuk (Ooligbuck Lake)
- Willard Ferdinand Wentzel (Wentzel Lake)
- Thoolezzah, a Dene guide (Thoolezzah Lake)

Ullebuk is also memorialized by Ooligbuck Point, in the Northwest Territories.

Augustine Tataneuck is also memorialized by the naming of a butterfly, *Incisalia augustus*.

ACKNOWLEDGEMENTS

THIRTY YEARS AGO, I READ A SINGLE SENTENCE IN ONE OF Churchill Post's daily journals that mentioned that a youngster, an Inuk that the post's men called Augustine, was living at the post. For the next decade I made a note of every snippet of information about him that I came across. I wrote the first draft of this book between 2001 and 2005 while wintering in the desert near a small Arizona town, spent the next twelve years teaching, and finished the project on Vancouver Island while in pandemic lockdown. The moral here might be that writing is best done in isolation. The moral, I have discovered, is not accurate. It takes much more than a village to produce a book. My village has been occupied by archives and archivists, libraries and librarians, bookstores and booksellers, online services, friends who had spare bedrooms, and my family.

First among the archives is the Hudson's Bay Company Archives in Winnipeg. Without the records of the Company we would know nothing or nearly nothing about Canada's deep history. I am grateful for them. First among the HBCA archivists are Judith Hudson Beattie and Anne Morton. Thank you, Judith and Anne, for research assistance and great conversations over lunch.

Many thanks are also due to librarians at the University of Manitoba's interlibrary loan desk, in the microfilm room at the University of Regina, and in the periodicals annex of the University of Arizona (Tempe). Two universities on Vancouver Island have found books and journals for me, and the senior librarian at the local branch of the Vancouver Island Regional Library has been more than helpful at finding obscure documents at libraries all over North America and making borrowing arrangements.

Professors Jennifer S.H. Brown and Timothy F. Ball encouraged me through ten years at the University of Winnipeg's Rupert's Land Research Centre. From them I learned to find history within the disciplines of anthropology and climatology. I owe their mentoring and caring attention more than I can express in words. I am also grateful to Professor Laura Peers, who unexpectedly came across a copy of Augustine's signature while searching the John West Collection at the Manitoba Archives for something entirely different and shared the news with me. The fact that a signature actually existed confirmed my belief that small, seemingly unimportant clues can lead to big conclusions.

When I fled the summer heat of the Arizona desert, there were friends who went as far as giving me a room to write in. To Jerry and Donna MacNeil, Midge and Bill Jory, Jim Daschuk and Giselle Marcotte, Karen Morrow, and Dr. David Miller: thank you.

Thank you also to Scott MacNeil, who has been Augustine's biggest fan over the years. We have discussed, on the phone, in emails, and at rare get-togethers, nearly all aspects of Augustine's life. Scott has without fail supported me in my long crusade to make Augustine known to all Canadians.

During the COVID-19 pandemic, support has come from another source that should be recognized. The online services of JSTOR and many library catalogues have been a boon for researchers, writers, teachers, and students working in isolation by offering free and unlimited access to books and journals. We should all be grateful for that.

I am eternally grateful to A4, an unknown person who vetted my manuscript and gave me short and useful lessons in Inuktitut grammar and Inuit naming practice.

My family has been the rock and manna that have sustained me for a lifetime. They are everything to me, and I thank them, as one of my grandchildren said, "to the other side of the universe and back again." My everlasting love and gratitude to Andrew, Connor, Fabienne, Mairi, Sarah, and William.

And finally I would like to acknowledge the Inuit children I taught two generations ago. They were so much fun in the classroom, so eager to learn, and so quick to pick up each bit of new information. They also went to a lot of trouble to look after me. When I had laryngitis for a week and had to use signs and the chalkboard to talk to them, they all whispered in the classroom. When I fell down crossing one of the water pipe tunnels on a Saturday, they came from all directions to make sure that I was okay. Many of them have become leaders, judges, legislators, authors, and educators, as well as nurses and helicopter pilots. They are all Elders now, and have created Nunavut. I am very proud of them.

GLOSSARY

Athapascan: people of the North American Subarctic, and their linguistic family, both sometimes referred to as Dene or Dené today

barming: the phase of making beer when the yeast begins to foam, indicating fermentation and alcohol production have begun

bateau (singular), bateaux (plural): flat-bottomed shallow-draft boat propelled by oars or one sail, used primarily for river travel

bermed: an adjective describing an energy-efficient structure usually built above or partially below grade with earth-covered walls and roof

bouletts: meatballs

bosses: roasted bisons' humps

capote: a hooded, usually knee- or shin-length coat, without buttons, closed by a sash or belt; an HBC capote is usually white

carriole: a sled with sidewalls for carrying a passenger

cartouche knife: *See* knives.

Chipewyan: an Athapascan-speaking Dene Nation of the Arctic and Subarctic east of Great Slave Lake

clasp knife: *See* knives.

Congou tea: *See* tea.

cooper: a tradesman specializing in the making of casks and other wooden containers

crash/crush sugar: *See* sugar.

Dutch cap: a woman's lace cap with triangular flaps

ferretting: a narrow strip of cloth sewn to seams to keep fabric from stretching or fraying

Inuk (singular), Inuit (plural): Indigenous Peoples inhabiting the Arctic and subarctic regions of Greenland, Labrador, Quebec, Nunavut, the Northwest Territories, and Alaska

Kabloona: See Qallunaaq.

knives: a *cartouche knife* has a full-length tang inside the handle; a *clasp knife* blade folds back into the handle; a *roach knife* has a short blade that curves upward for skinning fish

Labrador tea (*Ledum decumbens*): a flowering plant said to have a calming quality; contains a toxic element that makes it dangerous to human beings if taken in large quantities

made beaver (MB): a unit of exchange equivalent to the value of one prime beaver pelt, used in buying furs and bartering provisions. The value of the MB fluctuated according to the fur auctions in London after 1670.

needles, glover's: steel needles thicker than other needles, with a triangular point that can pierce animal hides, highly valued by Inuit women

partridge/ptarmigan/grouse: terms used in HBC documents for all small ground-nesting birds that inhabit the Canadian Arctic

pease: protein-rich legumes such as chickpeas and other leguminous plants

pipes, oil: barrels made at HBC fur trade posts to store liquids such as seal or whale oil

pistol lock: the firing mechanism that sparks and ignites the propellant in a firearm

pyrite: a gemstone containing sulphur that produces sparks when struck against metal or stone and lights tinder such as moss or muskox woolly hair

Qabloona/Qabluna: See Qallunaaq.

Qallunaaq: refers to all non-Inuit people but is primarily used for Europeans

roach knife: See knives.

sateen: a fabric with a weft-faced structure (i.e., the front side is smooth and the back is rough and dense)

staged or stagey (skins, pelts, hides): refers to pelts taken in summer before they have reached the "stage" when an animal's guard hairs have reached maximum thickness. The guard hairs that develop in the fall and early winter are what make the furs valuable as clothing and as a trade item. "Prime" is the fur trade word for the best pelts.

Souchong tea: *See* tea.

stroud: coarse woollen fabric

sugar, loaf and crash/crush: sugar loaf is made from boiled and filtered raw sugar poured into a cone-shaped mould and hardened by drying in a heated room. Crash or crush sugar is granulated sugar as we know it today.

tea: *Congou* is high-quality black tea grown in China, now called English Breakfast. *Souchong* is a black tea made from the fourth tier of leaves and partially dried and fermented.

tobacco: dried leaves of the *nicotiana* plant native to North and South America, without additives, for chewing, snuffing, and pipe-smoking in the early 1800s

tracking: man-hauling a canoe through very shallow water or dangerous rapids by walking along the shore pulling canoes with sturdy ropes. Also known as "lining."

NOTES

PREFACE

1   Stephen B. Oates, *Biography as History*, Charles Edmondson Historical Lecture, no. 12 (Waco, TX: Baylor University Press, 1990), 7.

INTRODUCTION TO AUGUSTINE'S WORLD

1   Audrey N. Clark, *The New Penguin Dictionary of Geography* (London: Penguin, 1990).
2   The latitude of the Arctic Circle is, more precisely, 66°33′47.7″ as of August 20, 2019. Because of Earth's axial tilt, the Arctic Circle fluctuates by plus or minus 2° over 41,000 years and is currently moving north about 49 feet every year. A region is "an area of the earth's surface with one or more features or characteristics (natural or the result of human activity) which give it a measure of unity and make it differ from the areas surrounding it." Clark, *New Penguin Dictionary*.
3   Average temperatures are from the mid-twentieth century. Overall, the earth had been slowly warming since the last great ice sheets began to melt.
4   Nancy Fogelson, *Arctic Exploration and International Relations 1900–1932* (Fairbanks: University of Alaska Press, 1992), 1. See also J. Brian Bird, "Arctic: Northernmost Region of the Earth," in *Encyclopedia Britannica*, last updated August 11, 2022, https://www.britannica.com/place/Arctic. The treeline moves either north or south during extended periods of warming or cooling.
5   A second ice sheet, the Cordilleran, covered Canada's far west from the Pacific Ocean to just east of the Rocky Mountains. At their greatest extent, the two ice sheets met.
6   John T. Andrews, "Satellite Image Atlas of Glaciers of the World" (U.S. Geological Survey Professional Paper 1386-J-1, n.d.). BCE means Before Common Era and replaces BC (Before Christ). CE means Common Era and replaces AD (Anno Domini, Latin for "year of the Lord"), used by the Roman Empire since 525. BCE has been used by Jewish scholars since 1708. In the late twentieth century, BCE and CE became more widely used out of respect for non-Christian readers and writers.

7   Brian Fagan, *The Great Warming: Climate Change and the Rise and Fall of Civilizations* (New York: Bloomsbury, 2008); Brian Fagan, *The Little Ice Age: How Climate Made History, 1300–1850* (New York: Basic Books, 2000); Raymond S. Bradley, *Climate of the Last Millenium* (Climate System Research Center, 2003); Reid A. Bryson and Thomas J. Murray, *Climates of Hunger: Mankind and the World's Changing Weather* (Madison: University of Wisconsin Press, 1977); Emmanuel Le Roy Ladurie, *Times of Feast, Times of Famine: A History of Climate since the Year 1000* (New York: Farrar, Straus and Giroux, 1988); H.H. Lamb, *The Changing Climate* (London: Wiley, 1966; London: Routledge, 1977); H.H. Lamb, *Climate: Present, Past and Future*, vol. 2, *Climate History and the Future* (London: Routledge, 1972); H.H. Lamb, *Climate History and the Modern World* (London: Routledge, 1982); H.H. Lamb, *Weather, Climate and Human Affairs* (London: Routledge, 1988). In 2011, Routledge Revivals published these as ebooks.

8   Fagan, *Little Ice Age*, 122–23.

9   Drew T. Shindell, Gavin A. Schmidt, Michael E. Mann, David Rind, and Anne Waple, "Solar Forcing of Regional Climate Change during the Maunder Minimum," *Science*, December 7, 2001, 2149–52; Drew T. Shindell, "Glaciers, Old Masters, and Galileo: The Puzzle of the Chilly 17th Century," NASA Science Briefs, December 2002, https://www.giss.nasa.gov/research/briefs/2002_shindell_06/. See also "Chilly Temperatures during the Maunder Minimum" (last updated 2006, accessed July 29, 2022, https://earthobservatory.nasa.gov/images/7122/chilly-temperatures-during-the-maunder-minimum), on the computer model created by Dr. Shindell and his team at NASA's Goddard Institute for Space Studies.

10 Stuart A. Harris, "Permafrost," in *The Canadian Encyclopedia*, Historica Canada, article published July 7, 2010, last modified August 10, 2015, https://www.thecanadianencyclopedia.ca/en/article/permafrost. See also Stuart A. Harris, *The Permafrost Environment* (Lanham, MD: Rowman and Littlefield, 1986).

11 Feng Sheng Hu and Lawrence C. Bliss, "Tundra," in *Encyclopedia Britannica*, article published May 4, 1999, last modified March 12, 2022, https://www.britannica.com/science/tundra. See also "The Tundra Biome," UC Museum of Paleontology, University of California (Berkeley), accessed July 29, 2022, https://ucmp.berkeley.edu/glossary/gloss5/biome/tundra.html.

12 Donald F. Acton, J.M. Ryder, Hugh French, Olav Slaymaker, and I.A. Brookes, "Physiographic Regions," in *The Canadian Encyclopedia*, Historica Canada, article published February 27, 2012, last modified March 4, 2015, https://www.thecanadianencyclopedia.ca/en/article/physiographic-regions.

13 Robert W. Park, "The Dorset-Thule Transition," in T. Max Friesen and Owen K. Mason, eds., *Oxford Handbook of the Prehistoric Arctic* (Oxford: Oxford University Press, 2016), 807.

14 Renee Fossett, *In Order to Live Untroubled* (Winnipeg: University of Manitoba Press, 2001), 11–14, 17–18, 24–25. The autonym "Inuit" has replaced "Eskimo" in general usage but is not appropriate when referring to the spectrum of genetically related Arctic people from Siberia to Greenland, including Alaskan Yu'pik, who do not have the words *Inuk* (person) and *Inuit* (people) in their dialect. "Eskimo" and "Eskimoan" continue to be useful when speaking or writing of all related Arctic peoples from far

eastern Siberia to Greenland. While archaeologist T. Max Friesen has made a case for replacing the name "Paleoeskimo" with "Paleo-Inuit," in accord with the Inuit Circumpolar Council's preference, but there is no evidence that the Paleoeskimo were actually Eskimoan. Nor were they Thule, who are generally recognized as the first Inuit. See T. Max Friesen, "On the Naming of Arctic Archaeological Traditions: The Case for Paleo-Inuit," *Arctic* 68, no. 3 (2015): iii–iv.

15 Robert McGhee, *Canadian Arctic Prehistory* (New York: Van Nostrand Reinhold, 1978).

16 Maanasa Raghaven, Michael DeGiorgio, Anders Albrechtsen, Ida Moltke, Pontus Skoglund, Thorfinn S. Korneliussen, Bjarne Grønnow, et al., "The Genetic Prehistory of the New World Arctic," *Science*, August 29, 2014, 1012–15.

17 Park, "Dorset-Thule Transition," 807.

18 T. Max Friesen, Introduction to "Pan-Arctic Population Movements: The Early Paleo-Inuit and Thule Inuit Migrations," chap. 28 in Friesen and Mason, eds., *Oxford Handbook of the Prehistoric Arctic*, 679–80.

19 David Morrison, "The Earliest Thule Migration," *Canadian Journal of Archaeology* 22, no. 2 (1999): 151–52; Peter Whitridge, "Classic Thule [Classic Precontact Inuit]," in Friesen and Mason, eds., *Oxford Handbook of the Prehistoric Arctic*, 831. The Neo-Atlantic climatic episode (900–1250 CE) was a period of significant warming throughout the northern hemisphere, with a rise of average temperatures estimated to have been about 3.6° Fahrenheit. Lamb, *Climate: Present, Past and Future*, 2:438.

20 Wendy Stephenson and Charles Arnold, *Taimani: At That Time: Inuvialuit Timeline Visual Guide*, 2nd ed. (Inuvik: Inuvialuit Regional Corporation, 2011), 20–22.

21 Laurence Marcellus Larsen, "The Church in North America (Greenland) in the Middle Ages," *Catholic Historical Review* 5, no. 2–3 (1919): 190.

22 Friesen, Introduction to "Pan-Arctic Population Movements," 680.

23 The newly dated Thule sites are at the Beaufort Sea coast, Banks Island, Victoria Island, south coast of Amundsen Gulf, Bellot Strait, Lancaster Sound, Devon Island, Ellesmere Island, the eastern and western coasts of Baffin Island, Naujan (Repulse Bay) on the west coast of Hudson Bay, and Cape York in Greenland.

24 The first Europeans to see the Copper Inuit were Samuel Hearne, at the mouth of the Coppermine River in 1771, and John Franklin and his men, at Coronation Gulf in 1821.

25 Diamond Jenness, "The Copper Eskimos," in *Encyclopedia Arctica*, vol. 8, *Anthropology and Archeology* (unpublished reference work, 1947–51), 50, Dartmouth College Library, Hanover, NH.

26 Louis-Jacques Dorais, *The Language of the Inuit: Syntax, Semantics, and Society in the Arctic* (Montreal: McGill-Queen's University Press, 2010), 28; Diamond Jenness, "Origin of the Copper Eskimos and Their Copper Culture," *Geographical Review* 13, no. 4 (1923): 545. Netsilik means "the seal place"; Netsilingmiut means "people of the seal place." Both can be used in referring to the people of the area.

27 Bryan C. Gordon, "Nadlok and the Origin of the Copper Inuit," in *Threads of Arctic Prehistory: Papers in Honour of William E. Taylor Jr.*, eds. David Morrison and Jean-Luc Pilon, Archaeological Survey of Canada Paper No. 149 (Hull: Canadian Museum of Civilization, 1994), 325, 336–37.

28 Kevin Timoney, "Tree and Tundra Cover Anomalies in the Subarctic Forest-Tundra of Northwestern Canada," *Arctic* 48, no. 1 (1995): 13–21. In 1927 the river and forest became a wildlife sanctuary covering about 20,077 square miles.

29 Many trade gathering places existed across the Arctic, from Siberia to Greenland. At least one, on the east coast of Greenland, was called Akilineq. Robert Brown wrote that "Akilinek [sic] signified a fabulous [sic; fabled] country beyond the seas." Henry Rink, *Tales and Traditions of the Eskimo: With a Sketch of Their Habits, Religion, Language and Other Peculiarities*, trans. Henry Rink, ed. Robert Brown (London and Edinburgh: William Blackwood and Sons, 1875), 169, editor's note. See also Fossett, *In Order to Live Untroubled*, 23, 25–27, 119; Gordon, "Nadlok and the Origin of the Copper Inuit," 336–37.

30 John Richardson, *Arctic Ordeal: The Journal of John Richardson, Surgeon Naturalist with Franklin, 1820–1822* (Kingston and Montreal: McGill-Queen's University Press, 1984), 28.

31 Curated relocations are deliberate, carefully planned moves that do not tend to create refugees. Curation's opposite is a "fragmented" or "panic" move, a response to an unexpected catastrophe such as an earthquake, volcanic eruption, tsunami, or enemy attack, when there is no time to prepare and people flee empty-handed in all directions.

32 George F. Lyon, *The Private Journal of Captain G.F. Lyon of H.M.S. Hecla during the Recent Voyage of Discovery under Captain Parry* (London: John Murray, 1824), 342. Lyon recognized that well-travelled Inuit were highly esteemed and noted that "the importance assumed by a great Eskimaux traveller is fully equal to that displayed by Europeans who have seen the world."

33 Ernest S. Burch Jr., "Caribou Eskimo Origins: An Old Problem Reconsidered," *Arctic Anthropology* 15, no. 1 (1978): 26–28.

34 Ernest S. Burch Jr., "The Thule-Historic Eskimo Transition on the West Coast of Hudson Bay," in *Thule Eskimo Culture: An Anthropological Retrospective*, ed. Allen P. McCartney, Archaeological Survey Paper No. 88 (Ottawa: National Museums of Canada, 1979), 194.

35 Burch, "Caribou Eskimo Origins"; Burch, "Thule-Historic Eskimo Transition," 194; Brenda L. Clark, *The Development of Caribou Eskimo Culture*, Archaeological Survey of Canada Paper No. 59 (Ottawa: National Museum of Man, 1977); William E. Taylor, "Hypothesis on the Origin of Canadian Thule Culture," *American Antiquity* 28, no. 2 (1963): 456–64.

36 Richardson, *Arctic Ordeal*, 28.

37 David Damas, "The Eskimo," in *Science, History and Hudson Bay*, ed. C.S. Beals (Ottawa: Dept. of Energy, Mines and Resources, 1968), 146.

38 In 1977 Eben Nanauq Hopson (Inupiaq) invited representatives of Inuit (Canada), Eskimo (United States), and Kallaalit (Greenland, Denmark) to a meeting in Barrow, Alaska, to discuss how Indigenous peoples across the Arctic could draw attention to their concerns about threats to the Arctic environment and to the Inuit language and cultural traditions. The meeting established the Inuit Circumpolar Conference (ICC), later renamed the Inuit Circumpolar Council (ICC), which is now an internationally recognized non-governmental organization with consultative status to the United

Nations. The Chukotka people (Russia) have since joined the organization. For a discussion of obstacles to Pan-Inuitism, see Daniel Chartier, "'Pan-Inuit' Written Heritage: Institutions, Goals, Projects, Perspectives," in *Heritage and Change in the Arctic: Resources for the Present, and the Future*, eds. Robert C. Thomsen and Lill Rastad Bjørst (Aalborg, Denmark: Aalborg University Press, 2017), 41–67.

39   Along with rights to all mineral resources and obligations to search for a northwest passage.

40   *Keewatin* is a Cree word meaning "big wind." *Kivallit* is Inuktitut for "people of the south." Statistics Canada continued to use the place name *Keewatin* in the 2016 census year, and some archaeological and anthropological publications also continue to use the old name as of 2020.

41   English in Rupert's Land, French in Lower Canada, German in Labrador, and Danish in Greenland.

42   Noelle Palmer, "The Role of Translation in Linguistic Standardisation across Inuit Nunangat" (MA thesis, Concordia University, 2016), iii.

43   Quoted in Palmer, 42.

CHAPTER 1. The Inuit, the Company, and Churchill Post, 1812

1   Provincial Archives of Manitoba, Hudson's Bay Company Archives (hereafter cited as HBCA), Churchill Post Journals, B.42/a/138:2v-3 (29 August 1812), B.42/a/138:27v (4 December 1812); Churchill Meteorological Journal, 1811–13, B.42/a/139a. Although there was probably a mechanical time-keeping device at the post in 1812, Topping did not mention one. His use of "night" may have referred to any time between sunset, defined as the moment the sun dips below the horizon, and the end of twilight, the roughly forty- to forty-five-minute period after the sun sets when there is still enough light to see by. See the Time and Date Corporation, Stavanger, Norway (timeanddate.com); and NOAA, the U.S. National Oceanic and Atmospheric Administration (https://gml.noaa.gov/grad/solcalc).

2   The Churchill River is about three miles wide between its west bank where the post was and its east bank where the supply ships anchored. Frederick J. Alcock, "The Churchill River," *Geographical Review* 2, no. 6 (1916): 443.

3   HBCA, Churchill Post Journals, B.42/a/138:2v.

4   HBC traders at all posts knew at least a few words related to trading, fur, food, locations, animals, and weather in the Indigenous languages their clients spoke. Some officers and labourers who spent years at one post became proficient in one or more Indigenous languages.

5   HBCA, Private Records, E.2/12:611–12; Andrew Graham, *Andrew Graham's Observations on Hudson's Bay*, ed. Glyndwr Williams (1791; London: Hudson's Bay Record Society, 1969), 239.

6   HBCA, Churchill Post Journals, B.42/a/57:19, B.42/a/63, 65, 77; York Factory Journals, B.239/a/5 (10 August 1720); York Factory Correspondence Books, B.239/b/1:25, 29; Richard Glover, "Introduction," in Graham, *Observations on Hudson's Bay*, 1, 236.

7   In Inuit belief, sharing a name means also sharing a soul. An infant may be named after a deceased person who, in life, had skills or other characteristics that benefitted the community and that the community hoped to replace in the newborn child.
8   The Iglulingmiut (People of the House Place) are the people of Melville Peninsula. Renee Fossett, *In Order to Live Untroubled* (Winnipeg: University of Manitoba Press, 2001), 125–31, 171–72, 190–91. See also Bernard Saladin d'Anglure, *Inuit Stories of Being and Rebirth: Gender, Shamanism, and the Third Sex* (Winnipeg: University of Manitoba Press, 2018).
9   George F. Lyon, *The Private Journal of Captain G.F. Lyon of H.M.S. Hecla during the Recent Voyage of Discovery under Captain Parry* (London: John Murray, 1824), 351. Lyon thought that only boys were treated this way, but there are a few known instances when girls were as well. Lyon seems to have thought that only the wealthy lent their children, but poorer people did also, and possibly with better reasons for the practice. Today the practice is often called "custom adoption" (*tiguaq, tiguarsiye*) by Inuit.
10 Samuel Hearne, *A Journey from Prince of Wales's Fort in Hudson's Bay to the Northern Ocean...in the Years 1769, 1770, 1771, & 1772*, ed. Richard Glover (1795; Toronto: Macmillan of Canada, 1958), 218n.
11 The man was Francis Loyer, described as "native of Hudson Bay" in the 1811–12 List of Servants. HBCA, Churchill Fort, List of Servants, 1812, B.42/f/7, #24.
12 HBCA, Churchill Account Book, 1794–1815, B.42/d/103a:24; List of Servants, 1815–16, B.42/f/9.
13 HBCA, Churchill Post Journals, B.42/a/137; List of Servants, 1812–13, B.42/a/138.
14 HBCA, Churchill Post Journals, B.42/a/138 (30 August 1812). Topping's comment confirms that Augustine's home community was not at Arviat but some distance north of it.
15 HBCA, Churchill Post Journals, B.42/a/138:27d.
16 Why the British explorers chose to call him "Augustus" instead of the HBC name "Augustine" is unclear. It may have been as simple as a spelling mistake in the correspondence between the British Admiralty or the HBC London Committee. In this book, "Augustine" is used in the title and throughout because it was the name given to him by the HBC officers he regarded as fictive kin, while "Augustus" was a temporary name, used for only five years by British explorers. Augustine's Inuit name is spelled "Tataneuck" because that is how he spelled it when he wrote it at the request of the missionary John West in 1823. In Churchill's 1824 Eskimo Trading Book, his English and Inuit names were written as "Augustine Tataniak." The handwriting does not look like that of the 1823 signatures we know to be Augustine's, so it is possible that one of the Churchill officers wrote it. HBCA, Eskimo Trading Book, 1824.
17 E.W. Maunder, *Notes to the Royal Astronomical Society* 50 (1890); E.W. Maunder, "A Prolonged Sunspot Minimum," *Knowledge* 17 (1894); Maunder, "A Prolonged Sunspot Minimum," *Journal of the British Astronomical Association* 32 (1922); John A. Eddy, "The Maunder Minimum: Sunspots and Climate in the Reign of Louis XIV," *Science* 92 (1976): 1189–202. Until the early twenty-first century, the Dalton Minimum (1790–1830) was known as the Second Maunder Minimum.
18 HBCA, Churchill Post Journals, B.42/a/108 (28–29 May 1787).

19 HBCA, Churchill Post Journals, B.42/a/111 (1788). Log book kept by Captain George Taylor.
20 William Auld (c.1770–post-1830) was surgeon at Churchill and at Reindeer Lake between 1790 and 1804, Chief (1795–1810), Superintendent of Northern Factories (1810–14), and retired in 1815. HBCA, Biographical Sheet, William Auld; *Dictionary of Canadian Biography*, vol. 6, 1821–1835 (University of Toronto/Université Laval, 1985); Colin Robertson, *Correspondence Book, September 1817 to September 1822*, ed. E.E. Rich ([London]: Hudson's Bay Record Society, 1939), 203–5, Appendix A ("Biographical").
21 HBCA, Churchill Post Journals, B.42/a/128:4v (July 1803), B.42/a/130 (3 September 1804), B.42/a/132 (1807), B.42/a/135:7v (1 July 1810).
22 The essential reference work on the physical plant at Churchill Post is Martha McCarthy's *Churchill: A Land-Use History, 1782–1930* (Ottawa: Parks Canada, 1985), based on the original documents of the Hudson's Bay Company.
23 "James Knight's Journal," *The Beaver*, Summer 1963, 20–21; E.E. Rich, "Introduction," in *James Isham's Observations on Hudsons Bay, 1743* ([Toronto]: Champlain Society; [London]: Hudson's Bay Record Society, 1949), xli.
24 William Wales, "Journal of a Voyage in 1768," *Philosophical Transactions of the Royal Society* 60 (1771): 191.
25 In the 1960s, residents of many Arctic homes, including mine, were still getting water by cutting blocks of ice from ponds and small lakes and melting the ice blocks in barrels or in reservoirs attached to kitchen stoves. The "necessary" was a large pail lined with a plastic bag and topped with a wooden toilet seat and lid. Twice a week the bag was tied off and hauled out on the sea ice where it floated or sank during the summer thaw. Similar arrangements, with the exception of the plastic bags, are likely to have prevailed at Churchill in Augustine's time. Martha McCarthy notes that "necessaries, or privies, were built" but does not give details of when, where, or how. McCarthy, *Churchill*, 31.
26 "Mister" is derived from the Latin *magister* meaning "one having control or authority," which evolved to "master" during the sixteenth and seventeenth centuries and was used to speak to or about men who did not have a higher or professional title—such as doctor, general, bishop—or who were wealthy landowners. By the late eighteenth century it had become an honorific that could be used in speaking to or of any man. *A New English Dictionary on Historical Principles*, vol. 6 (Oxford: Clarendon, 1908).
27 *The Compact Oxford English Dictionary* (Oxford University Press, 1971) dates the first in-print appearance of "servants" in this context to 1683, thirteen years after the establishment of the Hudson's Bay Company.
28 HBCA, Churchill Post Journals, William Auld's Memorandum Book, 1810, B.42/a/136a.
29 John Charles was born in London and was hired by HBC in 1799. He worked at Churchill and Churchill District until 1825, was Chief Factor at Athapasca from 1825 to 1836 and at York Factory from 1836 to 1839, and retired to Red River in 1843. HBCA, Biographical Sheet, John Charles.
30 William Ross (1783–1855), accountant, was Officer in Charge at Churchill in 1812–13 and in 1819–20. W. Stewart Wallace, ed., *Documents Relating to the North West Company* (Toronto: Champlain Society, 2013), 22:496.

31 HBCA, Biographical Sheets, John Pocock Holmes, John Charles, William Oman Sr., Joseph Spence, Peter Wishart.
32 HBCA, Churchill Post Servants' Accounts, B.42/f/7 (1812–13).
33 HBCA, Churchill Post Servants' Accounts, B.42/f/7 (1812–13). The date of a trading year, or Outfit, varied. In theory, Outfits started on June 1 every year. In practice, an Outfit for any particular post began when its stock of furs was ready for the supply ship. The exact date depended on how long it took to transport the furs to York Factory.
34 HBCA, Churchill Post Servants' Accounts, B.42/f/7 (1812–13).
35 The term is used in Hudson's Bay Company Biographical Sheets and other documents to describe anyone born in Rupert's Land regardless of parental ethnicity.
36 HBCA, Servants' Contracts (1780–c.1926), A.32/17, fo. 23; Churchill District Report for Outfit 1828–29, B.42/e/6; Michael Payne, "Fort Churchill, 1821–1900: An Outpost Community in the Fur Trade," *Manitoba History* 20 (Autumn 1990): 2–15.
37 James G.E. Smith, "Chipewyan," in *Handbook of North American Indians*, vol. 6, *Subarctic*, ed. June Helm (Washington, DC: Smithsonian Institution, 1981), 271. Smith identifies them as Elthen-eldèli, known as a significant population of Caribou-eater Dene and, at a more granular level, as Sayisi Dene (Rising Sun People). Smith noted that as of 1981, they were known as "dwellers at Stone Fort." Their home village was, at different times, near Nueltin Lake, Tadoule Lake, and Little Duck Lake as much as 250 miles northwest of Churchill Post. See Sydney Augustus Keighley, *Trader, Tripper, Trapper: The Life of a Bay Man*, with Renee Fossett Jones and David Kirkby Riddle (Winnipeg: Watson and Dwyer, 1989), 140, 159, 164.
38 McCarthy, *Churchill*, 75.
39 HBCA, Churchill Post Journals, B.42/a/159, fo. 5 (19 September 1822).
40 Stayner, born 1770 in London, was Writer and Assistant Trader at Churchill from 1782 to 1797 and Chief Factor from 1798 to 1801. He retired in 1801 to England with his two daughters, Ann and Sarah. HBCA, Biographical Sheet, Thomas Stayner; Raymond Shirritt-Beaumont, personal communication, March 2003.
41 HBCA, Churchill Post Journals, B.42/a/138:27v, Letter from Topping to Auld (4 December 1812).
42 HBCA, Churchill Post Journals, B.42/a/138 (September–December 1812), *passim*.
43 HBCA, Churchill Post Journals, B.42/a/138 (January–February 1813). "House" in this context referred to the post in its entirety. Similarly, buildings that housed the senior offices and their staff such as Winnipeg's Hudson's Bay House were always called "The House" in conversation among the men and families of the Northern Stores division of the HBC.
44 HBCA, Churchill Post Journals, B.42/a/138:35, Letter from John Spencer to Thomas Topping (4 June 1813); B.42/a/138:36, Letter from Topping to Auld at York Factory (7 June 1813); B.42/a/138:37, Letter from Auld to Topping (27 June 1813).
45 HBCA, Churchill Post Journals, B.42/a/148:29, 31d, 34, Letter from Topping to Auld (3 March, 16 April 1813).
46 The post's journal never mentioned Augustine's father after he left Churchill in 1812.
47 HBCA, Churchill Post Journals, B.42/a/138:7d.

48 HBCA, Churchill Post Journals, B.42/a/140:4.
49 HBCA, Churchill Post Journals, B.42/a/140:42d.

CHAPTER 2. The Apprentice, 1813–1820

1   HBCA, York Factory Journals, B.239/a/124:30d (4 August 1813); Churchill Post Journals, B.42/a/140:5v (14 August 1813).
2   HBCA, Churchill Journals, B.42/a/138, B.42/a/140. Both journals tell the story of the typhus outbreak but do not always agree on the dates of events and on the numbers of the sick, the healthy, and the dead. Other sources—such as *The Dictionary of Canadian Biography* (University of Toronto/Université Laval, 1985); *The Selkirk Settlers of Red River and Their Descendants, 1812–1992* (Winnipeg: Lord Selkirk Association of Rupert's Land, 1992), A3–A4; and a number of websites—also cite different numbers.
3   *Prince of Wales I* (1793–1833), the first HBC vessel with this name.
4   The other two colonists who died at sea were Hugh McDonald, a carpenter from Fort William, Argyleshire, and Samuel Lamont, a millwright from Bowmore, Islay, Argyleshire. Both men died on August 3, 1813, and were buried at sea. *Selkirk Settlers*, A4.
5   Typhus is not communicable person-to-person. It is carried by fleas, which most commonly live on rodents but also survive in animal hides, sawdust, sacking, and bedding, all of which would have been on the two HBC ships. Professor Paul Hackett, personal communication.
6   HBCA, Churchill Post Journals, B.42/a/140:5–6 (19–22 October 1813).
7   HBCA, Churchill Post Journals, B.42/a/138:41 (21 August 1813). Joseph Howse was on furlough in 1812–13 and had just returned to Churchill on *Prince of Wales*.
8   HBCA, Churchill Post Journals, B.42/a/138:41v; *Selkirk Settlers*.
9   HBCA, Churchill Post Journals, B.42/a/138:41v, B.42/a/140 (18, 19, 20–22, 25 August 1813). For a description of the Inuit method of making leather, see Andrew Graham, *Andrew Graham's Observations on Hudson's Bay*, ed. Glyndwr Williams (1791; London: Hudson's Bay Record Society, 1969), 188. See also James G.E. Smith, "Chipewyan," in *Handbook of North American Indians*, vol. 6, Subarctic, ed. June Helm (Washington, DC: Smithsonian Institution, 1981); and Matt Richards, *Deerskins into Buckskins: How to Tan with Brains, Soap and Eggs* (Cave Junction, OR: Backcountry, 1997).
10 HBCA, Churchill Post Journals, B.42/a/138, Letter from Topping to Auld (24 August 1813).
11 HBCA, Biographical Sheet, William Auld.
12 About 54 gallons or 238 litres.
13 HBCA, Churchill Post Journals, B.42/a/138, B.42/a/140 (30 August 1813). Katherine Gunn, age twenty, died on August 30; George McDonald, age forty-eight, died on September 1; John Sutherland, age fifty, died on September 2. *Selkirk Settlers*, A3.
14 HBCA, Churchill Post Journals, B.42/a/138.
15 HBCA, York Factory Journals, B.239/a/124:33 (6–7 September 1813).
16 HBCA, Churchill Post Journals, B.42/a/140 (9 September 1813).
17 HBCA, Churchill Post Journals, B.42/a/140:8.

18 HBCA, Churchill Post Journals, B.42/a/140. The woman who died on September 19 was Christian Gunn, the fifty-year-old wife of Alexander Gunn. *Selkirk Settlers*.
19 HBCA, York Factory Journals, B.239/a/120.
20 Churchill Creek is now Herriot Creek.
21 HBCA, Churchill Post Journals, B.42/a/140.
22 In the sixteenth century, "lumber" was a term applied to unused items of furniture, tools, and household utensils. In seventeenth- and eighteenth-century Britain, pawnshops were called "lumber-houses." Lumber rooms in houses were rooms where inconvenient, useless, and cumbrous items were stored. By the early nineteenth century, the word had taken on the meaning of "junk" (*The Compact Oxford English Dictionary*). In parts of Scotland today, large houses (including my sister-in-law's house at Stirling) often have "lumber-rooms" in the attic where seasonal clothing, unused furniture, and luggage are stored.
23 Donald Bannerman, age fifty, the last of the colonists to die, was from Badflinch. *Selkirk Settlers*.
24 HBCA, Churchill Post Journals, B.42/a/140 (24 September 1813).
25 HBCA, Churchill Post Journals, B.42/a/140 (12–17 October 1813).
26 Quoted in J.M. Bumsted, *Lord Selkirk: A Life* (Winnipeg: University of Manitoba Press, 2008), 243, attributed to Jean Murray Cole, *Exile in the Wilderness: The Life of Chief Factor Archibald McDonald, 1790–1853* (Toronto: Burns and McEachern, 1979), 18; Donald Gunn and Charles Tuttle, *A History of Manitoba* (Ottawa: MacLean, Roger, 1880), 100.
27 HBCA, Churchill Post Journals, B.42/a/141 (25–31 October 1813).
28 HBCA, Churchill Post Journals, B.42/a/140 (19 November 1813).
29 HBCA, Churchill Post Journals, B.42/a/140.
30 HBCA, Churchill Post Journals, B.42/a/140.
31 HBCA, Churchill Post Journals, B.42/a/140 (26 November 1813).
32 According to Archibald McDonald's great-great-granddaughter, Jean Murray Cole, McDonald believed the fire was caused by cracks in the trading room chimney, not by the settlers. Cole, *Exile in the Wilderness*.
33 HBCA, Churchill Post Journals, B.42/a/140 (29 November 1813). The Woody Islands are about twenty-six miles upriver from the post.
34 HBCA, Churchill Post Journals, B.42/a/140; "Settlers List," in *Selkirk Settlers*.
35 HBCA, Churchill Post Journals, B.42/a/140.
36 HBCA, Churchill Post Journals, B.42/a/140 (20 January 1814).
37 HBCA, Churchill Post Journals, B.42/a/140 (1 February 1814).
38 When airflow in a fireplace or stove is inadequate, oils in the wood may not be completely burned, becoming gaseous instead and rising with the smoke. As smoke rises it condenses inside the chimney, leaving a residue of flammable creosote.
39 HBCA, Churchill Post Journals, B.42/a/140 (27 November 1813).
40 HBCA, Churchill Post Journals, B.42/a/140 (5–6 April 1814).
41 HBCA, Churchill Post Journals, B.42/a/140 (7 April 1814).
42 HBCA, Churchill Post Journals, B.42/a/140 (4 June 1814).
43 HBCA, Churchill Post Journals, B.42/a/140 (4–10 June 1814).
44 HBCA, Churchill Post Journals, B.42/a/140 (4–10 June 1814).

45 HBCA, Churchill Post Journals, B.42/a/141 (24 September 1814).
46 HBCA, Churchill Post Journals, B.42/a/140 (16–18 June 1814).
47 HBCA, Churchill Post Journals, B.42/a/140:29d (10 July 1814); Robin Ridington, "Wechuge and Windigo: A Comparison of Cannibal Belief among Boreal Forest Athapaskans and Algonkians," *Anthropologica* 18, no. 2 (1976): 107–29; Jennifer S.H. Brown and Robert Brightman, "Introduction," in *The Orders of the Dreamed: George Nelson on Cree and Northern Ojibwa Religion and Myth, 1823* (Winnipeg: University of Manitoba Press, 1990); Martha McCarthy, *Churchill: A Land-Use History, 1782–1930* (Ottawa: Parks Canada, 1985), 44. McCarthy wrote, "Oddly enough such fears were common among the Chipewyan, who were often said to have refused to stay in a place because they heard strange Indians around their tents."
48 HBCA, Churchill Post Journals, B.42/a/140 (10 July 1814).
49 HBC journals were written in pencil during winter because the ink froze. They were called "rough copies." HBC hired Writers, men whose job it was to rewrite all the rough copies during the summer to send to the London Committee, and these were called "fair copies."
50 HBCA, Churchill Post Journals, B.42/a/140:29d, B.42/a/148:22d.
51 HBCA, Churchill Post Journals, B.42/a/125 (1800–1801), B.42/a/128 (1802–3), B.42/a/132 (1807), B.42/a/140 (1815).
52 HBCA, Churchill Post Journals, B.42/a/141:15v (3 May 1815).
53 HBCA, Churchill Post Journals, B.42/a/141 (29 May 1815).
54 HBCA, Churchill Post Journals, B.42/a/141 (1 May 1815).
55 HBCA, Churchill Post Journals, B.42/a/140 (21 June 1815), B.42/a/141:18b–18bd (24 June 1815), B.42/a/148:36d (22 June 1815). The entry appears in three different logbooks with slightly different dates and comments, which may have been the result of copying errors when the rough copy was rewritten or deliberate changes to correct grammar and spelling by the Writer.
56 HBCA, Churchill Post Journals, B.42/a/141:18b–18bd, B.42/a/148:36d; B.42/a/138, Letter from Thomas Topping to William Auld (4 December 1814).
57 HBCA, Churchill Post Journals, B.42/a/140 (24 June 1815).
58 HBCA, Servants' Contracts, 1780 to c.1826, A.32/16, fo. 17; George Simpson's Character Book, 1832, A.43/2; Colin Robertson, *Correspondence Book, September 1817 to September 1822*, ed. E.E. Rich ([London]: Hudson's Bay Record Society, 1939), Appendix A ("Biographical").
59 HBCA, Churchill Post Journals, B.42/a/148, fo. 38d (19 August 1815).
60 HBCA, Churchill Post Journals, B.42/a/142:3 (21 August 1815), B.42/a/148, fo. 19 (21 August 1815).
61 HBCA, Biographical Sheet, William Hemmings Cook. William Hemmings Cook was York Factory's Chief in Charge from 1809 to 1815. He resigned in 1819.
62 HBCA, Churchill Post Journals, B.42/a/142. Medical geographer Paul Hackett notes that "one of the most striking features of this period was the great frequency of 'colds' of varying descriptions and epidemic sore throats, as diseases of the respiratory tract emerged as by far the most common diseases at this time.... The colds that the traders noted encompassed a wide body of human sicknesses with roughly similar symptoms, collectively known as Acute Respiratory Diseases (ARDS)." See Paul Hackett, *A Very*

Remarkable Sickness: Patterns of Disease Diffusion in the Petit Nord (Winnipeg: University of Manitoba Press, 2002), 87.
63 HBCA, Churchill Post Account Book, 1823, B.42/d/112.
64 Medical kits were issued to all HBC trading posts well into the twentieth century, until a community had a government-run nursing station and a telephone or single sideband radio to call for help. For readers interested in early nineteenth-century medical practice, see Shepard Krech III, "The Death of Barbue, a Kutchin Chief," *Arctic* 36, no. 3 (1982): 437, Appendix ("Hudson's Bay Company Medical Practices in the Early Nineteenth Century").
65 HBCA, Churchill Post Journals, B.42/a/142 (18 November 1815).
66 HBCA, Churchill Post Journals, B.42/a/142 (1 December 1815).
67 HBCA, Churchill Post Journals, B.42/a/142 (12 January 1816). James Swain Sr. was Assistant Trader at York Factory.
68 HBCA, Churchill Post Journals, B.42/a/142, Letter from Adam Snodie to James Swain Sr. (8 January 1816). James Swain Sr. has been tentatively identified by HBCA as the brother of Thomas Swain, the Churchill Clerk who took seven healthy Selkirk settlers to York Factory and delivered a letter to Auld during the typhus threat in 1813.
69 HBCA, Churchill Post Journals, B.42/a/142 (12–27 January 1816).
70 HBCA, Churchill Post Journals, B.42/a/142 (4 February 1816).
71 HBCA, Churchill Post Journals, B.42/a/142 (6 February 1816).
72 HBCA, Churchill Post Journals, B.42/a/142 (5–6, 8 February 1816).
73 C.R. Harington, ed., *The Year without a Summer? World Climate in 1816* (Ottawa: Canadian Museum of Nature, 1992).
74 HBCA, Churchill Post Journals, B.42/a/142 (1–19 April 1816); Professor Paul Hackett, personal communication, September 10, 2002.
75 HBCA, Churchill Post Journals, B.42/a/142 (10 April 1816).
76 HBCA, Churchill Post Journals, B.42/a/142:16.
77 HBCA, Churchill Post Journals, B.42/a/142:18.
78 HBCA, Churchill Post Journals, B.42/a/142 (15–26 May 1816).
79 HBCA, Churchill Post Journals, B.42/a/142 (25–28 May 1816).
80 HBCA, Churchill Post Journals, B.42/a/142:19d, B.42/a/148:44d.
81 HBCA, Churchill Post Journals, B.42/a/142:20d.
82 HBCA, Churchill Account Book, 1815–16, B.42/d/104; Churchill Post Journals, B.42/a/138:38d.
83 HBCA, Churchill Post Journals, B.42/a/144, Letter from Adam Snodie to William Williams (2 March 1819).
84 Letter from Alexander Mackenzie to John Franklin, London, May 21, 1819, in John Franklin, *Journals and Correspondence: The First Arctic Land Expedition, 1819–1822*, ed. Richard C. Davis (Toronto: Champlain Society, 1995), 289.

INTERLUDE 1. The First Arctic Overland Expedition, 1819–1822

1 G.M. Thomson, *The Search for the North-West Passage* (New York: Macmillan, 1975), 146. Warm conditions in the Greenland Sea were a result of changes in the

frontal boundary of the northern jet stream. The usually steady jet stream had become highly sinuous in response to dramatically changed wind conditions related to the atmosphere's burden of volcanic debris from the 1815 eruption of Mount Tambora in Indonesia. Instead of lying in a more or less smooth belt around the globe between 40 and 60 degrees of latitude (zonal configuration), the jet stream developed long fingers of cold air that extended far to the south, alternating with deep troughs of warm air extending far to the north (meridional configuration). One of the cold troughs lay over the eastern Atlantic Ocean and western Europe, another hovered over central North America. Between them was a finger of much warmer air stretching from the western Atlantic northward into the Greenland Sea, which accounted for increased glacial calving and thinner, less extensive ice pack than usual. C.R. Harington, ed., *The Year without a Summer? World Climate in 1816* (Ottawa: Canadian Museum of Nature, 1992); Dr. T.F. Ball, personal communication, May 27, 2006.

2 Daniel Francis, *Discovery of the North: The Exploration of Canada's Arctic* (Edmonton: Hurtig, 1986), 71–72.
3 John Franklin, *Narrative of a Journey to the Shores of the Polar Sea, in the Years 1819-20-21-22*, 3rd ed. (London: John Murray, 1824), 36–37.
4 Robert Hood, *To the Arctic by Canoe 1819–1821: The Journal and Paintings of Robert Hood, Midshipman with Franklin*, ed. C. Stuart Houston (Montreal: McGill-Queen's University Press, 1974), 21.
5 Hood, 43.
6 John Richardson, "Dr Richardson's Residence at Cumberland House," in Franklin, *Narrative of a Journey*, 1:131–32.
7 Hood, *To the Arctic*, 46.
8 Hood, 48; HBCA, Cumberland House Journals, B.49/a/34 (3 January 1820).
9 HBCA, Cumberland House Journals, B.49/a/35 (18 January 1820).
10 William Williams, Governor of HBC Southern Department, arrived in Rupert's Land in 1818, set up headquarters at Cumberland House (1821–22), was at Moose Factory (1822–26), and retired in London. As Governor of the Southern Department he was subordinate to George Simpson, Governor of the Northern Department.
11 Hood, *To the Arctic*, 66–67.
12 Hood, 66.
13 In his edition of Richardson's journal, Dr. C. Stuart Houston included a table of travel dates for the expedition, which is a helpful aid for keeping track of who was where in the several periods in which the expedition split up into two or more separate parties. C. Stuart Houston, "Preface," in John Richardson, *Arctic Ordeal: The Journal of John Richardson, Surgeon Naturalist with Franklin, 1820–1822* (Kingston and Montreal: McGill-Queen's University Press, 1984), xii–xiii.
14 HBCA, Fort Resolution Journals, B.181/a/1-3 (December 1819, January–July 1820); Robertson's letter, July 1, 1820. Colin Robertson was not the only person to have difficulty with Pierre St. Germain's name; the expedition officers frequently referred to him as Perez or Parrish.
15 HBCA, Fort Resolution Journals, B.181/a/3, Letter from Franklin to McVicar, July 26, 1820, copy in McVicar's Letter Book. The letter is not included in John Franklin,

Journals and Correspondence: The First Arctic Land Expedition, 1819–1822, ed. Richard C. Davis (Toronto: Champlain Society, 1995).

16   Franklin, *Journals and Correspondence…1819–1822*, 86; C. Stuart Houston, "Introduction," in Richardson, *Arctic Ordeal*, xxv–xxvi.

17   Timothy C. Losey, ed., *An Interdisciplinary Investigation of Fort Enterprise, Northwest Territories* (Edmonton: Boreal Institute for Northern Studies, 1973), 15; George Back, *Arctic Artist: The Journal and Paintings of George Back, Midshipman with Franklin, 1819–1822*, ed. C. Stuart Houston (Montreal and Kingston: McGill-Queen's University Press, 1994), 74–83.

18   John Richardson, "Letter to His Wife," in Richardson, *Arctic Ordeal*, xxvi.

19   Franklin, *Narrative of a Journey*, 1:345–46.

20   Hood, *To the Arctic*, 145; Losey, *Interdisciplinary Investigation*, 15.

21   Hood, *To the Arctic*, 145.

22   Hood, 145; Franklin, *Narrative of a Journey*, 2:4; Richardson, *Arctic Ordeal*, 15.

CHAPTER 3. First Journey to the Western Arctic, 1820–1821

1   HBCA, Churchill Post Journals, B/a/145 (18 May 1820). William Ross (1783–1855) joined HBC in 1810 and served until 1813 at Churchill as Writer and accountant; as Trader at Oxford House from 1815 to 1816; as District Master at Nelson House from 1816 to 1819; and at Churchill from 1819 to 1821. W. Stewart Wallace, ed., *Documents Relating to the North West Company* ([Toronto]: Champlain Society, n.d.), 22:496.

2   HBCA, Churchill Post Journals, B.42/a/145 (12 May 1820), B.42/a/148 (19 May 1820).

3   HBCA, Churchill Post Journals, B.42/a/148:81–82 (29 May 1820).

4   HBCA, Churchill Post Journals, B42/a/148 (1 June 1820), B.42/a/145, fo. 5. William Ross spelled Junius's Inuit name the way he heard it, "Hootooreak." In modern Inuktitut his name would probably have been Hiutiruq.

5   Made beaver (MB) was a unit of value used as currency by fur trade companies in Canada. One MB could buy eight knives, one pair of trousers, two hatchets, one blanket, and twelve dozen buttons. One musket could be purchased for eleven MB. David A. Morrison, "The North West Company, 1779–1821," in *The Canadian Encyclopedia*, Historica Canada, article published October 18, 2013, last modified March 4, 2015, https://www.thecanadianencyclopedia.ca/en/article/the-north-west-company-17791821-feature.

6   HBCA, Churchill Post Journals, B.42/a/148, B.42/a/145:5.

7   HBCA, Churchill Post Journals, B.42/a/145:14.

8   "Slops" were knee- or ankle-length wide-leg trousers, but in the nineteenth century the term was used for any of the cheap, ready-made clothing issued to navy recruits from the ship's stores. *The Compact Oxford English Dictionary* (Oxford University Press, 1971).

9   Duck is a linen or cotton fabric, heavy but finer than canvas, used mainly for small boat sails and for men's, especially sailors', trousers. *The Compact Oxford English Dictionary*.

10   HBCA, Churchill Post Journals, B.42/a/145:22.

11 HBCA, Churchill Post Journals, B.42/a/148:85.
12 HBCA, Churchill Post Journals, B.42/a/145 (15 June 1820); York Factory Post Journals, B.239/a/127 (30 June 1820), B.239/a/129:23d.
13 HBCA, Norway House Journals, B.154/a/9, 4a dorso–4b. A possible explanation may be that Alexander Kennedy, Master at Norway House, left the post on June 24 to take the post's pelts and records for the Outfit year 1819–20 to York Factory in time for the arrival of the supply ship, and no one had been appointed to keep the journal in his absence.
14 For brief biographical information on Lamallice and Magnion, see George Simpson, *Journal of Occurrences in the Athabasca Department, 1820–1821, and Report*, ed. E.E. Rich (London: Champlain Society for the Hudson's Bay Record Society, 1938).
15 A year later, when the Hudson's Bay Company and the North West Company merged, Simpson was appointed Overseas Governor.
16 Simpson, *Journal of Occurrences*, 5, 7, 8.
17 Robert Hood, *To the Arctic by Canoe 1819–1821: The Journal and Paintings of Robert Hood, Midshipman with Franklin*, ed. C. Stuart Houston (Montreal: McGill-Queen's University Press, 1974), 46.
18 Simpson, *Journal of Occurrences*, 16–21, 25, 28 (17–30 August 1820).
19 Simpson, 71. Simpson's account of the weather and conditions of life in a canoe from Norway House to Lake Athabasca also describes what the two Inuit interpreters experienced as the two brigade leaders jockeyed for the superior position among brigade leaders. Simpson, 6–16.
20 HBCA, Fort Resolution Journals, B.181/a/3:16-17d (7–8 October 1820).
21 HBCA, Fort Resolution Journals, B.181/a/3 (21, 29 October 1820); George Back to Robert McVicar, July 16, 1822, in *Transactions of the Women's Canadian History Society of Toronto*, vol. 17 (1917–18), 15–16. McVicar's country wife was Margaret and they had a young daughter named Ellen.
22 John Franklin, *Narrative of a Journey to the Shores of the Polar Sea, in the Years 1819–20–21–22*, 3rd ed. (London: John Murray, 1824), 2:12–13; George Back, *Arctic Artist: The Journal and Paintings of George Back, Midshipman with Franklin, 1819–1822*, ed. C. Stuart Houston (Montreal and Kingston: McGill-Queen's University Press, 1994), 103.
23 C. Stuart Houston, Appendix 3, in Back, *Arctic Artist*, 339; Simpson, *Journal of Occurrences*, 206, 243.
24 George Back, "Account of a Trip to Fort Providence," in Franklin, *Journey to the Shores*, 2:64.
25 Franklin, *Narrative of a Journey*, 2:38; John Franklin, *Journals and Correspondence: The First Arctic Land Expedition, 1819–1822*, ed. Richard C. Davis (Toronto: Champlain Society, 1995), 94; HBCA, Fort Resolution Journals, B.181/a/3:16–17d; John Richardson, *Arctic Ordeal: The Journal of John Richardson, Surgeon Naturalist with Franklin, 1820–1822* (Kingston and Montreal: McGill-Queen's University Press, 1984), xxix, 25. Richardson puts the date of arrival at Fort Enterprise at January 25.
26 Richardson, *Arctic Ordeal*, 28. My best guess on the home country of the "strangers" is Repulse Bay on the western shore of Foxe Basin. It fulfills both of Augustine's descriptors—a place from which strangers could have come "overland" or along the salty "sea-coast" in their "canoes."

27 Back, *Arctic Artist*, 118–19; Franklin, *Narrative of a Journey*, 2:63.
28 Back, *Arctic Artist*, 118–19.
29 Franklin, *Narrative of a Journey*, 2:38–39.
30 Franklin, 2:94, 2:111.
31 Franklin, 2: 89–90.
32 Franklin, 2:91–92; Richardson, *Arctic Ordeal*, 30, 34; Back, *Arctic Artist*, 119.
33 Back, *Arctic Artist*, 119; Franklin, *Narrative of a Journey*, 2:95, 2:99–111; Richardson, *Arctic Ordeal*, 41. Akaitcho's ritual demands were fairly typical of many First Nations at the time, but Inuit rejected such ceremonials.
34 Back, *Arctic Artist*, 120.
35 Back, 120–21; Franklin, *Journals and Correspondence…1819–1822*, 137; Franklin, *Narrative of a Journey*, 2:101–2; Richardson, *Arctic Ordeal*, 40–42.
36 Back, *Arctic Artist*, 121; Franklin, *Narrative of a Journey*, 2:104; Richardson, *Arctic Ordeal*, 40–41.
37 Franklin, *Narrative of a Journey*, 2:105.
38 Franklin's *Narrative* makes the date June 13. Franklin, 2:116–17; Hood, *To the Arctic*, 157; C. Stuart Houston in Back, *Arctic Artist*, 124n8; Richardson, *Arctic Ordeal*, 45.
39 Back, *Arctic Artist*, 125; Franklin, *Narrative of a Journey*, 2:123. Franklin estimated the average load carried by each of the men at close to 180 pounds, an even hundred pounds more than Back thought. Franklin's figure is unlikely to be correct. The disparity may have risen when Franklin copied parts of Back's journal after his own was lost in a river crossing on the barrens.
40 Back, *Arctic Artist*, 125–30; Franklin, *Journals and Correspondence…1819–1822*, 155.
41 Back, *Arctic Artist*, 126–27, 129; Richardson, *Arctic Ordeal*, 54.
42 Back, *Arctic Artist*, 129–30.
43 Franklin, *Narrative of a Journey*, 2:161.
44 Richardson, *Arctic Ordeal*, 75.
45 Franklin, *Narrative of a Journey*, 2:165–66.
46 Back, *Arctic Artist*, 143.
47 Back, 145.
48 Richardson, *Arctic Ordeal*, 83.
49 Richardson, 80, 83; Back, *Arctic Artist*, 146; Hood, *To the Arctic*, 201.

CHAPTER 4. Death and Survival, 1821–1822

1 John Franklin, *Narrative of a Journey to the Shores of the Polar Sea, in the Years 1819–20–21–22*, 3rd ed. (London: John Murray, 1824), 2:193–94; John Richardson, *Arctic Ordeal: The Journal of John Richardson, Surgeon Naturalist with Franklin, 1820–1822* (Kingston and Montreal: McGill-Queen's University Press, 1984), 83–84; George Back, *Arctic Artist: The Journal and Paintings of George Back, Midshipman with Franklin, 1819–1822*, ed. C. Stuart Houston (Montreal and Kingston: McGill-Queen's University Press, 1994), 128, 130, 147.
2 Franklin, *Narrative of a Journey*, 2:193–94; Richardson, *Arctic Ordeal*, 96.
3 Franklin, *Narrative of a Journey*, 2:204–5.

4   Richardson, *Arctic Ordeal*, 89, 92–95; C. Stuart Houston, Commentary, in Richardson, *Arctic Ordeal*, 192, 195. Dr. Houston estimated an adult male caribou provided about 125 pounds of meat, a yearling about 60 pounds, and a rough average of 100 pounds of edible meat for a barren-ground caribou of unstated age.
5   Richardson, 96–97; Franklin, *Narrative of a Journey*, 2:204, 2:209, 2:211–12; Houston, Commentary, in Richardson, *Arctic Ordeal*, 195. The fresh game included an estimated 580 pounds of caribou, 185 pounds of muskox, 600 pounds of bear, plus occasional arctic hares, arctic foxes, and some ptarmigan, geese, and swans, according to Dr. Houston's analysis.
6   Back, *Arctic Artist*, 152, 159; Richardson, *Arctic Ordeal*, 110; Franklin, *Narrative of a Journey*, 2:201.
7   Back, *Arctic Artist*, 159; Richardson, *Arctic Ordeal*, 110; Franklin, *Narrative of a Journey*, 2:228. Coasting Bathurst Inlet while heading east had occupied the expedition for nine unproductive days.
8   Back, *Arctic Artist*, 160; Richardson, *Arctic Ordeal*, 110–11; Franklin, *Narrative of a Journey*, 2:229.
9   Franklin, *Narrative of a Journey*, 2:231–32, 2:238–39.
10 Franklin, 2:240, 2:242–44; Back, *Arctic Artist*, 163, 164; Richardson, *Arctic Ordeal*, 116, 118–19.
11 Richardson, 119; Back, *Arctic Artist*, 165n2.
12 Back, 165; Richardson, *Arctic Ordeal*, 119–20.
13 Back, *Arctic Artist*, 165; Richardson, *Arctic Ordeal*, 119–21.
14 Back, *Arctic Artist*, 166; Richardson, *Arctic Ordeal*, 122, 123.
15 Back, *Arctic Artist*, 166–67; Richardson, *Arctic Ordeal*, 123.
16 Back, *Arctic Artist*, 168; Richardson, *Arctic Ordeal*, 126.
17 Back, *Arctic Artist*, 168; Franklin, *Narrative of a Journey*, 2:254. Arrowroot is an easily digested and nutritious starch native to the West Indies, introduced to England about 1732. When dissolved in hot liquid and then cooled, it sets to a jelly useful for feeding babies or invalids. *Tripe de roche* was "four kinds of lichen," some of which were "noxious to several of the party, producing severe bowel complaints." C. Stuart Houston in Richardson, *Arctic Ordeal*, 127n21.
18 Richardson, *Arctic Ordeal*, 127; Franklin, *Narrative of a Journey*, 11:256–57; Back, *Arctic Artist*, 169.
19 Back, *Arctic Artist*, 169; Richardson, *Arctic Ordeal*, 128–29.
20 Franklin, *Narrative of a Journey*, 2:259.
21 Back, *Arctic Artist*, 169–70; Richardson, *Arctic Ordeal*, 128–29.
22 Franklin, *Narrative of a Journey*, 2:261–62; Richardson, *Arctic Ordeal*, 129–30; Back, *Arctic Artist*, 170–71.
23 Franklin, *Narrative of a Journey*, 2:264–65; Back, *Arctic Artist*, 172. Between September 3 and September 14, the daily food allowance averaged 1.8 pounds of fresh meat per man. Houston, Commentary, in Richardson, *Arctic Ordeal*, 195.
24 Back, *Arctic Artist*, 172; Franklin, *Narrative of a Journey*, 2:264–65; Richardson, *Arctic Ordeal*, 132–33.
25 Back, *Arctic Artist*, 172–73; Richardson, *Arctic Ordeal*, 133–34.
26 Franklin, *Narrative of a Journey*, 2:267–70; Back, *Arctic Artist*, 173.

27 Back, *Arctic Artist*, 175, 176; Richardson, *Arctic Ordeal*, 136–37; Franklin, *Narrative of a Journey*, 2:272, 2:274.
28 Back, *Arctic Artist*, 177; Richardson, *Arctic Ordeal*, 138; Franklin, *Narrative of a Journey*, 273. By "the contents of the stomach" Back meant the excrement they found in the animals' bowels.
29 Richardson, *Arctic Ordeal*, 140.
30 A coracle is a small, more or less round boat made of interwoven wicker or thin, bendable willow branches and covered with a watertight material such as leather.
31 Richardson, *Arctic Ordeal*, 142–43; Franklin, *Narrative of a Journey*, 2:288–91.
32 Back, *Arctic Artist*, 181; Richardson, *Arctic Ordeal*, 144–45; Franklin, *Narrative of a Journey*, 2:293, 2:295–96.
33 Back, *Arctic Artist*, 184; Back's account in Franklin, *Narrative of a Journey*, 2:374–81.
34 Fort Enterprise overlooked Winter Lake, which drains into the northern end of Roundrock Lake, about five miles distance from the fort. All the expedition men were familiar with the area from hunting and fishing. Peter Steele, *The Man Who Mapped the Arctic* (Vancouver: Raincoast Books, 2003), 98. Back and his men had travelled closer to fifteen miles along the lakeshore during their three-day search. Its coordinates are latitude 64°23'1" N, and longitude 113°25'5" W. Canadian Geographical Names Database.
35 Back, *Arctic Artist*, 185–86.
36 Back, 182–87; Back's account in Franklin, *Narrative of a Journey*, 2:382.
37 Back, *Arctic Artist*, 187.
38 Back, 188.
39 Richardson, *Arctic Ordeal*, 145–46.
40 Richardson, 145–47; Franklin, *Narrative of a Journey*, 2:297. From September 15 to October 4, the daily food allowance averaged about 1.6 pounds per man. For more on the starvation diet, see Houston, Commentary, in Richardson, *Arctic Ordeal*, 195.
41 Richardson, *Arctic Ordeal*, 146–47; Franklin, *Narrative of a Journey*, 2:302.
42 Franklin, *Narrative of a Journey*, 2:304–5.
43 Franklin, 2:306–7. Labrador tea, *Ledum decumbens*, is said to have a calming quality, and its flowers add sweetness to the drink. It does, however, contain a toxic element, which makes it dangerous if taken in large quantities. See Judy Farrow, "The Power of Plants," *Up Here: Life at the Top of the World* (September 2001: 38).
44 Franklin, *Narrative of a Journey*, 2:307–9.
45 Franklin, 2:309–11.
46 Franklin, 2:313–14, 2:315. Franklin did not give specific dates for the events at Fort Enterprise, but Augustine must have arrived on October 12 or 13.
47 Franklin, 2:315–16; "Mr Back's Narrative," in Franklin, 2:386.
48 Franklin, 2:318–19.
49 Franklin, 2:320–22.
50 Back, *Arctic Artist*, 193–94; Franklin, *Narrative of a Journey*, 2:320–22.
51 Franklin, *Narrative of a Journey*, 2:323–27. The four men already at Fort Enterprise were Franklin, Adam, Peltier, and Semandré.
52 Richardson, *Arctic Ordeal*, 148–49.
53 Richardson, 148–50.

54 Richardson, 150–54.
55 Richardson, 152–57.
56 Richardson, 155–56.
57 Richardson, 154–55.
58 Richardson, 156–59.
59 Franklin, *Narrative of a Journey*, 2:350–51, 2:356; Richardson, *Arctic Ordeal*, 163.
60 Back, *Arctic Artist*, 193–94.
61 Franklin, *Narrative of a Journey*, 2:357–58; Richardson, *Arctic Ordeal*, 164–65.
62 Timothy C. Losey, ed., *An Interdisciplinary Investigation of Fort Enterprise, Northwest Territories* (Edmonton: Boreal Institute for Northern Studies, 1973), 20. There have been reports that human remains were found in the caved-in cellar below the floor of Structure C, the officers' house, sometime during the 1960s by unauthorized "visitors" to the site (p. 37).
63 Franklin, *Narrative of a Journey*, 2:358–59.
64 John Franklin, *Journals and Correspondence: The First Arctic Land Expedition, 1819–1822*, ed. Richard C. Davis (Toronto: Champlain Society, 1995), 221; Richardson, *Arctic Ordeal*, 167.
65 Franklin, *Narrative of a Journey*, 2:362–64.
66 Richardson, *Arctic Ordeal*, 173.
67 Franklin, *Journals and Correspondence…1819–1822*, 229; Franklin, *Narrative of a Journey*, 2:365; Richardson, *Arctic Ordeal*, 173–76.
68 Franklin, *Narrative of a Journey*, 2:367–68; Richardson, *Arctic Ordeal*, 176–78. From 1815 to 1822, Fort Resolution Post was on Moose Deer Island. In 1822, after the merger of the two trading companies, it was moved to the mainland about a mile from the island. HBCA, Fort Resolution Journals, B.181/a/2; David M. Smith, "Fort Resolution, Northwest Territories," in *Handbook of North American Indians*, vol. 6, *Subarctic*, ed. June Helm (Washington, DC: Smithsonian Institution, 1981), 683–93.
69 HBCA, Fort Resolution Journals, B.181/a/4; Back, *Arctic Artist*, 201; Franklin, *Narrative of a Journey*, 2:371; Richardson, *Arctic Ordeal*, 178.
70 HBCA, Fort Chipewyan Journals, B.39/a/20; Back, *Arctic Artist*, 201–2.
71 HBCA, Fort Chipewyan Journals, B.39/a/20 (8 February 1822).
72 HBCA, Fort Resolution Journals, B.181/a/4:61; Fort Resolution Correspondence Book, 1825–26, B.181/b/1; Franklin, *Narrative of a Journey*, 2:395–96.
73 HBCA, Fort Chipewyan Journals, 1822, B.39/a/20; Franklin, *Narrative of a Journey*, 2:396.
74 HBCA, Fort Chipewyan Journals, 1821–22, B.39/a/20; Cumberland House Journals, 1821–22, B.49/a/38; Back, *Arctic Artist*, 212; Franklin, *Narrative of a Journey*, 2:396, 2:399.

INTERLUDE 2. Reorganizing and Retrenching the Company, 1822–1824

1 Ann M. Carlos and Frank D. Lewis, "Smallpox and Native American Mortality: The 1780s Epidemic in the Hudson Bay Region," *Explorations in Economic History* 49, no. 3 (2012): 277–90, citing J.B. Tyrell, ed., *Journals of Samuel Hearne and Philip Turnor Between the Years 1774 and 1792* (Toronto: Champlain Society, 1874), lx; R. Glover,

David Thompson's Narrative (Toronto: Champlain Society, 1962), 236; HBCA, York Factory Journals, B.239/a/80 (2 June 1782); Paul Hackett, *A Very Remarkable Sickness: Patterns of Disease Diffusion in the Petit Nord* (Winnipeg: University of Manitoba Press, 2002).

2 Ann Carlos, "The Causes and Origins of the North American Fur Trade Rivalry: 1804–1810," *Journal of Economic History* 41, no. 4 (1981): 778, 783.
3 Carlos and Lewis, "Smallpox and Native American Mortality."
4 Carlos, "Causes and Origins," 780–81.
5 HBCA, Biographical Sheet, Thomas Thomas. Born in Wales c.1766, Thomas Thomas was Surgeon at York Factory from 1789 to 1796, Master at Severn House from 1796 to 1810, Superintendent of Southern Factories from 1810 to 1814, Governor of Northern Department from 1814 to 1815, and retired to Red River in 1818.
6 HBCA, Churchill Fort, List of Servants, 1811, B.42/f/6; List of Servants, 1812, B.42/f/7. The staff at Churchill went down quickly after that: from thirty in 1812–13 to eleven in 1824–25, five in 1829–30, thirteen in 1834–35, and between seven and nine every year from 1839 to 1889. Michael Payne, "Fort Churchill, 1821–1900: An Outpost Community in the Fur Trade," *Manitoba History* 20 (Autumn 1990): 12. Names and numbers of servants vary depending on where they are recorded. Tallies of any particular years, such as Lists of Servants, Servants' Accounts, or daily post journals, do not always agree.

CHAPTER 5. The "Engaged Servant," 1822–1824

1 Letter from John West to the Governor and Gentlemen of the Council at York Factory, Hudson Bay, n.d., in John West, *The British North West American Indians with Free Thoughts on the Red River Settlement* (1823), 19, typescript copy of original held at St. John's College Library, University of Manitoba, Winnipeg.
2 Envelope from John West at York Factory to Emma West Atkinson, August 20, 1822, John West Papers, Archives of the Ecclesiastical Province of Rupert's Land, Provincial Archives of Manitoba.
3 The first HBC ship with this name; in service from 1793 to 1838.
4 HBCA, Churchill Post Journals, B.42/a/149:7–8, Letter from George Simpson at York Factory to Hugh Leslie at Churchill (12 August 1822). The letter was copied into the Churchill journal several weeks later.
5 HBCA, Churchill Post Journals, B.42/a/149, B.42/a/150; York Factory Journals, B.239/a/131.
6 HBCA, Churchill Post Journals, B.42/a/147 (7 July 1822).
7 HBCA, Churchill Post Journals, B.42/a/147 (28 September 1822).
8 HBCA, Churchill Account Books, B.42/d/108 (November 1822).
9 HBCA, Churchill Post Journals, B.42/a/149:13, B.42/a/150:12.
10 HBCA, Churchill Post Journals, B.42/a/149:13–14.
11 HBCA, Churchill Post Journals, B.42/a/149 (26 November, 10 and 14 December 1822).
12 HBCA, Churchill Post Journals, B.42/a/149 (12 January 1823).
13 HBCA, Churchill Post Journals, B.42/a/149 (26–27 February, 17 March, 13 April 1823).

14   HBCA, Churchill Post Journals, B.42/a/149 (6 June 1823), B.42/a/150:21.
15   HBCA, Churchill Post Journals, B.42/a/149:33 (8 June 1823), B.42/a/150:21d.
16   HBCA, Churchill Post Account Books, B.42/d/111; Eskimo Trading Book, 1823. A capote is a long, hooded cloak or coat, sometimes with buttons, other times held closed at the front by a sash.
17   HBCA, Churchill Post Journals, B.42/a/149 (13 June 1823).
18   HBCA, Churchill Post Journals, B.42/a/149:33 (8 June 1823), B.42/a/150:21d.
19   The spelling of these proper names follows the spellings used in the account books of the time. Pingnahewak's name appears in the Churchill Account Books in a number of variations, including Pingnashuack and Benachewak. Atahoona may be the same person as the man referred to as Atongana.
20   HBCA, Churchill Post Journals, B.42/a/149, B.42/a/154:23d, 26.
21   HBCA, Churchill Post Journals, B.42/a/154:23d.
22   On clothing design and production, see Betty Kobayashi Issenman, *Sinews of Survival: The Living Legacy of Inuit Clothing* (Vancouver: UBC Press, 1997). On men's clothing, see David Morrison and Georges-Hébert Germain, *Inuit: Glimpses of an Arctic Past* (Hull: Canadian Museum of Civilization, 1995), 62–63.
23   HBCA, Churchill Post Journals, B.42/a/149 (21 July 1823).
24   Letter from John Franklin to John Richardson, December 15, 1823, in John Franklin, *Journals and Correspondence: The Second Arctic Land Expedition, 1825–1827*, ed. Richard C. Davis (Toronto: Champlain Society, 1998), 279. Franklin's letter from London reports on his meeting with John West after West's return to England.
25   HBCA, Churchill Post Journals, B.42/a/149; John West, *The Substance of a Journal during a Residence at the Red River Colony...in the Years 1820–1823* (London: L.B. Seeley and Son, 1824), 152, 167–68. After Augustine's death, the Company followed what appears to have been his instructions and provided his widow with a yearly sum from his estate, and after she died gave equal portions of his estate to three heirs, two sons and one daughter, at their request.
26   HBCA, Churchill Post Journals, B.42/a/154:23d–26.
27   Letter from Franklin to Richardson, December 15, 1823, in Franklin, *Journals and Correspondence...1825–1827*.
28   One wonders, how did West hear from Ackshanook and his wife when neither spoke English and West spoke no Inuktitut?
29   West, *Substance of a Journal*, 154–55, 170–71.
30   West, 175.
31   HBCA, Churchill Post Journals, B.42/a/149:150.
32   HBCA, Churchill Post Journals, B.42/a/149; West, *Substance of a Journal*, 175–76.
33   Emile Petitot (1876), 90–92, cited in Derek G. Smith, "Mackenzie Delta Eskimo," in *Handbook of North American Indians*, vol. 5, *The Arctic* (Washington, DC: Smithsonian Institution, 1984), 347–58; Knud Rasmussen, *The Netsilik Eskimos: Social Life and Spiritual Culture*, Report of the Fifth Thule Expedition, 1921–24 (1931), 234–319, cited in Asen Balikci, "Netsilik," in *Handbook of North American Indians*, 5:426. See also Renee Fossett, *In Order to Live Untroubled* (Winnipeg: University of Manitoba Press, 2001), 207–8, 212–13.
34   Franklin, *Journals and Correspondence...1825–1827*, 279.

35 Franklin, 279.
36 Fossett, *In Order to Live Untroubled*, 206.
37 HBCA, Churchill Post Journals, B.42/a/149:46; West, *Substance of a Journal*, 181–82.

INTERLUDE 3. The Second Arctic Overland Expedition, 1824–1825

1   Letter from John Franklin to John Richardson, June 13 and July 24, 1823, in John Franklin, *Journals and Correspondence: The Second Arctic Land Expedition, 1825–1827*, ed. Richard C. Davis (Toronto: Champlain Society, 1998), 267–71.
2   Letter from Franklin to Richardson, August 1, 1823, in Franklin, *Journals and Correspondence...1825–1827*, 271.
3   Letter from Franklin to Richardson, August 1, 1823, 271–72.
4   John Barrow, *Quarterly Review* 18 (October 1817): 219.
5   Bering Sea Tribunal of Arbitration, *Fur Seal Arbitration, Proceedings of the Tribunal of Arbitration, Convened at Paris under the Treaty between the United States of America and Great Britain, Concluded at Washington February 29, 1892 for the Determination of Questions between the Two Governments concerning the Jurisdictional Rights of the United States in the Waters of Bering Sea*, vol. 7 ([1892]), 176.
6   Letter from Franklin to Barrow, November 26, 1823, in Franklin, *Journals and Correspondence...1825–1827*, 273–77.
7   Letter from Franklin to Richardson, December 15 and December 30, 1823, in Franklin, *Journals and Correspondence...1825–1827*, 278, 281. Henry, 3rd Earl Bathurst, was Secretary for War and the Colonies from 1812 to 1827.
8   Letter from Franklin to Richardson, December 15, 1823, 278.
9   Richard C. Davis, "Introduction," in *Journals and Correspondence...1825–1827*, xxvii.
10 Sylvia Van Kirk, *Many Tender Ties: Women in Fur-Trade Society, 1670–1870* (Norman: University of Oklahoma Press, 1983), 179–80; Letter from Simpson to Franklin, August 8, 1824, in Franklin, *Journals and Correspondence...1825–1827*, 335.
11 John Franklin, *Narrative of a Second Expedition to the Shores of the Polar Sea in the Years 1825, 1826, and 1827* (1828; Rutland, VT: Charles E. Tuttle, 1971), xxiv–xxix, 5–6.
12 Franklin, xviii–xxix.
13 Franklin, xxv–xxvi, 55–56; Franklin, *Journals and Correspondence...1825–1827*, 2–3.
14 Franklin, 2–3.
15 C. Stuart Houston and Mary I. Houston, "Franklin's Advance Party, 1824–1825," *The Beaver* 66, no. 5 (1986): 20; Franklin, *Journals and Correspondence...1825–1827*, 326–28; Davis, "Introduction," in Franklin, *Journals and Correspondence...1825–1827*, xliii.
16 Letter from Franklin to John Rae Sr., May 28, 1824, in Franklin, *Journals and Correspondence...1825–1827*, xliii, 326–30.
17 Letter from McTavish to Franklin, September 8, 1824, in Franklin, *Journals and Correspondence...1825–1827*, xliii, 326–30, 341–45.
18 Letter from Franklin to Richardson, December 30, 1823, in Franklin, *Journals and Correspondence...1825–1827*, 283.
19 Letter from Franklin to Richardson, August 24, 1824, in Franklin, *Journals and Correspondence...1825–1827*, 338.

20   Letter from Franklin to Richardson, September 26, 1824, in Franklin, *Journals and Correspondence…1825–1827*, 346.
21   Davis, "Introduction," in Franklin, *Journals and Correspondence…1825–1827*, xxxi–xxxii.
22   Franklin, *Journals and Correspondence…1825–1827*, 9, emphasis in original.
23   Letter from Franklin to Simpson, February 27, 1824, in Franklin, *Journals and Correspondence…1825–1827*, 295–98, emphasis in original.

CHAPTER 6. Second Journey to the Western Arctic, 1824–1826

1   HBCA, Churchill Post Journals, B.42/a/150:42d, B.42/a/151:32. Ullebuk was from Augustine's village and may have been either biologically or fictively kin to Augustine, or an in-law. He was probably near the same age as Augustine, and, like Augustine, he would have been married. *See also* Shirlee Anne Smith, "Ooligbuck," in *Dictionary of Canadian Biography*, vol. 8, 1851–1860 (University of Toronto/Université Laval, 1985).
2   HBCA, Churchill Post Journals, B.42/a/151:28–31.
3   HBCA, Churchill Post Journals, B.42/a/151 (7 July 1824).
4   HBCA, Churchill Post Journals, B.42/a/151 (7 July 1824); Letter from Franklin to Simpson, February 27, 1824, in John Franklin, *Journals and Correspondence: The Second Arctic Land Expedition, 1825–1827*, ed. Richard C. Davis (Toronto: Champlain Society, 1998), 298; Letter from Simpson to Franklin, August 8, 1824, in Franklin, *Journals and Correspondence…1825–1827*, 336.
5   Letter from Franklin to Richardson, December 15, 1823, in Franklin, *Journals and Correspondence…1825–1827*, 279.
6   Letter from Simpson to Franklin, August 8, 1824, in Franklin, *Journals and Correspondence…1825–1827*, 336.
7   HBCA, Churchill Post Journals, B.42/a/150:49d (13 August 1824); Churchill Post Journals, B.42/a/151 (16 August 1824); York Factory Journals, B.239/a/136 (28–29 August 1824).
8   HBCA, York Factory Journals, B.239/a/136 (31 August 1824); Letter from Simpson to Franklin, August 8, 1824, in Franklin, *Journals and Correspondence…1825–1827*, 336.
9   Letter from Franklin to Simpson, June 4, 1824, in Franklin, *Journals and Correspondence…1825–1827*, 328–30; HBCA, York Factory Journals, B.239/a/136 (1 September 1824).
10 "Bills of Lading for Boats Belonging to His Majesty's Land Arctic Expedition," in Franklin, *Journals and Correspondence…1825–1827*, 341–45.
11 Letter from McTavish to Franklin, September 8, 1824, in Franklin, *Journals and Correspondence…1825–1827*, 340–42; "Bills of Lading," 342–45.
12 Letter from Franklin to Simpson, June 4, 1824, in Franklin, *Journals and Correspondence…1825–1827*, 329.
13 Letter from McTavish to Franklin, September 8, 1824, in Franklin, *Journals and Correspondence…1825–1827*, 341.
14 HBCA, Cumberland House Journals, B.49/a/40 (18–25 October 1824).

15 HBCA, Cumberland House Journals, B.49/a/40 (21–22 October, 25 November 1824). The men who went to Carlton House were Neil McDonald, John Hodgson, John MacLea, Charles McKenzie, James Spence, Gustavus Aird, John McDuffie, and Alex Currie.
16 HBCA, Carlton House Journals, B.27/a/14 (5 December 1824).
17 HBCA, Carlton House Journals, B.27/a/14 (5 December 1824).
18 HBCA, Carlton House Journals, B.27/a/22 (17 October 1824).
19 Walter M. Hlady, "Indian Migrations in Manitoba and the West," *Manitoba Historical Society Transactions*, series 3 (1960–61), http://www.mhs.mb.ca/docs/transactions/3/indianmigrations.shtml; HBCA, Cumberland House Journals, B.49/a/40 (21 December 1824).
20 HBCA, Edmonton House Journals, B.60/a/23 (9 October 1825).
21 HBCA, Cumberland House Journals, B.49/a/40 (24–25 December 1824).
22 HBCA, Cumberland House Journals, B.49/a/40 (1 January 1825). Shrub is rum diluted with fruit juice or water.
23 HBCA, Carlton House Journals, B.27/a/14 (1 January 1825).
24 HBCA, Cumberland House Journals, B.49/a/40 (29 January 1826). Barm is yeast that forms on top of fermenting liquids. *The Compact Oxford English Dictionary* (Oxford University Press, 1971).
25 HBCA, Cumberland House Journals, B.49/a/40.
26 HBCA, Carlton House Journals, B.27/a/14; Cumberland House Journals, B.49/a/40.
27 John Franklin, *Narrative of a Second Expedition to the Shores of the Polar Sea in the Years 1825, 1826, and 1827* (1828; Rutland, VT: Charles E. Tuttle, 1971), xxx.
28 Franklin, xxx–xxxii.
29 Exactly what the relationship of the two Iroquois men was depends on the kinship vocabulary of the Iroquois people. A good place to start on Iroquois ethnography is Bruce G. Trigger, ed., *Handbook of North American Indians*, vol. 15, *Northeast* (Washington, DC: Smithsonian Institution, 1990).
30 Franklin, *Journals and Correspondence…1825–1827*, 27, 32n119.
31 Franklin, 27–28.
32 Franklin, 35–36.
33 HBCA, Cumberland House Journals, B.49/a/40 (1 June 1825).
34 HBCA, Cumberland House Journals, B.49/a/40 (2 June 1825).
35 Franklin, *Narrative of a Second Expedition*, xxxiii. In his journal, Franklin gave the healing time as "a month or five weeks." For greater detail, see Franklin, *Journals and Correspondence…1825–1827*, 59.
36 Franklin, *Narrative of a Second Expedition*, 2.
37 Franklin, 2–3; Franklin, *Journals and Correspondence…1825–1827*, 69–70.
38 Franklin, *Narrative of a Second Expedition*, 3; Franklin, *Journals and Correspondence…1825–1827*, 69–70. Methye Portage was renamed La Loche Portage in 1957.
39 It is more than disappointing that I have not been able to find a description or illustration of the drawings.
40 Franklin, *Narrative of a Second Expedition*, 4–6.
41 Franklin, 6–9.

42 Franklin, 9–11.
43 Franklin, 13–15.
44 HBCA, Fort Norman Journals, B.152/a/5 (7 August 1825). "This morning...at ten or eleven, Captain Franklin, accompanied by two officers in two canoes, arrived; a moment later, two other canoes arrived. The men numbered forty-two, all Canadians...and English soldiers."
45 Franklin, *Narrative of a Second Expedition*, 17–18.
46 Franklin, 19–21.
47 Franklin, 23–24. Charles Dease was a brother of Peter Warren Dease.
48 Franklin, 25–26.
49 Franklin, 27.
50 Franklin, 35–36.
51 Franklin, 37.
52 Franklin, 41–44.
53 Franklin, 43, 44.
54 Franklin, 45–46; Franklin, *Journals and Correspondence...1825–1827*, 113.
55 Franklin, 113.
56 Franklin, *Narrative of a Second Expedition*, 47–48.
57 Franklin, 48–49.
58 Franklin, 51–53.
59 Franklin, 51–53, 57.
60 Franklin, 53–54.
61 Franklin, 59; Franklin, *Journals and Correspondence...1825–1827*, 131.
62 Franklin, *Narrative of a Second Expedition*, 54–56.
63 Franklin, 53–56.
64 Franklin, 59–60.
65 Franklin, 62, 65.
66 Franklin, 66.
67 Franklin, 66.
68 Franklin, 66–67; Franklin, *Journals and Correspondence...1825–1827*, 150–51.
69 Franklin, *Narrative of a Second Expedition*, 68–69; Franklin, *Journals and Correspondence...1825–1827*, 153.
70 Franklin, *Narrative of a Second Expedition*, 69.
71 Franklin, 73, 76–77; Franklin, *Journals and Correspondence...1825–1827*, 160–69.
72 Franklin, *Narrative of a Second Expedition*, 73, 77, 80–81; Franklin, *Journals and Correspondence...1825–1827*, 165–67, 169, 171–72, 177–78.
73 Franklin, *Narrative of a Second Expedition*, 83; Franklin, *Journals and Correspondence...1825–1827*, 175–77.
74 Franklin, *Narrative of a Second Expedition*, 83–85.

CHAPTER 7. Journey to the Polar Sea, 1826–1827

1 John Franklin, *Narrative of a Second Expedition to the Shores of the Polar Sea in the Years 1825, 1826, and 1827* (1828; Rutland, VT: Charles E. Tuttle, 1971), 86–87.

2   John Richardson, "Observations for Latitude, Longitude, and Magnetic Observation," Appendix v in Franklin, *Narrative of a Second Expedition*, cxxxiv. Fort Norman was relocated several times. From 1825 to 1828, it was on the bank of the Mackenzie River at 64°40'38", upriver from the Bear Lake River outlet.
3   Franklin, *Narrative of a Second Expedition*, 88.
4   Franklin, 89–90.
5   A tributary to the Mackenzie River seen by Alexander Mackenzie in 1789, which he named Red River. Confusion with Red River in Manitoba led to traders informally calling it Mackenzie's Red River. Later it was renamed Arctic Red River.
6   Franklin, *Narrative of a Second Expedition*, 89–90.
7   Franklin, 90–92; John Franklin, *Journals and Correspondence: The Second Arctic Land Expedition, 1825–1827*, ed. Richard C. Davis (Toronto: Champlain Society, 1998), 186–88.
8   Franklin, *Narrative of a Second Expedition*, 93.
9   Franklin, 94–95; Franklin, *Journals and Correspondence...1825–1827*, 192–93.
10 Franklin, *Narrative of a Second Expedition*, 95; Franklin, *Journals and Correspondence...1825–1827*, 193–94.
11 "Dr. Richardson's Narrative of the Proceedings of the Eastern Detachment of the Expedition," in Franklin, *Narrative of a Second Expedition*, 188–89.
12 "Dr. Richardson's Narrative," 189, 191.
13 "Dr. Richardson's Narrative," 193–94.
14 "Dr. Richardson's Narrative," 194–95.
15 "Dr. Richardson's Narrative," 195–96. Ullebuk's ease with the western dialect is evidence that supports Ernest S. Burch's conclusion that Ullebuk's (and Augustine's) ancestors had relocated from the Arctic coast to west Hudson Bay in the last quarter of the seventeenth century.
16 "Dr. Richardson's Narrative," 198–99, 204.
17 "Dr. Richardson's Narrative," 199.
18 "Dr. Richardson's Narrative," 199–200.
19 "Dr. Richardson's Narrative," 200–201, 203.
20 "Dr. Richardson's Narrative," 204–5.
21 "Dr. Richardson's Narrative," 205–6.
22 "Dr. Richardson's Narrative," 206.
23 Franklin, *Narrative of a Second Expedition*, 99.
24 Franklin, 99; Franklin, *Journals and Correspondence...1825–1827*, 198.
25 Franklin, *Narrative of a Second Expedition*, 99–100; Franklin, *Journals and Correspondence...1825–1827*, 198–99.
26 Franklin, *Narrative of a Second Expedition*, 101, 102; Franklin, *Journals and Correspondence...1825–1827*, 200.
27 Franklin, *Narrative of a Second Expedition*, 102–3; Franklin, *Journals and Correspondence...1825–1827*, 200–201.
28 Franklin, *Narrative of a Second Expedition*, 104–5; Franklin, *Journals and Correspondence...1825–1827*, 201–4.
29 Franklin, *Narrative of a Second Expedition*, 105; Franklin, *Journals and Correspondence...1825–1827*, 204.

30 Franklin, *Narrative of a Second Expedition*, 106–7; Franklin, *Journals and Correspondence…1825–1827*, 203–4. A musket is long-barrelled, muzzle-loading gun that is fired from the shoulder.
31 Franklin, *Narrative of a Second Expedition*, 107–8.
32 Franklin, 108–9; Franklin, *Journals and Correspondence…1825–1827*, 205.
33 Franklin, *Narrative of a Second Expedition*, 109–10; Franklin, *Journals and Correspondence…1825–1827*, 206.
34 Franklin, *Narrative of a Second Expedition*, 105–6; Franklin, *Journals and Correspondence…1825–1827*, 204.
35 Franklin, *Narrative of a Second Expedition*, 111; Franklin, *Journals and Correspondence…1825–1827*, 207.
36 "Dr. Richardson's Narrative," 207–10.
37 "Dr. Richardson's Narrative," 210–11.
38 "Dr. Richardson's Narrative," 213.
39 "Dr. Richardson's Narrative," 213, 217–20.
40 "Dr. Richardson's Narrative," 220–25.
41 "Dr. Richardson's Narrative," 225–26.
42 "Dr. Richardson's Narrative," 226–30.
43 "Dr. Richardson's Narrative," 230, 234, 236.
44 "Dr. Richardson's Narrative," 236, 237, 238.
45 "Dr. Richardson's Narrative," 236–45.
46 "Dr. Richardson's Narrative," 245–52.
47 "Dr. Richardson's Narrative," 252–53. The island Kendall sighted was Victoria Island. The strait is still known as Dolphin and Union Strait.
48 Franklin, *Narrative of a Second Expedition*, 113–14.
49 Franklin, 114–15.
50 Franklin, 115–16.
51 Franklin, 115–16.
52 Franklin, 117, 120; Franklin, *Journals and Correspondence…1825–1827*, 210, 212.
53 Franklin, *Narrative of a Second Expedition*, 121–22.
54 Franklin, 122.
55 Franklin, 124–29.
56 Franklin, 129–31.
57 Franklin, 141–42, 146–47; Franklin, *Journals and Correspondence…1825–1827*, 248.
58 Franklin, *Narrative of a Second Expedition*, 147, 149.
59 Franklin, 151–53.
60 Franklin, 151–58.
61 Franklin, 254–55.
62 "Dr. Richardson's Narrative," 257–60.
63 Franklin, *Narrative of a Second Expedition*, 158–59. Barter Island, Point Heald, and Prudhoe Bay are in what is now Alaskan territory.
64 Franklin, 160–62.
65 Franklin, 162, 167.
66 Franklin, 167, 168, 170.
67 Franklin, 171–72, 173.

68 Franklin, 173–74.
69 Franklin, 112.
70 Franklin, 174–75, 176.
71 Franklin, 180.
72 Franklin, 176–77.
73 Franklin, 177–78.
74 Franklin, 179–80.
75 Franklin, 183.
76 "Dr. Richardson's Narrative," 268–69.
77 "Dr. Richardson's Narrative," 268–69.
78 "Dr. Richardson's Narrative," 269–71.
79 "Dr. Richardson's Narrative," 271–72.
80 "Dr. Richardson's Narrative," 273–74.
81 "Dr. Richardson's Narrative," 273–75.
82 "Dr. Richardson's Narrative," 277.
83 "Dr. Richardson's Narrative," 277–82.
84 "Dr. Richardson's Narrative," 282–83.
85 Franklin, *Narrative of a Second Expedition*, 184, 303; "Dr. Richardson's Narrative," 282, 283.
86 Franklin, *Narrative of a Second Expedition*, 184, 287–91, 303.
87 Franklin, 295–96.
88 Franklin, 297.
89 Franklin, 298, 302.
90 Franklin, 298–302; HBCA, Fort Simpson Journals, B.200/a/8.
91 Franklin, *Narrative of a Second Expedition*, 303–7; HBCA, Fort Resolution Journals, B.181/a/7.
92 HBCA, Fort Chipewyan Journals, B.39/a/25.
93 HBCA, Cumberland House Journals, B.49/a/42:47, B.49/a/43; Norway House Journals, B.154/a/15.
94 HBCA, Fort Chipewyan Journals, B.39/a/26; Franklin, *Narrative of a Second Expedition*, 313–14.

CHAPTER 8. Augustine, Ullebuk, and Moses, 1827–1830

1 Franklin to Back, Letter of Instruction, February 26, 1827, in John Franklin, *Journals and Correspondence: The Second Arctic Land Expedition, 1825–1827*, ed. Richard C. Davis (Toronto: Champlain Society, 1998), 389; HBCA, York Factory Journals, B.239/a/135 (1 September 1827); York Factory Account Books, General Shop, B.239/d/402:139.
2 John Franklin, *Narrative of a Second Expedition to the Shores of the Polar Sea in the Years 1825, 1826, and 1827* (1828; Rutland, VT: Charles E. Tuttle, 1971), 314n.
3 HBCA, Churchill Post Journals, B.42/a/155 (14 September 1827).
4 HBCA, Churchill Post Journals, B.42/a/153 (9 July 1826); Churchill Post Account Books, Eskimo Trading Book, 1828–32, B.42/d/139, 5, 25d, 27, 67. How widely the

disease had spread to other Inuit communities inland or on the north coast is not known; nor is there any written description of the disease.

5   Martha McCarthy, *Churchill: A Land-Use History, 1782–1930* (Ottawa: Parks Canada, 2002 and 2003), 45–47.
6   HBCA, Churchill Post Journals, B.42/a/152 (May and June 1825); McCarthy, *Churchill*, 93, 97, 99, 421, 423.
7   HBCA, Churchill Post Journals, B.42/a/154 (1824–27), fo. 62 (22 March 1827). Mallette has not been identified as an employee in the Company's archives or names index, including Servants' Contracts and Biographical Sheets.
8   HBCA, Churchill Post Journals, B.42/a/155 (15 September 1827).
9   HBCA, Churchill Post Journals, B.42/a/155 (17 September 1827).
10   HBCA, Churchill Post Journals, B.42/a/155 (4, 8 October 1827).
11   HBCA, Churchill Post Journals, B.42/a/155 (22 October 1827).
12   HBCA, Churchill Post Journals, B.42/a/155 (21 February 1828).
13   HBCA, Churchill Post Journals, B.42/a/155 (March and April 1828), *passim*.
14   HBCA, Churchill Post Journals, B.42/a/155, B.42/a/156 (May 1828), *passim*.
15   HBCA, Churchill District Report, 1827–28, B.42/e/5:2 (15 June 1828).
16   HBCA, Churchill Post Journals, B.42/a/156:7. Harding added his description of the trip south immediately after Dunnet's entry of July 13 after he returned from York Factory in August.
17   HBCA, Churchill Post Account Books, Men's Debts, B.42/d/126 (13 August 1828), B.42/d/127:3d; York Factory Account Books, 1828–29, B.239/d/327; Churchill Account Books, B.42/d/327.
18   HBCA, Churchill Post Account Books, Men's Debts, B.42/d/126 (13 August 1828), B.42/d/127:3d; York Factory Account Books, 1828–29, B.239/d/327; Churchill Account Books, B.42/d/327.
19   HBCA, Churchill Post Account Books, B.42/d/127:3d (11, 29 October 1828).
20   Letter from Franklin to Richardson, December 15, 1823, in Franklin, *Journals and Correspondence…1825–1827*, 279.
21   HBCA, Churchill Post Journals, B.42/a/156 (2 March 1829).
22   HBCA, Churchill Post Journals, B.42/a/156 (6 May 1829); Churchill Servants' Account Book, 1827–32, B.42/d/138 (6 May 1829).
23   HBCA, Churchill Post Journals, B.42/a/157:4d (8 July 1829). In Outfit 1829–30, Churchill's workforce consisted of one officer, one tradesman, and three labourers. Michael Payne, "Fort Churchill, 1821–1900: An Outpost Community in the Fur Trade," *Manitoba History* 20 (Autumn 1990): 12.
24   HBCA, Churchill Post Journals, District Report, 1828–29, B.42/a/6; York Factory, Abstract of Servants' Accounts, 1828–29, B.239/g/8.
25   HBCA, Churchill District Report, 1828–29, B.42/e/6:2. Franklin's two narratives note that at the New Year's festivities liquor was offered to expedition members and to local people, and Franklin himself enjoyed a drink with McVicar. No mention is made of Augustine imbibing in the expeditions' memoirs, with either Junius or Ullebuk.
26   HBCA, Fort Churchill Account Book, 1829, B.42/d/129; York Factory Abstracts of Servants' Accounts, 1828–29, Northern Department, B.239/g/8 (1 June 1829).

27 HBCA, Churchill Post Account Books, Men's Debts, B.42/d/131 (15, 22, 27 June 1829).
28 HBCA, Churchill Post Account Books, 1827–32, B.42/d/138 (9 June 1829).
29 HBCA, Churchill Post Journals, B.42/a/157 (17 July 1829).
30 HBCA, Churchill Post Journals, B.42/a/157:6 (18 July 1829). The rough copy and fair copy do not agree on the date, which is given as July 18 and July 20, respectively.
31 HBCA, Churchill Post Journals, B.42/a/157 (19 July 1829); Biographical Sheet, Baikie Sinclair. Plans for Sinclair to go to Lac La Pluie in 1829 were changed and he was sent to Oxford House as labourer and cattle herder (1829–39) and then to Cumberland House (1839–44). He retired to Red River.
32 HBCA, Churchill Post Journals, B.42/a/157 (28 July 1829).
33 HBCA, Churchill Post Journals, B.42/a/157 (17 August 1829).
34 HBCA, Churchill Post Journals, B.42/a/157 (19 August 1829).
35 HBCA, Churchill Post Journals, B.42/a/157 (30 August 1829).
36 HBCA, Churchill Post Journals, B.42/a/157 (19 September 1829); Churchill District Report, 1829–30, B.42/e/7.
37 HBCA, Churchill Post Journals, B.42/a/157 (19–29 September 1829).
38 HBCA, Churchill Post Journals, B.42/a/157 (1–14 October 1829).
39 HBCA, York Factory Journals, B.239/a/141 (6 October 1829).
40 HBCA, York Factory Journals, B.239/a/141 (15 October 1829).
41 HBCA, Churchill Post Journals, B.42/a/157 (16 October 1829).
42 HBCA, Churchill Account Books, B.42/d/131 (16 October 1829).
43 HBCA, Churchill Account Books, 1829, B.42/d/129:15.
44 HBCA, York Factory Journals, B.239/a/141 (7 November 1829).
45 HBCA, York Factory Account Books, B.239/d/356 (15 November 1829).
46 HBCA, York Factory Account Books, B.239/d/356 (16 November 1829).
47 HBCA, York Factory Journals, B.239/a/141 (22 November 1829).
48 HBCA, George Simpson's Correspondence Book, D.4/123:44, Letter from Robert Miles to George Simpson (23 November 1829). Given Moses's apparent age and frailty, Miles's recommendation that he be the first choice seems unlikely. Miles may have confused their names.
49 HBCA, Albany Fort Journals, B.3/a/134 (14 January 1830).
50 HBCA, Albany Fort Journals, B.3/a/134 (18 January 1830); Moose Fort Journals, B.135/a/135 (23 January 1830).
51 HBCA, Moose Factory, District Report, 1828–29, B.135/e/21 (29 July 1829).
52 HBCA, Moose Factory Journals, B.135/a/135:30; Moose Factory Abstracts of Servants' Accounts, 1829–30, B.135/g/111.
53 HBCA, Moose Factory Journals, B.135/a/135 (18 February 1830).
54 HBCA, Moose Factory Journals, B.135/a/135 (17, 22, 24 February 1830).
55 HBCA, Moose Factory Journals, B.135/a/135 (22–25 February 1830).
56 HBCA, Moose Factory Journals, B.135/a/135 (22 March–1 June 1830).
57 HBCA, Moose Factory Journals, B.135/a/135 (21–23 April 1830).
58 HBCA, Churchill Post Journals, B.42/a/157:22d. In fur trade terms, parchment is a skin, usually caribou, that has been scraped so that no flesh, fat, hair, or blood remain on it. Making parchment is a long and demanding job usually done by women. Inuit use it to make drums and as windows to let light into a snowhouse, among other things.

59 HBCA, Churchill Post Journals, B.42/a/154 (9 June 1827).
60 HBCA, Churchill Post Journals, B.42/a/157:22d.
61 HBCA, York Factory Account Book, Balances of Servants Accounts at the Northern Department, 1829, B.239/d/363:2d, 4 (1 June 1830).
62 HBCA, York Factory Correspondence Book, B.239/b/90:4
63 HBCA, Churchill Post Journals, B.42/a/157; Churchill District Report, 1829–30, B.42/e/7:4.
64 HBCA, York Factory Account Books, B.239/d/363:2d.
65 HBCA, York Factory Correspondence Book, Abstracts of Servants' Accounts for the Northern Department, 1830–31, B.239/b/90:42; York Factory, Abstracts of Servants' Accounts, 1831–33, B.239/g/70:58, 71–72. Augustine's wage for the three years of his engagement was £17 per annum.
66 The oldest child would have been about twelve years old, based on John West's comments.
67 HBCA, York Factory Correspondence Book, B.239/b/90:44.

INTERLUDE 4. The Northeast Expedition, 1830

1 Glyndwr Williams, "Introduction," in *Northern Quebec and Labrador Journals and Correspondence, 1819–35*, ed. K.G. Davies (London: Hudson's Bay Record Society, 1963) (hereafter cited as *NQLJC*), xix, xxi; HBCA, Governors Papers, Governor and Committee, Inward Correspondence, A.11/57:2; Official Reports to the Governor and Committee, D.4/89:106 (1824–26); D.4/91:15d–16d, 55–57 (1826–29); D.4/92:11d–12 (1826–29).
2 Benjamin Kohlmeister and George Kmoch, *Journal of a Voyage from Okkak on the Coast of Labrador, to Ungava Bay, Westward of Cape Chudleigh* (London: Brethren's Society for the Furtherance of the Gospel among the Heathen, 1814).
3 James McKenzie, "The King's Posts and Journal of a Canoe Jaunt through the King's Domains, 1808," in *Les Bourgeois de la Compagnie du Nord-Ouest*, ed. L.R. Masson (Quebec City: A. Coté, 1890), 408.
4 The Hudson's Bay Company's Royal Charter of 1670 gave the Company all and sole rights to trade in Rupert's Land, a territory defined as that portion of North America drained by rivers flowing into Hudson Bay. All rivers west of the height of land in Labrador and northern Quebec flowed to Ungava Bay; rivers east of the height of land flowed into the Atlantic Ocean, the St. Lawrence River, or Ungava Bay and therefore did not fall within England's legal definition of Rupert's Land.
5 HBCA, Rupert's House Post, B.186/b/15:10–11, George Atkinson's 1816 Journal; Great Whale Post Journals, B.372/a/4; Fort George Post Journals, B:77/a/5, George Atkinson's 1818 Journal (written by John Stewart); Williams, "Introduction," and K.G. Davies, Appendix B, in Davies, *NQLJC*, xxxix, xl–xli, 338–49.
6 HBCA, Second Journal of James Clouston, 1819–20, B.143/1/21. Published as "A Journal of a Journey in the Interior of the Peninsula of New Britain," in Davies, *NQLJC*, 41–42, 45, 47, 67–68, 338–40, 348–49; Williams, "Introduction," in Davies, *NQLJC*, xxxix–xli, xliv–xlix.
7 HBCA, Official Reports to the Governor and Committee, D.4/89:106, D.4/81:15d–16d, D.4/92:11d–12, 55–57.

8   HBCA, Rupert's House Correspondence Book, B.186/b/15:10–11; Williams, "Introduction," in Davies, NQLJC, lv.
9   HBCA, Official Reports to the Governor and Committee, D.4/92, fos. 1d-2, liii.
10 HBCA, General Correspondence Outward, D.4/18:111, Letter from G. Simpson to N. Finlayson (2 July 1831).
11 Williams, "Introduction," in Davies, NQLJC, liii, lix.
12 Letter from Nicol Finlayson to Governor Simpson and the Committee, September 20, 1830, in Davies, NQLJC, 178.
13 HBCA, George Simpson's Character Book, 1830, A.34/1:82d; Williams, "Introduction," in Davies, NQLJC, lix.
14 Unattributed, in E.E. Rich, *Hudson's Bay Company, 1670–1870*, vol. 3, *1821–1870* (Toronto: McClelland and Stewart, 1960), 462–63.

CHAPTER 9. The Ungava Adventure, 1830–1833

1   HBCA, Moose Factory Journals, B.135/a/135 (22 March 1830); Eastmain Journals, B.59/a/114, Letter from Erlandson to CF Joseph Beioly (29 May, 13 June 1830).
2   HBCA, Moose Factory Journals, B.135/a/135 (10 June 1830). The Cree guides were identified as Saunders and his son John.
3   Finlayson's Journal, June 22–25, 1830, in Davies, NQLJC, 102–3.
4   Finlayson's Journal, June 23, 1830; HBCA, Eastmain Journals, B.59/a/114, 115 (25 June 1830). Andrew Moar was a retired HBC man living at Eastmain. In the early nineteenth century, the Kaniapiscau River was known to Europeans as the South River and was often seen as the main branch of the Koksoak River.
5   Finlayson's Journal, July 7–9, 1830.
6   Finlayson's Journal, July 11–13, 1830.
7   Finlayson's Journal, July 14, 1830.
8   A "stage" in riverman speech is about 220 yards.
9   Finlayson's Journal, July 16–24, 1830.
10 Finlayson's Journal, July 25–29, 1830.
11 Finlayson's Journal, July 27 and 29–31, 1830.
12 Finlayson's Journal, August 2–3, 1830.
13 Finlayson's Journal, August 4–5, 1830; Benjamin Kohlmeister and George Kmoch, *Journal of a Voyage from Okkak on the Coast of Labrador, to Ungava Bay, Westward of Cape Chudleigh* (London: Brethren's Society for the Furtherance of the Gospel among the Heathen, 1814).
14 Robert J. Flaherty, "Two Traverses across Ungava Peninsula, Labrador," *Geographical Review* 6, no. 2 (August 1918): 125.
15 Finlayson's Journal, August 9–16, 1830.
16 Finlayson's Journal, August 12, 1830.
17 Finlayson's Journal, August 16–22, 1830.
18 Ross W. Wein and David A MacLean, eds., *The Role of Fire in Northern Circumpolar Ecosystems* (Chichester, England: Wiley for the Scientific Committee on Problems of the Environment of the International Council of Scientific Unions, 1983); Andrew M.

NOTES · 359

    Jones, personal communication for information on trees, mosses, and lichen species' reactivity with fire.
19 Finlayson's Journal, August 23–29, 1830.
20 Glyndwr Williams, "Introduction," in Davies, NQLJC, lvii, lx, lxv.
21 HBCA, Ships' Miscellaneous Papers: Montcalm, 1829, C.7/95, 1–3; RG20/6C/12, "Ships on Hudson's Bay Company Business Sailing between England and York Factory, 1670–1900," typescript, 28, 45–46; York Factory Journals, B.239/b/89a:10. Because *Montcalm* was a chartered vessel, its captain was not bound to submit logs and ship's paper to the London Committee. Only a few scraps of information concerning *Montcalm* made their way into the Company's archives. The garboard is the first range (or strake) of planks laid next to the keel of a wooden ship.
22 HBCA, Governor's Papers, Correspondence Book Outwards, D.4/17, Letter from Simpson to Royal (25 August 1830), 104–6; Davies, NQLJC, 118–19nn1–2.
23 HBCA, Governor's Papers, Correspondence Book Outwards, D.4/17, 102, 104–7, Letter from Simpson to Finlayson (25 August 1830).
24 HBCA, Fort Chimo Correspondence, Letter from Finlayson to J.G. Mactavish (14 February 1831); Davies, NQLJC, 182–86.
25 Finlayson's Journal, August 30–September 11, 1830.
26 Finlayson's Journal, August 31–September 3, 1830.
27 Finlayson's Journal, September 13, 1830.
28 HBCA, Fort Chimo Correspondence Books Outward, B.38/b/1, Letter from Nicol Finlayson to George Simpson (20 September 1830); Davies, NQLJC, 180.
29 Finlayson's Journal, September 13, 1830.
30 HBCA, Fort Chimo, Correspondence Books Outward, B.38/b/1, Letter from Nicol Finlayson to George Simpson (20 September 1830). The letter has not survived in the Company's archives. Extracts as they appeared in *In the Matter of the Boundary between the Dominion of Canada and the Colony of Newfoundland in the Labrador Peninsula*, (vol. VI of Joint Appendix, Pt VSII, no. 1106, 2783-4) are in Davies, NQLJC, 177–80.
31 Finlayson's Journal, September 14–20, 1830; HBCA, Governor's Papers, D:4/17:101, Letter from Simpson to Finlayson (22 August 1830).
32 Finlayson's Journal, October 12–18, 1830.
33 Finlayson's Journal, October 17–24, 1830. How people were housed is never mentioned in the Fort Chimo journals, but during the first month the carpenters built two houses. One may have been reserved for Finlayson, whose wife and son joined him in 1831. Augustine and his family lived in their tent.
34 Finlayson's Journal, November 1, 1830.
35 Finlayson's Journal, November 8 and 12, 1830.
36 Finlayson's Journal, December 19 and 25, 1830, and January 3, 1831.
37 Finlayson's Journal, January 10 and 15, 1831.
38 Finlayson's Journal, February 1, 7, and 12–14, 1831.
39 HBCA, York Factory Correspondence Inward, B.239/c/2, Letter from Finlayson to Mactavish (14 February 1831); Davies, NQLJC, 185. Finlayson's letter to Simpson has not survived.

40 Finlayson's Journal, February 20, 1831.
41 Finlayson's Journal, March 17–19, 21–22, and 24, 1831.
42 Finlayson's Journal, March 24–31, 1831.
43 Finlayson's Journal, April 9 and 22, 1831.
44 Finlayson's Journal, April 23–29, 1831.
45 Finlayson's Journal, April 26 and May 19, 1831.
46 Finlayson's Journal, May 20–23, 1831.
47 Finlayson's Journal, June 3, 1831.
48 Finlayson's Journal, July 4–5 and 7, 1831; Instructions to George McKay, July 11, 1831, in Davies, NQLJC, 187–88.
49 Finlayson's Journal, Instructions to William Taylor, July 13, 1831, in Davies, NQLJC, 186–87.
50 Finlayson's Journal, July 11 and 13–14, 1831.
51 Finlayson's Journal, August 29, 1831.
52 Finlayson's Journal, September 3, 1831.
53 Finlayson's Journal, 156n2, 158n1, 159nn1–3; HBCA, Churchill District Report, 1829–30, B.42/e/7.
54 The Company's records do not mention Mrs. Finlayson's journey or its date or means. There are three possible times when she could have reached Ungava: with the canoe brigade in the summer of 1830, on *Montcalm* in September 1830, or on *Beaver* in September 1831. When the Ungava expedition left Moose Factory on June 3, 1830, she was within two months of giving birth to her first child and it is unlikely that she was in the canoe brigade. Such a journey could have had deadly consequences for her and her baby. When *Montcalm* left York Factory on August 27, 1830, the baby (born August 6, 1830, in Red River) was three weeks old, the mother was recovering from the birth, and a canoe journey from Red River to York Factory in order to sail on *Montcalm* is very unlikely. The most likely time and means was 1831 on *Beaver*.
55 Finlayson's Journal, September 5–7, 1831.
56 Finlayson's Journal, September 3, 1831; Davies, NQLJC, 156n.
57 Minutes of June 29, 1831, in *Minutes of Council of the Northern Department of Rupert's Land, 1821–31*, vol. 3, ed. R. Harvey Fleming (Toronto: Champlain Society for Hudson's Bay Record Society, 1940), 283.
58 Finlayson's Journal, September 14–16, 23–24, 27–28, and 30, 1831.
59 Finlayson's Journal, November 5–6 and 12, 1831.
60 The Company's records do not name the nearest Indigenous communities, but they were probably Nascapi. Other inhabitants were Montagnais hunters, but their territory was too far south for them to be frequent visitors near Ungava Bay.
61 Finlayson's Journal, November 19–21, 1831.
62 Finlayson's Journal, December 17–31, 1831. All temperatures were read on a mercury thermometer and are in degrees Fahrenheit.
63 Finlayson's Journal, January 7, 1832. A sewn sled was made without nails. Rope, usually made from animal gut, held the parts together. Because braided sinew rope "gives" a bit when pulled or tautened, a sewn sled's various parts can move just enough to bounce over rough snow and ice without breaking.
64 Finlayson's Journal, January 28, 1832.
65 Finlayson's Journal, January 28, 1832.

66 Finlayson's Journal, February 4, 11, and 25, 1832.
67 Finlayson's Journal, March 17 and 24, 1832.
68 Finlayson's Journal, April 14, 21, and 28, 1832.
69 Finlayson's Journal, May 5 and 15, 1832.
70 Finlayson's Journal, June 2, 1832.
71 Finlayson's Instructions to Erlandson, June 23, 1832, in Davies, NQLJC, 188–89.
72 Erlandson's Journal, Letter to Finlayson from South River, July 4, 1832, in Davies, NQLJC.
73 HBCA, Fort Chimo Correspondence, 1830–33, Letter from Finlayson to Erlandson, July 16, 1832, in Davies, NQLJC, 189–90.
74 HBCA, Fort Chimo Correspondence, 1830–33, Finlayson's Instructions to Captain Thomas Duncan, August 6, 1832, in Davies, NQLJC, 189.
75 Erlandson's Journal, Letter from Erlandson to Finlayson, September 7, 1832.
76 HBCA, Fort Chimo Correspondence, 1830–33, Letter from Finlayson to Erlandson, September 12, 1832.
77 Augustine's wife was on board *Montcalm* with Augustine and their son in 1830, Betsy Finlayson was on board *Beaver* in 1831 with her year-old son, and Ullebuk was married before the birth of his son, William, at Fort Chimo in 1831 or 1832. The birth is reported in Letitia Hargrave's letters. Ullebuk also had a daughter, born at the post before 1836.
78 Finlayson's Journal, September 29–October 6 and November 10, 1832.
79 Erlandson's Journal, October 17–November 4, 1832.
80 Finlayson's Journal, November 17, 1832.
81 HBCA, Fort Chimo Correspondence, 1830–33, Letter from Finlayson to Erlandson, November 19, 1832, in Davies, NQLJC, 190.
82 HBCA, Fort Chimo Correspondence, 1830–33, Letter from Finlayson to Duncan, August 6, 1832, in Davies, NQLJC, 189; Letter from Finlayson to Erlandson, September 12, 1832, in Davies, NQLJC, 190.
83 HBCA, Fort Chimo Correspondence, 1830–33, Letter from Finlayson to Simpson, December 10, 1832, in Davies, NQLJC, p. 194.
84 Letter from Finalyson to Simpson, December 10, 1832, in Davies, NQLJC, 193–94.
85 Finlayson's Journal, February 21 and March 2, 1833.
86 HBCA, Fort Chimo Correspondence, 1830–33, Letter from Finlayson to Erlandson, March 27, 1833, in Davies, NQLJC, 195–96.
87 Letter from Finlayson to Erlandson, March 27, 1833, in Davies, NQLJC, 195.
88 Finlayson's Journal, March 30 and April 14, 1833.
89 Erlandson's Journal, May 5–13, 1833, in Davies, NQLJC, 219–20.
90 HBCA, Fort Chimo Report on District, 1833, B.38/e/1, 1833, fo. 1, Servants' Assessments.
91 HBCA, Fort Chimo Correspondence, 1830–33, Letter from Finlayson to Erlandson, June 17, 1833, in Davies, NQLJC, 196–97.

CHAPTER 10. "Faithful, Disinterested, Kind-Hearted Creature," 1833–1834

1 HBCA, Norway House Journals, B.154/a/24; George Back, *Narrative of the Arctic Land Expedition to the Mouth of the Great Fish River and along the Shores of the Arctic Ocean, in the Years 1833, 1834, and 1835* (Paris: Baudry's European Library, 1836), 27–28.

2   Back, *Narrative*, 25–26, 28–29.
3   Letter from Alexander Christie to Captain George Back, September 5, 1833, in Back, *Narrative*, 23, 28–29; HBCA, York Factory Correspondence Books, B.239/b/90 (9 September 1833).
4   HBCA, Fort Chimo District Reports, 1833–35, B.38/e/3.
5   HBCA, York Factory Correspondence Book, B.239/b/90, Letter from Alexander Christie to Chief Factors and Chief Traders of the Southern Department (14 September 1833).
6   HBCA, York Factory Correspondence Book, 1829–34, B.239/b/90, Letter from Alexander Christie to Chief Factors and Chief Traders (9 September 1833). A copy of Christie's letter was received and entered in the Athabasca District Correspondence Book, B.39/b/5 (2 February 1834).
7   HBCA, York Factory Correspondence Book, B.239/b/90, Letter from Alexander Christie to George Back (9 September 1833).
8   John Hutchinson was a newcomer to Rupert's Land, having been hired at Orkney in 1832, although probably born in Shetland. HBCA, Servants' Contracts, A.32/7, fo. 45 (1780–c.1926).
9   HBCA, Norway House Journals, B.154/a/24 (31 October 1833); Carlton House Journals, B.27/a/20 (31 October 1833).
10 HBCA, Carlton House Journals, B.27/a/20 (31 October 1833).
11 HBCA, Carlton House Journals, B.27/a/20 (24–31 October 1833).
12 HBCA, Carlton House Journals, B.27/a/20 (24 October–28 November 1833).
13 HBCA, Carlton House Journals, B.27/a/20 (21–30 November 1833).
14 Augustine's wife and son remained at Carlton House and were expected to stay there until Augustine's return.
15 HBCA, Carlton House Journals, B.27/a/20 (20–31 December 1833).
16 HBCA, Ile à la Crosse Journals, B.89/a/16 (5 February 1834).
17 HBCA, Ile à la Crosse Journals, B.89/a/16:85-87; Athabasca District Correspondence Book, B.39/b/5, Letter from Charles to Back (2 February 1834).
18 HBCA, Carlton House Journals, 1823–37, B.27/a/20-23.
19 HBCA, Carlton House Journals, B.27/a/20 (27 February; 5–6 March; 8, 20–26 April 1834); Athabasca District Correspondence Book, B.39/b/5:44, 55b–56a, Letter from George Back to John Charles (20 February 1834).
20 HBCA, Carlton House Journals, B.27/a/20 (31 December 1833, 6 January and 16 February 1834); Fort Chipewyan Journals, B.39/a/29 (25 January 1834); Athabasca District Correspondence Book, B.39/b/5:41b–43a, Letter from George Back to John Charles.
21 HBCA, Athabasca District Correspondence Book, B.29/b/5, Letter from John Charles to William Mcdonnell.
22 Augustine may already have known Blondin; they were both working at York Factory in 1828.
23 HBCA, Fort Chipewyan Journals, B.39/a/29 (3 February 1834); Fort Chipewyan Correspondence Books, B.39/b/5:61–63, Letter from John Charles to William McIntosh.
24 HBCA, Athabasca Post Journals, B.39/a/29, Letters from William Mcdonnell to John Charles; Athabasca District Correspondence Books, B.39/b/5:44a-b, 56a-b

(16 February, 13 April 1834); Back, *Narrative*, 109. The "strangeness of the weather" was widespread. At Fort Reliance on January 17, Back recorded a high of 45°F and a low of minus 70°F. At the end of May, Back recorded air temperature in the shade at 72°F, and 106°F in the sun. Back, *Narrative*, 131, and Appendix v, *Meteorological Journal*, 291, 295. Back's winter headquarters, Fort Reliance, was later renamed and is now simply Reliance.

25 Back, *Narrative*, 125. Back believed that the three men, "having no language in common, were unable to convey their sentiments to each other." This seems unlikely; the two guides were able to communicate with Mcdonnell, who spoke English and possibly French.
26 Back, *Narrative*, 125–27; HBCA, Fort Chipewyan Journals, 1834, B.39/a/29.
27 Back, *Narrative*, 125–27; HBCA, Fort Chipewyan Journals, 1834, B.39/a/29.
28 Back, *Narrative*, 126.
29 Back, 125–26; HBCA, Fort Chipewyan Journals, B.39/a/29; Athabasca District Correspondence Book, B.39/b/5, John Charles's Report to Governor, Chief Factors, & Chief Traders (May 1834).
30 HBCA, Fort Chipewyan Journals, B.39/a/29; Back, *Narrative*, 127.
31 Back, *Narrative*, 130–31.
32 Back, 131–32.
33 Charles's Report to Governor, Chief Factors, & Chief Traders, May 1834.
34 Back, 130–32.
35 HBCA, Fort Chipewyan Correspondence Book, B.39/b/5 (3 June 1834).
36 HBCA, Athabasca District Correspondence Book, B.39/b/4:61–63, Letter from John Charles to William McIntosh (22 May 1834).

CHAPTER 11. The Families, 1834–1863

1 HBCA, Cumberland House Account Book, B.49/a/48 (15 August 1834).
2 HBCA, Churchill Post Journals, B.42/a/163.
3 HBCA, Churchill Account Book, 1830–35, B.42/b/149b, Provision Blotter (1834). Pease are protein-rich legumes such as chickpeas, black-eyed peas, and other leguminous plants. Pease porridge is made by simmering the grain in water for several hours until soft and mushy.
4 HBCA, Churchill Account Book, 1830–35, B.42/b/149b, Provision Blotter (1834).
5 HBCA, Churchill Post Journals, B.42/a/163.
6 HBCA, Churchill Post Journals, B.42/a/163.
7 HBCA, Churchill Post Journals, B.42/a/163. Added to the roughly twenty-seven pounds of provisions, the Widow Augustine would have had sewing, cooking, and hunting equipment, as well as some bedding and clothing, making a total of at least fifty pounds to carry in her backpack and shoulder sling on the nearly three-hundred-mile walk north.
8 HBCA, Churchill Post Journals, B.42/a/166:21–21d.
9 HBCA, Churchill Post Journals, B.42/a/169:6.
10 HBCA, York Factory, Abstracts of Servants' Accounts, B.239/g/17–34.

11   HBCA, Churchill Correspondence Book, B.42/b/61:49d, Letter from James Hackland to James Hargrave (1 July 1858). Hackland's estimate of Augustine's estate was correct within a few pennies. At the end of Outfit 1832–33, two months before Augustine left Fort Chimo, his account stood at £75/3/7. HBCA, Fort Chimo, Miscellaneous Items, B.38/z/1:2–3.
12   HBCA, Fort Chimo, Miscellaneous Items, B.38/z/1:2–3.
13   HBCA, York Factory, Abstracts of Servants' Accounts, B.239/g/14:80; B.239/g/13–17.
14   The daughter was one of three children born before her parents went to Ungava and must have been in her late thirties by 1858.
15   HBCA, Churchill Correspondence Book, B.42/b/61:49d, 50d.
16   HBCA, Churchill Correspondence Book, B.42/a/189a, B.42/b/61.
17   HBCA, Churchill Correspondence Book, B.42/b/61:65d–66.
18   HBCA, Fort Chimo Journals, B.38/a/5 (13–18 July 1836).
19   HBCA, Fort Chimo Journals, B.38/a/5/ (15 August and 23 October 1836, 5 February 1837). There are no hints in the Company's records to suggest that Moses and his wife had children.
20   HBCA, Fort Chimo Journals, B.30/a/5 (15 August 1836).
21   HBCA, Fort Chimo Journals, B.38/a/5 (11 April 1837).
22   HBCA, Fort Chimo Journals, B.38/a/5 (13 July 1837).
23   HBCA, Albany Fort Journals, B.3/a/134; Fort George Journals, B.77/a/11:4; Moose Factory Journals, B.135/a/142:25; Rupert House Journals, B.186/a/55:32; Rupert House Correspondence, B.186/b/34:31; Fort George District Report, 1838, B.77/e/8.
24   HBCA, Fort George/Big River District Report, 1837–38, B.77/e/8:11.
25   HBCA, Fort George Journals, B.77/a/8–9.
26   HBCA, Fort George Journals, Fort George/Big River District Report, 1838–39, B.77/e/9.
27   HBCA, Fort George Journals, 1837–46, B.77/a/11–24; Fort George Correspondence Books, B.77/b/1–4; Fort George District Reports, 1837–40, B.77/e/8–10; Rupert's House Correspondence Books, 1837–53, B.186/b/42–63.
28   HBCA, Sir George Simpson, Correspondence Inward, D.5/33:14–15d (1852).
29   HBCA, Rupert House's Journals, B.186/b/63, 68; Sir George Simpson's Correspondence Inward, D.5/31:280.
30   HBCA, Churchill Correspondence Books, B.42/b/61:75–76, Letter from Charles Griffin.
31   E.E. Rich, *Hudson's Bay Company, 1670–1870*, vol. 3, *1821–1870* (Toronto: McClelland and Stewart, 1960), 647.
32   HBCA, York Factory Correspondence Books, B.239/b/92, Letter from John Charles to Robert Harding (July 1836); Letter from Charles to Thomas Simpson (27 July 1836); Letter from Charles to Harding (9 April 1837).
33   HBCA, York Factory Correspondence Book, B.239/c/3, Robert Harding to John Charles (30 June 1837). The son Harding refers to was Donald Ullebuk.
34   HBCA, Fort Chimo Journals, B.38/a/7, Letter from Erlandson to George Keith (4 August 1837).
35   HBCA, Rupert's House Correspondence Books, B.186/b/34:30; Moose Factory Journal, B.135/a/142.

36   HBCA, Moose Journal, B.135/a/142 (15 December 1837).
37   HBCA, Albany Correspondence Book, B.3/b/62, Letter from George Keith to Jacob Corrigal (18 December 1837); Letter from Jacob Corrigal to George Keith (26 December 1837).
38   HBCA, B.3/b/62, Letter from Jacob Corrigal to Charles McKenzie (9 July 1838).
39   Thomas Simpson, *Narrative of the Discoveries on the North Coast of America, Effected by the Officers of the Hudson's Bay Company during the Years 1836–39* (London: Richard Bentley, 1843), 334.
40   Letitia Hargrave to Florence MacTavish, September 10, 1843, in *The Letters of Letitia Hargrave*, ed. Margaret Arnett McLeod (Toronto: Champlain Society, 1947), 164. Ullebuk's son mentioned here was William Ullebuk, born at Fort Chimo in 1831 or 1832. During Ullebuk Sr.'s lifetime, William was known as William Ullebuk; in later years, he was often known to a new generation of fur traders as Buck and sometimes as Ouligbuck or Ullebuk, which causes confusion today. To the Inuit he was known as Marko, or possibly Makkok, meaning "the second one." William Ullebuk did not speak ten languages but, according to John Rae, he spoke Cree, English, and French as well as Inuktitut. He had apparently learned enough Cree to get by from the Cree guides he had known at Fort Chimo, and English as well from the post's people and his playmates, the Finlayson boys. His noted fluency in "Indian" may be an Athapascan dialect learned during the four years the family was in the Mackenzie region. *See also* Kenn Harper, "William Ouligbuck, John Rae's Interpreter," *Nunatsiaq Online*, November 28, 2008, https://nunatsiaq.com/stories/article/William_Ouligbuck_John_Raes_Interpreter/.
41   HBCA, Fort Chimo Journals, B.38/a/5 (13–18 July 1836). George Simpson McTavish, *Behind the Palisades: An Autobiography* (privately published; distributed by Gray's Publishing, Sidney, BC, 1963), 140.
42   HBCA, D.15/12:145d, Letter from Robert Harding to George Simpson (7 August 1844).
43   Letter from George Simpson to John Rae, June 15, 1846, Red River Settlement, in John Rae, *Narrative of an Expedition to the Shores of the Arctic Sea in 1846 and 1847* (London: Boone, 1850; Project Gutenberg, 2012), 9, https://www.gutenberg.org/ebooks/39917.
44   HBCA, Governor's Papers, D.15/12:135d, Letter from Harding to George Simpson (7 August 1844).
45   HBCA, Governor's Papers, D.15/12:135d, Letter from George Simpson to James Hargrave (2 December 1844); York Factory Correspondence Book, Letter from James Hargrave to Harding, B.239/b/99 (20 January 1845).
46   Hargrave to Harding (20 January 1845); John Rae to George Simpson, February 24, 1846, in John Rae, *John Rae's Correspondence with the Hudson's Bay Company on Arctic Exploration, 1844–1855*, ed. E.E. Rich (London: Hudson's Bay Record Society, 1953), 22.
47   Rae, *John Rae's Correspondence*, 27–30; George Back, *Narrative of the Arctic Land Expedition to the Mouth of the Great Fish River and along the Shores of the Arctic Ocean, in the Years 1833, 1834, and 1835* (Paris: Baudry's European Library, 1836), 10, 19, 34.
48   During his 1833–34 trek north to Lancaster Sound, Ross had missed the opening to Bellot Strait, which might have qualified as a passage for a small vessel. Rae did not scout the east shore of Committee Bay north of Lord Mayor's Bay, so he was also not aware of its existence.

49 Rae, *Narrative of an Expedition*, 27, 35.
50 Rae, 39, 40.
51 Rae, 55. "Fatigue party" is a military name for soldiers assigned to chores in support of armed front-line soldiers, such as preparing food, doing laundry, cleaning barracks, and digging latrines or other trenches.
52 Rae, 55.
53 Rae, 57.
54 Rae, 115.
55 Rae, 115.
56 HBCA, Biographical Sheets; Abstracts of Servants' Accounts, B.239/g/36:52. The five-year gap between Ullebuk's death and the closing of his account with the Company indicates that his children and his wife (if she outlived him), as his heirs, received payments from the account until all his savings were gone.
57 HBCA, B.42/a/61:14. William was born between 1831 and 1833 and so was probably closer to twenty-two years of age by 1853.
58 Letter from John Rae to Chief Factor William McTavish, November 26, 1852, in Rae, *John Rae's Correspondence*, 238–39.
59 Letter from Rae to McTavish, November 26, 1852, 238–39.
60 Letter from John Rae to George Simpson, July 13, 1853, in Rae, *John Rae's Correspondence*, 256.
61 Letter from John Rae to Archibald Barclay, September 1, 1854, in Rae, *John Rae's Correspondence*, 273.
62 Letter from Rae to Barclay, September 1, 1854, 274–77.
63 Letter from Rae to Barclay, September 1, 1854, 279, 283, 284, 286–87.
64 HBCA, Private Records, E.15/9, 285, John Rae's Report to Archibald Barclay, Secretary, London Committee (1 September 1854).
65 E.E. Rich, "Introduction," in Rae, *John Rae's Correspondence*, xci–xcii.
66 "William Ullebuk," in Rae, *John Rae's Correspondence*, 373–74, Appendix B ("Biographical").
67 HBCA, Churchill Post Journals, B.42/61:49d, 50d.
68 McTavish, *Behind the Palisades*, 133.
69 "William Ullebuk," 373–74.

EPILOGUE

1 Vita Sackville-West, "Introduction," in *The Diaries of the Lady Anne Clifford* (London: William Heinemann, 1923), xxiv–xxv.
2 Edgar Lutyens, spoken while he was thinking of writing a biography of Vita Sackville-West, overheard, and quoted by Carol Anshaw in the stage drama *Right After the Weather* (New York: Atria Books by Simon & Schuster, 1931), 163.
3 E.E. Rich, *The History of the Hudson's Bay Company: 1670–1870*, vol. 2, 1763–1870 (London: Hudson's Bay Record Society, 1959), 44.
4 Rich, 45, 46. Twenty thousand pounds in 1775 is worth just under nine million Canadian dollars in 2020.

5   These were the Kivallirmiut, Inuit who had moved from the central Arctic coast to the Hudson Bay coast in the 1680s. When Churchill was established in 1717, they were still newcomers, first-generation migrants to the region, and were spending most of their time learning about their new environment and making suitable changes to their economy and lifestyle.
6   Rich, *History of the Hudson's Bay Company*, 173, 176.
7   River geography limited the routes western and northern clients could choose to get to Churchill. Unlike the large forts at York, Severn, Albany, and Moose, situated at or near the mouths of navigable rivers flowing east or southeast, Churchill River flowed north and was blocked by ice and flood during meltdown. Eastern Chipewyan had no choice but to walk to Churchill, carrying their canoes for crossing small rivers and lakes, along with survival gear and furs for trade. Inuit could choose to walk to Churchill while, like the Chipewyan, carrying gear and trade furs on their backs, or they could choose to risk a very dangerous journey in kayaks.
8   Michael Payne, "Fort Churchill, 1821–1900: An Outpost Community in the Fur Trade," *Manitoba History* 20 (Autumn 1990): 15.
9   E.E. Rich, *Hudson's Bay Company 1670–1870*, vol. 2, 1763–1829 (Toronto: McClelland and Stewart, 1960), 176. Geography was the cause of failure there. All north-flowing rivers melt first at their southern headwaters and are impassable as ice blocks their northward flow and causes widespread annual flooding.
10 Rich, *History of the Hudson's Bay Company*, 284.
11 Rich, 486.
12 Payne, "Fort Churchill, 1821–1900," 2–15.
13 HBCA, Servants' Contracts, A.42/32/2, fo. 27, A.42/17, fo. 23 (1780–c.1926).
14 Payne, "Fort Churchill, 1821–1900," 11.
15 Inuit were never a Homeguard in the sense that the Chipewyan were. In the severe economic times of the Dalton Minimum, Inuit from the closest villages hunted seals at Seal River roughly fifty kilometres north of the post for a few weeks and were paid in trade goods. Their visits to the post itself were rare and short and only occasionally included wives and children. No Inuit families chose to settle permanently near the post. Churchill's Homeguards were eastern barrenland Chipewyan who chose to live close to the trading post and provide services as guides and hunters while hunting for themselves and maintaining their traditional lifestyle and their independence. Their elders and families who were not able to live on the land, usually for health reasons, lived year-round in cabins they or the Company's employees built outside the palisades. One of these families was Shenandoah's.
16 There is no record that Churchill men married Inuit women or even thought about it. This may be due to the Inuit practice of betrothing babies soon after birth as a way of ensuring that orphaned children had a second family if their birth parents died before their children were old enough to live independently. In theory all Inuit were in arranged marriages in early childhood. It may also have been because the Inuit had chosen *not* to live near the post, preferring to stay aloof and unbothered in their own country. Although we know that the families of Augustine and Ullebuk Sr. lived in their home villages when the two men were away on the Admiralty expeditions, we do not know if their wives and children lived at Churchill when the men worked and

lived there. George Simpson McTavish noted that "Ullebuk's second wife" had lived at Churchill, but which Ullebuk he meant is unclear.

17 We do not know when Ullebuk's first wife, Donald's mother, died, but if she was alive in 1824, Ullebuk would have made arrangements for her support as well.

18 Augustine's reason for not leaving them in the care of their village may have been due to the troubles that arose in Junius's family during his (Augustine's) first expedition absence.

19 He probably had some help from his colleagues, who might have known Inuktitut, Cree, and Chipewyan words related to food, animals, and trading, but I do not think that most Company officers and labourers were fluent speakers. Robert Harding may have been exceptional in language learning, but Viljhalmur Stefansson admitted that it took him five years living among Inuit to *acquire* the language, and I was told by Oblate junior missionaries that they were expected to spend the first five years of their tenure *learning* from books and an experienced senior colleague before taking up their priestly duties. To some degree they would also have *acquired* Inuktitut by being in the room when the senior missionary was chatting with potential parishioners. Augustine spent three full years and several summers *acquiring* English before being hired by the Admiralty.

20 Anne Rothwell, "This Is Why the Language You Speak Can Change How You Perceive Time," World Economic Forum, May 5, 2017, https://www.weforum.org/agenda/2017/05/this-is-why-the-language-you-speak-can-change-how-you-perceive-time/.

21 Alex Gray, "A Neuroscientist Explains Why Being Bilingual Makes Your Brain More Robust," World Economic Forum, July 2017, https://www.weforum.org/agenda/2017/07/bilingual-brain-better-neuroscience/.

22 Catherine L. Caldwell-Harris, "Emotionality Differences between a Native and Foreign Language: Theoretical Implications," *Frontiers of Psychology* 5 (2014): 1055.

INDEX

Page numbers in *italics* refer to maps.

Ackshanook (Inuk), 131–32, 347n24
Adam, Jean Baptiste (interpreter 1st Franklin expedition), 62–63, 77–80, 92–93, 95, 100, 102, 106–11, 344n51
Admiralty. *See* British Admiralty
Aird, Gustavus (Franklin 2nd middleman), 145, 152, 167, 186, 350n15
Akaitcho, Yellowknife Chief: Augustine's relationship, 78, 106–9, 219, 315; ceremonial visits, 78, 342n33; Copper Inuit relations, 62, 77–79, 82–86; family, 161–62, 168; Fort Enterprise, *xii*, 63–65, 76, 106–12, 162; Franklin's 1st expedition, 62–66, 76–86, 97–98, 101–3, 106–12, 162, 315; Franklin's 2nd expedition, 141, 161–62; gifts for, 111, 162; interpreters, 77–79. *See also* Yellowknives
Akaiyazza (Yellowknife hunter), 73
Akilineq (Inuit trading market), *xii*, *xiii*, xxix–xxxi, 330n29
Alaska: Franklin's 2nd expedition, *xi*, 194, 197, 353n63; Inuit trade, 193–94, 197; Loucheux trade, 176–77; map and locations, *xi*, 197, 353n63; Russian claims and trade, 139, 193–94, 198, 316; Russian traders, 193–94, 198; Thule, xxv–xxxviii, 328n14, 329n23; Yu'pik, 328n14
Albany, Fort, *xiii*, 118, 227, 228–29, 237, 244, 293, 297–98
alcohol: beer, 12, 15, 18–19, 30, 35, 157; HBC policies, 15, 221, 264; health benefits of beer, 19, 30; shrub, 156, 159, 350n22;

spirits (brandy, rum, whiskey), 12, 18, 77, 124, 152, 156, 159, 165, 171–72, 174, 288; wine, 12, 18, 111, 112
Alecamik (Inuk), 127
Amundsen Gulf, *xii*, xxvii–xxviii, 329n23
Angelique, 62, 63
Annagyniak (Inuk, Astanik's stepson), 133, 136, 210, 222, 307
Arctic: about, xxiii–xxvi; Arctic Circle, xxiii–xxiv, 327n2; landscape, xxiv–xxvi, xxix–xxx, 330n29; temperatures, xxiv, 327n3, 329n19; treeline, xxiv, xxvi, 327n4. *See also* climate
Arctic prehistory: archaeological sites, 329n23; Dorset (Tuniit), xxvi–xxvii, 328n14; maps, *xi*, *xii*; migrations, xxvi–xxxi, 308, 330n31, 352n15, 367n5; oral histories, xxvi, xxx; terminology, xxvi, 328n14; Thule, xxv–xxxviii, 328n14, 329n23
Arctic expedition to Ungava. *See* expedition, Ungava (1830–33)
Arctic expeditions, Franklin's. *See* Augustine, Franklin's first overland expedition (1820–21); expedition, Franklin's second overland (1824–25)
Arctic land expedition. *See* Back, George, Arctic overland expedition (1833–35)
Arctic Red River (Mackenzie's), 176, 202, 208, 298, 352n5
Arohauté, Charlois, 158, 350n29
arrowroot, 92, 343n17
Arviat, *xii*, *xiii*, xxx, 7–8, 332n14. *See also* Knapp's Bay (near Arviat)

Astanik (Augustine's brother), 123, 132–33, 136, 210, 290, 307
Atahoona, 127, 347n19
Athabasca, Lake, *xii*, 60–61, 70, 72, 111, 142, 151, 161, 341n19
Athapascan peoples: defined, 323; epidemics, 115–16; oral histories, 44–45, 337n47; trade with NWC, 309. *See also* Chipewyan, eastern (Churchill area); Chipewyan, western (Dene Arctic and Subarctic); Dogribs; Yellowknives
Atkinson, Emma (née West), 135
Atkinson, George, Jr., 239–40
Atongana, 127
Augustine Tataneuck: about, xxiii, 307–8, 313–17; birth, 10, 307; climate, xviii, xxv–xxvi; historical sources, xviii–xxi, xxxiii, 308, 316; known and unknown facts, xxii, xxiii, 7–8, 56, 307–8; location of home village, *xiii*, 1, 7–8, 75, 307, 332n14; memorials, 317; names, 7, 75, 332n16
Augustine, languages: about, 313–14; Inuktun dialect (Mackenzie Delta), 352n15; language learning, 313–14, 368n19; night classes in literacy, 76, 135, 170; reports on learning, 23, 24, 39; translation difficulties, 133–34; written English, xviii, 7, 76, 122, 135–36
Augustine, personal qualities: about, 307–8, 313–16; agency over his own life, xx, 152, 311–12, 315–16; character, xxi, 134, 147, 307–8; close relations with British, 135–36, 208, 313; clothing, 31–32, 69, 80, 83, 131, 191–92, 216–19; courage, 185–86; multiple identities and *Inuttitut* (behaving in the style of the Inuit), 315–16; physical size and appearance, 74, 127; reports on, 22–23, 24, 39, 55–56, 75–76, 122, 215, 221, 272, 285–86, 307–8; survival skills, xx, 308; tolerance, 316
Augustine, family: about, 45–46, 287–92; after Augustine's death (1834–63), 287–92, 347n25, 363n7, 364n11; arranged marriages, 45–46, 48, 367n16; brother (Astanik), 123, 132–33, 136, 210, 290, 307; children (daughter and two sons), 56, 131, 134, 149, 235, 290–92, 307, 347n25, 357n66, 364n14; Churchill visits, 232–35, 288–90; family care during absences, 68–69, 151, 235, 312–13; HBC accounts for provisions, 216–19, 221–22, 234, 235, 288–92, 347n25, 364n11; kinship (biological and fictive), xxxi, 4–5, 134, 312–13; known and unknown facts, xviii, xxii, 7–8, 56, 307–8; nephew (Annagyniak), 133, 136, 210, 222, 223, 307; wife, 7, 45–46, 48, 56, 131, 149, 221–22; wife and son on Back's expedition, 277–78, 280, 315, 362n14; wife and son on Ungava expedition, 235, 253, 255, 273, 315, 361n77; wife as widow, 287–91, 347n25, 363n7, 364n11; wife "lending" tradition, 132–34
Augustine, home village: Augustine's return to live (1814–15, 1816–20, 1823–24, 1829), 45–46, 55–56, 68–69, 136, 149, 223, 311; Churchill apprentices, 3–9, 308; Churchill visits, 9, 131, 220–21, 232–33, 289–90, 308; climate and landscape, xviii, xxv–xxvi, xxix; epidemic (1825–26), 210–11, 354n4; food shortages and starvation, 24, 55–56, 130, 233–34; Kivallirmiut kin, xxxii, 308, 367n5; known and unknown facts, xxii, xxiii, 7–8, 56, 307–8; location, estimated, *xiii*, 1, 7–8, 75, 307, 332n14; map, *xiii*; meeting place (Akilineq), *xii*, *xiii*, xxix, xxxi, 330n29; prehistoric migrations, xxvii–xxxi, 303, 330n31, 352n15, 367n5; threats to Augustine by Junius's relatives, 123, 131–36, 346n28, 368n18; trade, 1–3, 9, 55, 75
Augustine, Churchill, early years (1812–20): about, 22–24; absences, 45–48, 55–56, 119, 122–24; apprenticeship, 3–9, 14–16; arrival and adoption (1812–13), xviii, 1–7, 9, 24, 308, 311, 313, 332n9; climatic conditions, xviii, 23, 46; fire and rebuilding (1813–14), 37–42, 48, 310, 336n32, 336n38; firearms, 23, 35, 83, 132–33; firewood supply, 6, 18, 23; friendships, 20–21, 135–36; gardening, 15–16, 35, 47, 48; HBC contract (1815–16), 48–56; HBC reorganization, 118–19; hunter, 18, 124, 149–50; illnesses, 49–51; reports on, 22–23, 24, 55; Selkirk settlers (1813–14), 29, 31, 34–35,

40–45. *See also* Augustine, languages; Churchill, Fort

Augustine, Franklin's first overland expedition (1820–21): accounts for provisions, 68–69, 80; agency over his own life, 311–12, 315; British clothing, 69; climatic conditions, 67–69; Copper Inuit encounters, 82–88, 329n24; family arrangements, 68–69, 312; Fort Chipewyan, 112; Fort Enterprise, 69–77, 100–103, 344n34; Fort Providence, 102–3; Fort Resolution, 111; hunter, 88, 92–93, 103, 106; interpreter, 68–69, 79, 82–86, 313–14; interpreter, search for, 56, 59, 60–61; map, *xii*; starvation, 101, 103, 311–12; travel to Coppermine River, 80–84; Yellowknives' relations, 78, 106–7. *See also* expedition, Franklin's first overland (1820–21)

Augustine, Franklin's second overland expedition (1824–25): about, 147–48, 316; accounts for provisions, 150–51, 209–10; Cumberland House, 153–57; expedition's western detachment, 173–74, 177, 182–86, 190–202; family arrangements, 151; Fort Franklin, 170, 172; gifts, 191–94; hunter, 170, 172, 195; injuries, 160; interpreter, 164–65; Inuit encounters, 176–86, 190–93, 198–202; Loucheux, 164–65, 176–77; map, *xi*; Pillage Point attacks, *xi*, 182–86, 199–201, 219, 314–16; return to Churchill, 206–10; travel to Fort Norman, 160–62, 351n44; uniform, 191–92; wanderings, 166–67, 192–93. *See also* expedition, Franklin's second overland (1824–25)

Augustine, Churchill, later years (1827–34): accounts for provisions, 216–19, 221–22, 233–34, 288–92, 357n65; employee (1827–29), 212–20, 357n65; family after his death (1834–63), 287–92, 347n25, 364n11; return to home village (1829), 223; transfer to York and return, 216–20, 357n65. *See also* Augustine, Ungava expedition (1830–33); Augustine, Back's expedition (1833–35)

Augustine, Ungava expedition (1830–33): accounts for provisions, 234, 364n11; Fort Chimo, 254–64, 266–69; hunting and fishing, 255–58, 260, 263–64, 266–67, 269–71; interpreter, 225–28, 234–35, 244–45; reports on, 272; travel to/from Ungava, 251–53, 268–70, 273, 275–77; wife and son, 235, 253, 255, 273, 359n33, 361n77; York Factory, 234–35. *See also* expedition, Ungava (1830–33)

Augustine, Back's expedition (1833–35): climatic conditions, 279–80, 282; disappearance and death (1834), 282–87; family arrangements, 277–78, 280, 312–13, 315, 362n14; interpreter, 275–77; travel from York to Reliance, 277–83. *See also* Back, George, Arctic overland expedition (1833–35)

Augustus Lake, 317

Auld, Jane (William's daughter), 22, 38, 151

Auld, Mary, and family (William's wife), 22, 33, 35, 38, 151

Auld, William: Augustine's relationship, 22, 27, 35–36, 55, 313; biographical details, 333n20; Churchill chief officer (1795–1810), 310, 333n20; Churchill's typhus crisis and fire (1813–14), 31–33, 36–42, 310, 335n5, 336n32, 336n38; climatic conditions, 10, 23–24, 46; marriage and family, 22, 33, 35, 38, 151; Northern Superintendent (1810–14), 22–23, 27, 29–31, 118, 333n20; surgeon, 10, 30, 333n20

Back, George: Augustine's relationship, 75–76, 122, 135, 275–77, 286; career, 58, 275; Fort Chipewyan, 112; Fort Enterprise, 63–66, 97–98, 344n34; Fort Franklin, 168–70, 173–74, 206; Fort Providence, 98; Fort Resolution, 109–10, 111, 161; Franklin's 1st expedition, 58, 61–64, 73–76, 78–82, 85, 87–92, 95–96, 145–46; Franklin's 1st expedition, Back's party, 97–99, 101–2, 107–13, 344n34; Franklin's 2nd expedition, 137, 145–47, 157–63, 168–70, 173–74, 206, 208–9; Franklin's 2nd expedition, western detachment, 173–74, 177, 182–86, 190–202; interests, 76, 170, 171, 192–93, 206

Back, George, Arctic overland expedition (1833–35): accounts for provisions, 287, 291; Augustine's disappearance and death (1834), 282–87; Chipewyan and Cree, 279–81; climatic conditions, 281–85, 362n24; food shortages, 279–81; Fort Reliance (Great Slave Lake), 281–85, 362n24; Fort Resolution, 282–84; Iroquois guides, 282–84; Norway House, 275–76; plans, 275, 286; search for Ross's expedition, 275, 234, 301, 313, 365n48; workforce, 275–76, 282–83, 362n22
Back Bay, 125–26, 131, 220
Back Inlet, 196
Back River (Great Fish River), xii, xiii, 275, 303
Baffin Island, xiv, xxvii, 239, 243, 329n23
Baikie, Peter, 53
Baker Lake, xii, xiii, xxix, xxx, 233
Banks, Joseph, 57–58
Bannerman, John, 39
bannock, 289
Baptiste (Loucheux), 164–66
Barbue, Chief, 202
barming, defined, 323, 350n24
Barnston, George, 130
Barrow, John, 138–39, 145–47
Barrow, Point, 198, 298
Barter Island, xi, 194, 198, 353n63
bateau, bateaux, defined, 323
Bathurst, Cape, xi, 189
Bathurst, Lord, 139–40, 209–10, 348n7
Bathurst Inlet, xii, xiii, 88, 90, 94, 343n7
Bay of Hopes Advance, 269
BCE and CE, as abbreviations, 327n6
beads and beadwork, xix, 126, 128–30, 222
Bear Lake. See Great Bear Lake
bears, 88, 343n5
Beaulieu, François, 168–69, 174, 204, 207
Beauparlant, Gabriel (voyageur), 63, 73, 81, 97–99, 101
Beaver (HBC sloop): Moose Factory, 232; Ungava expedition, 243, 249, 252–53, 255, 257, 261–62, 267–70, 273, 275–77, 360n54, 361n77
beer. See alcohol
Belanger, Jean Baptiste ("le rouge"), 63, 81, 90, 100, 103

Belanger, Solomon ("le gros"), 63, 73, 81, 94, 96–98, 101–2, 107, 109–12
Belcher Islands, 295
Bell, John, 176, 202, 298
Belleau, Jean Baptiste (voyageur), 63
Bellot Strait, 302, 329n23, 365n48
Benoit, Joseph (voyageur), 63, 81, 100, 102–3, 106–7, 109–12, 315
Berens, Joseph, Jr., 137–38, 145
bermed, defined, 323
Beverly caribou herd, 334n37
Blackfoot and Cree hostilities, 155
Blondin, Pierre, 282–83, 362n22
Bloody Fall, 84–85, 202
Boas, Franz, xix
Boisvert, Jean Baptiste (voyageur), 219–20
Boothia Peninsula, xii, xiii, xxviii, 135, 275, 301, 304–5
Boucher, Paul (Lamallice), 70, 71–72, 277–78, 341n14
Boulanger, Charles, 282–85
HMS Brazen, 27–29, 32, 33, 69
Brisbois, Charles (HBC clerk, Fort Norman), 162, 176, 206
British Admiralty: about, 56–58; Franklin's 2nd expedition, 137–40, 143–44, 146, 154, 162 194; hires Augustine, 313–14; Napoleonic Wars, 57–58, 116–17; naval discipline, 31–32; Rae's discovery of Franklin relics recognized by, 304–305; scientific research, 57, 143; threats to British sovereignty, 139–40; uniforms, 31–32, 69, 80
Buchan, David, 58
Buchanan, James, 157–58
Buffalo Lake (now Peter Pond lake), 160
Burch, Ernest S., 352n15
Burnside River, 93–94
Bushy Island, xv, 39, 213
butterfly (*Incisalia augustus*), memorial to Augustine, 317
Button Bay, xv, 48

cannibals and monsters (wittigo, windigo, wechuge), 44–45, 337n47
capotes: construction and fabric, 126–27, 323, 347n16; expedition uniforms, 140, 153, 323; for Inuit, 126–27, 216, 217, 218, 219, 234

caribou: caribou-based economy, xxx; climatic conditions, 8, 46, 116; edible meat, 88, 93, 343n4; "frozen in ice" incident, 98–99; parchment, 60, 65, 356n58; Sayisi hunters, 20, 334n37; Ungava Naskapi, 271

Caribou-eater Dene (Sayisi Dene), 20, 334n37. *See also* Chipewyan, eastern (Churchill area)

Carlton House: Augustine's wife and son, 277–78, 280, 287, 315, 362n14; climatic conditions, 278–79, 280–81; food shortages, 278, 281; Franklin's 2nd expedition, 153–57, 207–8, 350n15; map, *xiii*; Richardson's visit (1827), 205, 208; tribal hostilities, 278, 280–81; wildfires, 281

Carmichael, Archibald (Franklin 2nd, middleman), 144

carrioles, 60, 111, 206–7, 323

Castor and Pollux River, 299, 302–4

CE and BCE, as abbreviations, 327n6

Ceghannack (Inuk), 299

Chantrey Inlet, *xii*, *xiii*, 298, 304

chaplains, HBC, 121. *See also* West, John

Charles, Jane Auld and children, 22, 38, 151–52

Charles, John: Augustine's disappearance and death (1834), 285–86; Augustine's friendship, 152, 278, 285–86, 312, 313; biographical details, 333n29; Fort Chipewyan officer, 280–82, 285–86; language skills, 227; marriage and family, 22, 38, 151–52; Nelson River officer, 49, 151–52; travel to Norway House, 208; York Factory officer, 227, 296, 333n29

Charles, John, Fort Churchill: Augustine's friendship, 19, 22, 24–25, 45–46, 48, 55; climatic conditions, 46–48; excursions, 19, 24–25, 35–36; fire and rebuilding (1813–14), 36–42, 48, 310, 336n32, 336n38; Franklin's first expedition, 58–59; officer, 19, 33–49, 58, 311, 333n29; Selkirk settlers (1813–14), 33–45, 335n5

Chesterfield Inlet, *xii*, *xiii*, xxix, xxx, xxxix, 136, 233, 303

children. *See* women and children

Chimo, Fort: alcohol, 264; anchorages and moorings, 249, 253–54, 262; care for the hungry, 265, 269; climatic conditions, 255, 257–59, 264–66, 271; construction, 249–51, 255–59, 262, 359n33; fire risks, 250–51, 268; fisheries, 255–58, 263–64; food supply, 250–51, 255–59, 263–64, 266–73, 292–93; illnesses and injuries, 258, 261, 266–67, 269; Inuit, 259–61, 263–67, 269–70; isolation, 242–43, 256, 263; map and landscape, *xiv*, 249; Moses, 273, 292–93, 295; name, 262; Naskapi, 264, 267, 271; reorganization and return to York, 273; South River House, 267–73; trade and gifts, 259–60, 264–65, 268, 270–71, 273; Ullebuk's residency, 273, 292–93, 296–99, 361n77. *See also* Augustine, Ungava expedition (1830–33); expedition, Ungava (1830–33)

Chipewyan, eastern (Churchill area): about, 20–21, 323, 334n37; climatic conditions, 23–24, 46, 51–55, 67–68, 116; country born, as term, xx; epidemics, 115–16; extended families, 211–12, 311; HBC care for invalids, 20–21, 43–44, 367n15; Homeguard for HBC posts, 20–21, 30, 311, 367n15; hunting and trapping, 43; Inuit contact, xxix; locations, xxix, 20–21, 334n37; marriage and children, 20–21, 211, 311; as "natives of Hudson Bay," 20, 334n35; Sayisi Dene, 20–21, 43–44, 334n37; Selkirk settlers crisis (1813–14), 28–30, 43; starvation, 54–55, 67–68; trade, 20–21, 23, 55, 214, 309, 367n7; women, 20–22, 214

Chipewyan, western (Dene Arctic and Subarctic): Athapascan dialects, 4, 323, 365n40; Back's expedition (1833–35), 281, 283, 284; Beaulieu's party, 168–69, 174, 204, 207; climatic conditions, 46, 279–81, 283; epidemics, 115–16; Fort Franklin, 168–69; oral histories, 44–45, 337n47; trade, 309. *See also* Akaitcho, Chief; Yellowknives

Chipewyan, Fort: Back's expedition (1833–35), 279, 281–83; climatic conditions, 282–83, 362n24; Franklin's 1st expedition, 60–61, 74, 86, 111–12; Franklin's 2nd expedition, 141, 147–48, 160–61, 207, 208; map and locations, *xii*, 74

Christianity, 121–22, 169–70, 174, 187. *See also* missionaries; West, John
Christie, Alexander (HBC Chief Factor), 234–35, 276–78, 298
Christie, William J. (HBC Chief Factor), 228, 230
Christmas festivities, 155–56, 171–72, 206, 242, 256
Churchill, Fort: about, 309–11; history of, 9–16, 118–19, 211, 309–11, 346n6; Homeguard, 20–21, 30, 311, 367n15; landscape, xxvi, 11–13; maps and locations, *xii*, *xiii*, *xv*, 1, 7, 11; names and sites, 11–12; York Factory role, 118. *See also* Augustine, Churchill, early years (1812–20); Augustine, Churchill, later years (1827–34); Hudson's Bay Company (HBC)
Churchill, buildings and physical plant: All-Purpose House, 12–13, 14; construction materials, 12–14, 15; distillery, 15, 211; early history, 9–16; fence, 12–13; fire and rebuilding (1813), 37–42, 48, 211, 310, 336n32, 336n38; garden, 15–16, 35, 47, 214; gunpowder storage, 14, 15, 37–38; kitchen and cooking, 6, 14, 15, 39–40, 213, 310; latrines, 16, 333n25, 366n51; Men's House, 13–14, 211, 212, 213, 310; names and sites, 11–12; officers' quarters, 13, 211; packing shed, 39; scholarly works on, 333n22; tents, 18, 35, 39–41, 310; trading room (Indian House), 13–14, 37–38, 42, 47, 48
Churchill, Chipewyan relations. *See* Chipewyan, eastern (Churchill area)
Churchill, climate: conditions (1802–28), 10, 46–48, 51–56, 125–27, 130, 213, 215; Dalton Minimum (1790–1830), xxv, 8–10, 46, 116, 332n17, 367n15. *See also* climate
Churchill, Cree relations. *See* Cree, Hudson Bay area (northwest and east)
Churchill, HBC personnel and other residents: about, 16–19, 309–11; Augustine's contract (1815–16), 49–56; care for invalids, 20–21, 43–44, 367n15; country born, as term, xx; number of residents, 54; Orcadian labourers, 17; reassignments (1815), 49; senior officers, 309–10; status and social relations, 16–19, 22, 310–12, 315; surgeons, 17, 19, 50; wages, 19, 357n65; women and children, 21–22; workforce, xix, 16–19, 118, 211, 346n6, 355n23. *See also* Hearne, Samuel; Hudson's Bay Company (HBC); Leask, John; Stayner, Thomas; Topping, Thomas
Churchill, Inuit relations. *See* Augustine, home village; Inuit, Churchill area
Churchill, living conditions: about, 16–19; extreme cold, 12–16; firewood, 12, 14, 18, 38; flooding, 12; food supply, 16, 18, 41, 43, 55–56; illnesses and injuries, 15, 16, 19, 39, 49–50, 338n63; lack of class differences, 18, 310–11; latrines, 16, 333n25, 366n51; mosquitoes, 11, 12, 16; rations, 15, 18, 124, 288–89; water supply, 12, 16, 19. *See also* Churchill, buildings and physical plant
Churchill, nearby features: Back Bay, 125–26, 131, 220; Button Bay, *xv*, 48; Cape Merry, *xv*, 2, 12, 223, 224; Churchill Creek cabins, 33–36, 38, 42; Haymarsh House, *xv*, 34–35, 40–41; hunting and wooding tents, 23, 35–36, 40–41, 51–52, 55, 310; map, *xv*; Seahorse Gully, *xv*, 1–2, 44–45, 48, 214, 220, 223; Stone Fort (Prince of Wales), *xii*, *xiii*, *xv*, 9, 11–13, 15; Woody Islands, *xv*, 39, 41, 336n33
Churchill, river port: bateau (*Hope*), 31, 32–33; cargo transfer, 2, 12, 16, 31, 32–33; east bank anchorage, 2, 12, 331n2; river features, *xv*, 11, 331n2, 367n7, 367n9; west bank pier, 2, 12, 14–15, 331n2
Churchill, Selkirk settlers (1813–14): about, 27–45, 335n2; Augustine's assistance, 29, 31, 34–35, 40–45; Chipewyan assistance, 29, 30, 43; Churchill Creek cabins, 33–36, 38, 42; climatic conditions, 35, 46; fire and rebuilding, 37–42, 48, 310, 336n32, 336n38; food supply, 29, 41, 43; Haymarsh House, 34–35, 40–41; historical sources, 335n2; living conditions, 27–35; Seahorse Gully, 44–45; surgeons, 30, 32, 34–35; tent camps, 28–30, 32, 34; typhus fatalities, 28–30, 32, 34, 335n2, 335n4,

335n13, 336n18; typhus prevention, 28–30, 32, 335n5; Woody Islands cabins, *xv*, 39, 41, 336n33; York Factory residents, 29–30, 31, 42–45, 338n68
Churchill, trade: about, 309–10; difficulties, 309, 367n7; lack of competition, 15; MB currency (made beaver), 324, 340n5; trade goods, 1, 9, 20, 23, 126–30; trading room, 13–14, 38, 42, 47, 48; visitors' settlements, 1–2
Churchill Creek (now Herriot Creek), *xv*, 33–36, 38, 44, 124, 336n20
Churchill River, *xv*, 11, 331n2, 367n7, 367n9
Churchill (HBC sloop), 9, 151
climate: about, xxiv–xxvi; climatic regimes, xxiv–xxvii, 8–10; Dalton Minimum (1790–1830), xxv, 8–10, 46, 116, 240, 332n17, 367n15; HBC daily journals, 46, 337n49; jet stream, 338n1; Last Glacial Maximum, xxiv; Little Ice Age (1350–1850), xxv, xxviii, 8; Maunder Minimum (1645–1715), xxv, xxviii; migrations, xxvi–xxxi, 330n31, 367n5; sunspots and change in, xxv, 8; temperatures, xxiii–xxv, 360n62; volcanic eruption (1815), 53, 338n1. *See also* Churchill, climate
clothing and uniforms: capotes, 126–27, 323; duck cloth, 340n9; ell (measure of cloth), 127; expedition uniforms and clothing, 140, 142, 152–53, 174, 191–92, 203–4; Mackintosh waterproof cloth, 143, 153, 173, 174; naval uniforms, 31–32, 69, 80; shopping at York (1828–29), 216–19, 221–22, 227; slops, 69, 340n8. *See also* Inuit, clothing
Clouston, James, 240
Columbia (US ship), 157
Comer, George (American whaling captain), xix
Company. *See* Hudson's Bay Company (HBC)
Confidence, Fort, 298
Congou tea, 217, 325
The Conjuror (Inuit shaman), 260
Contwoyto Lake, 94
Cook, William Hemmings (York Factory Chief in Charge), 49
cooper, defined. *See* Glossary, page 323
Copper Indians. *See* Yellowknives

Copper Inuit (Inuinnait), xxviii–xxix, 62, 77–78, 82–88, 162, 164, 314, 329n24
Coppermine River: Bloody Fall, 84–85, 202; Franklin's 1st expedition, 56, 58, 62–63, 77–79, 82–86, 95–97, 103, 111–12, 196, 202, 329n24; Franklin's 2nd expedition, 163, 189, 190, 196, 202–3; link of 1st to 2nd expedition, 196; map and locations, *xii*, 63, 96, 190
coracle, described, 344n30
Corcoran, Thomas (HBC senior officer, Fort George), 293–95
Coronation Gulf, *xii*, xxvii–xxviii, xxix, 196, 329n24
Corrigal (Chief Factor Jacob), 297, 301–2
Corston, Thomas (death of), 6
Coté, Pascal, 170
country born, meaning of, xx
Cournoyée, Emanual, (voyageur) 63
Cracroft River, 92
Craigie, John, 49
Cree, Hudson Bay area (northwest and east): Churchill trade and employment, 2, 214–15, 224–25; climatic conditions, 23–24, 46, 51–55; country born, as term, xx; James Bay Cree, 229, 241, 243, 245–48, 293; as "natives of Hudson Bay," 20, 334n35; oral histories, 44–45, 337n47; York Factory, 224–25
Cree, western, 155, 278–81
Cumberland House: Augustine's stay (1824–25), 154–57; Augustine's wife and son (1834), 287; Back's expedition, 287, 291; Christmas (1824), 155–56; Franklin's 1st expedition, 59–61, 71–72, 112; Franklin's 2nd expedition, 153–57, 159–61, 173, 205, 207–8; map, *xiii*
Currie, Alexander (Franklin 2nd, middleman), 144, 152, 350n15

Dalhousie, Cape, *xi*, 188
Dalton Minimum (1790–1830), xxv, 8–10, 46, 116, 332n17, 367n15. *See also* climate
dance. *See* music and dance
Davidson, James, 232
Dawson Inlet (Neville's Bay), xxx
Dease, Charles (Peter's brother), 171, 351n47
Dease, Elizabeth Chouinard, and children (Peter's family), 168, 169

Dease, Peter Warren: Dease-Simpson survey (1838–39), 296–98; Fort Franklin, 168–74, 204, 207; Franklin's 2nd expedition, 141–43, 162–64, 166, 168–74, 176, 204, 207, 275
Dease River, 204
Deer River, 247–48
Deerness, William, 224–25, 261–62, 266–67, 269, 272–73
Dene. See Chipewyan, western (Dene Arctic and Subarctic); Yellowknives
Dene, Caribou-eater, 20, 334n37. See also Chipewyan, eastern (Churchill area)
disabilities and hunger. See invalids, elderly, and the hungry
diseases. See illnesses and injuries; illnesses and injuries, medical care
Dogribs, 162, 168–70, 204–5, 206, 219
dogs, 67–68, 206, 289–90
Dogskin (boat), 222
Dolphin (oar and sail boat): Franklin's 2nd expedition, 141–42, 145, 151–52, 173, 176–82, 190, 196, 202
Dolphin and Union Strait, xii, 190, 196, 353n47
Doré, François, 221
HMS *Dorothea*, 58
Dorset (Tuniit), xxvi–xxvii, 328n14
Driver, William (HBC cooper), 224
Drummond, Thomas (naturalist), 205
Dubawnt River, xii, xiii, xxx
Dumas, Pierre (voyageur), 63, 81, 111
Duncan, Thomas (Captain of *Beaver*), 261, 267–71, 273, 277
Duncan, William (British sailor), 144, 152, 173, 183–84, 186, 193
Dunnet, Alex (Churchill labourer), 213, 215, 221, 224, 355n16
Dunning, James: Augustine's friendship, 19–20, 51, 123–24, 210, 311; biographical details, 20, 310–11; Churchill employee, 210–16, 222; family, 20, 21, 124, 211, 288, 310–11; hunting and fishing, 54, 125, 223; rations, 124, 288; reports on, 221; travel to York Factory, 219, 222
Dunning, James, Sr., 20, 310–11
Dutch cap, defined, 323

eastern detachment, Franklin's. See expedition, Franklin's second overland (1824–25)
Eastmain (HBC schooner), 33
Eastmain House, xiv, 118, 229, 237, 242–47, 270, 297, 358n4
Eddystone (HBC supply ship), 27, 29, 335n5
Edmonton, Fort, 155
Edwards, Abel (HBC surgeon), 32, 34–35, 36, 44
elderly. See invalids, elderly, and the hungry
Ellesmere Island, xxvii, 329n23
Ellthen-eldéli (Caribou-eater Dene), 20, 334n37. See also Chipewyan, eastern (Churchill area)
Encounter, Point, 179–81, 187
Endeavour (boat), 222, 224–25, 261
English literacy. See languages and literacy
Enterprise, Fort: Akaitcho's Yellowknives, 63–65, 76, 106–10, 162; Franklin's 1st expedition, 63–66, 74–77, 96–98, 101–11; map and locations, xii, 344n34; Winter Lake and Winter River, xii, 63–65, 171, 312, 344n34
Erlandson, Erland: Chimo clerk, 273, 296, 297; South River House, 267–73; Ungava expedition officer, 229, 243–51, 254, 256–57, 262, 265, 267–73, 292–93. See also Chimo, Fort
Eskimo, usage of replaced by Inuit, 328n14
expedition, Back's. See Back, George, Arctic overland expedition (1833–35)
expedition, Dease-Simpson survey (1838–39), 296–98
expedition, Franklin's first overland (1820–21): about, 56–66; Augustine as interpreter, 56, 59, 60–63, 79, 82–86, 311–15; Bathurst Inlet, xii, 88, 90, 94, 343n7; climatic conditions, 89–92, 95, 116; Copper Inuit, xxviii–xxix, 62, 77–78, 82–86, 329n24; deaths, 99, 103, 106, 111, 138, 139, 158; evaluation of, 140, 143; flag raisings, 86; food shortages, 87–93, 95–96, 343n23; Fort Chipewyan, 60–61; Fort Enterprise, xii, 63–65, 344n34; Fort Enterprise, return to, 99–113; Hood River, 88–91, 96; lack of local knowledge, 64–65, 74, 78–82, 86, 88–89, 94; link to 2nd expedition, 196;

map and locations, xii, 113; members and supplies, 61–63; plans, 56–58, 63, 82–83; South River House, 267–73; starvation, 90, 95–108, 315, 343n23, 344n40; travel eastward, coastal to Pt. Turnagain, 86–90, 296, 298; travel to Coppermine River, 80–84; travel westward, inland from Pt. Turnagain, 90–97; travel westward, inland return (Back's party), 97–99; travel westward, inland return (Franklin's party), 99–102, 311–12; women and children, 63. *See also* Akaitcho, Chief; Augustine, Franklin's first overland expedition (1820–21); Franklin, John, first overland expedition (1820–21); Yellowknives
expedition, Franklin's second overland (1824–25): about, 137–48; Admiralty support, 137–40, 143–44, 194; boats, 141–42, 157, 173, 176–77; canoes, 142, 158; Carlton House, 153–57, 350n15; climatic conditions, 175; Cumberland House, 153–57, 159–61; distance covered, 204; *Dolphin* (boat), 141, 145, 173, 176, 178–81, 190, 196, 202; eastern detachment, 173–74, 177–82, 186–90, 196, 202–5; firearms, 142, 177, 183–86, 187, 188, 191; flag raising, 202; Fort Franklin, 168–75; Fort Norman, 175; HBC support, 137–42, 145; Herschel Island, xi, 193–94, 198, 201; Inuit, 176–86, 190–93, 198–202; link to 1st expedition, 196; *Lion* (boat), 141, 145, 160, 162–67, 176–77, 182–84, 186, 193, 195, 198, 201; map, xi; medical supplies, 142; officers' travel to Fort Norman, 157–62, 351n44; Pillage Point attacks, xi, 182–86, 199–201, 219, 314–16; plans, 138, 140–41, 162–63, 173–74, 204–8; Point Encounter attacks, 178–81, 187; *Reliance* (boat), 173, 176, 182–86; retreat date, 194, 197; rumours, 200–202; supplies, 141–42; trade and gifts, 178–81, 187, 188, 191–93, 198–202; uniforms and clothing, 140, 142–43, 152–53, 174, 191–92, 203–4; *Union* (boat), 141–42, 145, 151–52, 173, 176, 178–81, 187, 189–90, 196, 232; *Walnut-Shell* (boat), 141, 142, 145, 202–3; western detachment, 173–74, 177, 182–86, 190–202, 205–6; workforce, 158, 351n44. *See also* Augustine, Franklin's second overland expedition (1824–25); Franklin, Fort; Franklin, John, second overland expedition (1824–25)
expedition, Rae (1846–47), 299–305, 365n40, 365n48
expedition, Ungava (1830–33): accounts for provisions, 227–28, 256, 263–64; Augustine's hiring, 225–28, 234–35, 244; canoes, 246–49; climatic conditions, 229; Cree, 229, 241, 243, 245–48, 293; Erlandson as officer, 229, 243–51, 254, 256–57, 262, 265, 267–73, 292–93; Finlayson as senior officer, 229, 241–73, 359n33, 360n54; HBC's information on Labrador, 237–42; Inuit, 229, 241–43, 248, 259–61, 263–66; *Montcalm* (supply ship), 249, 252–54, 277, 359n21, 360n54, 361n77; Moose Factory, 225–32, 244–46; Moses, 226–27; mosquitoes, 248, 251; plans, 229, 238, 241–44, 252, 267; reorganization and return to York, 273; reports on, 254, 256–57, 267–68, 272; South River House, 267–73; trade and gifts, 241–42, 253, 265; Ungava landscape, 229, 238–43; warnings of hardships, 247; workforce, 245–46; York Factory, 225–27. *See also* Augustine, Ungava expedition (1830–33); *Beaver* (HBC sloop); Chimo, Fort; Ullebuk; Ungava Bay and Peninsula

False River, 258, 266
Faries, Frederick (labourer at Ft Chimo), 245, 256, 262, 266–68, 270
fatigue party, defined, 366n51
Felix, François (voyageur), 158
females. *See* Inuit, women; women and children
ferretting, defined, 323
Fidler, Peter, 233
Finlayson, Betsy and son (Nicol's family), 262, 359n33, 360n54, 361n77
Finlayson, Nicol: Clerk in Charge at Fort Chimo, 229, 241–43, 245–73 passim, 292–93 passim, 298–99 passim; South River House, 267–73; Ungava expedition officer, 229, 241–73. *See also* Chimo, Fort

fires: Churchill (1813), 37–42, 310, 336n32, 336n38; plains wildfires, 281; Ungava area, 250–51, 265–66, 268
fishnets, 250, 251
Flaxman Island, xi, 195, 198
Flett, George (Orcadian), 261–63, 267, 270, 273
Foggy Island, 195, 197–98
Folster, John (oarsman with Rae), 300–302
Fontano, Antonio (voyageur), 63, 81, 100–101, 103
Forcier, Joseph (voyageur), 63, 81, 111
Fort Enterprise. *See* Enterprise, Fort
Fort Prince of Wales. *See* Prince of Wales's Fort (Stone Fort)
Fossett, Renee, xxi–xxii, 333n25
foxes, 1, 45, 260
France, wars, 11, 57–58, 116–17
Franklin, Fort: about, 168–69; Back's expedition (1833–35), 281; Beaulieu's party, 168–69, 174, 204, 207; Chipewyans, 168–69, 204; climatic conditions, 205–6; Franklin's 2nd expedition, 168–74, 177, 204–6; living conditions, 168–73, 206; maps and landscape, xi, xii, 168; name changes, 141, 168–69
Franklin, John: about, 58; Eleanor and Isabella (wife and daughter), 140, 145, 158, 165; location of remains (1854), 304–5; *Narrative of a Journey*, 138, 139; *Narrative of a Second Expedition*, 210
Franklin, John, first overland expedition (1820–21): Augustine's friendship, 122, 131–32, 135–36; Cumberland House, 59–60; Fort Chipewyan, 60–61, 112; Fort Enterprise, xii, 63–66, 72–74, 76–77; Fort Enterprise, return to (Franklin's party), 99–110, 344n34; HBC and NWC supplies and crews, 61, 72–74; HBC outfitting system, 74, 334n33; Hood's death, 103–6, 111, 138, 139, 158; lack of local knowledge, 64–65, 74, 78–82, 86, 88–89, 94; link to 2nd expedition, 196; loss of portfolio, 95; map, xii; travel to Coppermine River, 80–84; travel westward from Pt. Turnaround, 93–97; Winter River and Winter Lake, xii, 63–65, 171, 312;

York Factory, 112. *See also* Augustine, Franklin's first overland expedition (1820–21); expedition, Franklin's first overland (1820–21)
Franklin, John, second overland expedition (1824–25): about, 138–48; Admiralty support, 137–40, 143–44, 194; Augustine's friendship, 150, 160, 185–86, 208, 219; Cumberland House, 159–60; flag raisings, 165; Fort Franklin, 168–75, 205–6; gifts, 191–94; HBC support, 137–39, 145; Herschel Island, xi, 193–94, 198, 201; link to 1st expedition, 196; Loucheux, 164–65, 176–77; map, xi; Pillage Point attacks, xi, 182–86, 199–201, 219, 314–16; plans, 140–41, 162–63, 173–74; scientific interests, 170; travel party in northwest, 163–68; travel to Fort Norman, 157–63, 351n44; western detachment, 173–74, 177, 182–86, 190–202. *See also* Augustine, Franklin's second overland expedition (1824–25); expedition, Franklin's second overland (1824–25)
Franklin Bay, xi, xii, 189
Fraser, Paul (HBC junior officer), 159–61
Fuller, Thomas, 144, 152, 156–57, 167, 170–71, 173, 196
fur trade, xix, 70–72. *See also* Hudson's Bay Company (HBC); North West Company (NWC)
Fury and Hecla Strait, xiii, 299, 301–2

Gagné, Joseph (voyageur), 63, 81, 111
garboard, defined, 359n21
Garrock, Robert (HBC Churchill), 49
Garry, Fort, 18
Garry, Nicholas, 137–38, 145
Garry Island, 165, 200
Garson, George and Thomas, 261–62, 267, 271, 273
Garton brothers (Inuit), 266
geese, 43, 67, 125, 214, 299
George, Fort, xiv, 292–95, 297
George River, 260
Gibeault, Belonie (York Factory labourer), 224
Gibson, Hugh (HBC guide), 154–55
Gibson Cove, 300

INDEX · 379

Gillet, Thomas (Franklin 2nd, seaman), 144, 152, 196
Gladman, George, Jr. (Clerk in Charge, Moose Factory), and family, 229–32, 295
Gladman, Joseph, 295
Good Hope, Fort, *xi*, 163–64, 166, 171, 176, 202
Goose Creek and Goose Lake, *xv*, 124
goose hunt (Churchill), 20, 43, 214
Great Bear Lake: Dease Arm, 298; Franklin's 2nd expedition, 158, 161, 168, 173, 175, 203–4; maps and landscape, *xi*, *xii*, *xxvi*, 173. *See also* Franklin, Fort
Great Bear River, *xi*, 167
Great Fish River (Back River), *xii*, *xiii*, 275, 303
Great Slave Lake: climatic conditions, 282–83, 285; map and landscape, *xii*, *xxvi*; Moose Deer Island, *xii*, 61, 72–73, 111, 345n68; Reliance, 281–85, 362n24. *See also* Providence, Fort; Resolution, Fort
Great Whale River and Little Whale River, *xiv*, 239–40, 247, 294–95
Green Lake, 279
Greenland, *xxvi–xxvii*, 328n14
HMS *Griper*, 4, 146
grouse. *See* partridge/ptarmigan/grouse

Hackland, James (Churchill Master, 1850s), 291–92, 364n11
Halcrow, Thomas (HBC blacksmith), 39, 51, 53
Hallcom, Robert (British marine), 157
Harcus, George, 159
Harding, Robert: Augustine's relationship, 132, 213–14; biographical details, 119; Churchill officer (1821–45), 119, 123, 130, 150, 211–29, 232–35, 261–62, 288, 296–97; languages, 119, 150, 368n19; personal qualities, 130; Rae expedition (1846-47), 299–300; shopping at York (1828), 216–17; Ungava expedition, 225–27, 232–35; York visits, 125, 355n16
Hare (First Nations), 163, 168, 203–4
Hargrave, Chief Factor James, 291
Hargrave, Letitia, 298
Hay, Henry (Churchill labourer), 49

Hay, John (boatbuilder, Fort Chimo), 245, 256–57, 262, 267–69, 272, 273
Hayes River, *xii*, *xiii*, 70, 151, 209
Haymarsh Creek and Haymarsh House, *xv*, 34–35, 40–41
HBC. *See* Hudson's Bay Company (HBC)
Heald, Point, 197, 353n63
health care. *See* illnesses and injuries, medical care
Hearne, Samuel, 5, 11–14, 16, 84, 116, 309, 329n24
HMS *Hecla* (10-gun-bomb vessel), 4, 89, 301, 332n8
Hecla Strait, 299
Hendry, William, 241
Hepburn, John: Augustine's relationship, 122; biographical details, 58; Franklin's 1st expedition, *xii*, 60–61, 66, 80–82, 85–86, 88–90, 100, 103–12, 138, 344n34; Hood's death, 103–6, 138
Herriot Creek. *See* Churchill Creek (now Herriot Creek)
Herschel Island, *xi*, 193–94, 198, 201
historiography: author's life in the Arctic, *xxi–xxii*; biographies as incomplete, *xxi*, 307–8; sources on Augustine's life, *xviii–xxi*, *xxxiii*, 308, 316; women's absence in records, 22, 230, 247, 253, 298–99
Hodgson, John, 145, 152, 157, 350n15
Holmes, John Pocock (HBC surgeon) and Betsy, 19, 21–22
home village, Augustine's. *See* Augustine, home village
homebrew. *See* alcohol
Homeguard (Fort Churchill), 20, 21, 30, 42–43, 267n15, 269, 311. *See also* Sayisi
Hood, Robert: biographical details, 58; death, 103–6, 111, 138, 139, 158; Fort Enterprise, *xii*, 63–66, 99–100, 103–6, 344n34; Franklin's 1st expedition, 58–61, 76–77, 80–82, 93, 95; health, 77, 93, 95, 99–100, 104
Hood River, 88–91, 96
Hope, Fort, 300–303
House, definition of, 334n43
House, John, 224
Howse, Joseph, 29–30, 31, 335n7
Hudson Bay, *xii–xv*

Hudson Strait, xiv, 2, 31, 260, 268–70, 273, 276–77
Hudson's Bay Company (HBC): about, 16–19, 115–19, 309; departments, 118; historical sources, xviii–xxi; history of, xxxii, 16–19, 115–19, 309, 366n4; NWC competition, 15, 117–18, 239–40, 309; NWC merger (1821), 112–13, 240, 341n15; outfitting system, 74, 334n33; personnel status, 16–19, 243, 310, 311–12, 315; Red River Colony, 117–18; reorganizations, 49, 238; Rupert's Land as HBC territory, xxxi–xxxii, 117–18, 357n4; supply ships, 27, 335n5; trade restrictions, 117–18, 239–40; workforce numbers, 19, 118, 355n23. See also Simpson, George; and entries beginning with expedition
Hudson's Bay Company (HBC), London Committee: alcohol policies, 15; care for invalids and the hungry, 20–21, 265, 367n15; companions for excursions, 49; HBC daily journals, xviii–xix, 46, 337n49; Labrador information, 237–38, 241–42; local labourers at home posts, 216; marriage policies, 21–22
Hutchinson, John, 277–79, 280, 281, 362n8

Icy Cape, 194
Iglulik, xiii
Iglulingmiut (Place of Houses), 4–5, 332n8
Ile á la Crosse, xii, 61, 70, 159, 208, 279–80
illnesses and injuries: bowel distress, 92–93, 95–96, 99, 103, 166, 343n17; broken bones, 159; burns, 96; colds and respiratory diseases, 49–51, 53, 337n62; consumption, 39; dysentery, 166; frostbite, 90, 101; hypothermia, 94, 96; Indigenous epidemics, 115–16, 210–11, 354n4; injuries, xix, 16, 50–51, 82, 91–92, 96, 181–82; mental conditions, 102, 105; rheumatic fever, 169; scurvy, 15, 19, 24, 35, 39, 261, 266–68; snowblindness, 258; starvation, 95–108, 343n23, 344n40; swellings, 106, 195, 228; typhus, 335n5; typhus among Selkirk settlers, 28–30, 32, 34, 335n2, 335n13, 335nn4–5, 336n18
illnesses and injuries, medical care: historical sources, xix; medical kits, 50–51, 338n64; medicinal beer, 30, 35; surgeons, 19, 50, 106
Indigenous people. See Chipewyan, eastern (Churchill area); Chipewyan, western (Dene Arctic and Subarctic); Cree, Hudson Bay area (northwest and east); Cree, western; Inuit; Iroquois; Loucheux; Yellowknives
Inuinnait (Copper Inuit), xxviii–xxix, 62, 78, 82–86, 329n24
Inuit: about, 324; communities, xxxi; conjurers and sorcery, 131–32, 134–35; cosmology, 128–29; Dalton Minimum (1790–1830), xxv, 8–10, 46, 116, 332n17, 367n15; Eskimo, usage of replaced as "Inuit" and "Inuk," 328n14; historical sources, xviii–xxi, xx–xxi, xxxiii; Hudson Bay Inuit, 7–8; Inuit and Inuk replace Eskimo as ethonym, 324, 328n14; oral histories, xix, xxvi, xxviii–xxix; Paleoeskimo and Paleo-Inuit, 328n14; Pan-Inuit relations, xxxi, 330n38; territorial size and food resources, xxxi. See also Arctic; Arctic prehistory; climate
Inuit, Churchill area: adoption, 3–5, 9, 308, 311, 313, 332n9; apprentices, 3–9; climatic conditions, 10, 46, 51–55, 116, 125–27; early contact, xxx; epidemic (1825–26), 210–11, 354n4; frequency of contact, 9; HBC gifts for, 127–28, 149, 220, 222; migrations, xxv–xxxi, 308, 330n31, 352n15, 367n5; as "natives of Hudson Bay," 20, 334n35; starvation, 55–56, 130; trade, 55, 315, 367n7. See also Augustine, home village; Churchill, trade; Inuit, trade relations; Inuit, women
Inuit, clothing: adaptation for local area, 83; beads and beadwork, xix, 126, 128–30, 222; clothing construction, 21, 128–30; European fabrics and styles, 126–27, 216–19; symbols and patterns, 126, 129, 222; women seamstresses, xix, 128–30, 222
Inuit, Labrador. See Labrador
Inuit, languages: about, xxxiii, 313–14; dialects, xxviii, xxxi, 176, 179, 187, 193, 314, 352n15; historical sources, xviii, xxxiii, 7, 331n41; interpreters, 3–4, 313–14, 365n40; Inuktitut, xxviii, xxxiii, 7, 164–65, 179; languages of observers,

xxxiii, 331n41, 340n4; missionary influences, xxxiii; name changes, 7; writing systems, xxxi, xxxiii, 7, 179. *See also* Augustine, languages

Inuit, social relations: adoption, 3–5, 9, 308, 311, 313, 332n9; arranged marriages, 45–46, 48, 367n16; celebrations, 185–86; family relationships, 4–5; independence as trait, xxxi, 311–13; kinship (biological and fictive), xxxi, 4–5, 134, 312–13; liking, loving, and care, 135; names, 7, 332n7; sharing, xxxi, 4–5, 165, 233, 312, 316, 332n7; snowhouses, 75; status of well-travelled Inuit, xxix–xxx, xxxi, 330n32; wife "lending," 132–34

Inuit, trade relations: about, 315, 367n7; apprenticeships as support for, 5, 7, 315; climatic conditions, 55, 130; European clothing, 126–27; Franklin's 2nd expedition, 178–86, 190–93, 198–202; Moravians in Labrador, 239; shopping at York (1828–29), 216–19, 221–22, 227; summer gatherings, xxxi; Ungava Inuit, 253, 259–61, 264–65. *See also* Churchill, trade

Inuit, women: beads and beadwork, xix, 126, 128–30, 222; firearms, 128; HBC gifts for, 127–28; hunters, 128; marriage to Inuit men, 21, 45–46, 367n16; parchment making, 356n58; seamstresses, xix, 128–30, 222; trade goods, 21, 126–30. *See also* Augustine, family

Inuit Circumpolar Council (ICC), 328n14, 330n38

Inuk, as term, 324, 328n14

Inuvialuit (The Real People), xxvii

invalids, elderly, and the hungry: care at HBC posts, 20–21, 43–45, 269, 367n15; care for the hungry, 265

Iroquois, 276, 282–84, 350n29. *See also* Kanaquassé, Pierre; Teroahauté, Michel

Isbister, Thomas, 154–57

Itchinnah, Chief, 204

Itiviana (Junius's brother), 132–33, 210–11, 368n18

Itqujaq (Inuk), 187–88

James Bay: HBC explorations (1816–20), 237–41; HBC Southern Department, 118, 238; James Bay Cree, 229, 241, 243, 245–48, 293; landscape, 237–43; maps, *xiii, xiv*; Ungava expedition, 245–47, 296. *See also* Eastmain House; Moose Factory

Junius Hiutiruk: Augustine's home village, 68; disappearance and death, 97, 110, 131–35, 167; Franklin's 1st expedition, 69–76, 78, 80–94, 97, 110, 124, 277; memorial, 317; name, 68, 340n4; threats to Augustine by relatives of, 123, 131–36, 347n24, 368n18

Kabloona (*Qallunaaq*), defined, 324
Kanaquassé, Pierre (Iroquois), 276, 282–85
Kaniapiskau (South River), 240, 246–47, 249, 260, 268, 358n4
Kazan River, *xii, xiii,* xxx
Keewatin people, 8–10. *See also* Augustine Tataneuck; Inuit; Kivallirmiut; Moses; Ullebuk
Keewatin (later Kivalliq) Region, xxxii, 331n40. *See also* Augustine, home village
Keith, George, 262, 292, 297–98
Keith, James, 252
Kelsey, Henry, 3
Kendall, Cape, 196
Kendall, Edward Nicholas: biographical details, 146; Franklin's 2nd expedition, 146, 157–58, 161–67, 170, 173, 205–6, 208–9; Franklin's 2nd expedition, eastern detachment, 178, 181–82, 190, 196, 203–5, 353n47; surveyor-artist and playwright, 146, 170, 178, 206; travel to Fort Norman, 157–58, 161–62; York Factory, 209
Kennedy, Alexander, 341n13
Keskarrah (Akaitcho's older brother), 161–62
King George III (HBC vessel), 2
King William Island, *xii, xiii,* xxviii
Kinney, Surgeon, 32
Kivalliq (formerly Keewatin), xxxii, 331n40
Kivallirmiut, xxxii, 308, 367n5. *See also* Augustine, home village
Kivallit, 331n40
Knapp's Bay (near Arviat): Augustine's home village as nearby, 8, 46, 289; climatic conditions, 9, 46; Inuit, xxx, 7–9, 132; Inuit at Churchill, 3, 9, 132, 289–90; map, *xiii*; seal hunts, 9, 55, 136, 220

Knight, James, 11–12, 16
knives, types of, 324
Koksoak River: HBC explorations, 239–41; Inuit, 229; map and landscape, xiv, 240–43, 249–50, 358n4; Moravians, 238, 249; South River (Kaniapiskau), 240, 246–47, 249, 260, 263, 358n4; South River House, 267–73; Ungava expedition, 229, 243, 249, 267–73
Kusugak, Jose, xxxiii

La Loche River, 160
Labrador: hardships, 239–43; HBC's information on, 237–42; Inuit, xxvii, 237, 241, 253, 259–61, 263; Moravians, 238–39, 241–42, 249. *See also* expedition, Ungava (1830–33)
Labrador tea (*Ledum decumbens*), 100, 101, 103, 324, 344n43
Lac la Pluie, 216, 221, 222, 223, 229, 356n31
Lake, Point, 80, 97
Lamallice (Paul Boucher), 70–72, 277–78, 341n14
languages and literacy: Churchill languages, 4, 311; English language, 17, 135; formal education of HBC personnel, 17; Gaelic, 156, 172; HBC personnel's knowledge of languages, 5, 119, 331n4, 368n19; language learning, 314–15, 368n19; night classes in literacy, 76, 135, 170; Orcadian Scots, 17. *See also* Augustine, languages; Inuit, languages
Larch River (Netwakamy), xiv, 240, 248–49
larch trees, 249, 251
Laserre, Peter, 28
Le Fond, Louis, 245, 257, 259–60, 266, 270
Leask, John, 5–6, 10–11, 14, 18, 34, 37–42, 49, 311
Leith, Chief Factor James, 153–56, 159–61
Leslie, Hugh: Augustine's relationship, 27, 123–24, 132, 136; Churchill officer, 27, 122–27, 130–33, 150, 346n4; Franklin's 2nd expedition, 149–50, 210; Moses's relationship, 124, 293; Selkirk settlers (1813–14), 36, 38, 41
Lewes, John Lee, 276
lichens and mosses, 92, 95, 250–51, 343n17
Linklater, Mr. (Selkirk settler), 34, 39

Lion (boat): damage and repairs, 167–68, 173, 195; Franklin's 2nd expedition, western detachment, 165–68, 176–77, 182–86, 190–93, 195, 198, 199, 201; travel to Fort Norman, 141–42, 145, 151–52, 160–63, 175–76
liquor. *See* alcohol
Little Duck Lake, 20, 334n37
Little Ice Age (1350–1850), xxv, xxviii, 8
Little Whale River and Great Whale River, xiv, 239–40, 247, 294–95
locations of villages, xiii, 7–8, 46
London Committee. *See* Hudson's Bay Company (HBC), London Committee
Loucheux: Franklin's 2nd expedition, 140, 162–66, 171, 176–77, 202, 219
Loyer, Francis, 332n11
lumber, 42, 336n22
Lutyens, Edwin, 307, 366n2
Lyon, Cape, xi, xii, 189
Lyon, George Francis, 4–5, 146, 330n32, 332n9

Macarthur, Alexander (Franklin 2nd, middleman), 144
Macduffie, John (Franklin 2nd, middleman), 144, 152
Mackenzie, Alexander, 56, 352n5
Mackenzie River and Delta: Arctic Red River (Mackenzie's), 176, 202, 208, 298, 352n5; Franklin's 2nd expedition, 175–76; Franklin's 2nd expedition (eastern detachment), 177–82; Franklin's 2nd expedition (western detachment), 163–66, 173–74, 182–86, 196–202; Inuit, xxvii–xxxi, 135, 171, 176–87, 314; map, xi; Point Separation, xi, 177, 201–2. *See also* Good Hope, Fort; Norman, Fort (Tulita); Pillage Point
Mackenzie's Red River. *See* Arctic Red River (Mackenzie's)
Mackintosh waterproof cloth, 143, 153, 173, 174
MacLea, John, 350n15
made beaver (MB), 324, 340n5
Magnet (Rae expedition), 300
Magnion, 70–72, 341n14
Malcolm, William, 261–62, 266–68, 270–73
Mallette, 212, 355n7

Manitoba, *xii*, *xiii*
maps, *xi–xv*
Marble Island, *xii*, *xiii*, *xxix*, 7–8, 9, 75, 305
Marko, 365n40. *See also* Ullebuk, William (Ullebuk's son)
Matthews, Thomas, 144, 152, 156–57, 159–60, 169, 171, 173, 195
MB (made beaver), 324, 340n5
McAuley, Auley, 112
McCarthy, Martha, 333n22, 333n25, 337n47
McDonald, Archibald, 28, 30–32, 35, 40–42, 70, 336n32
McDonald, Neil, 144, 151–55, 157, 159, 312, 350n15
Mcdonnell, William, 281–84, 363n25
McDuffie, John, 350n15
McEachern, John, 144, 152
McGillivray, William and Katherine, 207
McKay, George, 228, 245, 257, 260, 263–67, 271, 273
McKenzie, Charles, 145, 152, 350n15
McKenzie, James, 239, 253
McKenzie, Roderick, 60, 280
McLea, John (Franklin 2nd, steersman), 145, 152, 196, 203–4, 206
McLellan, William (Franklin 2nd, middleman), 144, 152, 159
McLennan, John (Franklin 2nd, bowman), 145, 152, 159
McLeod, Alexander Roderick, 275, 285
McTavish, George Simpson, 305, 367n16
McTavish, John George, 130–31, 144–45, 150–52, 212–13, 224, 229, 257, 262, 305
McVicar, Christy McBeath and son, 142, 207
McVicar, Margaret and Ellen, 112, 341n21
McVicar, Robert: Franklin's 1st expedition, 61–62, 72–74, 111–12; Franklin's 2nd expedition, 140–42, 161, 205, 207–8, 341n21, 355n25; Resolution, officer, 61–62, 141–42, 207
medical care. *See* illnesses and injuries, medical care
Melville Peninsula and Sound, *xiii*, *xxvii*, 4, 89, 301, 332n8
Merry, Cape, *xv*, 2, 12, 223, 224
Methye Portage (now La Loche Portage), *xii*, 160, 350n38
Miles, Robert, 225, 227, 234, 252, 294, 297, 303, 356n48
Millette, Joseph, 261–62, 265–67, 272–73
missionaries: HBC chaplains, 121; historical sources, xx–xxi, xxxiii; Moravians, 238–39, 241–42, 249. *See also* West, John
mister, as term, 17, 333n26
mixed parentage, as term, 20
Moar, Andrew (HBC retired), 247, 358n4
Moar, James (HBC Churchill), 49
Money, William (British marine), 157
Montcalm (chartered ship), 249, 252–54, 277, 359n21, 360n54, 361n77
Moore, George (HBC York Factory), 230–31
Moore, James (HBC sailor), 23, 38, 40
Moose Deer Island, *xii*, 61, 72–73, 111, 345n68. *See also* Great Slave Lake
Moose Factory: HBC Southern Department, 118, 339n10; living conditions, 18, 230–32; maps, *xiii*, *xiv*; Ungava expedition, 225–32, 244–46, 256, 262, 270, 360n54
Moravians, 238–39, 241–42, 249
Morin, Antoine, 282–83
Morwick, James, 232, 245, 253, 255–56, 260, 262–63, 267–69, 271, 273
Moses (Inuk): about, 124, 292–96; accounts for provisions, 217–18, 221, 226–27, 293, 295–96; Chimo residency and visits, 273, 292–93, 295; Churchill (1822, 1827–29), 125, 210, 212–15, 224; George residency, 293–94; health and age, 124, 228–31, 255, 293–95, 356n48; hunting and fishing, 125, 258, 267–71, 273, 292–93; interpreter, 260–61, 293–95; marriage and family, 292–93, 295–96, 364n19; Moose Factory, 226–32, 234–35; personal qualities, 214–15, 221, 272, 293–95; reports on, 221; retirement, 292–95; Richmond Gulf Inuit, 294–95; Ungava expedition, 226–29, 234–35, 246, 250–51, 255, 258–60, 264, 266–71, 273
mosquitoes: at Churchill, 11, 12, 16; on journeys, 72, 81, 160, 173, 175–76, 224; Ungava Bay, 248, 250, 251
mosses and lichens, 92, 95, 250–51, 343n17
Munro (Inuk interpreter), 303
Munro, George (voyageur), 158
Murray, John, 138–39

music and dance: Christmas celebrations, 155–56, 172; Fort Enterprise, 76–77; Fort Franklin, 169, 174; Inuit celebrations, 185–86, 193, 199; languages, 156; musical instruments, 161, 169, 172, 177
musket, defined, 353n30
muskox, 93, 343n5

Naeukghahie, 127
Nagjuktormiut, 85. See also Copper Inuit (Inuinnait)
Nainsby, Surgeon, 28, 30, 32
Napoleonic Wars, 57, 58, 116–17
narwhal, 133
Naskapi, Ungava, 264, 267, 271, 360n60
natives of Hudson Bay, as term, 20, 231, 334n35. See also Chipewyan, eastern (Churchill area); Inuit
needles, steel, 129–30, 191, 222, 234, 324
Nelson River Post and District, 24, 49, 151–52, 219–20, 224
Netsilik, xxviii, 135, 303–5, 329n25
Netsilingmiut, xxviii, 329n26
Neville's Bay (Dawson Inlet), xxx
New Year's festivities, 111, 155–56, 172, 206, 256, 355n25
Newfoundland, xxvii
Norman, Fort (Tulita), xi, 162–63, 169, 171–76, 205, 351n44, 352n2
North Knife River, xv, 41, 51–52, 54–55
North Pole (Rae expedition), 30c
North West Company (NWC): Franklin's 1st expedition, 61–62, 72–74; HBC relations, 15, 117, 240, 341n15; in Labrador, 239–40, 271. See also Wentzel, Willard Ferdinand
northeastern expedition. See Chimo, Fort; expedition, Ungava (1830–33); Ungava Bay and Peninsula
Northwest Territories, xi, xii, xiii
Norway House: Back's expedition, 275–78, 291; Franklin's 1st expedition, 70, 72, 112, 341n13, 341n19; Franklin's 2nd expedition, 142, 206, 208; map, xiii
Nueltin Lake, 334n37
Nunavut, xii, xiii
NWC. See North West Company (NWC)

Oman, William: Augustine's friendship, 19–20, 210, 303, 311; Churchill employee (1827–29), 212–16, 219–21, 225–26; family, 20, 21, 211, 214, 288, 310–11
Oman, William, Sr., 19, 310–11
Ontario, xiii
Ooligbuck, 365n40. See also Ullebuk, William (Ullebuk's son)
Ooligbuck Lake and Point, 317
Oostineedjue, 295
Orcadians, 17, 49, 261, 311
Owl River, 122–23, 215

Paleoeskimo (Dorset or Tuniit), xxvi–xxvii, 328n14
Paleo-Inuit, as term, 328n14
parchment (caribou skin), 60, 65, 356n58
Parent, Jean Baptiste (voyageur), 63, 80–81
Parry, Cape, xi, xii, 189
Parry, Edward, 4, 89, 144, 189, 198
partridge/ptarmigan/grouse, 51–52, 97, 203, 257, 264, 270, 324
pease, defined, 324, 363n3
Peel River, 298
Pelly Bay, xiii, 301, 303
Pelonquin, Matthew ("Crédit"), 63, 81, 91, 92–93, 99
Peltier, Joseph, 63, 81, 93, 95, 100, 102, 106–8, 344n51
Penetanguishene depot, 143, 147, 158
Perrault, Ignace, 63, 81, 95, 100, 103, 111
Peter Pond Lake (was Buffalo Lake), 160
Pillage Point, xi, 182–86, 199–201, 219, 314–16
Pingnahewak (Inuk), 127, 347n19
pipes, oil, defined, 324
pistol lock, defined, 324
Prince, Richard, 245, 253, 256, 262
Prince of Wales I (HBC supply ship), 27–33, 121–22, 142, 144–45, 151, 276, 335n3, 335n5, 335n7
Prince of Wales's Fort (Stone Fort), xii, xiii, xv, 9, 11–13, 15
Prince Rupert III (HBC supply ship), 12
Providence, Fort, xii, 62–63, 73, 89, 98, 102, 109–11
Pruden, John Peter, 278–81, 287
Prudhoe Bay, xi, 197, 353n63
ptarmigan. See partridge/ptarmigan/grouse
pyrites, xxxi, 324

Qallunaaq, defined, 324
Quebec, *xiv*, 357n4
Queen Maud Gulf, *xii, xiii*, xxviii

Rae, John, 299–305, 365n40, 365n48
Rankin Inlet: Augustine's home village near, 8, 46, 75; author's life in, xxi–xxii; Inuit migrations, 308; maps and distances, *xii, xiii*, 7–8; oral histories, xxviii; Thule, xxvi–xxviii, 328n14, 329n23
recreation at forts, 77, 159, 169–70, 171–72
Red River. *See* Arctic Red River (Mackenzie's)
Red River Colony, 117–18, 333n29, 346n5, 356n31
Red River settlers, typhus crisis. *See* Churchill, Selkirk settlers (1813–14)
Reed, Daniel, 230–31
Refuge Cove, 181, 186–87
Reliance (Franklin 2nd, boat), 173, 176, 182–86, 193, 195, 199, 201
Reliance, Fort (Great Slave Lake), 281–85, 362n24
Reliance, Fort (later Fort Franklin, Great Bear Lake), name changes, 141, 168–69. *See also* Franklin, Fort
religion. *See* Christianity
Repulse Bay, *xiii*, 4, 58, 89, 146, 300, 302–4, 329n23, 341n26
Resolution, Fort: Back's expedition (1833–35), 281–83; Franklin's 1st expedition, 61, 72–74, 111; Franklin's 2nd expedition, 142, 160–61, 205, 207, 242, 281–86; map and distances, *xii*, 61, 72–73, 111, 345n68; Moose Deer Island, *xii*, 61, 72–73, 111, 345n68
Richardson, John: Augustine's friendship, 75, 122, 131–32, 135–36, 150, 208, 219; biographical details, 58; connection of 1st and 2nd expeditions, 196; Cumberland House, 159, 208; Fort Enterprise, *xii*, 63–66, 75–76, 99–100, 103–10, 344n34; Fort Franklin, 168–74, 204–5; Franklin's 1st expedition, 54, 58–61, 63–66, 75–82, 87–88, 90–91, 94, 99–113, 339n13; Franklin's 2nd expedition, 142, 145–46, 150, 168–69, 204–5; Franklin's 2nd expedition, eastern detachment, 173–74, 178–82, 186–90, 196, 200–204; health, 96, 99, 106; Hood's death, 103–6, 138; scientific interests, 76, 86, 105–6, 109, 170, 172–73, 178, 179, 189, 205; surgeon, 76, 82, 94, 106, 108, 109, 159, 170, 182
Richmond Gulf, *xiv*, 229, 237–38, 240, 243, 247, 293–95, 297
Rivers, George, 230
Robertson, Colin, 61, 211, 310, 339n14
Rocher, Joseph, 245, 256, 259–60, 263–66, 270–73
Ross, Alexander, 19
Ross, Donald, 142, 159
Ross, John, 275, 284, 301, 313, 365n48
Ross, William, 19, 67–70, 333n30, 340n1, 340n4
Roundrock Lake, 98, 101–2, 344n34
Rowand, John, 276
Royal, Robert, 252–54
Rupert's House, 297
Rupert's Land: as birthplace for "natives of Hudson Bay," 20, 334n35; HBC territory, xxxi–xxxii, 117–18, 357n4
Russia, 139, 193–94, 328n14, 330n38

St. Germain, Pierre, 61–63, 75, 77–81, 91–99, 101, 107–11, 339n14
Saskatchewan, *xii, xiii*
sateen, defined, 324
Saunders, John, 230–31, 358n2
Sayisi Dene (Rising Sun People), 20, 43–44, 334n37. *See also* Chipewyan, eastern (Churchill area)
Scottish colonists. *See* Churchill, Selkirk settlers (1813–14); Red River Colony
scurvy, 15, 19, 24, 35, 39, 261, 266–68
Seahorse Gully, *xv*, 1–2, 44–45, 48, 214, 220, 223
Seal River: climatic conditions, 125–26, 130, 367n15; fishery, 24–25, 126, 127–28, 130, 149–50, 220, 367n15; maps and distances, *xii, xiii, xv*, 25, 367n15
seals and seal hunts: Churchill, 9, 10, 55, 125–26, 130; climatic conditions, 8, 9, 10, 116, 125–26, 130, 367n15; sealskin clothing, 21, 192, 199; trade, 149–50, 235; whales, 127
Second Maunder Minimum (Dalton Minimum), 332n17. *See also* climate
Selkirk, Lord, 27, 117–18

Selkirk settlers. *See* Churchill, Selkirk settlers (1813–14); Red River Colony
Semandré, François, 63, 81, 100, 102, 106–8, 344n51
Separation, Point, *xi*, 177, 201–2
servant, as term, 17–18, 333n27
settlers. *See* Red River Colony
settlers, typhus crisis. *See* Churchill, Selkirk settlers (1813–14)
Severn, Fort, *xiii*, 346n5
sewn sleds, 360n63
Shenandoah, 21, 23, 35, 40–41, 43–45, 310, 367n15
shrub (diluted rum), 156, 159, 350n22
Simpson, Fort, *xi*, *xii*, 162, 207
Simpson, George: Augustine's relationship, 252; Back's expedition (1833–35), 275–76, 285; career, 70, 72, 112–13, 341n15, 341n19; Franklin's 1st expedition, 70, 72, 74, 112–13, 121; Franklin's 2nd expedition, 121, 122, 145, 147, 150–51; HBC's information on Labrador, 237–42; Rae expedition (1846-47), 299–300; Ungava expedition, 225, 227–29, 240–44, 252–54, 256–57, 262, 267, 270–71
Simpson, Thomas, 296–98
Simpson Peninsula, *xiii*, 301
Sinclair, Baikie, 149, 210, 214–15, 221, 223, 356n31
singing. *See* music and dance
Slater, James, 245, 251, 254–56, 258, 264, 268–69, 272–73
Slave Lake. *See* Great Slave Lake
sleds, sewn, 360n63
Sloop's Cove, 28–30, 32, 34
Smith, Edward (NWC clerk), 72–74, 112, 162, 207
Snodie, Adam, 24, 49–56, 58–59, 122
Somerset Island, xxviii
Souchong tea, 325
South River (Kaniapiskau), 240, 246–47, 249, 260, 268, 358n4
South River House, 267–73
Southampton Island, *xiii*, *xiv*
Spence, James (Franklin 2nd, middleman), 145, 152, 350n15
Spence, John (HBC, York Factory), 23
Spence, Joseph (blacksmith), 19

Spence, Thomas (Churchill cook), 6, 15, 17, 36–42, 310, 311
Spinks, Robert (Admiralty sailor), 144, 152, 192, 200–201
spirits. *See* alcohol
Split Lake, 152, 312
sports and games, 77
stage (distance), defined, 358n8
staged or stagey, defined, 324–25
Stapylton Bay, *xii*, 190
Starvation Cove, 304
starvation, symptoms of: Adam, 102, 106; Peltier, 106; Semandré, 102, 106
Stayner, Chief Factor Thomas, 10, 13, 14–16, 22, 46, 310, 334n40
Stefansson, Viljhalmur, 368n18
Stewart, Chief Factor Alexander, 207–8
Stewart, Archibald (Franklin 2nd, middleman), 145, 152
Stewart, John, exploration of Ungava Peninsula, 239–40
Stirling, James (officer on *Brazen*), 27–29, 31–32
Stone Fort (Prince of Wales's Fort), *xii*, *xiii*, *xv*, 9, 11–13, 15. *See also* Churchill, Fort
Stoney, 278, 280–81
stroud, defined, 325
Stuart, John, exploration of Great Whale River, 154–57
sugar terminology, 325
Swain, James, Sr., 52, 338nn67–68
Swain, Thomas, 29–30, 31, 338n68

Tadoule Lake, 334n37
Tambora, Mount, eruption, 53, 338n1
Tataneuck. *See* Augustine Tataneuck
Taylor, George (HBC sloop captain), 9, 210, 215–17, 233, 245
Taylor, William: Ungava expedition, 228, 244–45, 247, 250–51, 255–58, 260, 263, 265–67, 273
tea, 59, 217, 218, 289, 325
tea, Labrador, 100–101, 103, 344n43
tea and beer, pine, 30, 35
temperature measurements, 360n62
Teroahauté, Michel (Iroquois), 63, 81, 90, 100, 103–5, 138, 158, 350n29
Thelon River, *xii*, *xiii*, xxix–xxx, 233, 330n28
Thomas, Thomas (HBC Overseas Governor), 49, 118, 346n5

Thoolezzah Lake, 317
Thule, expansion of, xxv–xxxviii, 328n14, 329n23
time-keeping devices, 331n1
Tiriganniaq (Inuk, Copper), 85–86, 87, 88
tobacco, defined, 325
Topping, Thomas: Augustine's mentor, 3, 5–8, 55, 121, 122, 332n14; Churchill chief officer, 1, 3, 5–8, 19, 23–24, 55, 121–22, 331n1; climatic conditions, 23–24, 46; typhus crisis (1813), 28–33, 335n5. *See also* Churchill, Selkirk settlers (1813–14)
tracking, canoe, 325
Tree River, *xii*, xxix, 96
HMS *Trent*, 58, 144, 146
tripe de roche (lichen), 92, 95, 343n17
Tuniit (Dorset), xxvi–xxvii, 328n14
Turnagain, Point, 90, 296, 298
Turner, John (Captain, *King George III*), 2, 27–29, 31–32
typhus outbreak. *See* Churchill, Selkirk settlers (1813–14)
Tysoe, Shadrach (British marine), 157

Ullebuk: accounts for provisions, 150, 209–10, 216–17, 221, 227, 234, 302, 366n56; biographical details, 302, 349n1; Chimo residency, 273, 292–93, 296–99; Churchill employee, 149–50, 212–16, 223–25; Franklin's 2nd expedition, 150, 153–57, 160, 170, 172, 206–10, 312; Franklin's 2nd expedition, eastern detachment, 177–82, 186–90, 196, 202–5; health, 255, 258, 297–98, 300–302; hunting and fishing, 170, 172, 187, 189, 250, 251, 255–56, 267–71; interpreter, 150, 151, 179, 260–61, 296–97, 352n15; Lac la Pluie employee (1828–29), 216, 221, 222, 229; marriages and family, 296–305, 312, 349n1, 361n77, 365n40, 366n56, 367n16, 368n17; memorials, 317; Moose Factory, 226–32, 234–35; personal qualities, 150, 204–5, 208, 214, 272, 297; Rae expedition (1846–47), 299–302; Ungava expedition, 226–31, 234–35, 246, 250–51, 253–60, 266–73, 312, 365n40
Ullebuk, Donald (Ullebuk's son), 296–97, 299–300, 312, 364n33, 368n17

Ullebuk, William (Ullebuk's son), 292, 297–300, 302–5, 361n77, 365n40, 366n57
Ungava Bay and Peninsula: exclusion from Rupert's Land, 239, 357n4; hardships, 229, 238–43, 256, 263; HBC's information on, 237–42; Inuit, xxvii, 253, 259–61, 264–68, 270–71; map, *xiv*; Moravians, 238–39; Naskapi, 264, 267, 271. *See also* Chimo, Fort; expedition, Ungava (1830–33); Labrador
Union (boat): Franklin's 2nd expedition, 141–42, 145, 151–52, 176–82, 187, 189–90, 196; Moose Factory, 232; repairs, 173
United Nations, 330n38
United States: Inuit Circumpolar Council (ICC), 328n14, 330n38; Monroe Doctrine, 139–40. *See also* Alaska
Ussaq, Leo, xxi–xxii
Utuck, 127

Vaillant, Régiste, 63, 81, 93, 95, 99
Victoria Island, xxviii, 329n23, 353n47
Vivier, Alexis, 158, 184
volcanic eruption (1815), 53, 338n1
voyageurs, 70–71, 342n39

Wacacoo, 214
Wager Bay, 122, 130
Wales, William, 11
Walnut-Shell (boat), 141–42, 145, 202–3
warble fly larvae, 106
Wedderburn, Fort (Lake Athabasca), 70, 72
Wentzel, Willard Ferdinand: Franklin's 1st expedition, 62–63, 73–77, 81, 86, 140, 146, 275; Franklin's 1st expedition, return to Fort Chipewyan, 86, 98, 112; memorial, 317; Providence, NWC officer, 62–63
Wentzel Lake, 317
West, Reverend John, 121–23, 131–36, 146, 213, 219, 320, 332n16, 347n24, 357n66
western detachment, Franklin's. *See* expedition, Franklin's second overland (1824–25)
Whale Cove, *xii*, *xiii*, xxx, 7–8, 9, 289, 307. *See also* Augustine, home village
Whale River. *See* Great Whale River and Little Whale River
whales, 127, 132, 220, 260, 309

Wilberforce Falls, 91
wildlife: bears, 88, 343n5; foxes, 1, 45, 260; geese, 43, 67, 125, 214, 299; muskox, 93, 343n5; partridges, 51–52, 97, 203, 257, 264, 270; whales, 127, 132, 220, 260, 309; wolves, 1, 45, 172. *See also* caribou; seals and seal hunts
Wilkes, Samuel (sailor, Franklin 1st expedition), 58
William, Fort, 158, 262
Williams, William (HBC Overseas Governor), 56, 58–59, 61, 74, 339n10
Williamson, David, 235
Wilson, George (British marine), 157, 161, 169, 172, 177, 184, 186, 192
wine. *See* alcohol
Winnipeg, Lake, *xiii*, 70, 158
Winter River and Winter Lake, *xii*, 63–65, 171, 312, 344n34
Wishart, Peter (HBC master boat builder), 19, 34, 39, 53
wolves, 1, 45, 172
women and children: about, 21–22; absence in HBC journals, 22, 230, 247, 253, 298–99; British wives, 21–22; country born, as term, xx; country wives, 21–22, 73; mixed parentage, defined, 20; "natives of Hudson Bay," as term, 20, 334n35; rations, xix, 288–89
women and children, Inuit. *See* Augustine, family; Inuit, social relations; Inuit, women
Wood, Hugh (Churchill cooper), 19, 34
Wood, James (Churchill Post), 49
Woody Islands, *xv*, 39, 41, 336n33

Yellowknife, *xii*
Yellowknife River, *xii*, 63, 75
Yellowknives: Augustine's relationship, 78, 219; Back's drawings, 76; Back's expedition (1833–35), 281; ceremonial visits, 78, 342n33; Copper Inuit hostilities, 62, 77–79, 82–86; Dogrib hostilities, 162; food shortages, 77, 78, 281; Fort Enterprise, *xii*, 63–65, 76, 106–12, 162; Franklin's 1st expedition, 62, 76–86; Franklin's 2nd expedition, 140–41, 161–62, 168; Franklin's gifts of gratitude, 111, 162; interpreters, 62, 77–81; Yellowknife River site, 63–64. *See also* Akaitcho, Chief
York Factory: Augustine as employee, 216–19, 357n65; Augustine's visits, 27, 49–50, 112, 121, 216–19, 221–22, 277; climatic conditions, 23–24, 215; courier system, 242; Edwards as surgeon, 32, 34–35, 36, 44; Franklin's 2nd expedition, 142, 144–45, 147, 151, 154, 205; HBC Northern Department centre, 27, 118; HBC social hierarchies, 18, 219; living conditions, 15, 18; maps and distances, *xii*, *xiii*, 59, 122, 226; Rae expedition (1846-47), 299–300; scurvy, 15, 24; Selkirk settlers (1813–14), 29–30, 31, 42–45, 338n68; shopping at store, 216–19, 221–22, 226; Ungava expedition, 225–28, 273
Yukon Territory, *xi*

Source: Photo by Andrew Jones

Renee Fossett has a PhD in history from the University of Manitoba and was a Harington Fellow at the Centre for Rupert's Land Studies at the University of Winnipeg. She lived in the Arctic for ten years as a community teacher and organizer, and was a co-author with Sydney A. Keighley and David K. Riddle of *Trader, Tripper, Trapper: The Life of a Bay Man*. Dr. Fossett is also author of *In Order to Live Untroubled: Inuit of the Central Arctic, 1550 to 1940*, which won a Clio Award from the Canadian Historical Association for Best Regional Book in 2001. She is now retired, living on the Pacific Coast of British Columbia.